Legislating

Privacy

Priscilla M. Regan

Technology, Social Values, and Public Policy

Legislating

Privacy

The University of North Carolina Press *Chapel Hill & London*

© 1995 The University of North
Carolina Press
All rights reserved
Manufactured in the United States of
America

Library of Congress Cataloging-in-
Publication Data
Regan, Priscilla M.
Legislating privacy: technology, social
values, and public policy / by Priscilla
M. Regan.
    p. cm.
Includes bibliographical references
(p.   ) and index.
ISBN 0-8078-2226-4 (cloth : alk. paper)
1. Privacy, Right of — United States.
2. Computer security — Government
policy — United States. 3. Wiretapping —
Government policy — United States.
4. Lie detectors and detection —
Government policy — United States.
I. Title.
JC596.2.U5R44   1995
323.44'8'0973 — dc20   94-49544
                    CIP

The paper in this book meets the
guidelines for permanence and
durability of the Committee on
Production Guidelines for Book
Longevity of the Council on Library
Resources.

99 98 97 96 95   5 4 3 2 1

This book is dedicated to

CHRIS,

MICHAEL,

&

MARY

Contents

Tables and Figures

Preface

Beginning in the 1960s, an array of technological and social changes precipitated challenges to individual privacy. Computerization of record systems, wiretapping of telephone conversations, parabolic microphones, lie detector tests, personality tests, and miniaturized cameras presented an alarming potential for invading individual privacy. Press reports, television coverage, and scholarly studies increased public concern about surveillance, dehumanization, and behavior modification. George Orwell's *1984* represented a dreaded vision of the future that appeared all too possible given continuing advances in science and technology. By the mid-1960s, public and congressional concern fueled inquiries into the capabilities and uses of these techniques and the development of legislative actions to prevent or alleviate privacy invasions.

Technological and social changes continue to accelerate and, in some cases, have surpassed human imagination. Genetic mapping, retina scanning, brain-wave testing, Intelligent Transportation Systems, and smart homes are all techniques that appear futuristic but are currently available. Policy responses to these changes mirror those of the 1960s; apprehension about invasions of privacy, media and academic interest, and public concern prompt legislative inquiries and the introduction of legislation. Once again technology is perceived as having moved faster than legal protections. And once again the policy problem is defined in terms of invasions of individual privacy. Because problem definition affects political activity and policy outcomes, it is likely that legislative attempts to protect privacy in the 1990s will mirror prior legislative activity.

To help understand the congressional politics involved in resolving questions about fundamental values and technological change, this book examines the policy processes in three areas: information privacy, especially with regard to computerized databases; communication privacy, with an emphasis on wiretapping; and psychological privacy, with primary attention given to polygraph testing. In each of these areas, technological changes raised policy issues that initially were defined in terms of the invasion of personal privacy by technology. In each area, the policy problem was recognized shortly after the technology was first used, but it took years, if not decades, for Congress to formulate and adopt a policy to address the perceived problems. Also, for each issue, the emphasis on privacy diminished during the course of the policy debates. Legislation reflected not the importance of the value of privacy but an unbalanced compromise between those who benefited from the new technologies and those who advanced the importance of privacy. In each area, those who benefited from the technology exercised more influence over the final legislation.

Such an outcome is not necessarily surprising in American politics. Most legislation can be explained by examining the conflicts and compromises among the interests affected. In that sense, these areas of privacy and technology policy are fairly typical of policy making in the United States: the interests opposed to privacy protections were better organized and had greater resources and were therefore successful at delaying and weakening legislation. This viewpoint, however, leaves unanswered an important question: Why did the idea of privacy not serve as a lightning rod that sparked public support and timely legislation? In these cases, a cherished American value was threatened by technological change. Why was that value not accorded more importance throughout the policy process? Why was there no public outcry that privacy be protected? Why were competing interests able to trample over the value of privacy? And why did it take so many years to formulate and adopt policy?

The question of how values are treated in the policy process is not often explicitly analyzed. Most policies embody a preference for one set of values over another. Indeed, policy questions are increasingly being framed in terms of a conflict of values, a current example being jobs versus the environment. This example also illustrates one of the problems of examining policy questions from a value perspective, namely that it is often difficult to untangle values from interests. Most interests can point to values that support those interests, and most values have interests behind them. However, separating the relative importance of values and interests in the policy process is a critical step in developing not only a more complete understanding of the policy process but also an understanding of our values.[1]

The purpose of this book is twofold. First, it seeks to explicate the dynamics of congressional formulation and adoption of policy in situations where privacy was perceived to be threatened by new technologies. Political scientists often describe the policy process in the United States as untidy, messy, and complicated. The process reflects the concerns of the framers of the Constitution and the system they devised; the framers were, as Charles Jones points out, "more concerned about preventing tyranny than they were with facilitating policy development."[2] It is difficult to develop models that account for all the factors involved in policy making. In order to understand congressional policy making in the privacy and technology areas examined in this book, chapter 7 compares four features of congressional policy making — ideas, interests, policy communities, and policy entrepreneurs.

In analyzing the dynamics of congressional formulation and adoption of policy, policy scholars agree that how an issue is defined when it is placed on the public agenda is important to the politics of the policy process and the ultimate policy resolution. In all three areas of privacy and technology examined in this book, an analysis of congressional politics reveals that the conception of privacy contributed to limited congressional support for legislation. The congressional patterns of activity provide evidence for the dominance of interests over the idea of privacy. For those interested in protecting privacy, the dynamics of congressional policy making point to the need to rethink the importance and meaning of the value of privacy.

Second, the book seeks to explain why the accepted understanding of the value of privacy did not elicit more support for stronger legislation to protect privacy. In the areas of privacy and technology examined in this book, part of the explanation for why privacy did not draw more congressional advocates is that it is difficult to define "privacy." In virtually all philosophical and legal writing about privacy, authors begin by noting the difficulty in conceptualizing their subject. Definitional problems in determining what constitutes an invasion of privacy also occur in everyday conversations about privacy. A variety of issues are discussed under the rubric of privacy — abortion, the right to die, drug testing, and monitoring of employees. The focus in this book is on those issues resulting from the development of technological devices that alter individuals' control over access to themselves: the technologies that record our transactions, transmit our messages, and evaluate our well-being and predispositions.

Another problem in legislating to protect privacy is its definition as an individual right. Mary Ann Glendon argues that "our individual rights-laden public language" impoverishes our political discourse because issues "tend to be presented as absolute, individual, and independent of any necessary relation to responsibilities."[3] As we will see, policy discussions about privacy have followed this pattern. These difficulties not only are of interest to philosophers and legal scholars but also have profound implications for the formulation of public policy to protect privacy. My goal in this book is not to arrive at a definition of privacy with which all philosophers can concur. Instead, my concern is to explore the policy importance of the idea of privacy and to examine what happens when an individualistic conception of privacy serves as a goal in congressional policy making.

An individualistic conception of privacy does not provide a fruitful basis for the formulation of policy to protect privacy. When privacy is thought important primarily as an individual right and value, the scenario of policy responses described above occurs. If privacy is also regarded as being of social importance, different policy discourse and interest alignments are likely to follow. My analysis of congressional policy making reveals that little attention was given to the possibility of a broader social importance of privacy. As I reread the philosophical and legal literature on privacy, I began to understand why policy debates emphasized the importance of privacy to the individual. Although much of the earlier literature was provoked by concerns for the social implications of technological changes and the surveillance capabilities that these technologies offered government and private organizations, the policy problem was defined largely in terms of the impact of these changes on individual privacy. My reading of that literature and the links I found to policy discourse and congressional debates led to the conclusion that only part of the earlier understanding of the importance of privacy had been incorporated into the policy discussion.

The policy emphasis on individual privacy and policy solutions framed in terms of the protection of individual rights to privacy are not surprising given our liberal tradition. But this analysis of congressional policy making points to the need to rethink the value of privacy and to explore a path that has been largely uncharted in much of the philosophical thinking about privacy — the path that acknowledges the social importance of privacy. I argue that privacy serves not just individual interests but also common, public, and collective purposes. A recognition of the social importance of privacy will change the terms of policy debate and the patterns of interest-group and congressional activity.

In this effort, I am not attempting to refute or diminish the importance of the earlier literature on privacy. In the mid-1960s, the writings and thinking of Alan Westin, Charles Fried, and Arthur Miller were profoundly important in bringing attention to the privacy implications raised by new technologies. Their concern focused on the social changes that resulted from these new technologies. Although they defined these changes largely in terms of individual privacy, they were also very much concerned with organizational changes and effects on the democratic process. However, in policy debates and later philosophical writing, the emphasis on individual privacy flourishes while the social importance of privacy receives less attention. It is this focus on the social importance of privacy that I wish to return to and develop. In the earlier literature, a public importance of privacy — involving freedom of association, free speech, and voting, for example — was recognized. An implicit sense of a common value of privacy — that people shared some interest in privacy — was also expressed. I expand the understanding of privacy's importance in these areas and develop an analysis of privacy as a collective value, providing an additional basis for the social importance of privacy.

Because privacy played such a crucial role in defining each of these issues and in placing them on the public agenda, chapter 2 reviews the legal and philosophical development of the right to privacy. The analysis in that chapter emphasizes the difficulties in conceptualizing privacy and in viewing privacy as being of importance primarily to the individual. Chapter 3 examines the importance of privacy throughout American history as well as current public opinion about privacy and technology. The problems involved in capturing public opinion about privacy are also discussed.

The next three chapters examine each of the privacy areas — chapter 4 focuses on information privacy; chapter 5, on communication privacy; and chapter 6, on psychological privacy. Each of these chapters uses the policy process as the framework for comparison. For each area, the emergence of the privacy invasion as a public problem and its subsequent placement on the congressional agenda are first examined. The formulation of various alternatives for dealing with the problem is then analyzed. In each of the areas of privacy and technology policy, this stage of the policy process is the longest and the most acrimonious. Next, chapter 7 examines the politics of congressional adoption in some detail. The purpose of this analysis is to explain why Congress legislated as it did, at the time it did, and to set the stage for analyzing how Congress might respond to current privacy issues, including medical privacy, Intelligent Transportation Systems, personal communication systems, direct mail, and genetic screening.

In conclusion, chapter 8 suggests the logic for a new way of thinking about privacy — not solely as being important to an individual but also as having broader social importance. This social importance derives from the fact that privacy is a common value in that it is shared by individuals, a public value in that it has value to the democratic political system, and a collective value in that technology and market forces make it increasingly difficult for any one person to have privacy unless everyone has a similar minimum level of privacy. The policy implications of defining privacy as a social value are then explored and applied to several emerging issues involving privacy and technology.

In any analysis of public policy, events continue to unfold as books and articles are written. In this book, the primary period under study encompasses the early 1960s through the late 1980s. When relevant to the discussion, congressional activity on privacy issues through the 103d Congress (1993–94) is examined.

Acknowledgments

In writing this book, I have drawn upon more than ten years of interest, research, and involvement in privacy and technology issues. My doctoral dissertation, written at Cornell University in the late 1970s, was a comparative analysis of the formulation of information privacy policy in the United States and Britain. The advice that Theodore J. Lowi, Peter Katzenstein, and Woody Kelley offered during that time continues to influence my thinking and analysis. In the mid-1980s, I worked at the congressional Office of Technology Assessment and was the principal author of two reports on privacy and technology: *Electronic Record Systems and Individual Privacy* (1986) and *Electronic Surveillance and Civil Liberties* (1985). I also contributed to the OTA report on integrity testing. I was privileged to work at the OTA with a number of people upon whose knowledge and support I continue to draw, including Nancy Carson, Denise Dougherty, Gail Kouril, Jean Smith, Rick Weingarten, and Fred Wood.

Many individuals in Congress, in federal agencies, and in various interest groups were generous with their time in answering my questions and providing their insights on the dynamics of the policy process that occurred in the areas of privacy and technology discussed in this book. I am especially grateful to Jerry Berman, Robert M. Gellman, Mary Gerwin, Janlori Goldman, Robert W. Kastenmeier, Marcia MacNaughton, Ronald L. Plesser, Marc Rotenberg, Robert Veeder, Jon Weintraub, and Kristina Zahorik.

I am greatly indebted to four people who read the entire manuscript and made extensive and helpful comments: Christopher J. Deering, David H. Flaherty, Robert M. Gellman, and Alan F. Westin. All of them brought vast experience and knowledge to their reading of the manuscript, and I benefited enormously from their comments and advice. The reviews of two anonymous readers were also helpful in sharpening the argument and analysis. Over the last few years, a number of colleagues within the academic community as well as the policy community have read, discussed, and commented on sections of this book. At the risk of omitting someone, I would like to thank Colin Bennett, Timothy Conlan, Mary Culnan, Robert Dudley, Oscar Gandy, Miriam Golden, Janlori Goldman,

Robert Katzman, Barbara Knight, Judith Lichtenberg, Julie Mahler, Gary Marx, Joshua Mitchell, Helen Nissenbaum, James Piffner, Marc Rotenberg, James Rule, Paul Schwartz, and Conrad Waligorski.

Earlier versions of parts of the book's analysis and argument appear in other papers and articles. Some of the material on information privacy policy in chapter 4 appeared in "Privacy, Efficiency, and Surveillance: Policy Choices in an Age of Computers and Communication Technologies," in *Science, Technology, and Politics: Policy Analysis in Congress*, edited by Gary Bryner (Boulder, Colo.: Westview Press, 1992), reprinted by permission of Westview Press. The analysis about the passage of the Electronic Communications Privacy Act in chapter 5 and parts of the argument about the politics of ideas in chapter 7 were previously published in "Ideas or Interests: Privacy in Electronic Communications," *Policy Studies Journal* 21, no. 3 (Autumn 1993): 450–69. Parts of chapter 8, especially with respect to the policy issues raised by genetic testing and screening, can also be found in "Surveillance and New Technologies: The Changing Nature of Workplace Surveillance," in *New Technology, Surveillance, and Social Control*, edited by David Lyon and Elia Zureik (Minneapolis: University of Minnesota Press, forthcoming). Permission to use this published material is gratefully acknowledged.

In the course of thinking and writing about the social importance of privacy, I have presented parts of the argument in various settings, including a panel at the April 1991 Midwest Political Science Association meeting; a seminar at the May 1991 Computer Professionals for Social Responsibility meeting; a panel at the August 1992 Second Summer Symposium of the Honor Society of Phi Kappa Phi; a May 1993 Canadian workshop entitled "New Technology, Surveillance, and Social Control"; and a February 1994 seminar at the Center for Human Values at Princeton University. Comments and discussions at all of these forums were tremendously helpful in clarifying my analysis.

I greatly appreciate the support and encouragement of the chair of the Department of Public and International Affairs at George Mason University, Louise White, as well as the research assistance of Amy Bunger Pool and the help of Lisa Stimatz, a reference librarian at George Mason University's Fenwick Library. Discussions in my graduate courses on the policy process forced me to be more concrete and explicit about the dynamics of the policy process. I am also grateful to Lewis Bateman at the University of North Carolina Press for his editorial guidance and to Paula Wald for her careful editing.

Finally, I would like to acknowledge the support, encouragement, and help of friends and family. They are far too numerous to mention individually, but I thank them all. I owe a special and enormous debt to my husband and children, who endured my state of distraction while I concentrated my energy and time on writing; they provided much comfort and understanding, and it is to them that I dedicate this book.

Legislating

Privacy

Privacy, Technology, and Public Policy

When Robert Bork was nominated to the Supreme Court in 1987, a Washington, D.C., newspaper, after examining the computerized records of a video store, published the titles of movies he had rented. In 1989, while preparing an article on computers and privacy, a *Business Week* editor, claiming to be investigating a job applicant, gained access from his home computer to the database of a major credit bureau for a $500 fee and obtained the credit report of the vice president.[1] In 1991 allegations that aides of Virginia's junior senator Charles Robb had eavesdropped on the car phone conversations of Virginia's governor Douglas Wilder alarmed car phone users as well as politicians. Because of the prominence of the people involved, these "privacy" invasions received considerable attention and contributed to the development of legislative initiatives.

Every day millions of ordinary people are subject to a variety of technologies that invade their privacy. Frequent-shopper programs retain computerized databases on the buying habits of millions of consumers and then sell that information to marketing firms. Banks, department stores, malls, airports, and federal and state governments currently use sophisticated electronic surveillance equipment for security purposes. Cordless phone conversations can be picked up accidentally on a home or car radio or can be intercepted intentionally. Job applicants are subject to a variety of background checks and, for many jobs in the service sector, are required to take "honesty" or "integrity" tests to determine if they have engaged in prior actions that could be labeled dishonest or counterproductive and to gauge applicants' attitudes toward such actions.

Although these examples are contemporary, concerns about privacy and technology are not new. In 1928 Supreme Court Justice Louis Brandeis, in a now famous dissenting opinion in a case involving wiretapping, warned: "Subtler and more far reaching means of invading privacy have become available to the Government. . . . The progress of science in furnishing the Government with the means of espionage is not likely to stop with wiretapping. Ways may some day be developed by which the Government, without removing papers from secret drawers, can reproduce them in court, and by which it will be enabled to expose to a jury the most intimate occurrences of the home."[2] Science and technology have progressed and, as Justice Brandeis anticipated, have given government and other organizations the capability to invade privacy in new and different ways.

A number of technological innovations have an aura of science fiction but will soon become realities. Genetic mapping and screening will make possible the identification of genes associated with predispositions to certain diseases or behaviors. Medical researchers have already identified genes associated with cystic fibrosis, breast and colon cancer, osteoporosis, and alcoholism. Once genetic identifications can be made on an individual basis, a host of troubling privacy problems, especially in the areas of employment and insurance, will develop. Pilot projects utilizing Intelligent Transportation Systems (ITS) also raise privacy issues. These systems allow for the tracking of vehicles in real time and the collection of information on where vehicles have been and where they are headed. These communication and information systems will contain vast resources of personal information that have not been easily documented before and will be of great interest to direct marketers and law enforcement officials. Personal communication systems, which telephone companies see as a major trend in the future, will associate phone numbers with individuals rather than with phones. Although this will facilitate direct communication, it will also allow for monitoring the movements of individuals.

Uses of new technologies raise policy issues that are often defined in terms of an invasion of privacy. A new technology might allow for observation of actions regarded as "private," listening in on conversations thought to be "private," collection and exchange of information thought to be "private," or interpretation of physiological responses viewed as "private." At the same time, the new technology gives the organizations using it a new source of power over individuals. The power derives from the organizations' access to information about individuals' histories and activities, the content and pattern of their communications, and their thoughts and proclivities.

Technology enhances the ability of organizations to monitor individuals. Oscar Gandy refers to this as the "panoptic sort" — "a kind of high-tech cybernetic triage through which individuals and groups of people are being sorted according to their presumed economic or political value."[3]

Yet in policy debates in the United States, the emphasis has been on achieving the goal of protecting the privacy of individuals rather than curtailing the surveillance activities of organizations.[4] Instead of targeting the organizational aspects of surveillance, policy concern has been directed at the effect of surveillance on individual privacy. It was thought that by protecting individual privacy, the surveillance activities of organizations and the government would be checked. Individual rights were seen as a means of controlling power. This emphasis on privacy and individual rights makes for good political rhetoric and captures the initial attention of the public and policy makers. Privacy issues are easily placed on the public, and even the governmental, agenda. But as this book will illustrate, the focus on privacy and individual rights does not provide a sound basis on which to formulate public policy. As a value, privacy is important, but as a goal for public policy, privacy remains ambiguous.

One problem in legislating to protect privacy is that it is difficult to conceptualize privacy, especially for purposes of formulating policy. Authors of philosophical and legal works about privacy emphasize that their subject is difficult to define. Alan Westin's book *Privacy and Freedom* begins: "Few values so fundamental to society as privacy have been left so undefined in social theory or have been the subject of such vague and confused writing by social scientists."[5] Judith Jarvis Thomson's article "The Right to Privacy" opens: "Perhaps the most striking thing about the right to privacy is that nobody seems to have any very clear idea what it is."[6] Similarly, C. Herman Pritchett, in his foreword to David O'Brien's book *Privacy, Law, and Public Policy*, states: "Privacy is a confusing and complicated idea."[7] In the first chapter of her book *Privacy, Intimacy, and Isolation*, Julie Inness writes that in the legal and philosophical literature on privacy, "we find chaos; the literature lacks an accepted account of privacy's definition and value."[8] This view is echoed by Vincent Samar in the first chapter of his work *The Right to Privacy: Gays, Lesbians, and the Constitution* when he states: "After a century of development of the right to privacy in American law, the parameters of privacy and the arguments for its protection are still unclear."[9]

These difficulties in conceptualizing privacy not only are of philosophical importance but also have profound implications for the formulation of public policy to protect privacy. My interest here is not to arrive at a definition of privacy with which all philosophers can concur. I agree with Spiros Simitis, an internationally renowned privacy scholar and the former data protection commissioner for the German state of Hesse, that "the more the need for a convincing definition of privacy based on criteria free of inconsistencies has been stressed, the more abstract the language has grown."[10] Instead, I forego that debate entirely and use the definition of privacy that has provided the basis for most policy discussions in the United States, namely that privacy is the right to control information about and access to oneself.[11] My concern is to explore the policy importance of the idea of privacy, not to refine its definition, and to examine what happens when an individualistic conception of privacy serves as a goal for congressional policy making. As we will see, this individualistic conception of privacy does not provide a fruitful basis for the formulation of policy to protect privacy.

In addition to difficulties in conceptualizing privacy as a value, another problem in legislating to protect privacy is its definition as an individual right. In the American tradition, there are two types of rights — civil liberties and civil rights. Privacy is defined as a civil liberty, a right to be free of outside interference or what Isaiah Berlin terms a negative liberty.[12] Vincent Samar also makes the point that "legal privacy is a species of negative freedom."[13] Because privacy is viewed as a civil liberty, it loses some of the political power and legitimacy that attaches to rights in American political life.[14] Defining a problem in terms of rights has been a potent political resource for many issues — civil rights, women's rights, rights of the disabled — but these issues involve rights to some benefit or status and are defined not in terms of an atomistic individual but an individual as a member of a group. These civil rights issues raise different questions than do civil liberty issues about the use of government power and elicit different types of politics.

Because privacy is seen as an individual interest and choice, ambiguities about its meaning exist. It is assumed that different people define privacy differently. No individual right is absolute, and all need to be balanced against other competing rights and interests. Privacy is balanced against other values people regard as important, such as freedom of the press, law and order, detection of fraud, and national security. The ambiguous nature of privacy is further complicated because people assume they possess a certain level of privacy and appear unconcerned about privacy — until their privacy is threatened or invaded. When this occurs, the definition of privacy is dependent upon, or derived from, the nature of the threat to privacy.

In the United States, the formulation of policy to protect privacy in the face of technological change has been slow and incremental. Most recent analyses of the development of American privacy protections have focused on judicial formulation of policy. Both Julie Inness and Vincent

Samar base their analyses almost exclusively on legal protections for privacy that have resulted from Supreme Court decisions.[15] Congressional deliberations have received less attention. But several recent books point to weaknesses in American privacy legislation, especially in the area of personal information. Both David Flaherty[16] and Colin Bennett[17] compare the formulation and content of information privacy legislation, or data protection, in a number of Western democracies and point to shortcomings in the American approach. David Linowes,[18] Jeffrey Rothfeder,[19] and Jeff Smith[20] examine a number of situations, especially in the private sector, in which privacy is raised as an issue and suggest that existing statutes need to be strengthened and new ones adopted. In general, these authors advocate more congressional action. An understanding of the dynamics of congressional politics involving earlier privacy issues will provide a basis for determining what is likely to occur in policy formulation involving current and future privacy issues.

Three Areas of Privacy Concern

The U.S. Congress has passed more than a dozen laws protecting individual privacy, most of which have been enacted since 1974 (see figure 1.1). Most were placed on the congressional agenda in response to technological changes that were perceived as threatening an area of individual privacy. Concerns about information privacy—involving questions about the use of personal information collected by organizations such as credit card companies, banks, the federal government, educational institutions, and video stores—account for three-quarters of these laws. Communication privacy concerns—involving questions about who can legitimately intercept discussions between two parties, whether those discussions be printed, verbal, or electronic—are responsible for two-thirds of the remaining laws. Psychological privacy issues—involving questions about the degree and type of probing utilized in determining individuals' thoughts and attitudes—have resulted in the smallest percentage of privacy legislation.

Before discussing the selection of privacy areas, we should place these laws in perspective. The number of laws does not reflect enormous policy success by privacy advocates. Some of these laws, notably the Video Privacy Protection Act of 1988 and the Right to Financial Privacy Act of 1978, were passed in response to specific circumstances that highlighted threats to privacy. But more importantly, the actual number of laws passed pales in comparison to the amount of congressional activity de-

Figure 1.1
Selected Privacy Legislation

Title III of the Omnibus Crime Control and Safe Streets Act of 1968 (PL 90-351) protects the privacy of wire and oral communications by prohibiting electronic surveillance of aural communications except for law enforcement surveillance under a court order, specified telephone company monitoring for service purposes, and cases where one participant consents to the surveillance.

Fair Credit Reporting Act of 1970 (PL 91-508) requires credit investigations and reporting agencies to make their records available to the subjects of the records, provides procedures for correcting information, and permits disclosure only to authorized customers.

Family Educational Rights and Privacy Act of 1974 (PL 93-380) requires educational institutions to grant students or parents access to student records, establishes procedures to challenge and correct information, and limits disclosure to third parties.

Privacy Act of 1974 (PL 93-579) gives individuals rights of access to and correction of information held by federal agencies and places restrictions on federal agencies' collection, use, and disclosure of personally identifiable information.

Foreign Intelligence Surveillance Act of 1978 (PL 95-511) establishes legal standards and procedures for the use of electronic surveillance to collect foreign intelligence and counterintelligence within the United States.

Right to Financial Privacy Act of 1978 (PL 95-630) provides bank customers some privacy regarding their records held by banks and other financial institutions and stipulates procedures whereby federal agencies can gain access to such records.

Privacy Protection Act of 1980 (PL 96-440) prohibits government agencies from conducting unannounced searches of press offices and files if no one in the office is suspected of having committed a crime.

Cable Communications Policy Act of 1984 (PL 98-549) requires cable services to inform subscribers of the nature of personally identifiable information collected and the nature of the use of such information; the disclosures that may be made of such information; the period during which such information will be maintained; and the times during which subscribers may access such information about themselves. It also places restrictions on the cable services' collection and disclosure of such information.

Electronic Communications Privacy Act of 1986 (PL 99-508) extends Title III protections and requirements to new forms of voice, data, and video communications, including cellular phones, electronic mail, computer transmissions, and voice and display pagers.

Computer Matching and Privacy Protection Act of 1988 (PL 100-503) requires agencies to formulate procedural agreements before exchanging computerized record systems for purposes of searching or comparing those records and establishes Data Integrity Boards within each agency.

Employee Polygraph Protection Act of 1988 (PL 100-347) prohibits the private sector's use of lie detector tests for employment purposes, except in certain circumstances.

Video Privacy Protection Act of 1988 (PL 100-618) prohibits video stores from disclosing their customers' names and addresses and the specific videotapes rented or bought by customers except in certain circumstances.

Telemarketing Protections Act of 1991 (PL 102-243) restricts telemarketing calls, especially those made by autodialers.

Sources: Office of Technology Assessment, *Federal Government Information Technology: Electronic Record Systems and Individual Privacy*, OTA-CIT-296 (Washington, D.C.: Government Printing Office, 1986); Robert Aldrich, *Privacy Protection Law in the United States*, report 82-98 (Washington, D.C.: National Telecommunications and Information Administration, 1982); Sarah P. Collins, *Citizens' Control over Records Held by Third Parties*, CRS report 78-255 (Washington, D.C.: CRS, 1978).

voted to the subject and the number of laws not passed, involving, for example, medical privacy, personality tests, the sale of personal information, and the use of the social security number. From 1965 through 1974, nearly fifty congressional hearings and reports investigated a range of privacy issues including federal agency practices, use of personality tests and lie detectors, wiretapping, use of census information, and access to criminal history records. From 1965 through 1972, over 260 bills related to privacy were introduced, with the passage of only the Omnibus Crime Control and Safe Streets Act of 1968 and the Fair Credit Reporting Act of 1970.[21]

This book examines the course of legislation in one area of each of the major categories of privacy concern — information privacy, communication privacy, and psychological privacy.[22] Congress has been active in each of these areas. In the area of information privacy, there were more than 150 days of hearings from 1965 through 1988, excluding those on the privacy of credit records. Almost fifteen committee or staff reports on information privacy were released during the same period. On communication privacy issues, Congress held more than eighty days of hearings from 1958 through 1986, with the release of eight reports. In the area of polygraphs and privacy, Congress held over thirty days of hearings from 1974 through 1988 and issued ten committee or staff reports. (See appendixes A–C for details of congressional activity.)

Information privacy first appeared on the congressional agenda in

1965 in response to a proposal to establish a National Data Center. Computerized information systems were seen as a threat to the privacy of personal information held by many large organizations. The information activities of government agencies were of particular interest because of the sensitivity of the information they collected — financial information in tax files and criminal history records in Federal Bureau of Investigation (FBI) files, for example — and because of the nonvoluntary nature of government information collection. Computerized information called up the specter of a dossier society in which citizens are defined by their permanent records. In the 1960s, with the advent of mainframe computers, it was easier to store information for longer periods of time and to retrieve specific pieces of information from large databases. The Privacy Act was finally passed in 1974, largely because the revelation of government misuses of personal information that occurred during the Watergate scandal provided an opportunity for congressional consideration. Because of the work of the Privacy Protection Study Commission, congressional oversight of the Office of Management and Budget's (OMB) guidance on Privacy Act matters, and agency use of computer matching, whereby two or more computerized record systems are compared to identify individuals who appear in more than one record system, the issue of information privacy remained on the congressional agenda. When the power of computers was linked to that of telecommunications systems in the 1980s, it became easier to exchange information. The Computer Matching and Privacy Protection Act, passed in 1988, addressed some of the issues raised by computerized exchanges of information among government agencies.

Communication privacy initially appeared on the congressional agenda in the 1920s. Electronic eavesdropping and bugging devices made it possible for others to listen in on what were assumed to be private communications. Although Congress had made the interception and divulgence of communications illegal in 1927 and 1934,[23] these laws responded less to concerns about the privacy of the contents of communications than to concerns about the integrity of the communication system. Additionally, despite these laws, public and private wiretapping continued. Civil liberties advocates and law enforcement officials debated the merits and demerits of wiretapping throughout this period until legislation was passed in 1968. Title III of the Omnibus Crime Control and Safe Streets Act prohibited private interception of telephone conversations and required a court order for government interception, except in cases involving national security or cases in which one party consented to interception of the communication. This law was passed largely in response to the Supreme Court ruling in *Katz v. United States* (389 U.S. 347 [1967]) and because of congressional interest in organized crime. Telephone privacy reappeared on the congressional agenda in the early 1980s because of court decisions that revealed the gap in privacy protection created by new communication technologies, such as electronic mail and cellular phones. A consensus among civil liberties advocates, law enforcement officials, and representatives of the telephone industry facilitated the passage of the Electronic Communications Privacy Act in 1986.

Congressional debate about use of the polygraph began in the 1960s as part of a broader investigation of privacy invasions, including psychological testing. Use of the polygraph and other "lie detector" techniques made it possible to record a person's conscious, subconscious, or unconscious thoughts. These techniques raised the specter of not only Big Brother but also the *Clockwork Orange* depiction of dehumanization and brainwashing. The Employee Polygraph Protection Act was not passed until 1988, when the scientific evidence mounted that polygraph results were not valid for preemployment screening and when unions recognized that polygraphs could be used as a way of denying employment opportunities to selected people. Questions about privacy and employment screening continued to be raised with the increased use of paper-and-pencil honesty tests, and the issue remained on the congressional agenda.

These three areas of privacy and technology provide interesting comparisons for a number of reasons. First, all were defined as "privacy" issues, and yet the privacy invasion in each case took on a somewhat different character or definition. Therefore, the philosophical and legal concepts behind the privacy concern varied. With respect to information held by government agencies, privacy was defined as the right of individuals to exercise some control over the use of information about themselves. In the area of communication privacy, the roots of the privacy interest were found in the Fourth Amendment right of the people "to be secure in their persons, houses, papers, and effects, against unreasonable searches and seizures." For polygraph examinations, the privacy interest was defined as an invasion of intimate thoughts and bodily integrity, which were threatened by the probing nature of the questions and the physical intrusiveness of the polygraph technique. Fifth Amendment issues regarding protection against self-incrimination and Fourth Amendment questions involving searching and seizing a person's thoughts were also raised. For each area of privacy concern, these different philosophical and legal traditions established different policy histories or policy roots that affected the course of policy deliberation.

A second reason for comparing these areas is that in each case the technological component of the perceived privacy invasion is different. In information privacy, advances in computers and telecommunications enabled the collection, storage, exchange, and manipulation of vast reserves of personal information. With increased access to personal computers and networks, these capabilities became available to diverse types of users. In communication privacy, various communication-transmission technologies — copper wire, fiber, microwave, and satellite — were all somewhat vulnerable to interception by other technologies. In psychological privacy, technologies allowed the measurement of physiological responses, including respiration, perspiration, and blood pressure.

The role technology played in defining the policy problem and the ability to deal with the problem apart from the technology differed in each of these cases. For example, in the early debates regarding the computerization of information, many argued that the problems resulted from the maintaining of record systems, not the fact that they were computerized, and that policy should not focus on technology. Debates about the privacy of communications centered around the fact that the technological medium through which a communication was transmitted established the ability to intercept that particular communication. Much of the policy debate focused on selecting the appropriate preelectronic analogy for that type of communication. For example, is electronic mail similar to postal communications or voice communications? In the case of the polygraph, it was the existence of a technology that allowed the probing of the body's physiological reactions that created a policy problem.

Because technology played such a prominent role in defining these issues and in placing them on the congressional agenda, an understanding of the relationship between technology and privacy and of the debates about the relationship between technology and social change provides an important context for examining congressional debates.

Technology and Privacy

In each of these areas, technology was the catalyst for public concern about privacy. Technology played a pivotal role in defining these issues as public problems and in placing them on the policy agenda. In each area, however, it was possible to invade individual privacy before the particular technology involved was developed. Before the advent of computers and telecommunications, personal information was collected and stored by organizations and also exchanged among organizations. Before telegraph, telephone, and electronic mail, it was possible to listen in on or overhear the personal conversations of others. And before the invention of devices to measure physiological responses, judgments could be made about whether a person was telling the truth.

Despite the fact that it was possible to invade privacy before a particular technology was used, debate about technology and privacy inevitably revisited the question about the importance of the technology. Did the technology cause the privacy invasions? Or did technology exacerbate threats to privacy that already existed? Or was the technology itself neutral, not playing a direct role but making possible either increased privacy or diminished privacy depending upon those who applied the technology? The debate about the role of technology in bringing about social change is a long and colorful one, having persisted for centuries. It is not possible to either summarize or resolve that debate here, but it may be helpful to place the debate about privacy and technology into a broader perspective by introducing three schools of thought on the role of technology and social change: those of the technology determinists, the technology neutralists, and the technology realists.

The technology determinists believe that technology has become an end in itself, that is, an autonomous force subject to no external controls. In an important analysis of this perspective, Langdon Winner summarizes technological determinism as resting upon two hypotheses: "(1) that the technical base of society is the fundamental condition affecting all patterns of social existence and (2) that changes in technology are the single most important source of change in society."[24] Consistent with these hypotheses, anthropologist Leslie White states: "Social systems are in a very real sense secondary and subsidiary to technological systems. . . . The technology is the independent variable, the social system the dependent variable."[25] Economist John Kenneth Galbraith adopts a similar view: "We are becoming the servants in thought, as in action, of the machines we have created to serve us."[26] Probably the most influential of the technological determinists is Jacques Ellul, who asserts that "technique has become autonomous; it has fashioned an omnivorous world which obeys its own laws and which has renounced all tradition."[27] Other prominent thinkers such as Hannah Arendt, Lewis Mumford, and Herbert Marcuse have also adopted this view, fearing the inevitable emergence of a world in which the individual becomes a cog in a social machine whose course is dictated by technical processes beyond human control.

Opposed to this is the view of the technology neutralists that technology has no independent force. Rather, it is a tool that can be shaped by people to whatever ends they desire. Technology remains under human control. It is possible to anticipate all possible effects of technological change and to choose the end desired. As Edward Glaser describes it, "Technology is inherently neutral and plastic. It makes a fine servant and will do exactly what man commands."[28]

The middle ground in this debate is held by those who recognize that although technology has a force of its own, it is not independent of political and social forces. Technological developments create new opportunities and new problems, but the direction of social change is the result of the dynamic relationship between technological developments and political, economic, and social decisions. In this vein, Victor Ferkiss argues that "technology sets limits to man's activities and in large measure defines his existence" but adds that although "technology conditions civilizations and explains much about them . . . it never completely determines them or acts in isolation or independently of human choosing."[29] Somewhat similarly, Oscar Gandy claims that there is a "technological imperative. It resides not in the machines but in the people who use them."[30] The technological realists also see technology as arising from certain political, social, and economic decisions. The "invention" or "development" of technologies is a result not just of scientific or technical knowledge but also of larger social decisions that make the knowledge possible and create the need for the technology. James Beniger's analysis of the evolution of modern society as the attempt to gain increasing control over information and of the important roles that bureaucracy and the computer play in that evolution is in keeping with the argument that technological changes must be examined from a broad historical and cultural perspective.[31]

As technological innovations increase and come to dominate most areas of modern life — business, education, medicine, and government — the social responsibilities according to the technological realist perspective become somewhat overwhelming. Neil Postman, for example, introduces the image that culture "must negotiate with technology."[32] At the same time, he warns that the scope of these negotiations is broad: "Technological change is neither additive nor subtractive. It is ecological. . . . It changes everything."[33] Langdon Winner similarly concludes that technology is not "a monstrosity or evil in and of itself" but "an unfinished creation, largely forgotten and uncared for, which is forced to make its own way in the world."[34]

The question of privacy and technology can be examined from each of these approaches. Technology determinists see computers and telecommunications, electronic eavesdropping equipment, and the polygraph as the causes of privacy invasions. More importantly, they assert that the existence of such devices signals a subsequent set of events beyond human control. The kind of world described by Aldous Huxley in *Brave New World* and George Orwell in *1984* is inevitable. The sphere of individual life free from outside observation will only diminish further until it disappears. Little can be done to reverse the course that has been launched by the technology. Public policy is therefore largely irrelevant. Technology neutralists, on the other hand, regard privacy invasions as the result not of technology but of human decisions. The technologies are merely tools that are used by people to achieve certain ends. If the ends are unpopular, the technologies can be changed by human decision. Under this approach, public policy plays an active role in setting the course of technological development.

Technology realists adopt a more complicated view of privacy and technology. They see technology as an agent of change and believe the actual direction of change depends on both the capabilities of the technology and the uses to which it is put. Unlike the other two approaches, technology realism considers neither technology nor society alone the determining factor. Rather, realists maintain that a dynamic relationship exists between the two. Computer technology, for example, opens up new possibilities for information processing; those in charge of information processing choose certain uses of that technology that fit within the financial and ethical constraints set by their organizations. But the technology determines the range of choices, and not all consequences of a choice can be predicted. The role of public policy is largely reactive — technological changes are adopted, anticipated or unanticipated consequences occur, and those dissatisfied with the consequences press for change. But the reversal of the course that has been set is difficult not only because the technology itself pushes in a certain direction but also because powerful social, economic, and political actors may benefit from that course.

By the mid-1960s, concerns about privacy and technology were reflected in a "literature of alarm" that was instrumental in placing the issues of information privacy, communication privacy, and psychological privacy on the policy agenda. This literature also provided serious analyses of the policy problems and proposals for legislation. Prominent among these works are Samuel Dash, Richard Schwartz, and Robert Knowlton, *The Eavesdroppers* (1959); Myron Brenton, *The Privacy Invaders* (1964);

Vance Packard, *The Naked Society* (1964); Edward Long, *The Intruders* (1967); Alan Westin, *Privacy and Freedom* (1967); Jerry Rosenberg, *The Death of Privacy* (1969); Stanton Wheeler, *On Record: Files and Dossiers in American Life* (1969); and Arthur Miller, *The Assault on Privacy* (1971). Although the privacy concern and emphasis varied, all viewed technology, especially computer technology, as fundamentally changing the privacy of individuals. Senator Edward Long (D-Mich.), a member of the Senate Judiciary Committee, was most concerned with the "electronic snooping" that was made possible with miniature transmitters, telephone bugs, and wireless microphones. He took the position that "in this field, as in many others, modern science and technology seem to have run far ahead of man's ability to handle his new knowledge wisely."[35] Arthur Miller, a law professor at the University of Michigan, focused on the threat to privacy from computers, data banks, and dossiers and emphasized that "man must shape his tools lest they shape him."[36]

The most comprehensive volume in this literature is Alan Westin's *Privacy and Freedom*. Recognizing that the new surveillance capabilities of telephone tapping, electronic eavesdropping, television monitoring, polygraph testing, personality testing, and computerized databases were the result of technological changes, Westin saw a need to move beyond public awareness of the problem to "discussion of what can be done to protect privacy in an age when so many forces of science, technology, environment, and society press against it from all sides."[37] But for Westin, it was not the technology alone that threatened privacy but the fact that these technologies were developed "at a time when socio-cultural changes in American life have produced an acceptance of these surveillance techniques by many private and public authorities."[38] It was the organizational uses of these techniques and the benefits that various social, political, and economic actors gained through use of surveillance technologies that brought the threat to individual privacy.

Although technology was the catalyst for public concern, most analyses in this "literature of alarm" concluded that technology was not the policy problem. A Luddite solution of destroying the machines was neither appropriate nor possible. Instead, the problem concerned privacy invasions resulting from organizational uses of these new technologies — Internal Revenue Service (IRS) databases, FBI wiretapping, or employer polygraphing. The focus of the policy debate shifted from the technology alone to the best way to protect individual privacy that appeared threatened by organizational uses of new technologies.

This book adheres to the tradition of the technology realists. In each of the policy areas examined here, technology is important because it changed or influenced ideas and interests, brought new players into policy communities, and energized policy entrepreneurs. In this sense, technology is something of an intervening factor, lacking independent influence over policy but working primarily through ideas, interests, policy communities, and policy entrepreneurs. The technology was important in determining those who perceived themselves as affected. In each case, technology was thought to threaten individual privacy. Technology changed the relationship between individuals and organizations and thus changed the interests of the individuals and the organizations. Computerized information systems made it easier for organizations to collect, store, retrieve, and manipulate personal information; the technology gave them the capability to know more, and therefore potentially to control more, about individuals. Wiretapping and electronic surveillance gave law enforcement officials, as well as snoopers and private investigators, the ability to monitor personal communications; again, the technology gave them the capability to know more, and therefore potentially to control more, about individuals. Polygraph testing gave employers and law enforcement officials the capability to intimidate individuals into revealing facts and feelings; again, the technology brought with it a capacity to change the power relationship between the individual and others.

Congress and Privacy Legislation

In order to understand the dynamics of congressional formulation and adoption of policy when privacy is perceived to be threatened by new technologies, four factors involved in congressional policy making will be examined — ideas, interests, policy communities, and policy entrepreneurs. In each case, the idea of privacy was pivotal in the initial definition of the policy problem and in placing it on the congressional agenda. However, the idea of privacy turned out to be a weak basis for formulating public policy; it did not have the intellectual clarity or public support to become "an idea whose time has come."[39] The weakness of the idea of privacy as a policy goal exists in part because of the American legal and philosophical understanding of privacy. The definition of privacy as an individual right that derives from the Constitution did, in fact, hamper constructive policy formulation because discussion often became bogged down in court definitions. The association of these issues with the concept of privacy meant that a rich legal and ideological storehouse of ideas was available, but these ideas were not clear enough for successful policy discourse. Instead, legal phrases—such as an expectation of privacy—became symbols everyone could support, albeit with different meanings. In addition to the ambiguous meaning of privacy, other difficulties in policy formulation occurred because of its definition as a right. No right is absolute; all are balanced against other social and individual rights and interests.

Much of the policy formulation for each of these issues focused on such other social interests. The debate moved from the idea of privacy to an examination of the ideas that were supported by other interests and focused on how other ideas and interests would be compromised by privacy protections. In effect, this changed the policy debate from one of ideas to one of interests. In each case, opponents did not challenge privacy as a value but instead focused on the importance of the competing interest, and the value associated with that interest, and on the need to balance privacy against that interest. Balancing of interests is a major theme in congressional debates within the three privacy areas examined in this book. In the case of computerized information systems, the competing interest was the efficiency of organizational operations, in this case government agencies. The advantages of computers and telecommunications in collecting, processing, manipulating, and storing information were extolled by those opposed to regulations protecting privacy. In the debates about wiretapping and electronic surveillance, the major competing interest was the investigatory need of law enforcement officials. Protecting the privacy of communications was seen by opponents as limiting the ability of government agents to access the contents of communications that might provide evidence of illegal activities. Concerning the polygraph, the competing interest was the ability of employers to hire honest workers and reduce theft and fraud in the workplace. Those opposed to restrictions on the use of the polygraph argued that such restrictions were heavy-handed federal actions limiting the freedom of private employers and did not directly engage the arguments about the intrusiveness or invasiveness of the polygraph.

Advocates of privacy protections were therefore forced to respond to these interests. A policy community concerned about privacy emerged, with the American Civil Liberties Union (ACLU) forming the core. In the case of information privacy, the ACLU joined with allied computer experts in debates over the use of personal information. In communication privacy, civil liberties advocates worked primarily on their own during debates over Title III and cooperated with communications industry groups to gain passage of the Electronic Communications Privacy Act. In debates about the polygraph, the ACLU worked with unions and psychologists for passage of the Employee Polygraph Protection Act.

Given the fact that each of these issues remained on the congressional agenda for years, if not decades, before legislation was passed and that there were quite clearly two sides in the debate over privacy and technology, policy entrepreneurs were essential to successful policy resolution. In all three cases, leadership came from the chairs of the subcommittees with jurisdiction over the issues. But equally important were the efforts of congressional staff who worked within the policy communities, developed expertise in the areas, and sustained their interest even when there appeared to be no realistic political support for legislation.

The purpose of this analysis of the dynamics of ideas, interests, policy communities, and policy entrepreneurs in privacy policy formulation is to understand why Congress legislated as it did, at the time it did, and to set the stage for analyzing, in the concluding chapter, how Congress might respond to current privacy issues such as Caller ID, genetic testing, and increased private sector use of personal information. Because each of these factors is central to the analysis, they are briefly introduced here.

Ideas. Within the public policy literature, the "politics of ideas" is becoming an important new model for explaining policy making, providing "an alternative perspective that recognizes greater diversity in the motives of political action and a wider array of effective political forces."[40] In this new model, ideas about what is good for society, rather than individual self-interest, explain much of political activity and policy making. Indeed, ideas associated with the public interest, morality, justice, the collective good, and wise policy solutions are seen as forces that can overcome narrow interests in determining political choices. The exact features of this model are still evolving, and in chapter 7 I examine its contours more thoroughly. It is important at this point, however, to acknowledge that one difficulty with this model is that ideas and interests are not inherently contradictory in their influence or effect, nor do they operate independently within policy making. Kingdon notes that "self-interests and ideas are not opposite but are inseparable."[41] It is often difficult to disentangle the effects of ideas and interests. In most policy formulation, it is a safe bet that both are at work. But how ideas and interests interact and the policy effect of that interaction also need to be explored. This book seeks to shed some light on the interaction between ideas and interests. As Kingdon points out, an idea "might well be accompanied by and buttressed by self-interest, but it also has a life of its own."[42] My interest here is to reveal how privacy's "life of its own" shaped the interaction between ideas and interests and ultimately policy outcomes.

Much of the empirical support for the existence of a politics of ideas comes from case studies of policy making for legislation that was in the public interest but was opposed by interest groups. In these cases, a broad, unorganized public interest triumphed over organized special interests. Martha Derthick and Paul Quirk examined the deregulation of the trucking, airline, and telecommunications industries, three cases in which deregulation occurred despite the initial opposition of industry, unions, and regulatory agencies.[43] They concluded that deregulation was an "idea whose time had come" and that ideas could not be ignored in policy analysis. Timothy Conlan, Margaret Wrightson, and David Beam examined the passage of the Tax Reform Act of 1986, again a case in which organized special interests were opposed to legislation that arguably benefited the broad, unorganized public.[44] They credit the idea of comprehensive tax reform or tax fairness as playing a critical role in explaining the passage of the act. Peter Schuck examined immigration policy in the 1980s and concluded that a number of ideas — including diversity, civil rights, international human rights, competitiveness, due process and equal protection, and family fairness — were important causal forces.[45]

The areas of privacy and technology policy examined in this book offer a different opportunity for analysis because they involved an idea or value — privacy — that could have provided a force for policy making but did not.[46] The literature on the politics of ideas suggests several conditions under which ideas might play a central role in policy making. If an *exogenous factor* precipitates change, then the effect is often to establish a new arena for conflict or to broaden the scope of conflict for an existing issue. This would also allow for the definition of a new policy issue or the redefinition of an older issue, enabling new players or interests to join the policy community. At this point, ideas can play a role in defining the issue or in providing the basis for a new coalition. A second condition under which a politics of ideas might occur is the presence of *symbols and slogans* by which ideas can be popularized and introduced into public discourse. If an issue can be tied to symbols, then ideas could play an important role in policy making and possibly overcome interests. A related condition for the existence of a politics of ideas is the presence of a *latent public interest* that can be mobilized to be concerned about the issue. As we will see, these conditions are present in the cases of privacy and technology. We might therefore expect the formulation and passage of privacy and technology policies to reflect a politics of ideas; later chapters will examine why this did not occur.

Interests. The interest model of politics provides the framework for much analysis of policy formulation and adoption. Policy making is viewed as a process of bargaining, negotiation, and compromise among competing groups whose material interests are likely to be affected by the policy under debate.[47] The result is usually an incremental change in existing policy or a tentative step in a new direction, either of which represents a new equilibrium point that results from the group struggle. In the interest model, this group struggle occurs largely behind the scenes in subgovernments or "iron triangles" in which the groups affected work out their own compromises. In this model, the government — particularly legislative committees or subcommittees — provides a forum for group discussion, serves as a referee in group disputes, and ratifies group agreements.

In the three areas of privacy and technology examined in this book, the initial policy issue was defined as one of privacy. But policy in each area imposed costs on fairly well-defined interests — government agencies, law enforcement and intelligence officials, and employers. These interests were already organized and had easy access to congressional committees and members of Congress. In addition to possessing political access and support and a clear sense of their own interests, they were able to redirect the definition of the issue away from the idea of privacy to other ideas, such as efficiency, crime control, and an honest work force. In the process, the politics of interests dominated. The ambiguity of the idea of privacy and its definition as an individual right made it relatively easy to move from the politics of ideas to the politics of interests. In the introduction to *The Power of Public Ideas*, Robert Reich suggests that in some cases "to disregard . . . ideas is to miss the essential story."[48] But in these cases of privacy and technology, to disregard interests is to miss the essential story. Politics in these cases is similar to interest-group politics, with subcommittee chairs playing key roles, pro forma floor approval, and behind-the-scenes negotiations among a relatively small group of interested parties.

Policy communities. John Kingdon describes policy communities as specialists in a given policy area, including researchers, congressional staff, interest-group advocates, academics, and government analysts.[49] Such individuals constitute a largely self-selected, informal group concerned about a specific policy area. Policy community members formulate position papers and policy alternatives, discuss ideas, hold meetings to develop a consensus, and often draft legislative proposals. The concept of a policy community is similar to that of an "issue network," developed by Hugh Heclo as an alternative to the notions of iron triangles and sub-governments that dominated most earlier analyses of policy formulation.[50] Iron triangles and subgovernments imply a closed system of people from congressional committees, executive agencies, and interest groups. Although few in number, members of iron triangles exerted almost autonomous influence over particular policy areas. After examining policy making in the 1960s and 1970s, Heclo concluded that in many policy areas, "it is all but impossible to identify clearly who the dominant actors are."[51] Instead of a few key individuals, webs or networks of influence exist, comprised of a number of participants who move in and out of the network, are motivated by an intellectual or emotional commitment rather than a material interest, and operate in a nonhierarchical manner. Policy communities generally exhibit more stability than do issue networks but are similar in that interests alone do not dominate relationships within the community.[52]

The notion that such policy communities or issue networks exist in a number of policy areas and exert considerable influence over policy making in those areas is not disputed. What is somewhat less well understood is how these communities develop, change over time, and exercise influence in a variety of settings. In each of the three areas of privacy and technology policy examined in this book, the development of a policy community that advocated passage of legislation and monitored implementation and evaluation was critical in mobilizing support and keeping the issue on the congressional agenda. In the 1960s, the threats to individual privacy that technological changes raised were new issues. Privacy and technology issues did not fit neatly into an existing policy subsystem with established relationships among interest groups, congressional committees, and government agencies. Indeed, much of the early policy formulation focused on finding an appropriate definition for the policy problem — whether it was one of civil liberties and constitutional rights, one of controlling or managing technological change, or one of bureaucratic or organizational accountability.[53] Because the problem crossed the boundaries between traditional policy interests and committee jurisdictions, individuals with diverse perspectives were brought together in the early stages of policy discussion. At the time privacy issues were added to the public agenda in the 1960s, a privacy community interested in legislation had not yet formed. By the late 1970s, however, a core policy community interested in general privacy issues existed along with specialized privacy communities, or advocacy coalitions, concerned with specific aspects of privacy — including information privacy, communication privacy, and workplace privacy. Moreover, the creation of a group of privacy experts in the 1980s was critical in broadening the legitimacy of and the support for the issue and in facilitating learning within the policy community. Chapters 4, 5, and 6 will examine each of these trends — the establishment of a general privacy community, the development of advocacy coalitions, and the emergence of privacy experts — and analyze how learning occurred within and across these groups.

Policy entrepreneurs. Members of Congress operate under a variety of constraints and have a range of policy preferences. The particular mix of constraints and policy preferences varies significantly from member to member and often for one member in the course of a legislative career. Despite this variation, the literature on congressional behavior points to some commonalities. In a classic study of Congress, Richard Fenno identified three goals that motivate members' committee activity: reelection, good public policy, and influence within the chamber.[54] Of these, interest in reelection has tended to dominate much of the subsequent literature on congressional behavior.[55]

In general, privacy issues do not provoke great electoral support, however. Members are therefore unlikely to champion or adopt these issues just because they believe there will be an immediate electoral payoff. As will be shown in chapter 3, the public is increasingly concerned about privacy but is not mobilized to take political action to protect privacy. Privacy has not been an issue in the electoral arena at either the national or the state level. Constituency pressure or an "electoral connection" does not provide an explanation for why a member of Congress chooses to champion privacy issues.

In each of the three areas of privacy and technology policy examined in this book, congressional policy formulation and reformulation spanned over thirty years. For long periods of time, several key members of Congress gave sustained attention to each issue, and their leadership was critical to the passage of legislation and subsequent oversight. These members acted as "policy entrepreneurs."[56] Most congressional entrepreneurs on privacy issues have been highly respected members of their institutions. In the 1960s, Senators Sam Ervin and Edward Long and Representatives Cornelius Gallagher, Barry Goldwater, Jr., and Edward Koch were all visible and articulate members of their chambers who brought a great deal of personal credibility to privacy issues. In the 1980s, Senators William Cohen, Orrin Hatch, Edward Kennedy, Patrick Leahy, and Charles Mathias, and Representatives Don Edwards, Glenn English, Robert Kastenmeier, and Pat Williams were similarly visible, forceful, and credible proponents of privacy concerns. Privacy, then, has not suffered from a lack of respected congressional leaders. A question to be examined throughout the book is why these members of Congress adopted a leadership position on privacy-related issues. The answer is not simple; a number of factors affect members' behavior.

In each area of privacy and technology policy, subcommittee jurisdiction set the context for member interest and the staff kept the issue alive. The three areas involve different committees. Congressional debates about government collection of personal information occurred in four committees — the Senate Committee on Governmental Affairs, the House Committee on Government Operations, and the House and Senate Committees on the Judiciary. With respect to the interception of telephone communications, policy formulation occurred almost exclusively in the House and Senate Committees on the Judiciary. Policy deliberations regarding the polygraph began in the Judiciary and Government Operations committees and later moved to the House Committee on Post Office and Civil Service and then the House Committee on Education and Labor and the Senate Committee on Labor and Human Resources.

Privacy and Public Policy

In each of the three areas of privacy and technology policy examined in this book, a similar pattern regarding the dynamics of the congressional policy debate emerges — initial definition of the policy problem as one of privacy invaded by new technology; opposition by those who benefited from use of the new technology and from redefinition of the problem; continued pressure by a small but vigilant privacy community that relied for support on the members and staff of key congressional committees; and, after years, passage of weakened legislation.

The comparison of these three areas allows for the drawing of some general conclusions concerning the meaning of privacy in an advanced technological society and the ability of Congress to deal with issues involving fundamental values and technological change. The policy process began with an emphasis on the value of privacy, and much of the policy debate was framed in terms of an individual interest — privacy — in conflict with a societal interest — government efficiency, law enforcement, and an honest work force. In policy debates, the individual interest was on weaker footing than the societal interest. Privacy was on the defensive because those alleging a privacy invasion bore the burden of proving that a certain activity did indeed invade privacy and that the individual privacy interest was more important than the societal interest.

Missing from the debates was an explicit recognition of the social importance of privacy. Although privacy is viewed as a boundary separating the individual from society, the dominant assumption has been that only the individual has an interest in that boundary — that society has to concede control over certain areas to the individual for personal development. This is consistent with a liberal democratic tradition, which emphasizes the importance of the individual and the necessity of individual rights. But the social dimensions of privacy become apparent once one considers the source of threats to privacy. Threats to privacy from database surveillance, electronic eavesdropping, and polygraph testing do not come from other individuals and do not primarily affect one's personal relationships. Instead, these threats come from private and governmental organizations and affect how these organizations treat individuals and how they control an individual's opportunity to obtain a job, credit, or insurance in today's society. Privacy is important not only because of its protection of the individual as an individual but also because individuals share common perceptions about the importance and meaning of privacy, because it serves as a restraint on how organizations use their power, and because privacy — or the lack of privacy — is built into systems and organizational practices and procedures. These latter dimensions give privacy broader social, not only individual, significance.

This analysis of the policy processes resulting in Title III of the Omnibus Crime Control and Safe Streets Act of 1968, the Privacy Act of 1974, the Electronic Communications Privacy Act of 1986, the Computer Matching and Privacy Protection Act of 1988, and the Employee Polygraph Protection Act of 1988 offers insights into how to define more appropriately the policy problems presented by current privacy issues such as Caller ID, the use of the social security number as a national identifier, sale of transactional information such as consumers' buying habits, and genetic screening. For these new issues, it is important to recognize not only the individual rights problems they raise but also the collective interests affected by privacy invasions. In "Federalist Paper #10," James Madison refers to factions or particular interests opposed to the "permanent and aggregate interests of the community."[57] In chapter 8, I will argue that privacy is one of those permanent and aggregate interests.

Chapter 2

Privacy as a Philosophical and Legal Concept

Throughout American history and in philosophical and legal discussions, privacy has been viewed as important to the individual, as some type of boundary that shields the individual from others. The importance of privacy is rooted in liberal thinking — privacy inheres in the individual as an individual and is important to the individual primarily for self-development or for the establishment of intimate or human relationships. Given that the philosophical justification for privacy rests largely on its importance to the individual as an individual, policy discussions about protecting privacy focus on the goal of protecting an individual value or interest. The result has been an emphasis on an atomistic individual and the legal protection of his or her rights. This line of discourse has served to weaken the concept of privacy as a policy goal. But it is important to examine the evolution of the emphasis on the importance of privacy to the individual and the lack of development of a broader social importance to privacy.

Philosophical arguments about privacy's importance are paralleled by views on privacy in common law and constitutional law. Anglo-American legal thinking, especially constitutional thinking, places the individual at the center of concern. In the development of privacy law, the individual is indeed at the center, but the development of legal doctrines to protect individual privacy has been slow and fragmented.

In order to understand the philosophical and legal context that provides the backdrop for the discussion of privacy issues in the three privacy and technology areas examined in this book, this chapter briefly reviews the philosophical and legal development of a right to privacy. The intention here is not to provide an exhaustive discussion of philosophical and legal bases of privacy but to understand how philosophical and legal thinking shaped the definition of privacy as a value at the time that public and congressional attention turned to issues of privacy invasions.

Philosophical Views about Privacy

Concern for a right to privacy has been discussed primarily in terms of liberal thinking, especially Lockean liberalism, with its emphasis on the individual's possession of certain natural rights. In liberal thinking, a tension was established between the individual and the larger social/political entity of which the individual is a part. As Thomas McCollough points out: "Both Hobbes and Locke began in their political theorizing with the atomistic unit of the self-interested individual; the problem was how essentially separate individuals, with private and conflicting interests, could coexist in tolerable harmony."[1] The purpose of government was the protection of individual natural rights, and at the same time, these rights played an important role in limiting the power of government.

Within this liberal tradition, privacy is regarded as an individual right and its importance has been framed in individualistic terms — in terms that emphasize separateness and self-interest. This liberal view of the importance of privacy has dominated subsequent policy debate about privacy. To understand how the individualistic concept of privacy developed, this section reviews the early philosophical literature about privacy. It is this literature that shaped the conception of privacy that served as a policy goal during the first congressional debates about privacy in the 1960s. This literature continues to provide the intellectual backdrop for policy discussions about privacy.

American philosophical and legal thinking on privacy as a specific value and right takes as its point of departure Samuel Warren and Louis Brandeis's 1890 *Harvard Law Review* article. Their article, and subsequent philosophical and legal debate in the United States about a right to privacy, was provoked by a technological change — the ability of the press to report events without being physically present: "Instantaneous photographs and newspaper enterprise have invaded the sacred precincts of private and domestic life; and numerous mechanical devices threaten to make good the prediction that 'what is whispered in the closet shall be proclaimed from the housetops.'"[2] They argued that the common law protected a "right to privacy" and that "now the right to life has come to mean the right to enjoy life — the right to be let alone."[3]

Warren and Brandeis based this right on two common law developments. The first was the law relating to defamation, which they viewed as a weak basis for a right to privacy because "the wrongs and correlative rights recognized by the law of slander and libel are in their nature material rather than spiritual."[4] Instead, they anchored the right to privacy in the common law protection offered intellectual and artistic property: "The protection afforded to thoughts, sentiments, and emotions, expressed through the medium of writing or of the arts, so far as it consists in preventing publication, is merely an instance of the more general *right of the individual to be let alone.* . . . The principle which protects personal writings and all other personal productions, not against theft and physical appropriation, but against publication in any form, is in reality not the principle of private property, but that of an *inviolate personality*" (emphasis added).[5] Their argument emphasized the importance of privacy to the individual, who needed a "retreat from the world" and had a right "to be let alone." As they so eloquently stated, "The intensity and complexity of life, attendant upon advancing civilization, have rendered necessary some retreat from the world, and man, under the refining influence of culture, has become more sensitive to publicity, so that solitude and privacy have become more essential to the individual."[6] At the same time, they realized that "the dignity and convenience of the individual must yield to the demands of the public welfare or of private justice."[7]

Privacy was not again a major topic of philosophical interest in the United States until the 1960s, provoked both by technological changes that appeared to threaten privacy and also by renewed legal interest in the Warren and Brandeis article. These philosophical debates will be reviewed to show that the emphasis on the importance of privacy to the individual continued in modern thinking and also concealed another aspect of privacy — its social importance. In many of these inquiries, authors refer to a social value of privacy. But they do not develop the social importance of privacy. Instead, they use its social aspects as a context for examining the importance of privacy to the individual. The question of the social importance of privacy is a path that was not pursued thoroughly or aggressively in these philosophical and legal writings.

The 1960s debate between Dean William Prosser and Professor Edward Bloustein about whether the Warren and Brandeis "right to privacy" was a singular right or a composite of other rights illustrates that although privacy was recognized as existing in a social context, its social importance was not developed.[8] Bloustein acknowledged a social value in, and community concern with, privacy. He challenged Prosser's opinion that privacy rested on a number of different interests and argued that if Prosser was correct, then "the social value or interest we call privacy is not an independent one, but is only a composite of the value our society places on protecting mental tranquility, reputation and intangible forms of property."[9] Bloustein here referred to privacy as a social value, which when invaded involved "a blow to human dignity or an injury to personality,"[10] and he argued that there was a "community concern for the preservation of the individual's dignity."[11] But when he discussed specific instances in which privacy was threatened, he did not make explicit the social importance of privacy but instead emphasized the social importance of the competing interest. For example, with respect to the government's collection of information, Bloustein stated: "Most of us have agreed, however, that the social benefits to be gained in these instances require the information to be given and that the ends to be achieved are worth the price of diminished privacy."[12] This shift in emphasis is one that continues in subsequent philosophical treatments of privacy: a social value of privacy exists but only as it relates to the individual. When privacy competes with another social value or interest, the *social* basis of the other interest is explored while the *individual* basis of the privacy interest is examined.

This shift can also be seen in Alan Westin's seminal work *Privacy and Freedom*. Westin's writing is rooted in the social context; his concern is with larger social, economic, and political changes that diminish privacy. He argued that privacy is a basic need derived from animal roots, was important to people in primitive societies, and is part of the Western liberal political tradition of limiting the surveillance powers of government. Consistent with liberal thinking, he defined privacy in individual terms as "the claim of individuals, groups, or institutions to determine for themselves when, how, and to what extent information about them is communicated to others."[13] Westin concluded that "privacy is an irreducibly critical element in the operation of individuals, groups, and government in a democratic system with a liberal culture."[14] He recognized that privacy served broader social functions in liberal democracies, including providing support for religious tolerance, scholarly investigations, the integrity of the electoral system, and limits on police power.[15] He therefore furnished the bases for developing a broader social importance of privacy. But in two important areas Westin's analysis moves away from further development of that social importance of privacy: the first involves his discussion of the importance of privacy to the individual and the second his analysis of the balance between privacy and other interests.

Westin anchored privacy to the individual and each individual's relationship to society:

Viewed in terms of the relation of the individual to social participation, privacy is the voluntary and temporary withdrawal of a person from the general society through physical or psychological means, either in a state of solitude or small-group intimacy or, when among larger groups, in a condition of anonymity or reserve. The individual's desire for privacy is never absolute, since participation in society is an equally powerful desire. Thus each individual is continually engaged in a personal adjustment process in which he balances the desire for privacy with the desire for disclosure and communication of himself to others, in light of the environmental conditions and social norms set by the society in which he lives.[16]

After defining privacy as a withdrawal from society, Westin proceeded to examine the importance of privacy to the individual in quite individualistic terms. This value of privacy for individual withdrawal becomes even more apparent in Westin's discussion of the four basic states of individual privacy — solitude, intimacy, anonymity, and reserve — and of the functions that privacy performs "for individuals in democratic societies," providing them with personal autonomy, emotional release, self-evaluation, and limited and protected communication.[17] Westin stated that the core of the "right of individual privacy" was "the right of the individual to decide for himself, with only extraordinary exceptions in the interests of society, when and on what terms his acts should be revealed to the general public."[18] He therefore apparently regarded privacy as fundamentally at odds with social interests.

For Westin, privacy and social participation were competing desires, and each individual established a balance between the two that was best for that individual. Although the norms of society may have set some parameters on that balance, basically it was a "personal adjustment process." Thus, each individual might establish a unique balance between privacy and social participation. But Westin recognized that in that balancing process, the individual was at some disadvantage because of a social interest in what he termed "privacy-invading phenomena,"[19] especially when these were used to detect deviant behavior or enforce rules. He explained: "Each society sets socially approved machinery for penetrating the privacy of individuals or groups in order to protect personal and group rights and enforce the society's rules and taboos."[20] Although the "privacy-invading phenomenon" might have a social purpose, privacy still served primarily individual purposes within the context of organizational and democratic society. Privacy was "basically an instrument for achieving individual goals of self-realization."[21] The assumption was that privacy is a means by which individuals can voluntarily and temporarily withdraw from society — by which they can be, as Warren and Brandeis said, "let alone."

The focus on privacy as an aspect of individual dignity is also seen in the writing of Charles Fried, who again turned the analysis of privacy inward to the individual rather than outward to society. He defined privacy, in terms similar to Westin's, as "that aspect of social order by which persons control access to information about themselves"[22] and regarded privacy as "the necessary context for relationships which we would hardly be human if we had to do without — the relationships of love, friendship, and trust."[23] For Fried, privacy was part of the mutual respect between individuals in a society, it was not an essential ingredient of a society of individuals. He did not consider a more organic or collective importance of privacy. In other words, the importance of privacy was in forming the basis of relationships between individuals, not in forming a society of individuals. This distinction is revealed somewhat starkly in his discussion of the collection of information by third parties, which, in his view, threatened not the relationship of the individual with the third party but the relationship between the individual and an intimate friend: "The rupture of this balance [between friends] by a third party — the state perhaps — thrusting information concerning one friend upon another might well destroy the limited degree of intimacy the two have achieved."[24] Fried was not concerned that the disclosure or even knowledge of information might change the relationship between the individual and the third party, in this case the state. His primary concern with such disclosures was their effect on the context in which relationships of love, trust, and friendship occur between or among individuals. The effect on broader social relationships or on society in general was not discussed or even considered problematic.

An interest in a broader relevance of privacy entered the philosophical discussion about privacy in 1971 with the publication of a collection of essays by the American Society for Political and Legal Philosophy. In the preface, the editors framed the issue in terms of "the proper location of the boundaries between the private and the public."[25] They acknowledged that disputes about where to establish these boundaries increase "as modern polities grow more congested, complicated, and powerful vis-à-vis their citizens,"[26] but they still rooted privacy in the individual and related privacy to the concepts of individualism and liberty.

Within that volume, a number of writers began by acknowledging that privacy has some social importance or is derived from a social context. Carl Friedrich was concerned with the political implications of the boundary between public and private. Although he acknowledged that "privacy is closely related to individualism," he was "not concerned . . . with the private aspect of this privacy, individualistic and libertarian, but with the political interest that may be involved. Has it a distinctive function in particular political orders"?[27] He argued that both secrecy and privacy, which he defined as "private secrecy,"[28] were functional under some circumstances in a democratic government. What, then, was the functionality of privacy beyond ensuring the "dignity of the individual [which] is so crucial a constituent element of the democratic belief system that it calls for recognition except in a clear case of dysfunctional secrecy"?[29] Friedrich gave as examples the privacy of property, which was important to a competitive economy, and the privacy of the secret ballot, which ensured that voters were free to express their preferences. He then stated that "the individual's privacy needs (and hence the functionality of such privacy) spread to other facets of the individual's convictions, more especially in religious matters."[30] In this statement, Friedrich made it clear that although he was concerned with the political and not the individual aspect of privacy, the functionality of privacy was derived from its importance to the individual. Interestingly, in his discussion of totalitarianism, he revealed some appreciation for a broader social importance of privacy: "To some theorists this destruction of the private sphere appears to be the core of totalitarianism. . . . It is the consequence of the fact that privacy has lost most of its functionality."[31] Although he did not state it directly, he seems to imply that in such regimes, privacy has not lost its functionality for the individual but for the government. Thus, privacy may be functional for the individual, but the lack of privacy may be functional for the government.

Sharing Friedrich's interest in boundaries between private and public spheres, Arnold Simmel regarded privacy as "part and parcel of the system of values that regulates action in society."[32] His argument was that privacy was important "to the whole structure of human interaction and values, and to the nature of individual personality. If privacy prospers, much else will prosper. If privacy is extinguished, much else that we care about will be snuffed out. If privacy changes, much else will change."[33] He viewed privacy, then, as important not just to the individual but also to the "whole structure of human interaction and values," or the social system. But in his discussion of "privacy boundaries," his interest shifted from the importance of privacy to the social system to the "social processes that delimit the space of free movement of the individual, and thus define in the course of social interaction a socially agreed-upon concept of the individual, which is reflected in the individual's own definition of this self. Conversely, those individual definitions of self collectively become part of the social definition of the individual. This is important because the individual occupies a central position in our value system."[34] Simmel viewed privacy as one of the boundaries of the social system and argued that to protect privacy, agreement "on the proper boundaries of the self, the family, and any other social organization"[35] would be necessary. But he then shifted back to the individual, noting that there are "no final solutions to the conflicts over the rights of individuals,"[36] although his earlier statement would imply that these conflicts entail more than the rights of individuals as unique entities but also the interests or rights of the family and other social organizations.

Three articles in the summer 1975 issue of *Philosophy and Public Affairs* brought renewed attention to the debate about the status and nature of privacy. In the first, Judith Jarvis Thomson argued that privacy was not a separate right but was derived from clusters of other rights, especially "rights over our own persons" and "rights over our property."[37] Although her analysis did not explicitly raise the question of the social importance of privacy, she did base her study in a liberal tradition with an emphasis on rights as individual rights. Thomas Scanlon agreed with Thomson that there may not be a single overarching right to privacy but argued that the various privacy rights "have a common foundation in the special interests that we have in being able to be free from certain kinds of intrusions."[38] The "common foundation" here had a social origin and was composed of conventional norms and legal boundaries that specified "when, where, and in what ways we may and may not be observed, listened to, questioned, and in other ways kept track of."[39] Scanlon's emphasis on boundaries is similar to that of Simmel, as is his avoidance of the question regarding the criteria or processes by which such boundaries were established; he merely asserted instead that they were necessary: "Our zone of privacy could be defined in many different ways: what matters most is that *some* system of limits to observation should be generally understood and observed."[40] Scanlon viewed the zone of privacy as culturally and historically derived: "The foundations of privacy become a matter of practical concern when we are faced with open questions that are not resolved by our existing conventions. Such questions may be posed, for example, by the development of new technology, or by changes in social habits or relative values which present new conflicts or make our present conventions no longer seem reasonable. We then need to decide how to extend our old conventions to cover these new cases or whether to change our conventions in the face of the new situation."[41] Our zones of privacy may be threatened by new technologies, and a social decision may be necessary to reaffirm or redraw those boundaries, but a social interest in privacy was not necessarily one of the criteria for those boundaries.

In also responding to Thomson's article, James Rachels viewed privacy as being important to the individual and involving some control over who has access to oneself and to information about oneself. He argued that privacy was valued because "there is a close connection between our ability to control who has access to us and to information about us, and our ability to create and maintain different sorts of social relationships with different people."[42] Privacy was important because it allowed people to maintain different social relationships. Rachels noted that "new types of social institutions and practices sometimes make possible new sorts of human relationships, which in turn make it appropriate to behave around people, and to say things in their presence, that would have been inappropriate before."[43] It is interesting that in this passage he chose the phrase "human relationships" rather than "social relationships" and that as an example of these relationships he referred to group therapy rather than, for example, the new relationship between a credit agency and a consumer. He concluded by noting that "a fact about ourselves is someone's business if there is a specific social relationship between us which entitles them to know."[44] Social relationships then became the basis for invading privacy rather than a source for the protection of privacy.

In most of the works examined above, the importance of privacy finds its roots in liberal thinking—privacy inheres in the individual as an individual and is important to the individual for self-development or for the establishment of intimate or human relationships. Although many authors recognized that the realm of privacy was socially determined, the importance of that realm was for individual self-development or for human relationships. Some authors, such as Westin, Blaustein, and Friedrich, acknowledged that privacy was important to society but did not develop that aspect as fully as they examined the importance of privacy to the individual. For example, in discussing surveillance by observation, Westin quotes an important passage from Robert Merton's *Social Theory and Social Structure*: " 'Privacy' is not merely a personal predilection; it is an important functional requirement for the effective operation of social structure."[45] It appears that in much of the philosophical literature examined above, "the effective operation of social structure" translated rather quickly into "individual freedom and liberty." The result has been an emphasis on an atomistic individual and the legal protection of his or her rights.

Much of the more recent philosophical writing about privacy has similarly emphasized privacy's importance to the individual and for the development of personal relationships. Julie Inness sees privacy as important because it gives the individual control over intimate decisions, "decisions concerning matters that draw their meaning and value from the agent's love, liking, and caring."[46] Vincent Samar also emphasizes the importance of privacy for the development of individual autonomy.[47] In chapter 8, the policy implications of these philosophical questions about the importance of privacy are further explored. The primary point to be gained from this review is that the importance of privacy has been framed primarily in terms of its value to the individual. This philosophical view has shaped policy discussions about privacy.

Legal Issues in the Privacy Debate

Philosophical questions about the meaning and status of privacy are reflected in constitutional and common law developments regarding a right to privacy. Both bodies of law have provided some protection for privacy, but the protection is limited and not easily carried over into new areas. A phrase that recurs in legal writing about privacy is whether it is possible to put "old wine in new bottles."[48] Neither common law nor constitutional law provided a clear legal basis for protecting privacy when threatened by computerized databases, electronic eavesdropping, and polygraphs. In each case, new statutory protections were needed.[49] Common law and constitutional law developments provided the context for crafting new statutory protections. A review of each is therefore necessary for understanding the policy debates examined later. Given the vast legal literature on privacy and the increasing number of court decisions about privacy, it is important to emphasize that the purpose of this review is limited in chronology and content to those legal issues that were important in establishing the context for congressional policy formulation. Legal issues, especially those involving the scope or influence of Supreme Court decisions, that were especially important in congressional debates will be discussed in more detail in chapters 4, 5, and 6.

Common law basis for a right to privacy. Second only to the Warren and Brandeis article in its influence on the development of legal thinking regarding the protection of privacy in the United States is William Prosser's 1960 *California Law Review* article on privacy. His review of legal developments led him to conclude that "at the present time the right of privacy, in one form or another, is declared to exist by the overwhelming majority of the American courts."[50] Prosser isolated four distinct torts — intrusion, disclosure, false light, and appropriation — in state common law decisions that, he argued, represented four types of privacy invasions.[51] He saw these as invading four distinct kinds of interests of individuals. Privacy, then, was not a common interest but a common term denoting the ways in which one's "right to be let alone" could be invaded.

Although Prosser's analysis received wide acceptance as a way of categorizing tort law relating to privacy,[52] most legal scholars doubted whether these traditional privacy protections in common law could, or should, be extended to cover more general privacy concerns. Part of the difficulty was that, as Harry Kalven pointed out, "the deadening common sense of the Prosser approach"[53] divorced tort law privacy from the philosophical importance that Warren and Brandeis gave it. A less philosophical, but no less important, reason for questioning Prosser's approach is that tort law does not protect an individual prior to injury. When an individual's privacy is arguably threatened by government record keeping or by wiretapping, for example, tort law only supplies a means of redressing grievances after the invasion; it does not provide a means of preventing the invasion from occurring.[54]

Some legal scholars argued that these torts could be extended to protect privacy in certain circumstances. Writing in the mid-1960s, Kalven concluded that privacy and defamation actions were being combined in a "hybrid tort" in cases where "the use of a name without consent is held to be offensive because the attribution is false and where the answer to its being nondefamatory is that it is a use of the name without consent."[55] In this hybrid tort, consent to the use of one's name becomes a key concept in establishing a cause of action. Such a principle is similar to Charles Fried and Alan Westin's definition of privacy as control over information about oneself. However worthy the philosophical and legal reasoning behind such a hybrid tort, the courts did not adopt it. It did become, however, one of the primary principles of the Code of Fair Information Practices[56] and is incorporated in most information privacy legislation in the United States and abroad.

Others argued that property law could provide the basis for privacy protection. In this view, personal information or the content of personal communications was seen as the property of the person in question. Therefore, the person would have a legal right to control use of that information and could sue for misuse of information. For example, Alan Westin suggested that "personal information, thought of as the right of decision over one's private personality, should be defined as a property right."[57] Arthur Miller opposed this approach, arguing that "property concepts are irrelevant to the personal values that we are attempting to preserve by recognizing a right of privacy."[58] This approach was first rejected by Warren and Brandeis. In addition to this more philosophical question, there is a very real practical obstacle to the usefulness of a property approach—in many cases, the information that an individual seeks to protect is in the hands of a third-party record holder, for example, a government agency, telephone company, or employer. The attempt to use property law as a basis for protecting personal information, however, has by no means been abandoned, as there are currently proposals for giving individuals not only property interests in their personal records but also royalties when information from those records is used or sold.[59]

Constitutional basis for a right to privacy. Although a "right to privacy" is not mentioned in the Bill of Rights, the Supreme Court has ruled in favor of various privacy interests, deriving the right to privacy from the First, Third, Fourth, Fifth, and Ninth amendments. Since the late 1950s, the Court has upheld, under the First Amendment and due process clause, a series of privacy interests, such as "associational privacy,"[60] "political privacy,"[61] and the "right to anonymity in public expression."[62] The Court did not view these as privacy rights per se but saw privacy as important in supporting the values protected by the First Amendment. The Supreme Court also has found protection for a right to privacy against unreasonable surveillance and compulsory disclosure in the Third Amendment's prohibition against quartering soldiers.

The Court has viewed the Fourth Amendment as an important basis for privacy in its protection of "the right of the people to be secure in their persons, houses, papers, and effects, against unreasonable searches and seizures." The Fourth Amendment has both an individual rights component and a prohibition against arbitrary governmental action. Patrick Henry, in urging the adoption of the Bill of Rights, noted the importance of the prohibition: "The officers of congress may come upon you now, fortified with all the terrors of paramount federal authority. . . . They ought to be restrained within proper bounds."[63] The Supreme Court recognized that the Fourth Amendment protected privacy interests as early as 1886 in *Boyd v. United States.*[64]

The most important Fourth Amendment cases involving privacy interests have been those dealing with wiretapping. In *Olmstead v. United*

States,[65] the Court ruled in a 5–4 decision that the Fourth Amendment did not apply to wiretapping because no physical trespass was involved, which would be necessary for there to be a "search," because phone messages are not tangible items that can be "seized," and because there was no protection for voice communication projected outside the home. The Court adopted a privacy concept that was based largely on a property interest; people had privacy in their "persons, houses, papers, and effects." Justice Brandeis in dissent made an eloquent argument that the Fourth Amendment protected a right to privacy and that "invasions of individual security" could not be defined in such narrow property terms: "The progress of science in furnishing the Government with means of espionage is not likely to stop with wiretappings. Ways may some day be developed by which the Government, without removing papers from secret drawers, can reproduce them in court, and by which it will be enabled to expose to a jury the most intimate occurrences of the home. Advances in the psychic and related science may bring means of exploring unexpressed beliefs, thoughts and emotions. . . . Can it be that the Constitution affords no protection against such invasions of individual security?"[66] Justice Brandeis interpreted the Fourth Amendment as a limitation on the government as well as a protection for the individual and argued that the amendment protected against "every unjustifiable intrusion by the Government upon the privacy of the individual, whatever the means employed."[67]

Wiretapping continued to be a constitutionally sanctioned investigatory method until 1967, when the Court overruled *Olmstead* in *Katz v. United States*, holding that the Fourth Amendment protected people, not places, and did not require physical trespass or seizure of tangible material. But the Court warned in *Katz* that the "fourth amendment cannot be translated into a general 'right to privacy'" and that "virtually every governmental action interferes with personal privacy to some degree."[68] Following *Katz*, judicial determination of whether a "search or seizure" occurred depended on whether an individual had a "reasonable expectation of privacy" in the area or activity under surveillance. To determine this, the Supreme Court adopted as its test the two-part formulation from Justice John Marshall Harlan's concurring opinion: "first that a person have exhibited an actual (subjective) expectation of privacy and, second, that the expectation be one that society is prepared to recognize as 'reasonable.'"[69] The subjective part of the test entails an analysis of the means the individual employs to protect his or her privacy, for example, closing the door of a phone booth or closing curtains. The more objective part of the test looks to what society regards as a reasonable expectation of privacy. Although this is important in that it recognizes that there is indeed a societal interest in what is considered private, it does so without specifying an objective referent for "society." Is "society" represented by today's opinion polls, long-standing norms and traditions, a reasonable person, or the knowledge people have in common?

The result of the objective part of the test is that the Supreme Court in subsequent decisions has implicitly constructed a continuum of circumstances under which it assumes that society would regard an individual as having a reasonable expectation of privacy. The continuum ranges from public places ("open fields," "in plain view," "public highways"), in which there is no objective expectation of privacy except in unusual circumstances, to the inside of one's home with the windows and curtains shut and the door bolted, in which there is an objective expectation of privacy. The objective recognition of privacy along the continuum (shopping centers, motels, offices, cars, and yards) depends on judicial interpretation. In the late 1970s, the Court modified the objective component of the test, referring to it as a "legitimate" expectation of privacy.[70] In *Rakas v. Illinois*, Justice William Rehnquist referred to expectations of privacy "which the law recognizes as 'legitimate.'"[71] This modification gives the objective part of the test a positive-law, rather than societal-expectation, meaning. This has practical as well as theoretical importance in that the courts would not ask whether society regarded an expectation of privacy in a particular case as reasonable but would instead examine the laws to determine privacy expectations. Although this would require less subjective analysis by the courts, it seems to assume that the laws are correct and need not be evaluated against fundamental law, such as the Fourth Amendment.[72]

The *Katz* distinction that "the fourth amendment protects people, not places," has raised the question of whether the Fourth Amendment still protects property interests or whether it now protects only more personal interests. The issue of the protection afforded people as distinct from that afforded places has become more significant with the growth of third-party record keepers, such as banks and credit bureaus. But the Court has not expanded the Fourth Amendment protections. For example, in *United States v. Miller*, the Supreme Court ruled that "checks are not confidential communications but negotiable instruments to be used in commercial transactions"[73] and that the individual has no property interest or Fourth Amendment expectation of privacy in those records. In some rulings, the Court has treated privacy as the only interest protected by the Fourth Amendment, ignoring the more traditional property interests.[74] The result has been a further narrowing of Fourth Amendment protection, both because property interests are not considered and because of the problems of defining privacy. As one legal commentator has noted: "Privacy, like most concepts of fundamental value, is a relative, indeterminate concept that is not easily converted into a workable legal standard."[75]

The Fifth Amendment protection against self-incrimination also serves as a basis for a type of privacy protection, especially psychological privacy. But although the principle of the Fifth Amendment — that no person shall be compelled to be a witness against himself or herself — may be broad, its application is limited to criminal cases. Thus, the Fifth Amendment, in a way similar to the Fourth, has not been interpreted to provide anything close to comprehensive privacy protection. Courts have interpreted it to be a prohibition against disclosures of incriminating personal information that are compelled at some point during the criminal justice process or other governmental proceedings. The rationale for such Fifth Amendment protection varies — some adhere to the philosophy that the protection is necessary for fair treatment in accusatorial situations, others believe that it reflects a belief that it is inhumane to force people to give witness against themselves, and still others view compelled disclosures to be serious invasions of privacy.[76]

In general, the Court has adopted a rather narrow interpretation of the Fifth Amendment. One way it has done this is by making a distinction between testimonial evidence, involving communication by the individual, and physical evidence. This distinction was made most clearly in the Warren Court's decision in *Schmerber v. California*, in which the Court ruled that there was no Fifth Amendment protection against blood tests, viewed as physical evidence, to determine blood alcohol content after a car accident.[77] In the area of personal information, the Court has also developed a number of ways to limit the Fifth Amendment, for example, by requiring that the incriminating information that is being compelled is actually in the possession of the individual. In *Couch v. United States*, the Burger Court ruled that an individual could not claim Fifth Amendment protection for an Internal Revenue Service summons for records held by an accountant.[78] The Court has also ruled that information that is part of a "required record" is not protected by the Fifth Amendment. If records are required to fulfill a regulatory function, if the individual would normally keep such records, or if the records are analogous to public documents, then they fall into the category of "required record"[79] and are not protected by the Fifth Amendment.

In these Fourth and Fifth Amendment cases, privacy is viewed as essential to the protection of other, more well-established rights. The Supreme Court did not arrive at what Alan Westin has termed "a positive theory of privacy based on identifying the interests or functions of privacy in contemporary American society."[80] Instead, as William Beaney has noted, the Court had been tentatively insisting that "privacy-dignity claims deserved to be examined with care and to be denied only when an important countervailing interest is shown to be superior."[81]

In *Griswold v. Connecticut*,[82] the Court began to establish an independent right to privacy, although the source of this privacy right was unclear and its protection seemed to be limited to reproductive interests. In *Griswold*, the Court struck down a Connecticut statute that prohibited the prescription or use of contraceptives, ruling that it was an infringement on marital privacy. Justice William Douglas, in the majority opinion, viewed the case as concerning "a relationship lying within the zone of privacy created by several fundamental constitutional guarantees," the First, Third, Fourth, Fifth, and Ninth amendments, each of which creates "zones" or "penumbras" of privacy. Although the majority supported the notion of an independent right to privacy inherent in the marriage relationship, not all agreed with Justice Douglas as to its source. Justices Arthur Goldberg, Earl Warren, and William Brennan preferred to lodge the right under the Ninth Amendment.

Seven years later, in *Eisenstadt v. Baird*, the Court struck down a Massachusetts law that made it a felony to prescribe or distribute contraceptives to single persons. The Court extended the right to privacy beyond the marriage relationship, placing it with the individual: "If the right of privacy means anything, it is the right of the *individual*, married or single, to be free from unwarranted governmental intrusion into matters so fundamentally affecting a person as the decision whether to bear or beget a child."[83] In *Roe v. Wade*,[84] the Court struck down a Texas antiabortion statute and further extended the right to privacy "to encompass a woman's decision whether or not to terminate her pregnancy." In this case, the majority argued that the right to privacy was "founded in the Fourteenth Amendment's concept of personal liberty and restrictions upon state action." The district court had earlier concluded that the source of the right was the Ninth Amendment's reservation of other rights retained by the people, as had been earlier argued by Justices Goldberg, Warren, and Brennan in *Griswold*.

In 1976 in *Paul v. Davis*,[85] the Supreme Court refused to expand the areas of personal privacy considered "fundamental" to include erroneous information printed in a flyer listing active shoplifters. Instead, it limited these fundamental areas to "matters relating to marriage, procreation, contraception, family relationships, and child rearing and education."[86] A year later, in *Whalen v. Roe*,[87] the Court for the first time recognized a right to information privacy, noting that the constitutionally protected "zone of privacy" involved two kinds of individual interests: "One is the individual interest in avoiding disclosure of personal matters, and another is the interest in independence in making certain kinds of important decisions."[88] Although it recognized an expanded notion of privacy, the Court unanimously upheld a New York law that required the state to maintain computerized records of prescriptions for certain drugs because "the New York program does not, on its face, pose a sufficiently grievous threat to either interest to establish constitutional violation."[89] In reaching this conclusion, the Court took into account the security of the computer and restrictions on the disclosure of information.

In another 1977 case, the Court used a test similar to the one developed in *Whalen*, balancing the extent of the privacy intrusion against the interests that the intrusion advanced. In this case, *Nixon v. Administrator of General Services*,[90] the Court upheld a federal statute that required national archivists to examine written and recorded information accumulated by the president. Richard Nixon challenged the act's constitutionality on the grounds that it violated his right of privacy. Although the Court recognized that the "appellant has a legitimate expectation of privacy in his personal communications"[91] and that one element of privacy is "the individual interest in avoiding disclosure of personal matters,"[92] it stated that "the constitutionality of the Act must be viewed in the context of the limited intrusion of the screening process, of appellant's status as a public figure, of this lack of any expectation of privacy in the overwhelming majority of the materials, of the important public interest in preservation of the materials, and of the virtual impossibility of segregating the small quantity of private materials without comprehensive screening."[93] The appellant's interest in privacy was not a match for these competing interests.

Conclusion

From this brief review of the philosophical and legal development of privacy protections up to the time of congressional debates examined in this book, several themes emerge. First, it is difficult to pinpoint the types of claims that can be brought under the philosophical and legal rubric of privacy. Although privacy is widely recognized as an important value, neither philosophers nor jurists have been successful in converting the value into a clearly defined, protectable legal standard. Its contours have evolved, in part, in response to changing technological and social forces. A second theme that was fairly well established when congressional debates began in the 1960s is that privacy is generally viewed as deserving constitutional protection when it is tied to a specific constitutional principle, for example, the importance of privacy as a prelude to the exercise of First Amendment rights. In this sense, privacy as a derivative right is on stronger constitutional ground than privacy as an independent right, except in the areas of reproductive privacy. Third, privacy is not absolute but has to be balanced against other rights and interests and often loses to those rights and interests. This is true both in the area of invasions of privacy for law enforcement purposes and in the area of information collection for public purposes.

The final theme is that the courts have not been aggressive in expanding privacy protections, in both common law and constitutional law, to new areas of privacy and technology. As we will see in examining congressional policy formulation, court opinions are important in setting the stage for policy debate and exposing areas where privacy is unprotected, but they generally do not chart a course for legislative action. Although courts have increasingly played important roles in making public policy, their lack of aggressiveness and their reticence in charting new courses are not unique to these areas of privacy and technology policy. Donald Horowitz argues that the policy-making functions of the courts "have gradually been superimposed on a structure that evolved primarily to decide individual cases."[94] He points to several general constraints on the courts as policy-making institutions. The courts are passive institutions, responding only when litigants bring suits to them. Courts deal with cases and controversies and limit their review to the facts of the case and their remedy to the parties to the suit. Although the courts may be a natural venue for resolving legal questions, they provide a poor locus for policy making about issues of technological change and privacy because they deal with individual-level disputes and because their legal analysis is likely to reemphasize the individual character of the rights at issue rather than exploring the social implications.

Chapter 3

Privacy in American Society

One of the fundamental tenets of a representative democracy is that the public policies the government adopts should reflect the views of the people. The primary mechanism for translating popular preferences into public policies is through the actions of the legislature. The processes and procedures of the legislature constrain and control the ways in which popular views affect policy decisions. In the next several chapters, detailed attention will be given to the ways in which the U.S. Congress, largely through committees and subcommittees, has formulated and adopted policy to protect privacy. Chapter 1 demonstrated some of the ways in which policy problems become defined as privacy invasions and alluded to the symbolic power that privacy brings to political discourse. Chapter 2 introduced the philosophical and legal thinking about privacy. But what do "the people" think about privacy? Is privacy a modern value, or do its roots reach deeper into history? How important is privacy to people and in what contexts? Given popular views about privacy, is it appropriate to expect a representative legislature to take action to support those views?

Privacy does not exist in a vacuum but is part of a larger social, cultural, political, and economic world. As changes occur in other realms, privacy may be increased or diminished. Architectural changes in the eighteenth century, for example, created more separate spaces and, as a result, the possibility for more privacy. Technology is only one of a host of factors that can affect the possibilities for privacy. On the social level, cultural mores, organizational activities, political administrations, and international entanglements can all affect privacy. On the individual level, one's work experience, financial and consumer activities, family situation, and life style choices all have an effect on privacy.

To understand the larger context in which the policy debate about privacy takes place, this chapter examines aspects of the historical backdrop of privacy. This examination of some key aspects of privacy in the

United States supports the argument that privacy has always been important to individuals but also illustrates that the contours of individual privacy have been dependent on sociocultural developments. A review of the results of public opinion polls taken during the last twenty years demonstrates the context in which policy debate occurs.

Since the 1970s, Americans have been surveyed repeatedly about their attitudes toward privacy, especially in light of technological changes. Quite consistently during these years, Americans have indicated that they value privacy highly; in the decade since 1983, almost 80 percent of respondents to Harris public opinion polls have replied that they were very concerned or somewhat concerned about threats to privacy. (See table 3.1.) But public concern about privacy has not translated into public pressure on policy makers to take actions to curb technological developments and to protect privacy. Difficulties in conceptualizing privacy contribute to the absence of public pressure. But as the data in this chapter demonstrate, privacy is important to people both in the abstract and in concrete situations. Even when privacy is contrasted with social interests, such as catching criminals, or personal interests, such as the conveniences associated with using credit cards, it is still regarded as being quite important to individuals. Public opinion surveys suggest that privacy appears to be an important, perhaps even volatile, latent interest. The contours and meanings of that interest need to be explored.

Privacy in American History

Privacy — meaning some boundary between the individual and society or between what is, or should be, private and what is, or should be, public — is a concept that has existed throughout American history.[1] Its roots go back to England, as reflected in the political thinking of Thomas Hobbes and John Locke and the form of liberal democratic government that derived from that thinking. Although clearly privacy is important as part of this liberal tradition, its manifestation throughout American history is complicated both by difficulties in conceptualizing it and by technological and cultural changes that have affected the meaning of privacy and the ability to achieve privacy. It is important to emphasize that technological and cultural changes can have positive or negative implications; oftentimes they protect privacy while at other times they threaten privacy.

If privacy is viewed as a boundary between an individual and all other individuals, it is partly dependent on physical isolation. In this sense, privacy was difficult to find in a crowded colonial cottage but was easy to find on the American frontier. The attainment of this physical dimension of privacy depends on geographical location — it is easier in rural than in urban areas — and income — it is easier for the wealthy than for for those with few resources. But privacy as a boundary between individuals involves not only physical space but also social space. The social dimension was much harder for individuals to achieve and control. For example, eavesdroppers and gossipers have been a perennial problem throughout American history. In colonial times and through the early nineteenth century, they were regarded as nuisances and dealt with through social norms and mores rather than through legal redress. During this time, exchanging gossip or overhearing conversations carried less of a negative impact because people knew other people within a broader context and everyone knew that their own activities might be similarly revealed. The community character of this time period, or what Edward Bloustein calls the "mutual interdependence among neighbors,"[2] moderated the invasiveness of gossipers and eavesdroppers.

The privacy dimension we are most concerned with here involves the ability to retain a boundary between oneself and institutions. One of the best statements expressing this concept is that "a man's home is his castle," an idea that goes back to colonial times and is enshrined in the Fourth Amendment. Although this concept is a cornerstone of English jurisprudence, David Flaherty argues that it has its antecedents in "ancient times, biblical literature, and Roman law."[3] Alan Westin similarly finds privacy interests in both the animal world and primitive societies.[4] This need for privacy may be part of human nature, but it is most assuredly part of Western liberal thinking, with its unwavering Lockean respect for private property. As Flaherty points out: "The colonial concept of privacy, like so many rights and privileges, was essentially a negative one. The colonists expected to be left alone in their homes and families."[5] As part of a safeguard for the "privacy" of property, colonial laws protected the sanctity of homes against outsiders, especially officials of colonial governments, except in circumstances in which an official concern necessitated searches of homes without a specific search warrant. And in these cases, the legitimacy of the search was often challenged.

Although the privacy of one's home was established fairly early in America, as David Flaherty reports, a number of laws originating in Puritan times seem contradictory to a more general, less property-based concept of privacy. For example, in most New England towns, laws required that a newcomer receive permission before settling in the town.

The purpose of these residency laws was to ensure that newcomers would not be an economic or social burden on the community. To be allowed to reside in the town, a newcomer had to divulge extensive personal information. But the privacy implications of these laws never became much of an issue because so few people actually moved.[6] During the seventeenth century, many towns had laws that prohibited people from living alone. A Puritan belief that "vagrancy, pauperism, and social disorders were the anticipated consequences of single living"[7] appears to have motivated these laws. Many towns also had laws that required colonists to inform authorities about infractions committed by others.[8]

Based on private property interests represented by the expression that "a man's home is his castle," it is fairly easy to justify restrictions on entry into or searches of an individual's home. In examining the development of a more general concept of privacy involving the ability to retain a boundary between individuals and institutions, it is appropriate to consider social expectations about the privacy of mail communications and the census. Both raise privacy questions and allow us to examine early cases of privacy in light of social or technological changes. As will be seen, the questions raised in the eighteenth century are remarkably similar to the ones that confronted Congress in the three privacy areas examined in this book.

Before a formal postal system was established in the United States, letters and parcels were carried in an ad hoc fashion by ship captains, friends, or people hired for the purpose of delivering specific items.[9] The privacy of letters was also rather uncertain, depending primarily on the care of the carrier, although to secure a degree of privacy people could seal letters with wax or write in code. In some cases, especially when a ship captain brought many letters to a particular town, mail would be delivered to one central place where it might sit unattended until people collected their mail. A concern for privacy was reflected in the 1710 English Post Office Act's provision that forbade the opening of mail except by warrant, thus establishing a similar level of protection or expectation of privacy to that which existed for a home. In 1753 Benjamin Franklin, as postmaster general, issued a regulation that required postmasters to take an oath not to open mail.

At this point, expectations about the privacy of the content of a communication depended in large part on how possible it was to keep the contents private when others were interested in knowing them. Expectations also affected the concept of a need for privacy; if it was not possible to keep communications "private," then privacy was not considered relevant in the communications realm. But as it became possible to keep communications private, people insisted on privacy and actions were taken, either individually or legally, to ensure privacy. For example, prior to the American Revolution, mail was frequently opened by British officials, not Franklin's postmasters, who sought information about plots and conspiracies among the colonists. During the Revolutionary War, military authorities were known to open letters that they suspected contained intelligence information. In the early years of the Republic, partisan rivalries often provided an incentive to open letters. Both George Washington and Thomas Jefferson are reported to have complained that their letters were opened.[10] During this time, motives for opening letters derived from many sources, and it was fairly easy to gain access to mail and open it. With the introduction of locks on mailbags, the use of envelopes, and an increase in the volume of mail during the early nineteenth century, it became harder to invade the privacy of mail communications. Such invasions were also made more difficult by the major postal statutes of 1825, which prohibited not only postal employees but all persons from taking or opening a letter before it was delivered "with a design to obstruct the correspondence, to pry into another's business or secrets."[11] The law made no exemption for opening letters for official purposes. In 1878 the Supreme Court elevated this protection against examination of letters by extending Fourth Amendment coverage to postal letters in *Ex parte Jackson*.[12]

Privacy also became an issue after the government's establishment of a census.[13] The Constitution provides for a national census to be conducted every ten years in order to apportion seats in the House of Representatives and to assign the tax responsibility of each state. The first census in 1790 asked few questions, but some opposition was expressed because it represented the powers of the new national government as a force distinct from the state governments. The second census asked questions about the number and size of windows so that a house tax could be levied; some citizens opposed these questions. As the years passed, the number of questions and the amount of information requested increased. David Seipp reports that 4 details were asked in 1790, 20 in 1820, 82 in 1840, and 142 in 1860.[14] In each case, the increase in the number of details requested provoked some opposition. In 1849 a statistician is reported to have told Congress that when asked new questions in the census "the people sometimes look with a jealous eye upon the whole subject, without understanding the purpose of it, and refuse to give correct information, or give wrong information."[15]

In addition to concern about the sensitivity of questions asked, the census also raised privacy concerns about the confidentiality of the information collected. From the first census in 1790 until the census of 1870, copies of the census enumerators' lists were posted so that people could check the information for errors. As the census became more detailed, the posting of information became controversial. Concerns with confidentiality remained local until 1830, when copies of individual reports were first sent to Washington, D.C., along with the aggregate summaries of census data. In response to objections about divulging personal information, the circular for the 1840 census contained an official statement emphasizing the importance placed on the confidentiality of returns and the impossibility of linking statistical information to a particular individual.

The 1890 census provoked widespread objections because of the inclusion of questions about diseases, handicaps, and home mortgages. The "offensive impertinence" and "inquisitorial" character of the questions were criticized by the national press, including the *Boston Evening Transcript*, *Boston Globe*, *Los Angeles Times*, *New York Sun*, *New York Times*, and *New York Tribune* as well as a number of papers in smaller cities.[16] Some critics suggested a public strike of the census, while others advised people not to answer offensive questions. Public opposition to the 1890 census reflected both a concern for individual privacy and suspicion of the government. In an effort to address the criticisms of the 1890 census, the census of 1900 eliminated questions about debts and diseases. In 1900 Congress created a permanent census office and strengthened legal requirements for confidentiality. In 1919 unauthorized disclosure of census information became a felony, and the penalty was increased from a fine of $1,000 to imprisonment.[17]

The history of privacy concerns associated with postal communications and the census illustrates the importance that individuals attached to their individual privacy throughout American history — their desire to retain the personal nature of mail communications and their reluctance to divulge personal information. Privacy was an important value in the nineteenth century as new social arrangements became more important. But privacy became important within the context of those social arrangements. It was not just a concern for privacy that generated opposition to the census or mail openings but also a concern about limiting the powers of organizations. As social, economic, and political organizations took on a more prominent role in the mass society of the twentieth century, the theme of privacy continued to be important — but in the context of these larger changes, not in isolation from them.

Modern Views about Privacy

Numerous public opinion polls during the last twenty years have included questions about privacy. When asked their view of the importance of privacy, people respond that privacy, in principle, is very important and valued. In general, these polls reveal that most Americans regard privacy as a genuine value, not as a means of concealing improper activities or avoiding punishment or detection. Sixty-four percent of respondents disagreed with the statement, "Most people who complain about their privacy are engaged in immoral or illegal conduct."[18] In 1978 and 1990 support for privacy as a legitimate value was quite high, with three-quarters of respondents agreeing that privacy should be added to "life, liberty, and the pursuit of happiness" as a fundamental right.[19] When viewed as a fundamental right, privacy can be interpreted as being involved in a range of constitutional and moral issues — freedom from surveillance and searches, reproductive freedom, freedom to associate, confidentiality of communications, and family values.

Several public opinion surveys have asked about privacy in the context of other civil liberties issues. The Gallup Organization conducted the Opinion and Values Survey in 1976–77 and the Civil Liberties Survey in 1978–79.[20] Both surveys asked about a range of civil rights and civil liberties, including freedom of speech and press, freedom of religion, freedom of assembly, the rights of the accused, and privacy. In late 1992 the American Civil Liberties Union (ACLU) Foundation undertook a benchmark survey to measure public awareness of and concern about personal privacy.[21] Attitudes in eight privacy domains were investigated: the collection and use of personal information for employment purposes; the use of personal information for purposes other than that for which it was collected; the confidentiality of HIV test results; consideration of off-the-job activities in hiring and firing decisions; covert telephone monitoring in the workplace; urine testing for drugs; lesbian and gay rights; and choice in matters of reproduction.[22]

The public opinion surveys that are directly relevant to the policy issues covered in this book are those involving access to and knowledge about individuals — polls that ask questions about privacy in the context of information collection and use. Many of these studies have been privately sponsored, most often by credit-reporting, telephone, or insurance companies, but have been conducted by major public opinion research organizations.[23] The prime examples are the four public opinion surveys conducted by Louis Harris and Associates for Equifax, a credit-reporting company. These polls, as is also true of the civil liberties polls, are essentially "special-interest-group polls"[24] conducted to identify the public's preconceptions about the issue of privacy and to determine how knowledgeable the public is about the issues. The Harris-Equifax surveys and the civil liberties surveys are not, however, "advocacy polls," which are released only if the results support the position of the organization sponsoring the survey.

In evaluating the results of public opinion polls about privacy, a number of cautions are in order. Some of the difficulties involved, such as the impact of question wording and ordering, are common in any attempt to assess public opinion, and some are more peculiar to the measurement of opinion about privacy. Public opinion polls about privacy present two problems in accurately gauging the concern about privacy. The first is that those who are most concerned about or sensitive to privacy probably will not be willing to respond to public opinion surveys. Oscar Gandy argues that "any survey that is concerned about opinions related to privacy and personal information will be nonrandom and systematically biased."[25] Survey results, then, would tend to underestimate the level and intensity of concern about privacy. James Katz and Annette Tassone make a similar point and conclude that "there is little practical way to surmount this weakness since standard practices of estimating nonrespondent characteristics would not work well for this dimension of nonresponse."[26]

A second problem involves not underestimating but overestimating privacy concerns. Surveys that ask only about privacy, such as the Harris-Equifax polls, may exaggerate respondents' concerns about privacy.[27] Concerns may also be inflated in opinion polls that ask specifically about civil liberties issues. Overestimation of concern is possible in any public opinion survey that attempts to measure people's attitudes about a particular issue. It may be that the issue is one on which respondents do not have a genuine opinion. In this case, the survey may be measuring a nonattitude. The subject of the poll may be one that is somewhat remote from respondents' concerns and not one for which they have developed real views. But once the respondents know that the survey is about a specific subject, they may express views on that subject even if they did not have views before, and they may articulate views that they think the pollsters want to hear. The question then becomes whether the survey is measuring or creating attitudes about a particular issue. In focus groups, which involve a facilitated small-group discussion of an issue and provide more in-depth information than opinion polls, Oscar Gandy found that "privacy per se was not something most participants had given any thought to."[28] This finding would support the contention that surveys asking specifically about privacy exaggerate or create concerns about privacy. Those surveys that ask about privacy along with other issues (such as the Cambridge Reports and National Opinion Research Center) are probably better measures of concern about privacy and help determine the salience of the issue.[29]

GENERAL PRIVACY CONCERNS

Even if privacy appears to have some characteristics of a nonattitude and if surveys underrepresent those most concerned about privacy, there has been and continues to be a high level of latent public concern about privacy. From the 1970s to 1993, general concern about threats to personal privacy increased. Most Americans answered affirmatively when asked directly whether they were concerned about threats to personal privacy. In several Harris surveys, the following question was posed:[30] "How concerned are you about threats to your personal privacy in America today?" (See table 3.1.) The percentage of those who viewed themselves as very or somewhat concerned about privacy increased from 64 percent in 1978, to 77 percent in 1983, and to 79 percent in 1990. The percentage of those "not concerned at all" dropped from 19 percent in 1978 to about 7 percent in subsequent years. The levels of concern and nonconcern have remained stable over the four Harris surveys conducted in the 1990s.

Responses to a more general public opinion survey, the Cambridge Reports, are quite similar to those of the Harris-Equifax surveys. The Cambridge Reports asked three questions in 1988 and 1989 to gauge respondents' level of concern about privacy. As table 3.2 indicates, people's responses varied with the question asked. Personal privacy was very important to about 70 percent of respondents, but the percentage of those very concerned about the invasion of privacy, both at the time asked and in the future, was significantly lower, at about 42 percent. In the 1978–79 Civil Liberties Survey, an overwhelming majority rated the right to privacy in their correspondence or phone conversations as extremely important (79 percent) or important (17 percent).[31] In general, then, when surveys ask about privacy, respondents indicate a high level of concern. This concern could easily be heightened by media reports about privacy invasions and become more salient.

Although there is evidence of latent public concern about privacy, these survey responses do not indicate what it is about privacy that concerns

Table 3.1
Concern with Threats to Personal Privacy

	1978	1983	1990	1991	1992	1993
Base	1,511	1,256	2,254	1,255	1,254	1,000
Very concerned	31%	48%	46%	48%	47%	49%
Somewhat concerned	33	29	33	31	31	30
Not very concerned	17	15	14	12	13	11
Not concerned at all	19	7	6	7	8	6
Not sure	1	<.5	1	1	2	3

Sources: Louis Harris and Associates and Alan F. Westin, *Harris-Equifax Consumer Privacy Survey, 1992* (Atlanta: Equifax, Inc., 1992), table 1, p. 15, and *Harris-Equifax Health Information Privacy Survey, 1993* (Atlanta: Equifax, Inc., 1993), table 1-1, p. 23.

people. The construct of privacy that is being measured is not clear. A difficulty in interpreting results of survey data is that privacy is not defined or is defined in a variety of ways, ranging from autonomy, solitude, control over information, or freedom from neighbors to freedom from government or from employer surveillance. Respondents may be considering different aspects of privacy, which would make it hard to compare or aggregate responses. Gandy concurs that "there are no universal definitions of privacy, and individuals are likely to be responding to quite different things when they indicate the presence or absence of concerns."[32]

The ACLU Foundation's 1994 report confirms a lack of crossover on privacy issues. People have not connected concerns about privacy and personal autonomy in one situation to similar concerns in other situations. Indeed, Albert Cantril and Susan Davis Cantril conclude that "it is difficult to infer an individual's level of concern about privacy in one domain from the degree of concern expressed in another domain."[33] Their analysis of survey results revealed little consistency in the way sociodemographic factors account for concern about privacy across the domains.[34] Based on the results of this survey, it would not be easy to identify in demographic terms — by age, race, sex, education — which groups in the population are likely to be concerned about privacy invasions in a variety of contexts or which groups are likely to be supportive of stronger privacy protections generally. The Cantrils concluded that "although many of these aspects of privacy can be linked in terms of the fundamental principles at stake, as a general rule they have not yet been so linked in the collective thinking or experience of most of the American public."[35]

Table 3.2
Perceived Importance of Threats to Privacy

	1988	1989
Compared with other subjects on your mind, how important is personal privacy?		
Very important	70%	67%
Somewhat important	23	24
How concerned are you about the invasion of your personal privacy in the United States today?		
Very concerned	38	44
Somewhat concerned	37	32
What about in future years — how concerned are you about the invasion of your personal privacy in the future?		
Very concerned	45	—
Somewhat concerned	35	—

Source: Cambridge Reports, as discussed in James E. Katz and Annette R. Tassone, "Public Opinion Trends: Privacy and Information Technology," *Public Opinion Quarterly* 54, no. 1 (Spring 1990): 139–40.

Given the range of privacy issues covered in the ACLU Foundation survey — including employer monitoring, secondary use of information, reproductive rights, and gay and lesbian rights — it is not surprising that these aspects of privacy have not been linked.

The ACLU Foundation survey supports the position that views about privacy are quite dependent upon the context. As Gandy found in his focus groups, "participants apparently utilized quite distinct schema when thinking about privacy in relation to the government as compared to their employers, to organizations providing them with goods and services, or to their friends, neighbors, or coworkers."[36] James Katz and Merton Hyman similarly found that attitudes toward telephone privacy were not related to concerns about other aspects of privacy.[37] Attitudes about privacy vary from context to context, and it is not possible to predict from one context to another. Mary Culnan criticizes empirical research that has used privacy as the dependent variable and suggests instead that attitudes toward a specific information practice be used as the dependent variable.[38] The Harris-Equifax surveys ask questions about both general attitudes toward privacy and attitudes toward specific practices.

Given the importance of context in understanding attitudes about privacy, public opinion polls regarding the three privacy areas examined in this book will be reviewed briefly. In the employment context, the public has been queried with respect to the monitoring of employees and the collection of information for employment decisions. Since the late 1970s, respondents have indicated sensitivity about the kinds of information they considered appropriate for employers to request. Information about previous job record and education is seen as legitimate by overwhelming majorities: 96 percent for the former and 92 percent for the latter in the 1992 ACLU Foundation survey[39] and 91 percent and 94 percent, respectively, in the 1978 Harris survey for Sentry Insurance.[40] There is significantly less support for employer collection of other types of information, such as data on race, marital status, and drinking habits, as indicated in table 3.3. The 1992 survey sought respondents' views about employers asking employees or prospective employees about activities outside work. Overwhelming majorities were opposed to employers asking employees about playing dangerous sports (87 percent), smoking (89 percent), or having a beer with a friend (94 percent).[41]

The 1978 and 1992 surveys also reveal public skepticism about the monitoring of employees, especially involving the use of technological devices, but attitudes depend on the purposes of the monitoring. In 1978 a 66 percent majority of the public believed that use of "closed circuit television to obtain continuous checks on how fast workers perform" should be forbidden, while less than a majority (42 percent) thought that use of closed circuit television to prevent employee theft should be forbidden.[42] At that time, 83 percent of the public believed that "listening in on the conversations of employees to find out what they think about their supervisors and managers" should be forbidden.[43] The 1992 ACLU Foundation survey asked about telephone monitoring for assessing job performance and telephone monitoring without a specified purpose. Concerning use of monitoring for performance evaluation, 56 percent of the public said that employees should know when their calls are being monitored, while 32 percent thought supervisors should be able to listen in without employees' knowing. With regard to more general monitoring of employees' calls, 65 percent said an employer should not be able to do so, 21 percent thought employers could do so without employees' knowledge, and 8 percent thought employers could do so only if the employee

Table 3.3
Appropriateness of Information Collected by Employers

	1978	1992
Previous job record	91%	96%
Education	94	92
Age	78	56
Race	48	34
Marital status	58	38
Drinking habits	62	17

Sources: Albert H. Cantril and Susan Davis Cantril, *Live and Let Live: American Public Opinion about Privacy at Home and at Work* (New York: American Civil Liberties Union Foundation, 1994), table 1, p. 9; Louis Harris and Associates and Alan F. Westin, *The Dimensions of Privacy: A National Opinion Research Survey of Attitudes toward Privacy* (Stevens Point, Wis.: Sentry Insurance, 1979), table 3.1, p. 33.
Note: Cells reflect the percentage of respondents agreeing that the information is "appropriate."

was informed.[44] In the 1978 Harris–Sentry Insurance survey, support for employer use of lie detectors also appeared related to the purpose for which it was used, with 62 percent reporting that "asking a job applicant to take a lie detector test" should be forbidden, while 43 percent thought that "requiring an employee to take a lie detector test when there is suspicion of theft" should be forbidden.[45]

In the law enforcement context, survey results indicate support for privacy, but, as in the employment context, the character of that support is contingent upon the circumstances. In the 1976–77 Opinion and Values Survey, 36 percent of respondents believed that tapping telephones of people suspected of planning crimes should be prohibited as an invasion of privacy, while 46 percent believed it was necessary to reduce crime.[46] At the same time, an overwhelming number of respondents believed a court order should be required before wiretapping. In the 1978 Harris survey for Sentry Insurance, 87 percent of the public responded that the police, when they suspect that "members of an organization never convicted of a crime might engage in illegal actions in the future," should not be able to wiretap without obtaining a court order.[47] In the 1978–79 Civil Liberties Survey, 73 percent similarly responded that tapping telephones after obtaining a legal warrant "can be justified when used against known criminals suspected of planning new crimes," while 19 percent believed that even with a warrant, tapping "still violates personal privacy and should be outlawed by Congress."[48] Since law enforcement interests are

Table 3.4
Response to Statement: "Consumers Have Lost All Control over How Personal Information about Them Is Circulated and Used by Companies"

	1990	1991	1992	1993
Base	2,254	1,255	1,254	1,000
Agree strongly	71%[a]	37%	47%	47%
Agree somewhat		34	29	33
Disagree somewhat	27	20	13	15
Disagree strongly		3	7	4
Not sure	3	4	3	2

Source: Louis Harris and Associates and Alan F. Westin, *Harris-Equifax Health Information Privacy Survey, 1993* (Atlanta: Equifax, Inc., 1993), table 1-6, p. 30.
[a]In 1990, the question was asked on a three-scaled response: agree, disagree, or not sure.

defined in more concrete terms, a majority of respondents tend to support law enforcement rather than privacy. For example, 61 percent in 1978–79 responded that the police should be able to bug the meetings of the leaders of organized crime when they take place in a private home or office.[49] A slight majority of the public, 58 percent, responded in 1978 that it is "all right" for a government agency to make all employees who handled classified information that has been leaked to the press take a lie detector test to determine who leaked the information.[50] It is important to note that there are three qualifications for the approval of a lie detector test — that the employees involved handle classified information, that information has been leaked, and that the purpose of the test is to determine who leaked the classified information.

The area of organizational collection and use of personal information has been the subject of numerous public opinion surveys over the past twenty years. Respondents consistently report a high level of concern about their lack of knowledge about and control over how organizations use information about them. As table 3.4 indicates, over 70 percent of respondents during a four-year period agreed that "consumers have lost all control over how personal information about them is circulated and used by companies."

Survey questions have attempted to reach beneath this general sense of loss of control and pinpoint common areas of concern. In 1990 respondents were asked to categorize each of three activities as a major problem, a minor problem, or not a problem: 57 percent of the public viewed "consumers being asked to provide excessively personal information" as a major problem; 54 percent viewed "inaccuracy and mistakes" as a major problem; and 39 percent viewed the "sharing of information by companies in the same industry" as a major problem. Small minorities — 10, 6, and 16 percent, respectively — viewed these as not problems.[51] This perceived loss of control is not limited to records held by organizations in the private sector but also extends to those held by the federal government. In 1990 64 percent disagreed that "since the Nixon Watergate episode in the early 1970s, there haven't been any really serious attempts by the federal government at invading people's privacy."[52]

Part of the sense of loss of control comes from the perception that information is being used and exchanged in ways that individuals do not know. Indeed, 76 percent of respondents in 1978 agreed that "Americans begin surrendering their personal privacy the day they open their first charge account, take out a loan, buy something on the installment plan, or apply for a credit card."[53] An increasing number of Americans believe that personal information about them is being kept in "some files somewhere for purposes not known" to them, with 44 percent believing this to be true in 1974 and 67 percent in 1983.[54] In 1978 respondents split, 41 percent on each side, on whether organizations "have enough checks and safeguards against the misuse of personal information."[55] Most respondents in 1983 believed that organizations that did not keep information confidential were seriously invading privacy, with 82 percent believing that the Federal Bureau of Investigation's (FBI) not keeping information about individuals confidential constituted such an invasion and 77 percent believing this of credit bureaus' practice of selling credit-rating information.[56] Although such practices were regarded as invasions of privacy, 75 percent believed that credit bureaus shared information with others and 38 percent believed that the FBI did.[57] Although 84 percent of respondents in 1983 believed that master files of personal information could be compiled "fairly easily," 78 percent believed that assembling such files would constitute an invasion of privacy.[58] When asked about specific information practices, respondents were suspicious about what organizations were doing, or could do, and regarded them as invasions of privacy.

In 1990 respondents were also asked how much they trusted twelve types of organizations "to collect and use information about people like you in a responsible way." (See table 3.5.) Hospitals and the Census Bureau were rated most highly, while companies that sell products by

Table 3.5
Trust in Organizations' Use of Personal Information

	High 8–10	Moderate 4–6	Low 1–3
Health insurance companies	18%	49%	32%
Life insurance companies	20	48	30
Auto insurance companies	17	44	37
Companies soliciting by direct-mail or phone	6	28	64
Telephone companies	27	49	23
Credit bureaus	17	42	39
Employment-screening companies	17	48	31
Employers	28	49	20
Hospitals	37	44	18
Internal Revenue Service	28	39	32
Social Security Administration	34	42	22
Census Bureau	36	45	17

Source: Louis Harris and Associates and Alan F. Westin, *The Equifax Report on Consumers in the Information Age* (Atlanta: Equifax, Inc., 1990), table 2-7, pp. 20–22.

direct mail or telephone were rated poorly. Not surprisingly, most respondents rated most organizations in the moderate category. For over half of the organizations, the percentages indicating low trust were greater than those indicating high trust. Interestingly, although only 17 percent accorded high trust and 39 percent accorded low trust to credit bureaus, 46 percent agreed with the statement that "my privacy rights as a consumer in credit reporting are adequately protected today by law and business practices."[59] In 1991 this percentage dropped to 37, with 58 percent believing that their privacy rights in credit reporting were not adequately protected.[60]

The 1992 ACLU Foundation survey also gauged the level of concern about seven secondary uses of personal information (a use other than that for which the information was originally intended). The highest percentages indicating a "great deal" of concern involved three practices: "the telephone company giving records of calls to a private agency doing a background check on you" (66 percent); "credit card companies letting mail order companies know about things you have bought" (57 percent); and "a health insurance company putting medical information about you into a computer information bank that others have access to" (56 percent).[61]

Respondents were questioned not only about their concerns with organizational practices but also about their perceptions of the types of information exchanges that were taking place. The important findings in this area included the following: 40 percent thought credit ratings were given out very often; 41 percent thought information about credit card purchases was given to mail-order companies; 43 percent thought telephone companies never released records of calls; and 56 percent thought records of video rentals were never shared.[62]

In each of the three contexts of employment, law enforcement, and organizational collection and use of information, survey respondents indicate concern about privacy, perceptions of privacy invasions, and attitudes supportive of privacy. The question remains, however, whether surveys are measuring the respondents' sense of personal privacy loss or their perception of societal changes in the level or degree of privacy. In analyzing the 1990 Harris-Equifax data set, Gandy found a direct and statistically significant relationship between exposure to reports about privacy-related incidents involving misuse of computerized information and higher levels of concern about privacy.[63] The ACLU Foundation survey developed a composite measure of concern about and awareness of secondary uses of personal information (see table 3.6), which also indicated a strong relationship between awareness and concern. For all except two types of disclosures of information — those of telephone records and records of video rentals — the greatest percentage of respondents chose the "aware and concerned" category, expressing at least a "fair amount" of concern about disclosure and thinking that it happens at least "once in a while."

Survey questions generally address perceptions and attitudes about privacy rather than actual behaviors or experiences.[64] The question then is what this opinion about privacy actually means. Is the opinion a good indicator of an underlying attitude? Or was the respondent "guessing"? The more abstract the subject of the question, the more likely it is that the response will reflect a "nonattitude" rather than a coherent concern or preference. Moreover, as in other areas of public opinion polling, complex interrelationships exist among attitudes, cognitions, and behaviors in privacy responses; current survey data do not untangle these relationships. When measuring opinions that have no corresponding behaviors with which the responses can be compared, it is difficult to evaluate the accuracy or meaning of the poll results.[65]

When surveys ask directly about privacy-related behaviors or experiences, the number of reports of some form of privacy loss or invasion is

Table 3.6
Composite Measure of Awareness and Concern Regarding Secondary Uses of Personal Information

	Aware and concerned[a]	Unaware and concerned[b]	Unaware and unconcerned[c]	Aware and unconcerned[d]
Credit card company giving out information about bill paying	52%	11%	11%	27%
Insurance company getting more information than needed from your doctor	48	22	15	15
Mail-order company getting credit card information	54	21	11	13
Telephone records given out	35	46	13	5
Employer giving employee information to health insurance company	32	26	22	19
Health insurance company putting information into database accessible by others	46	29	11	14
Video rental records given out	16	40	36	7

Source: Albert H. Cantril and Susan Davis Cantril, *Live and Let Live: American Public Opinion about Privacy at Home and at Work* (New York: American Civil Liberties Union Foundation, 1994), p. 15, tables A-2a–2g, pp. 149–62.

[a] Those who express at least "a fair amount" of concern and think secondary uses happen at least "once in a while."

[b] Those who are concerned about secondary uses but do not think they happen.

[c] Those unperturbed by the possibility of secondary uses and doubt they happen.

[d] Those who seem most reconciled to secondary uses, which they think take place.

Table 3.7
Improper Disclosure of Medical Information

	Yes	No	Not Sure
Health insurance companies	15%	82%	3%
Clinics/hospitals	11	87	2
Public health agencies	10	86	4
Employers	9	89	1
Doctors	7	92	1
Pharmacists/druggists	3	95	1

Source: Louis Harris and Associates and Alan F. Westin, *Harris-Equifax Health Information Privacy Survey, 1993* (Atlanta: Equifax, Inc., 1993), table 4-4, p. 51.

generally lower than the concern about privacy loss or invasion. But the percentage of those reporting that they did not apply for credit, insurance, or a job because they did not want to provide certain information about themselves more than doubled in twelve years, from 14 percent in 1978 to 30 percent in 1990.[66] Forty-two percent refused to give information to a business or company because they "thought it was not really needed or was too personal," while 14 percent refused to give information to a government agency for the same reason.[67] The 1993 Harris-Equifax survey asked respondents whether they or a member of their immediate family had changed their behavior because of a concern about the confidentiality of medical records. Only 7 percent reported not seeking medical or psychological treatment because they did not want to harm their "job prospects or other life opportunities."[68] Eleven percent reported that they did not file insurance claims in order to protect their privacy and confidentiality.[69]

Despite general perceptions about a loss of control and some changes in individual behavior, few people believe that their privacy has actually been invaded. During the late 1970s, about 10 percent believed that their telephone had been tapped.[70] In 1991 only 25 percent reported that they had personally been the victim of an invasion of privacy. This reflected only a 6 percent increase in thirteen years, 19 percent having reported that they had been a victim in 1978.[71] The 1993 Harris-Equifax Health Information Privacy Survey asked respondents whether they believed that health care workers or organizations had ever improperly disclosed their personal medical information. As table 3.7 indicates, most respondents did not believe improper disclosure had occurred.

Although evaluating public opinion about privacy presents difficulties, the trends that appear in survey results are important to consider from a public policy perspective. A very important trend is that public support for laws to protect the privacy of personal information has been consistently high. In 1978 two-thirds of respondents thought laws could go a long way in helping to preserve our privacy.[72] In surveys conducted by the Roper Center for Public Opinion Research in 1982, large majorities believed that laws were needed to govern the ways in which organizations use personal information, with 85 percent supporting laws mandating that corrections of information be included in files, 82 percent believing that individuals should be notified of the existence and content of files and should be able to obtain copies of those files, and 71 percent advocating laws prohibiting most private parties from asking for social security numbers.[73] In the 1983 Harris survey, strong majorities of the public and majorities of all leadership groups supported new federal laws to deal with information abuse. The authors of the Harris analysis observed: "Particularly striking is the pervasiveness of support for tough new ground rules governing computers and other information technology. Americans are not willing to endure abuse or misuse of information, and they overwhelmingly support action to do something about it. This support permeates all subgroups in society and represents a mandate for initiatives in public policy."[74] Support for new initiatives to protect privacy was even more striking in 1990. Respondents were asked which of three policy options was needed "at the federal level to protect privacy." Forty-one percent of the public selected the strongest option: "Create a regulatory privacy protection commission with powers to issue enforceable rules for businesses handling consumer information." Significant minorities — from 25 to 30 percent — of the "privacy-intensive industries"[75] also favored the strongest option. Twenty-four percent of the public favored creation of a nonregulatory privacy protection board. Sixty-five percent of the public supported the establishment of some institutional mechanism, either regulatory or nonregulatory, to protect privacy, while 31 percent favored staying "with the present system of specific laws, Congressional oversight, and individual lawsuits."[76]

The responses to the 1993 Harris-Equifax survey on medical information also reflect public support for government action to protect the privacy and confidentiality of medical records. Fifty-six percent of the public favored new legislation, as compared to 39 percent who preferred "continuing with existing state and federal laws and professional stan-dards."[77] When asked about the need for an independent privacy board, 46 percent of the public responded that it was "extremely important" that one be established and 40 percent responded that it was "somewhat im-portant."[78] Almost three-quarters of respondents also believed that it was "extremely important" that new federal legislation give individuals the right to inspect and correct their medical records, specify who has access to records, and impose penalties for unauthorized disclosure.[79] These responses reflect overwhelming public support for aggressive federal ac-tion to protect the privacy of medical records.

A second policy implication revealed in survey responses is that the concern most Americans have for privacy is within the context of their relationships with institutions, not other individuals, and that this privacy concern is related more generally to attitudes toward societal institutions. This is reflected in the 1978 and 1990 responses to several questions. Ninety-three percent of respondents in 1990 and 94 percent in 1978 gave a positive response to the statement: "I have someone I can share my personal problems with when I need to." Ninety percent in 1990 and 88 percent in 1978 agreed with the statement: "I am generally able to be by myself when I need to be."[80]

In contrast, those who are most concerned about threats to individual privacy are also most distrustful of technology and government. The analysts of the 1990 Harris-Equifax survey created an index of distrust based on responses to four statements: technology has almost gotten out of control; government can generally be trusted to look after our inter-ests; the way one votes has no effect on what the government does; and, in general, business helps us more than it harms us. Survey analysts found that 23 percent of the public could be categorized as "highly distrustful of technology and the institutions of government and business," while 32 percent were moderately distrustful, 31 percent had a low level of dis-trust, and 14 percent were not distrustful. The responses of these groups were then matched to their responses regarding their concern about threats to their personal privacy. Eighty-five percent of the highly distrust-ful and 82 percent of the moderately distrustful were "very" or "some-what" concerned about threats to privacy.[81] This same distrust index was used in analyzing responses to the 1993 Harris-Equifax survey; 32 per-cent of the public was rated as highly distrustful (an increase of 9 percent from 1990) and 31 percent was rated as moderately distrustful. Eighty-four percent of the highly distrustful respondents were also "very" or "somewhat" concerned about privacy.[82]

Commenting on this relationship between distrust and privacy concern, Alan Westin, who served as academic adviser for the Harris-Equifax surveys, stated: "Given the continuing distrust of American institutions, it will not be easy in the 1990s to lessen general public concern about threats to privacy. The unusually high nonresponse rate to the 1990 Census exemplifies this problem."[83] In analyzing the results of the ACLU Foundation survey, the Cantrils came to a similar conclusion regarding the use of personal information and distrust of organizations: "The public's view of the secondary use of personal information can be characterized more as distrust of those engaged in the practice than as perceived vulnerability regarding the accuracy or amount of information that is involved."[84]

An additional reason for regarding institutions as the source of privacy concerns is that people are ambivalent about technology; they see both its benefits and its threats. Many surveys queried respondents about their views on computers and privacy. According to Harris polls, the percentage of Americans who perceive computers as a threat to privacy increased from 38 percent in 1974, to 41 percent in 1977, and to 54 percent in December 1978.[85] In 1983 the percentage perceiving computers as a threat decreased slightly to 51 percent, while the percentage believing that computers are not a threat increased from 33 percent to 42 percent.[86] This question was asked again in 1992, with 37 percent agreeing very strongly and 31 percent agreeing somewhat strongly that computers are an actual threat to privacy—a 17 percent increase over nine years.[87] The percentage of the public that does not believe that the privacy of personal information processed by computer is adequately safeguarded has also been increasing—from 52 percent in 1978, to 60 percent in 1983, and to 66 percent in 1992.[88] The Harris-Equifax surveys also indicate growth of the perception that computers have made it easier to obtain confidential personal information improperly, with 80 percent agreeing in 1978 and 1983 and 89 percent agreeing in 1992.[89]

Public attitudes toward computers, however, also reflect the benefits that computers bring. In 1978, 63 percent of respondents to a Harris survey agreed that computers have improved the quality of life in our society; the number increased to 79 percent in 1992 and 76 percent in 1993.[90] In 1983, 68 percent of the public believed that the use of computers must be sharply restricted in the future if privacy is to be preserved.[91] In 1993 the percentage of respondents sharing this belief had increased only 3 percentage points to 71 percent,[92] having dropped to 67 percent in 1992.[93]

In a complex environment of institutions and competing interests, survey results reveal that people do recognize that interests in privacy must be balanced against other interests, on a case-by-case basis, and that they regard privacy as an important value in this balancing process. In the 1990 Harris-Equifax survey, respondents were asked to weigh a number of government interests against a privacy interest; 56 percent opposed a requirement for a national work identification card to help identify illegal aliens, 59 percent favored a requirement that "extremist political groups" file membership lists with the government, and 64 percent agreed that the "press goes too far in investigating the private lives of politicians."[94] Respondents were also asked to balance a number of consumer/convenience interests against their privacy interests. Over half reported that they would not be very upset (17 percent) or would not be upset at all (37 percent) if they could not use a credit card.[95] Sixty-one percent reported that they would not be very upset (23 percent) or would not be upset at all (38 percent) if they could not receive mail offers or catalogs targeted to their interests.[96] Sixty-nine percent believed it was a "bad thing" that businesses could buy information about "your consumer characteristics — such as your income level, residential area, and credit card use — and use such information to offer goods and services to you."[97] Seventy-six percent found it unacceptable that companies ask credit-reporting bureaus to identify people meeting certain characteristics so that the companies can offer those people special products or services.[98] Fifty-five percent believed that telephone companies should be able to sell Caller ID, when it was described as a service that enables people "to see the telephone number of the person calling them."[99] When informed about the controversial aspects of this service — that although it allows people to screen incoming calls and enables companies to access customer records faster, it discloses unlisted numbers and makes it impossible to call hotlines anonymously — 55 percent thought it should be regulated by law, 25 percent thought it should be banned, and 17 percent thought it should be freely available.[100] Responses to questions about reuse of public record information also indicate that respondents recognize the implications of the reuse of information. For example, 77 percent do not object to auto insurance companies checking an applicant's driving record, but 32 percent do oppose the use of public record information by companies in order to create mailing lists.[101]

In terms of gauging the need and support for public policy, it is helpful to estimate whether concern about privacy will increase or decrease over time. In order to accurately predict change over time, it is necessary to have some understanding of the factors contributing to attitudes and beliefs about privacy. The most extensive and thorough recent attempt to

Table 3.8
Key Explanatory Variables of Privacy Concern

Privacy Concern	Key Explanatory Variables
Employer collection and use of personal information	Sex (being female) Age (being young) Region (outside the South) More education Independence of judgment Concern about unreasonable police searches
Secondary information uses	Distrust of big business Knowing someone who is HIV positive or has AIDS Less education Concern about unreasonable police searches
Covert monitoring at work	Support for opportunities for minorities Perceived threat of misuse of personal information Less education Optimism about the nation's future
Drug testing	Age (being young) Region (outside the South) Concern about unreasonable police searches Not having been asked to take a drug test Living in more urban areas Distrust of big business Confidence in Clinton

Source: Albert H. Cantril and Susan Davis Cantril, *Live and Let Live: American Public Opinion about Privacy at Home and at Work* (New York: American Civil Liberties Union Foundation, 1994), p. 138.

understand concern about privacy is found in the Cantrils' analysis of the 1993 ACLU Foundation survey. Through a series of multiple regression analyses for a variety of demographic[102] and nondemographic[103] factors, they found that demographic factors are more important than nondemographic factors in explaining levels of concern for only one privacy domain — employers' collection and use of personal information. In the area of drug testing, demographic and nondemographic factors are of relatively equal importance. Neither demographic nor nondemographic factors are important in explaining concern about secondary uses of information or covert monitoring.[104] Table 3.8 summarizes the most important

Table 3.9
Concern with Threats to Privacy, by Age

	18–29	30–49	50+
Very concerned	43%	47%	47%
Somewhat concerned	38	35	28
Only a little concerned	16	13	13
Not concerned at all	3	4	11

Source: Louis Harris and Associates and Alan F. Westin, *The Equifax Report on Consumers in the Information Age* (Atlanta: Equifax, Inc., 1990), table 1-1, p. 2.

factors explaining privacy concern in the contexts of employment, law enforcement, and organizational use of information.

In three of the four domains, concern about unreasonable searches is one of the key explanatory values. Education is also important in three domains, but not in similar ways: less education is important in explaining concerns about secondary uses of information and covert employee monitoring and more education is important for concerns about employer collection of information. Distrust of big business is a factor in two domains: secondary information uses and drug testing. Being young is also an element explaining privacy concerns in two domains: employer collection of information and drug testing.

In terms of information and consumer privacy, Alan Westin's analysis of the 1990 and 1991 Harris-Equifax surveys led him to conclude that age was "a more consistently significant factor than any other demographic characteristic."[105] He found that young people (18–29) were the least concerned, those from 30 to 49 were in the middle, and those 50 and older were the most concerned. These differences, however, do not fall into an easily identifiable pattern. In fact, responses to the 1990 question about general concern with threats to privacy do not follow the pattern Westin suggests and do not vary much by age, as table 3.9 indicates.

Responses to several specific questions in the 1990 survey do indicate age differences. For example, those over 50 would be less upset if they could not receive new offers of credit, mail offers, or catalogs than those in the young or middle-age ranges, as indicated by table 3.10. However, these questions seem to be evaluating attitudes toward marketing and consumer conveniences rather than attitudes toward privacy. A better question for evaluating attitudes toward privacy may be whether people decided not to apply for a job, credit, or insurance because of a require-

Table 3.10
Level of Concern with Loss of Conveniences Relating to Privacy, by Age

	18–29	30–49	50+
Could not obtain credit based on record			
Very upset	7%	5%	8%
Not upset at all	36	58	67
Could not receive new mail offers or catalogs			
Very upset	14	13	13
Not upset at all	32	35	47
Could not use credit card			
Very upset	18	19	19
Not upset at all	30	32	48

Source: Louis Harris and Associates and Alan F. Westin, *The Equifax Report on Consumers in the Information Age* (Atlanta: Equifax, Inc., 1990), pp. 26–30.

ment to provide personal information. The responses to this question appear counter to the trend Westin suggested, with 34 percent of both the 18–29 and 30–49 age groups responding affirmatively, while only 24 percent of the 50 and older group gave negative responses.[106]

Responses to the 1991 survey are also difficult to categorize. Age is a factor in respondents' interest in having their names removed from all mailing lists, with 12 percent of 18–29-year-olds selecting that option compared to 20 percent of those aged 30–49 and 31 percent of those 50 and over.[107] But these age differences are not necessarily consistent with responses to a question about interest in obtaining a copy of one's own credit report, with 24 percent of the 18–29 group being very interested compared to 16 percent of those 30–49 and 9 percent of those 50 and over.[108] Twenty-six percent of those 18–29 and 27 percent of those 50 and over had a great deal of confidence in the reliability of information used by companies to decide whether to offer credit, while only 19 percent of the 30–49 group expressed a great deal of confidence. Interestingly, the percentage expressing no confidence at all was quite similar across the three groups: 12 percent of those 18–29; 14 percent of those 30–49; and 10 percent of those 50 and over.[109]

Despite questions about generational differences, survey results suggest a public perception that privacy invasions will get worse in the future. The Roper Center for Public Opinion Research included "lack of privacy" on a list of different problems people might face in twenty-five to thirty years: those identifying "lack of privacy" as something they thought would be a "serious problem" in the future constituted 55 percent in 1975; 59 percent in 1979; 63 percent in 1983; and 61 percent in 1985.[110] In 1988 the Cambridge Reports asked about future concerns about invasion of personal privacy; 45 percent responded that they were "very concerned," and 35 percent were "somewhat concerned."[111] In 1992 respondents to the Harris-Equifax survey were asked to compare consumer privacy protection in the year 2000 to protection today. Fifty-five percent responded that consumer privacy protection would "get worse," 12 percent thought it would "get better," and 32 percent thought it would "remain the same."[112]

Conclusion

Both historical examples and the results of public opinion surveys demonstrate that people value privacy as an ideal that is important in the abstract and as a factor that is understood in real-life situations. Although privacy may not be voluntarily suggested as one of the five most pressing public policy issues, a great deal of latent public policy concern about privacy exists. Not only do people care about privacy in a number of social, political, and economic contexts, but they also support more government action to protect privacy. But the latent public support for privacy and for stronger legislation has not been translated easily into legislative action to protect privacy. In the areas of computerized databases, wiretapping, and polygraph testing, public concern and legislative proposals existed for years, if not decades, before legislation was passed. Also, the resulting statutes were weaker than the original proposals to protect privacy.

In the next three chapters, we will analyze these areas of privacy concern and congressional deliberations to develop an understanding of how privacy interests are defined in policy debates, the role that technology plays in threatening privacy, and the congressional politics involved in resolving questions about fundamental values. In chapter 1, four features of congressional policy making—ideas, interests, policy communities, and policy entrepreneurs—were introduced as important in the development of policy to protect privacy. Technology is viewed as an intervening factor; technology influences ideas and interests, brings new players into policy communities, and energizes policy leaders. This analysis of three areas of privacy and technology illustrates the importance and interplay among political factors in the formulation and adoption of policy.

Chapter 4

Information Privacy:
Recording Our Transactions

The collection and use of information about individuals is not a modern phenomenon. As far back as the eleventh century, William the Conqueror compiled the Doomsday Book, which contained information on each of his subjects, in order to plan taxation and other state policies. But the question of abuses arising from, and the proper scope of, information practices did not become a social or political issue until the 1960s. Two factors coalesced to bring the issue to the public agenda — an increase in record-keeping activities and the computerization of information processing. Until the twentieth century, record keeping about individuals was limited to specific activities and was largely local in nature. As political, economic, and social relationships became more complex and organizations developed more formal arrangements for dealing with clients and customers, the nature of record keeping changed significantly. Organizations relied upon records to mediate their relationships with individuals. Accompanying this change was a qualitative increase in the sensitivity and personal nature of the information contained in these records. As the government expanded its social welfare activities, as the economy became more credit oriented, and as society became more insurance conscious, more records containing information of a more sensitive and personal nature were maintained.

With the introduction of mainframe computers in the 1960s, large organizations, such as credit agencies, banks, and the federal government, began to store their records in computerized form. Many were apprehensive that with computerization more information would be collected and retained and then disclosed to or exchanged with other organizations. This was seen as a threat to individual privacy because more personal information would be collected and more people would have access to it. People also feared that the storage capacity, speed of retrieval, and searching capabilities of computers would fundamentally change relationships between individuals and organizations, with people's lives being governed by the contents of their computer files. The organizations using these computers, however, regarded computerization as a tool to enhance operational efficiency. Computers made it easier for organizations to retain records over a long period of time and faster for organizations to retrieve a particular record from a large system of records.

As computerization spread throughout public and private organizations, the legal protections for individuals in the new environment became an issue. In chapter 2, an examination of the constitutional and common law protections of privacy revealed that both areas of law were inadequate in dealing with the information privacy issues posed by computers. None of the common law categories of privacy protection — appropriation, intrusion, public disclosure, or false light[1] — provided an effective legal remedy for violation of information privacy. Arthur Miller also points out that "in some ways most significantly, the existing common-law structure does nothing to give the data subject a right to participate in decisions relating to personal information about him, a right that is essential if he is to learn whether he has been victimized by a privacy invasion."[2] Moreover, the common law approach, which involves filing a legal suit after an alleged injury, was itself inadequate given the scale and scope of personal information collection and use. This is especially true with respect to the federal government, as Miller maintains: "A suit against a unit of the federal government for an invasion of privacy involves a trek through what is surely the world's most arduous obstacle course."[3] Because of the inadequacies of constitutional and common law in covering information privacy, especially in an environment of rapid technological change, the need for new statutory protections and congressional actions was widely recognized in the legal and policy community interested in the issue.

The primary policy tension in the area of privacy and data collection has been between the privacy rights of individuals — defined as the rights of individuals to control information about themselves — and the needs of organizations to conduct their administrative functions and to make timely and accurate decisions about people. Over the thirty-year period of congressional policy making covered in this book, innovations in computer and communication technologies provided the catalyst for public concern and the backdrop for congressional legislation. But, as we will see, the congressional policy goal has not been to draft legislation addressing technological change but to articulate the privacy value that should govern the use of technology in an organizational setting. In pursuing this policy goal, the difficulties in balancing individual values against organizational interests became the focus of policy deliberations.

This chapter examines congressional policy making concerning federal agency use of personal information. Because of the extensiveness of government information collection and because the government/citizen relationship is so important in a democratic society, this area of personal information collection and use has been the subject of the most policy discussion. As figure 1.1 illustrates, information privacy laws were also enacted to control the personal information practices of other organizations, including the Fair Credit Reporting Act of 1970, the Family Educational Rights and Privacy Act of 1974, and the Right to Financial Privacy Act of 1978.

With regard to government information, two waves of policy discussions have resulted in two pieces of legislation. The first originated with the initial responses to computerization in the 1960s and resulted in the passage of the Privacy Act of 1974 and the establishment of the Privacy Protection Study Commission (PPSC). The second began with the large-scale use of computer matching by federal agencies and ended with the passage of the Computer Matching and Privacy Protection Act in 1988. Debate on the issue of the personal information practices of government agencies is by no means closed. The focus now is once again on the question of the need for the establishment of an effective oversight agency.[4] Supporters of privacy protection also point to weaknesses in legislating on a sector-by-sector basis, and some advocate a more comprehensive approach to privacy protection. Following media reports of misuses of and easy access to credit information, Congress has been engaged in the process of strengthening the Fair Credit Reporting Act. The issue of health care reform and the question of the role of the government in managing a system that collects comprehensive medical information on all Americans have placed the issue of medical privacy back on the policy agenda. The groundwork for understanding these debates will be established in this chapter, and the issues will be examined further in chapter 8.

The First Concern: Records and Privacy

In 1965 the Social Science Research Council (SSRC) proposed the establishment of a Federal Data Center to provide access to and coordinate the use of government statistical information. This proposal precipitated congressional hearings; both the House[5] and the Senate[6] committees holding the hearings focused on the invasions of privacy made possible by the creation of a computerized data center. The House had established a Special Subcommittee on Invasion of Privacy in 1964, largely at the request of Representative Cornelius Gallagher (D-N.J.), who became its chair.[7] Gallagher viewed the hearings on a Federal Data Center as an attempt to establish "a sense of balance" and to discover what information would be stored, who would have access, and how confidentiality and privacy would be protected. As Gallagher's statement reflects, his concern was with the possible effect of computers on individuals and their privacy: "It is our contention that if safeguards are not built into such a facility, it could lead to the creation of what I call 'The Computerized Man.' 'The Computerized Man,' as I see him, would be stripped of his individuality and privacy. Through the standardization ushered in by technological advance, his status in society would be measured by the computer, and he would lose his personal identity. His life, his talent, and his earning capacity would be reduced to a tape with very few alternatives available."[8]

The purpose of the hearings was largely to raise the level of public concern about the proposal and about possible abuses arising from such a computerized system. Privacy and computers were effective symbols in placing the issue on the congressional and public agendas. As Morris Ogul reports: "The committee evoked a series of images which could play on popular ambivalence toward computers. . . . The notion of a personal dossier bank with the overtones of totalitarianism attached thereto raised equally horrendous images."[9] Symbols rather than technical issues dominated the hearings in order "to demonstrate that the data bank had to be considered as a policy issue with *moral overtones*" (emphasis added).[10] Framing the issue in such terms would lead to a debate not about interests but about ideas.

Congress's first discussions concerning computerized record systems cast the issue in terms of the idea that individual privacy was threatened by technological change. But this idea of privacy did not exist in a vacuum, and once Congress began to seriously consider computerization of government information as a policy problem, it recognized the need to understand how federal agencies were handling personal information. If the computer was likely to change information practices and to threaten individual privacy, some knowledge about the current situation was necessary. As part of this effort, the Senate Subcommittee on Administrative Practice and Procedure sent a questionnaire to all federal agencies to determine the amount and nature of personal information collected and used by the agencies. This survey revealed that the federal government had accumulated a rather extraordinary number of records: in the mid-1960s, about 3.1 billion individual-person records existed, many of which were for persons counted more than once or persons no longer living. These files included 2.9 billion names, 2.4 billion present and past addresses, 264.5 million police records, 279.6 million mental health records, 916.4 million profiles on alcoholics and drug addicts, and over 1.2 billion income files.[11] The study concluded that "the majority of Government forms require either nonessential or too detailed information from the individual citizen"[12] and that confidentiality provisions were nonexistent or meaningless. Even without computerization, government record-keeping practices still appeared to present problems of privacy invasion. Even without the image of the computer, the symbol of "government dossiers," implying the secretiveness and completeness of the files, was compelling.

Although the first round of congressional hearings cast doubt on the wisdom of the SSRC proposal for a Federal Data Center, the Bureau of the Budget was still interested in improving the storage of and access to government statistics. A second study again recommended the establishment of a National Data Center, criticized the existing statistical operations of the government as inefficient and inadequate, and concluded that "freer access would not endanger personal privacy, but rather that the center's supervision could increase actual protection of confidentiality."[13] In 1967 and 1968 both the House and the Senate again held hearings,[14] and both rejected the proposal for a National Data Center, in part because of the fear that once such a center was established it would be difficult to ensure that it would maintain a limited role and because committee members were not convinced that such a center would adequately protect the privacy of individual records. But the drive to computerize federal agency information systems and the concerns about individual privacy, government efficiency, and congressional oversight did not disappear. Following the debate about a National Data Center, the public and Congress recognized that privacy, computers, and government information practices had introduced a policy problem that needed to be addressed.

GIVING MEANING TO PRIVACY

Once the problem of individual privacy was raised, the question became how Congress could best protect this value. Public concern and public interest existed, but the contours of the problem and the appropriate solution were uncertain. The attempt to formulate a policy response was made simultaneously in three forums — a congressional subcommittee, an executive agency, and a private foundation. This situation helped to develop a degree of political and intellectual synergy for the issue. The issue of privacy and computers was a new issue; no policy community had yet been organized around the issue. Computer scientists and civil liberties advocates, as well as those in organizational management, had to develop their own perspectives on the issue and then work together in formulating alternatives.

Senator Sam Ervin (D-N.C.), chair of the Senate Judiciary Committee's Subcommittee on Constitutional Rights, became interested in the issue and in 1970 initiated what became a four-year study of government data banks.[15] He explained the subcommittee's hearings as a response to the perceived fear of Americans that "the existing procedures are no longer sufficient to protect the privacy of the individual versus the 'information power of government.' "[16] In ten days of hearings, which received extensive press coverage, the subcommittee heard testimony regarding the effects of computerization on information handling, the use of information in surveillance activities, the legal status of privacy and personal information, and policy proposals for protecting individual privacy. The hearings raised the question of whether computers could provide more protection for information — whether the mix of administrative and technological safeguards offered by computers could provide more protection than was available in the file clerk and carbon paper era.

In building congressional support for legislation, Senator Ervin acknowledged the importance of providing detailed information on agency practices and their effect on individuals. The thousands of complaints that the subcommittee received increased Senator Ervin's commitment to the issue. He also routed the complaints of citizens to the senators who represented them, which worked to broaden the Senate's interest in and concern about the federal government's information practices. As part of its investigation, the subcommittee surveyed 54 federal agencies and discovered 858 data banks, noting that "there are without a doubt a great many more Federal data banks which the subcommittee, despite more than four years of patient effort, was unable to uncover."[17] The subcommittee found that the majority of these data banks existed under unclear statutory authority and that government agencies failed to notify individuals that personal information about them was maintained in a data bank. In terms of protecting individuals, the subcommittee revealed that over half of the agencies allowed individuals to review their own files, although agencies did not actively encourage or publicize this option. It also learned that information was readily passed on to other federal and state agencies but was not readily available to the general public.

In response to Senator Ervin's concerns, Elliot Richardson, then secretary of the Department of Health, Education, and Welfare (HEW), set up a Secretary's Advisory Committee on Automated Personal Data Systems. The purview of the HEW committee was to analyze and make recommendations regarding harmful consequences that could result from computerized information systems, including the use of the social security number.[18] In 1969 the Russell Sage Foundation and the National Academy of Sciences cosponsored a project directed by Alan Westin and Michael Baker, which gathered empirical information on how computer applications were being used by actual organizations. The conclusions of these two studies did not vary in significant ways. It was agreed that the computer was the catalyst for the problem but not the cause; that the problem was primarily one of protecting the privacy of individuals, defined as the right of individuals to control information about themselves; that the problem existed in both the public and private sectors; and that some control had to be exercised over the ways in which organizations used personal information.

The Westin and Baker study concluded that computerization of records was not the villain it was portrayed to be and shattered the illusions created by futurist hype about the early arrival of "1984." The policy problem was not one of "information security to be resolved by technical specialists" but one involving choices about "privacy, confidentiality and due process."[19] Westin and Baker recommended a number of policy actions to be applied to both manual and computerized records, including a "Citizen's Guide to Files"; rules for confidentiality and data sharing; limitations on unnecessary data collection; technological safeguards; restricted use of the social security number; and the creation of information trust agencies to manage sensitive data.

In 1973 the HEW committee released its report, *Records, Computers, and the Rights of Citizens*, which identified three consequences of the use of computerized record keeping: an increase in organizational data-processing capacity; more access to personal data; and the creation of technical record keepers.[20] The HEW committee emphasized the need for statutory protections because "the natural evolution of existing law will not protect personal privacy from the risks of computerized personal data systems. In our view the analysis also disposes of any expectation that enactment of a mere right of personal privacy would afford such protec-

Figure 4.1
Code of Fair Information Practices

There must be no personal record-keeping system whose very existence is secret.

There must be a way for an individual to find out what information about him or her is in a record and how it is used.

There must be a way for an individual to prevent information about him or her that was obtained for one purpose from being used or made available for other purposes without his or her consent.

There must be a way for an individual to correct or amend a record of identifiable information about him or her.

All organizations creating, maintaining, using, or disseminating records of identifiable personal data must assure the reliability of the data for their intended use and must take precautions to prevent misuse of the data.

Source: U.S. Department of Health Education and Welfare, Secretary's Advisory Committee on Automated Personal Data Systems, *Records, Computers, and the Rights of Citizens* (Washington, D.C.: Government Printing Office, 1973).

tion. . . . The development of legal principles comprehensive enough to accommodate a range of issues arising out of pervasive social operations, applications of a complex technology, and *conflicting interests of individuals, record-keeping organizations and society*, will have to be the work of legislative and administrative rule-making bodies" (emphasis added).[21] Its final recommendations focused on the enactment of a Code of Fair Information Practices, which would apply to both computerized and manual files. (See figure 4.1.)

The rationale for such a code derived from the definition of the policy problem as one of privacy, confidentiality, and due process. This definition can be found in the early Ervin hearings, the HEW report, and the Westin and Baker study as well as in books and articles on the subject. Specific components of the code can also be found in policy proposals suggesting that individuals be allowed to see and correct their own files; such proposals were frequently made in congressional hearings and scholarly writing. These proposals emphasized fairness in the treatment of individuals who were the subject of records and were in part borrowed from fair labor principles and proposals for fair credit reporting. The HEW report and its Code of Fair Information Practices were important because they assembled for the first time in the United States the components of fairness in record keeping.[22] The Code of Fair Information Practices provided both the meaning for the idea of information privacy and the framework for subsequent policy formulation. The code was framed around the concept of giving individuals the means to protect privacy as they saw fit; the problem, although endemic to all public and private organizations, was one affecting individuals, and the solution was to give individuals the legal basis to take action. The assumption was that delineating fairness in information practices would protect individual privacy. Although fairness became the policy goal, the problem was still defined in terms of privacy invasions and privacy continued to be utilized as a symbol in congressional and public discussions.

INTERESTS RESPOND

As support grew for the importance of individual privacy and a Code of Fair Information Practices, organizations began to recognize that giving individuals control over information about themselves would reduce organizational control over that information and would be likely to impose costs on organizations. These interests were not as vocal during the early stages of policy formulation, when attention concentrated on the role of computers and the meaning of privacy, but as policy proposals became more of a reality, these interests became more visible.

Following the revelations of misuse of personal information that occurred during Watergate, hearings on a number of privacy bills were held in both the Senate and the House in 1974. In the Senate, the Committee on Government Operations, through its Ad Hoc Subcommittee on Privacy and Information Systems, and the Judiciary Committee, through its Subcommittee on Constitutional Rights, held joint hearings on five privacy bills.[23] The major bill on which debate focused was S. 3418, introduced by Senators Sam Ervin (D-N.C.), Charles Percy (R-Ill.), and Edmund Muskie (D-Maine).[24] This bill was comprehensive in its scope, covering all automated and manual personal information systems in federal, state, and local governments as well as the private sector. It adopted a regulatory approach, providing for a Federal Privacy Board with authority to enter premises where information was held and by subpoena compel the production of documents, to hold hearings regarding violations and exemptions, and to order an organization to cease and desist unauthorized information practices. It also established fair information practices, similar to the HEW code, and gave individuals the rights to see and amend their files and to be informed of dissemination of information.

The House Committee on Government Operations also held hearings in 1974 on a Privacy Bill, H.R. 16373, which was less inclusive and provided weaker protections than the Senate bill; it covered only federal agencies, did not provide for an independent privacy board, and allowed for more exemptions.[25]

The congressional hearings highlighted the organizational interests that were threatened by proposals to strengthen individual privacy. The two most contentious issues were whether the public and private sectors should be subject to similar legislation and whether a Federal Privacy Board should be established. In both cases, those opposed — federal agencies and private sector organizations — were able to weaken the scope of the proposed legislation and to defer these policy decisions. These interests were able to prevail over those advocating protections for individual privacy and fairness in using personal information.

A major argument for removing the private sector from the purview of the 1974 legislation was that there was little concrete evidence of abuses in private sector personal information practices. This argument was made in congressional hearings by witnesses from private industry, for example, the American Life Insurance Association, and from the government, for example, the Department of Commerce.[26] Discussions about proof put the burden on those who wanted privacy protections to produce accounts about individuals who had been harmed by private sector practices or evidence about patterns of misuse of personal information by private sector firms. Private sector organizations also argued that they were already overburdened by government regulations and that the proposed legislation was unnecessary and costly. Their strategy was to urge companies to enact voluntary protections for personal information in order to lessen the pressure for government regulation. Private sector witnesses argued that Congress was setting itself an impossible task; too many factors had to be taken into account to devise a policy that protected individuals and did not unreasonably burden organizations, while also allowing for government oversight. One of the most vocal and most respected privacy advocates, Alan Westin, agreed that it was unwise, at that time, to impose statutory requirements on private organizations.[27]

The proposal to establish an agency to monitor personal information practices, which was contained in the Senate Privacy Bill (s. 3418), was regarded by some as an integral part of effective oversight of personal information practices. In the 1971 hearings, for example, Arthur Miller recommended the appointment of an "information ombudsman";[28] others had proposed the establishment of a "regulatory commission with full powers over the collection, use and dissemination of personal information."[29] But both the HEW committee and the Westin and Baker study were opposed to this approach. In fact, the HEW committee came out strongly against a regulatory scheme: "We doubt that the need exists or that the necessary public support could be marshalled at the present time for an agency of the scale and pervasiveness required to regulate all personal data systems. Such regulation or licensing, moreover, would be extremely complicated, costly and might uselessly impede desirable applications of computers to record keeping."[30] In hearings on the Senate bill, all federal agencies and many private sector organizations voiced opposition to the privacy board. Federal agencies testified that such a board was unnecessary because agencies could monitor their own compliance with information requirements and that the cost of such a board would be enormous. Roy Ash of the Office of Management and Budget (OMB) stated, "Implementation can best be accomplished by holding agencies accountable for implementing these policies and subjecting their performance to congressional and public scrutiny. To establish a separate agency would only serve to increase costs, fragment responsibility, and delay implementation of the bill while the Commission develops its guidelines and rules."[31] The Treasury Department also testified that the establishment of a separate oversight agency would "be disproportionate to the problem."[32] IBM also argued against the creation of an agency with rule-making powers, believing instead that the "establishment of fair information practices, supported by legal sanctions, should adequately protect individual rights of privacy."[33]

The Senate Judiciary and Government Operations subcommittees were persuaded that the creation of an independent agency with regulatory powers would constitute an "adversarial posture"[34] not needed at that time and that "a much more effective and less cumbersome procedure will permit an individual to seek enforcement of his rights under procedures established by each Federal agency."[35] But the Senate committees concluded that there was still a need for an investigatory and advisory agency with authority to monitor and inspect federal personal information systems; compile and publish information on federal information systems; develop model guidelines for implementation of information systems; investigate and hold hearings on violations and proposals for new systems; and study state and private sector information practices.[36]

In the House, proposals to establish a Federal Privacy Board were rejected by the Subcommittee on Foreign Operations and Government

Information and by the full Committee on Government Operations. On the floor, an amendment proposed by Representative Gilbert Gude (R-Md.) to establish such a board was rejected by a 29 to 9 vote. The following statement of President Gerald Ford in support of H.R. 16373 was quoted in floor debate and was quite influential in House deliberations: "I do not favor the establishment of a separate Commission or Board bureaucracy empowered to define privacy in its own terms and to second-guess citizens and agencies. I vastly prefer an approach which makes Federal agencies fully and publicly accountable for legally mandated privacy protections and which gives the individual adequate legal remedies to enforce what he deems to be in his own best privacy interest."[37] President Ford's emphasis on privacy as an individual concern and his focus on the legal remedies individuals should have were important themes in House and Senate floor debates.

The definition of privacy that was used most frequently in floor debates was that of Warren and Brandeis. Senator Ervin, for example, introduced his bill as "an important first step in the protection of our individual right to be left alone."[38] Senator Barry Goldwater, Jr. (R-Ariz.), speaking in support of legislation that his son had cosponsored in the House, stated: "By privacy I mean the right 'to be let alone' — from intrusions by Big Brother in all his guises."[39] Similarly, in the House, Representative Richard Ichord (D-Mo.) defined the right to privacy as the "right to be left alone . . . without a doubt a right inherent in our libertarian system."[40] As President Ford's comments reflect, if the core concern was protecting *individual* choices, then government should not define privacy — individuals should. But the floor debates also reflect the clash between the idea of individual privacy and the interests of organizations. Defining privacy as the right to be let alone had something of a hollow ring, given the organizational needs for information and the benefits individuals receive from those organizations. Members of Congress recognized that this privacy right was not absolute and needed to be balanced against other interests, primarily law enforcement, investigative concerns, and national security. Although support for the principle of privacy was unwavering, when Congress had to balance privacy against competing interests, the other interests generally prevailed. For example, in House floor votes, numerous types of information were exempted from restrictions in the Privacy Act, such as noncriminal justice investigatory material that revealed sources, testing materials for federal employment, and evaluation materials supporting promotion in the armed services.[41]

Throughout the floor debates in both chambers, the images of *1984* and Watergate were repeatedly evoked. This statement by Representative Ralph Regula (R-Ohio) was typical: "Almost without notice and in the name of efficiency our technological progress has moved us toward the 'big brother' supervision predicted in George Orwell's book *1984*."[42] Representative William S. Moorhead (D-Pa.), the House bill manager, noted that the proposed Privacy Act would "make it legally impossible for the Federal Government in the future to put together anything resembling a '1984' personal dossier on a citizen."[43] Supporters of legislation did not need to rely on fiction for images; the recent abuses of Watergate provided an example of the need for legislation. In the opening House debate, Representative Moorhead noted that "the events of the past several years have a lesson in them. Americans want to see more credibility in Government, and they want to see the removal of any undue Government power which could be used to invade their personal privacy."[44] Senator Ervin also pointed out that many witnesses had "said that the disclosures of Watergate highlighted the need for this bill" but that "the committee report makes clear that the bill is based on long-standing complaints of governmental threats to privacy which will haunt Americans in the years ahead unless this legislation is enacted."[45] Despite Senator Ervin's analysis of the general need for legislation, most observers believe that the legislation would not have been seriously debated and passed in 1974 without the Watergate revelations.

On November 21, 1974, the House adopted its version of the Privacy Act by a vote of 353 to 1 and the Senate adopted its version by a vote of 74 to 9. The acts that passed the two chambers differed primarily in the Senate's creation of a Privacy Protection Commission, its tighter restrictions on the use of information, and its extension of the bill's requirements to certain law enforcement files. Because of the brief time remaining in the Ninety-third Congress, members of the Senate and House Government Operations committees believed it more expedient to have the committee staffs work out a compromise rather than sending the bills to a conference committee.[46] The compromise bill reflected more of the original House bill in that it covered only federal agencies and did not provide for a separate agency to oversee agency information practices. It gave individuals rights of access, correction, and knowledge about personal records in computerized or manual files; subjected federal agencies to standards of fair information handling; charged OMB with responsibility for implementation and oversight of the act; and established the Privacy Protection

Study Commission to investigate the need for legislation over the private sector and the need for an oversight body over federal agencies. On December 17, the Senate approved the compromise substitute by a 77 to 8 roll call vote and sent it to the House, which approved the measure the following day by voice vote. President Ford signed the Privacy Act of 1974 on January 1, 1975.

Before turning to the next stage of policy making, it is important to evaluate what has occurred up to this point. (See appendix A for a summary of key congressional activity in the area of information privacy, 1965–88.) In 1965 a new problem was placed on the congressional agenda by subcommittee chairs in both the House and the Senate. The problem was defined as the invasion of privacy by computers and evoked images of *1984*, the "Computerized Man," and a dossier society. Press interest was high, public concern was generated and resulted in numerous letters being sent to members of Congress, and almost thirty days of congressional hearings were held in the late 1960s and early 1970s. In the early 1970s, analyses of the problem and possible alternatives were conducted by congressional subcommittees, a federal agency committee, and a National Academy of Sciences study. These groups all agreed that the problem was the invasion of individual privacy, not technology. They also agreed that the solution involved giving individuals new rights by which they could control information about themselves, as stated in the Code of Fair Information Practices. However, a number of points were disputed: whether all record systems, public and private, should be subject to the same requirements; what legal recourse individuals should have; and, most importantly, what oversight of personal information practices was necessary. The Privacy Act of 1974 includes all the points upon which there was agreement, but those who advocated more protection for privacy were not able to prevail on any of the points of disagreement.

The Privacy Act encompassed the minimum protection that was advocated at that time. Executive agencies and private sector organizations raised sufficient questions about the cost of privacy, the effect on efficiency, and the burdensome nature of additional regulation to thwart stronger privacy protection. When organizations argued against specific proposals, such as the establishment of a privacy board, they did not frame their opposition in terms of privacy but in terms of costs and burdens. Privacy, although an important part of the rhetoric in hearings and in floor debate, was not the center of the policy conflict. Congressional advocates of stronger privacy legislation knew the barriers they confronted, especially opposition from President Ford. Privacy advocates spoke repeatedly of the Privacy Act as an "important first step."[47] The more difficult questions were advanced to the second step, which the Privacy Act delegated to the Privacy Protection Study Commission.

BALANCE BETWEEN IDEAS AND INTERESTS

The mandate of the Privacy Protection Study Commission was to make "legislative recommendations . . . necessary to protect the privacy of individuals while meeting the legitimate needs of government and society for information."[48] This mandate reflected the tension between the idea of privacy and the interests of government and society in information, framed not just as an interest but also as a "legitimate need." One of the primary charges to the PPSC was to investigate the private sector's personal information practices and to make recommendations to Congress. Over 300 witnesses from the private sector testified in sixty-one days of hearings that were held on a sector-by-sector basis, including, for example, insurance, credit, banking, and medical sectors.[49] Articles in both business journals and data-processing trade magazines were similar in urging private sector firms to "aggressively present [their] views to the Privacy [Protection] Study Commission or the Congress as they consider future privacy legislation. The penalty for failure to do so may be unacceptable costs and difficulties in attempting to comply with the provision of such legislation."[50]

As was true with federal agencies in the debate over the Privacy Act, private sector organizations did not oppose the idea of privacy but emphasized the costs and burdens of complying with privacy protections. The commission also distributed questionnaires to 500 large companies to learn the extent and nature of private sector information handling as well as perceived problems and costs involved in complying with proposed legislation. Additionally, Representatives Edward Koch and Goldwater sent a similar questionnaire to another 1,000 firms. The PPSC assembled detailed descriptions of information practices, policies, and values for a broad range of private sector organizations, including insurance, credit reporting, direct mail, and employment firms. At times, the PPSC had to pry or demand cooperation in order to gain sufficient factual information.

The work of the PPSC provided an opportunity for growth and development in the privacy policy community. Those who had become committed to the privacy issue during the formulation of the Privacy Act now gravitated to the commission, and many who were new to the privacy issue became advocates during the time they worked with the commission. The PPSC continued to compile records of questionable information practices, to keep the issue on the government's agenda, and to secure legitimacy for the policy community. For members of Congress, the PPSC provided another forum in which they could play a visible role as protectors of individual privacy.

In considering the nature of the public policy interests involved in organizational information practices, the PPSC adopted the position that privacy was both a "societal value" and an "individual interest" because record-keeping relationships were "inherently social."[51] Starting with a recognition of the societal value of privacy, the PPSC developed a rationale for examining other "significant societal values and interests" against which privacy had to be balanced, including First Amendment interests, freedom of information interests, the societal interest in law enforcement, cost, and federal-state relations.[52] But in the analysis of how these societal interests are to be balanced against privacy, privacy is treated largely as an individual interest. The "societal value" of privacy is overlooked. For example, the discussion of federal-state relations and privacy begins as follows: "A major interest that must be weighed in the balance of organizations' needs for information against the *individual's interest in having his personal property* protected is *society's interest in maintaining the integrity of the Federal system*" (emphasis added).[53] Similarly, the first paragraph of the PPSC's 1977 report speaks of the need "to strike a proper balance between the individual's personal privacy interests and society's information needs."[54] As was true in the philosophical literature on privacy, there is a recognition that privacy has some social value, but that value is not further developed. Rather, there is a return to an emphasis on privacy as an individual value.

In its report, the PPSC concluded that a voluntary approach should be the initial means of implementing policy in the private sector. The PPSC reasoned that if individuals had the right to assert their interests, organizations would find it more attractive to comply voluntarily. If they did not, then additional enforcement mechanisms might be necessary. The PPSC indicated that existing federal agencies with regulatory authority over a sector, such as the Federal Trade Commission or state insurance departments, would be the appropriate control mechanisms, not a new information privacy agency.[55] The PPSC did recognize, however, that "improving the capability of the individual to protect himself can be an inadequate tool for resolving major systemic problems"[56] and recommended the establishment of a Federal Privacy Board. This "influential 'prodding' structure"[57] would be responsible for monitoring and evaluating implementation of privacy legislation, participating in federal administrative proceedings regarding privacy, issuing interpretive rules for federal agencies, and advising on the privacy implications of proposed statutes. The PPSC made it clear that this board would have no enforcement power over the private sector but only "in connection with the implementation by federal agencies of the Privacy Act itself."[58]

The recommendations of the PPSC were referred to numerous substantive congressional subcommittees. In the House, the Omnibus Right to Privacy Act (H.R. 10076) was introduced by Representative Richardson Preyer (D-N.C.) and cosponsored by Representatives Koch and Goldwater. This long and detailed bill filled 161 pages of a committee report and contained most of the recommendations of the PPSC. Although chances for passage were considered slim, the bill was referred to seven different House committees. Within the private sector, organizations began to establish voluntary privacy protections in order to thwart legislation. For example, a trade journal analysis of the PPSC report urged private organizations to voluntarily comply with the recommendations because it was in their self-interest to fashion their own guidelines: "Government will eventually, but always, fill in gaps left by private enterprise in self-regulating its own activities, much as air automatically moves to fill a vacuum. The message is clear: Private enterprise must thoroughly analyze its own activities, observe where shortcomings exist, decide on a course of action to remedy those shortcomings, and ACT. If this is not done, the propensity for Government to regulate our affairs will continue unabated."[59] Some firms began to emphasize protection of personal information in their advertising. For example, "Your privacy is our concern" became the slogan of the Aetna Insurance Company, whose executive vice president was a member of the PPSC. Civil liberty groups and other privacy advocates were critical of the report "for 'temporizing' on some of the really tough issues, and for over-emphasizing matters of procedure while avoiding judgments of substance and content."[60] Privacy advocates believed that the report left too much to voluntary self-regulation and relied too heavily on individual initiative.

Despite intensive information gathering, sixty-one days of hearings, a dedicated commission, a good staff, and an interested public, no legislation resulted directly from the recommendations of the Privacy Protection Study Commission. The continued involvement of many of the original congressional supporters, such as Representatives Koch and Goldwater — except for Senator Ervin, who had retired — failed to guarantee success.

Moreover, President Jimmy Carter had established a task force on privacy and supported efforts to protect privacy. But the quandary for President Carter was similar to that of many members of Congress who saw privacy as something that protected the individual but viewed big government, especially the Washington, D.C., bureaucracy, as antithetical to the individual. President Carter could not support the establishment of a Federal Privacy Board to protect individual privacy; such a plan conflicted with his liberal view of limited government and protection of individual rights. Interestingly, it was under President Carter that computer matching, initiated as an effort to make the government more effective, began raising the next set of privacy issues.

CLASH OF IDEAS: PRIVACY VERSUS EFFICIENCY

Following passage of the Privacy Act and the recommendations of the Privacy Protection Study Commission, congressional interest in privacy was overshadowed by congressional and executive interest in the efficiency and effectiveness of government programs. Consequently, the terms of debate shifted from an emphasis on individual rights to an emphasis on the detection of fraud, waste, and abuse. The policy arenas in which these issues were debated shifted within Congress from judiciary and individual rights committees and subcommittees to management and budget committees and subcommittees and, on the whole, shifted from Congress to the executive, especially to various presidential commissions, such as the President's Private Sector Survey on Cost Control (the Grace Commission) and the President's Council on Integrity and Efficiency (PCIE).

The Privacy Act's limitations on federal agency use of information and requirements that individuals consent to further uses of information were compromised and weakened by a series of executive and legislative actions. The first of these was Project Match, proposed by HEW secretary Joseph Califano in November 1977. In Project Match, the computerized files of federal employees would be compared to the computerized files of those receiving benefits through Aid to Families with Dependent Children (AFDC) in order to detect government employees who had given false information on an AFDC application.[61] Privacy advocates in Congress, members of the Privacy Protection Study Commission, the American Civil Liberties Union (ACLU), and others criticized the proposed matching of records as a "fishing expedition." Some federal agencies, including the Civil Service Commission and the Department of Defense, questioned whether the Privacy Act prohibited such a use of their files because the use was not compatible with the purpose for which the information was collected and hence required individual consent. Despite these criticisms and hesitations, the matching was done, and by March 1978 Project Match had identified thousands of employees who were possibly ineligible for AFDC benefits and had generated so much data that agency officials could not investigate all cases to determine the validity of the information.[62]

In response to congressional, presidential, and interest-group concerns about the privacy implications of Project Match, the OMB — with assistance from the President's Office of Telecommunications Policy and the White House staff working on President Carter's Privacy Initiative, involving legislative proposals to protect privacy — was given responsibility for writing guidelines for computer matching. The OMB guidelines, issued in March 1979, allowed computer matches to occur as a "routine use" exemption to the Privacy Act[63] and required any disclosures of personal information during a computer match to be made in accordance with the routine use limitations, for example, notice was to be given in the *Federal Register* prior to the match, allowing time for public comment. Under the OMB guidelines,[64] a match was to be performed only if there was a "demonstrable financial benefit," and, to this end, the guidelines required documentation of benefits, costs, potential harm, and alternatives. The guidelines also required agencies to submit a report describing the match to the director of the OMB, the Speaker of the House, and the president of the Senate.

The purpose of the guidelines was "to aid agencies in balancing the government's need to maintain the integrity of Federal programs with the individual's right to personal privacy." However, agencies did not follow the guidelines, the OMB did not monitor agencies' activities, the public and interest groups did not respond to *Federal Register* notices, and there was little congressional reaction. The ideas of integrity and efficiency complemented federal agencies' interests in matching records. But the idea of privacy did not complement the interests of any group with a role in computer matching, except the individuals under investigation, who generally were not aware that their records were being matched. The balance that might have been achievable between the two ideas was offset by the support of interests on one side and the lack of knowledge on the other. In this policy setting, agency use of computer matching increased.

During this same time period, Congress passed a number of laws whose purpose was either to reduce fraud, waste, and abuse in government

Figure 4.2
Laws Enhancing Efficiency and Affecting Privacy

Tax Reform Act of 1976 (PL 94-455) permits the Department of Health, Education, and Welfare to search the databases of other federal agencies to locate parents who are not making child-support payments.

Food Stamp Act Amendments of 1980 (PL 96-58) allow state food stamp agencies to use wage, benefit, and other information in the files of the Social Security Administration and of state unemployment compensation agencies.

Paperwork Reduction Act of 1980 (PL 96-511) gives the Office of Management and Budget oversight authority for federal agency information practices and the responsibility to promote the effective use of information technology. This law is perceived as encouraging data sharing among federal agencies.

Debt Collection Act of 1982 (PL 97-365) sets up a system of data sharing between federal agencies and private credit-reporting agencies in order to facilitate the collection of delinquent nontax debts. Specifically, the act permits federal agencies to refer delinquent nontax debts to credit bureaus to affect credit ratings; require applicants for federal loans to supply their taxpayer identification numbers; screen credit applicants against Internal Revenue Service files to check for tax delinquency; and turn over to private contractors the addresses of delinquent debtors obtained from the Internal Revenue Service.

Federal Managers Financial Integrity Act of 1982 (PL 97-255) requires periodic evaluations of and reports on federal agencies' systems of internal control and actions to reduce fraud, waste, abuse, and error and also encourages information sharing.

Department of Defense Authorization Act of 1983 (PL 97-252) requires the secretary of education to establish a method to verify that any individual receiving a federal grant or loan has complied with Selective Service registration requirements.

Deficit Reduction Act of 1984 (PL 98-369) calls for the most far-reaching data sharing at both the state and federal levels. It requires states to establish information systems containing income and wage information from employers for purposes of verifying eligibility for benefit programs and to exchange relevant information with other state agencies and with the Department of Health and Human Services.

PL 94-452, PL 94-505, and PL 97-252 establish *inspector general offices* in a number of federal agencies, including Health and Human Services, Labor, and Defense. These laws emphasize the public policy goal of detecting fraud, waste, abuse, and management deficiencies and give these offices discretionary power in initiating audits and investigations and in choosing techniques to meet these goals. Computer matching and other record searches have all been employed by inspectors general.

Source: Office of Technology Assessment, *Federal Government Information Technology: Electronic Record Systems and Individual Privacy*, OTA-CIT-296 (Washington, D.C.: Government Printing Office, 1986).

programs or to increase the overall efficiency of government programs. Each of these contributed to a political environment that condoned the sharing of personal information or authorized computer matches. (See figure 4.2.) Although many of these laws accorded certain due process rights to the individual, the use of personal information for a purpose other than that for which it was collected was further legitimated.

THE RETICENCE OF THE COURTS

Because legal and constitutional arguments could be used to challenge computer matching, the courts provided a forum in which privacy could receive support, but case law did not clarify all the legal questions involved. Computer-matching programs raise several constitutional questions, specifically, whether they violate protection against unreasonable searches and seizures, due process, and equal protection of the law.[65] The Fourth Amendment presumption is that searches are not warranted unless there is evidence of a crime. If probable cause for believing that a crime has been committed and that a particular individual was involved exists, then a court may issue a search warrant against that individual. Fourth Amendment case law has resulted in the concept of an "expectation of privacy." In 1975 a district court allowed a computer match of recipients of veterans' disability benefits and recipients of social security benefits in *Jaffess v. Secretary HEW.* The court held that the disclosure under the matching program was "for the purpose of proper administration."[66] Jaffess had not reported his social security income to the Veterans' Administration, and after the computer match, his veterans' benefits were reduced. He claimed that a constitutional right of privacy protected his record. The court rejected this claim, ruling that "the present thrust of decisional law does not include within its compass the right of an individual to prevent disclosure by one governmental agency to another of matters obtained in the course of transmitting agency's regular functions."[67] But the legal question of what kind of Fourth Amendment "expectation of privacy" an individual has in filling out a form and swearing that the information provided is true and correct was not specifically decided. The question of the rights of federal workers to the privacy of information provided and maintained for employment purposes was also not decided. In both instances, statutes, especially the Privacy Act of 1974, provided more precise legal guidance than the Constitution.

The scope of computer matches also raises Fourth Amendment questions. Computer matches are generalized electronic searches of millions of records. Under the Fourth Amendment, the Supreme Court has determined that searches must not be overly inclusive; no "fishing expeditions" or "dragnet investigations" are allowed. Yet in computer matches, many people who have not engaged in fraud or are not actually suspected of criminal activity are subject to the computer search. This raises questions about the presumption of innocence, as reflected in Fourth and Fifth Amendment case law. If matches are considered a Fourth Amendment search,[68] then some limitations on the breadth of the match and/or justifications for a match are necessary. For example, a government agency could be required to show that a less intrusive means of carrying out the search was not available and that procedural safeguards limiting the dangers of abuse and agency discretion were applied. Additionally, procedural safeguards are required under due process protections. A final constitutional issue is whether matching conflicts with the equal protection clause because categories of people, not individual suspects, are subject to computer matches. Two groups — federal employees and welfare recipients — are most often the subjects of computer matching.

Despite these arguments about the constitutionality of computer matches, the courts have generally not upheld individual privacy claims in cases challenging computer-matching programs. Moreover, there has been little litigation in this area for two reasons. First, the damage requirements of the Privacy Act are so difficult to prove that they serve as a deterrent to its use. The act does not provide injunctive relief and provides a civil remedy only if actual damages can be proved. Secondly, in large-scale computer matching, single individuals are rarely sufficiently harmed to litigate claims and most individuals are not even aware of the match. The cases that have gone to court have generally been brought by welfare rights organizations. Courts have not applied the Fourth Amendment "search and seizure" doctrine. In reviewing matching programs, the courts have required only that the programs be rational, that is, the means used must be reasonably related to a legitimate government purpose. The purpose of achieving efficiency and detecting fraud, waste, and abuse has been seen as legitimate. With respect to the choice of means, the courts have traditionally deferred to administrative discretion.

The Second Concern: Systems and Surveillance

While various exchanges of personal information were becoming routine among federal agencies, a number of congressional committees asked the Office of Technology Assessment (OTA) to evaluate some of the large computer systems proposed by major federal agencies. From 1976 to 1982, the OTA examined a range of information systems — the Internal Revenue Service's proposed Tax Administration System, the Federal Bureau of Investigation's National Crime Information Center and Computerized Criminal History System, electronic mail systems for the U.S. Postal Service, and electronic funds transfer systems.[69] The OTA panels and meetings provided forums for analysis of privacy issues, which was not being done within the federal agencies, and for communication among and further growth in the privacy community. For example, the tax system assessment drew together Marcia MacNaughton, previously on Senator Ervin's staff, as project director and Alan Westin as chair of the advisory panel. In general, these studies concluded that privacy, due process, and equity issues had not been adequately addressed in the design of new systems. A comprehensive report, *Computer-Based National Information Systems*, provided a survey of recent developments in computer and communication technologies and a framework for understanding the policy issues that might result. Included among these issues was privacy, especially questions concerning the effectiveness of the sector-by-sector, or selective, approach to protecting privacy that had been adopted in the United States.[70]

Beginning in 1982, the congressional committees with jurisdiction over the Privacy Act reentered the discussion and refocused congressional attention on privacy. In that year, the Subcommittee on Oversight of Government Management of the Senate Committee on Governmental Affairs held hearings on computer matching.[71] Senator William Cohen (R-Maine), chair of the subcommittee, in his opening remarks emphasized the congressional oversight responsibility "to determine whether the Government is striking a proper balance between the important concerns of Government efficiency and individual privacy."[72] Two panels of witnesses testified at this hearing — one of privacy experts and one of inspectors general and members of the PCIE. In 1983 the Government Information, Justice, and Agriculture Subcommittee of the House Committee on Government Operations held hearings.[73] Representative Glenn English (D-Okla.) noted that these were the first such hearings on the Privacy Act and that they were precipitated, in part, by the concern "that the bureaucracy has succeeded in avoiding most of the act's substantive limitations on the use of information."[74]

Both congressional hearings were important in establishing that there was a problem with the Privacy Act itself and OMB enforcement of it. The dimensions of the problem and the alternatives for dealing with it still needed to be determined. To this end, the General Accounting Office (GAO), initially at the request of some members of Congress and later on its own initiative, began a number of studies of the use of computer matching by federal and state agencies and of the implementation of the Privacy Act. From 1976 to 1984, the GAO produced ninety-two reports on eligibility verification programs at the state and federal levels and fifty-six reports relating to privacy and information systems.[75] Additionally, in 1983 the Senate Committee on Governmental Affairs and the House Committee on the Judiciary's Subcommittee on Courts, Civil Liberties, and the Administration of Justice requested that the OTA examine federal agency use of new information technologies and evaluate the implications both for congressional oversight of agency activities and for individual rights.

At this time, privacy had not disappeared as a congressional concern, but the importance of other governmental interests, especially efficiency and law enforcement, had become dominant. Catching "welfare cheats" was a more popular symbol than fear of Big Brother. There was a lack of interest in privacy and political pressure to protect privacy. Many privacy advocates were also beginning to recognize the difficulties in providing individual control over record exchanges given the technological ease of exchanges and organizational imperatives.

REASSESSING THE TECHNOLOGY AND THE PROBLEM

Increased use of computer matching during the late 1970s and early 1980s reawakened privacy advocates inside and outside the government and reopened the debate on the definition of this policy problem. As records were used and exchanged for more purposes, the policy concern focused more on surveillance and social control than on individual privacy. The capabilities of computerized databases and the merging of separate databases made it possible for the organizations using and maintaining databases to monitor the present and past activities of individuals. The technological component of the problem also reentered the policy debate. The surveillance potential of computerized information systems had been recognized in the early debates. For example, in 1973 sociologist James Rule in *Private Lives and Public Surveillance* argued that "the commonest solutions to the problem of mass surveillance in large-scale societies lie in the use of documentation. . . . The formal rendering of information about people comes to take the place of informal mechanisms of surveillance found in small-scale settings. The crucial function of such documentation is to link people to their pasts, and thereby to provide the surveillance necessary for the exercise of social control."[76]

As the use of computer matching and other record searches increased, scholars and journalists within this policy community began to reemphasize the surveillance aspect of the problems caused by computers. David Burnham's *Rise of the Computer State* adopted this perspective, arguing, for instance, that "without such general surveillance operations" as the computerized data banks of credit bureaus or car rental agencies, which contain records on each transaction of each customer, "the quick access to credit and the mobile life our society prizes would be impossible."[77] Similarly, Gary Marx and Nancy Reichman suggested that computers were "routinizing the discovery of secrets," in that systematic data searching "permits the joining of heretofore independent pieces of information in order to expose offenses and offenders that would remain hidden unless such links could be drawn."[78] John Shattuck, director of the Washington, D.C., office of the ACLU, referred to computer matching as "an effective way of combining personal data from a wide variety of separate record systems and using it to keep track of individuals."[79] This shift from the idea of privacy to the idea of surveillance refocused the concern from the individual to larger groups. Although an individual could be singled out and have his or her privacy invaded, it was more likely that, by virtue of performing rather routine tasks, one's activities would be monitored. The focus on surveillance also drew back into policy discussions those who were concerned about technology, which broadened the policy community to include computer professionals interested in the impact of computers and academics researching technology and social change.

With the arrival of the year 1984, the surveillance theme received more attention both inside and outside Congress. Representative Robert Kastenmeier's Subcommittee on Courts, Civil Liberties, and the Administration of Justice held a series of hearings entitled "1984 and the National Security State."[80] Senator William Cohen's Subcommittee on Oversight of Government Management held hearings on the computer matching of taxpayer records.[81] As it became clear that the technology made this type of record surveillance possible, the technological capabilities of computer and communication technologies became central issues in the policy debates. A number of interest groups also organized conferences around this theme. The American Bar Association (ABA) in August 1984 held a symposium entitled "Information Law and Ethics: In the Shadow of Orwell — The Citizen and Government." The ACLU and the Public Interest Computer Association (PICA) held two consultations, in June 1984 and January 1985, to explore privacy issues posed by new computer and communication technologies. Congressional staff from both the House and the Senate were participants in the ABA symposium and the ACLU/PICA conference. Following release of the Louis Harris poll, *The Road after 1984*, the House Subcommittee on Government Information, Justice, and Agriculture held hearings in which a number of witnesses testified that the Harris survey documented both a need for stronger privacy legislation and an increase in the public's support for such legislation.[82]

As was true in the congressional deliberations of the 1960s and 1970s, members of Congress perceived a need for accurate information on how federal agencies were using new information and communication technologies and with what effects. In response to requests from the Senate Committee on Governmental Affairs and the House Committee on the Judiciary, the OTA conducted a survey of federal agencies.[83] The most relevant findings of that survey were that the number of computer matches performed by federal agencies nearly tripled from 1980 to 1984 and that the number of separate records evaluated in the reported matching programs totaled over 2 billion, with the total number of records matched reported to be over 7 billion due to multiple matches of the same records. The survey was important in providing congressional committees with empirical data regarding the changes that had taken place in federal agency information practices since the Privacy Act deliberations in the early 1970s.

The OTA's analysis of federal agency use of electronic record systems — specifically for computer matching, front-end verification, and computer profiling — revealed four common policy problems:

> First, new applications of personal information have undermined the goal of the Privacy Act that individuals be able to control information about themselves. . . .
>
> Second, there is serious question as to the efficacy of the current institutional arrangements for oversight of federal agency compliance with the Privacy Act and related OMB guidelines. . . .
>
> Third, neither Congress nor the executive branch is providing a forum in which the privacy, management efficiency, and law enforcement implications of federal electronic record system applications can be fully debated and resolved. . . .
>
> Fourth, within the federal government, the broader social, economic, and political context of information policy, which includes privacy-related issues, is not being considered.[84]

The OTA concluded that the widespread use of computerized databases, electronic record searches and matches, and computer networking was rapidly leading to the creation of a de facto national database containing personal information on most Americans. The use of the social security number as a de facto electronic national identifier facilitated the development of this database.[85] The press attention the report received focused on the idea that a national database did not have to contain all records about people stored in one computer; the linking of computers allowed for the creation of a de facto national database.[86]

In 1986 Senators Cohen and Carl Levin (D-Mich.) introduced the Computer Matching and Privacy Protection Act (s. 2756), which sought to ensure the privacy, integrity, and verification of data disclosed in computer matching and to establish Data Integrity Boards within federal agencies. In opening hearings on the bill before the Subcommittee on Oversight of Government Management, Senator Cohen remarked: "The subcommittee's investigation and past hearings have revealed tremendous potential for abuse in computer matching, because there are no mandatory rules for agencies to follow when performing matches, little protection for the person whose records are matched, and inadequate oversight of how these programs are being conducted."[87] Testifying at these hearings were representatives from the OMB, GAO, OTA, ACLU, and ABA. The most pressing policy problems identified were questions about whether computer matches were authorized by law and what justifications were given; concerns for the rights of individuals subject to computer matches; the accuracy of records used in matches; and the cost-effectiveness of using matches to uncover fraud, waste, and abuse. As these concerns were examined, it became apparent that the idea of efficiency, which was used to justify computer matching, was not being achieved by computer matching. Records contained many inaccuracies, and no evidence of cost-effectiveness was apparent.

Because computer matching was purportedly used to enhance the efficiency and effectiveness of the delivery of government programs and services, it is logical to expect that computer matches should themselves be cost-effective. Under the 1979 OMB computer-matching guidelines, a match was to be performed "only if a demonstrable financial benefit can be realized that significantly outweighs the costs of the match and any potential harm to individuals that could be caused by the matching program." However, this stipulation was rarely observed; cost-benefit analyses were not done in a systematic fashion but were usually sketched out quickly when requested by the OMB. The cost-benefit requirement was dropped from the 1982 OMB guidelines, largely in response to criticisms of the requirement from the inspectors general and the PCIE.

In the early 1980s, advocates and users of computer matching — including the OMB, the Grace Commission, and various inspectors general — repeatedly asserted that computer matches were cost-beneficial but offered little empirical evidence in support.[88] In response to the 1986 OTA survey, 7 out of 37 (19 percent) agencies participating in computer matches reported that they did cost-benefit analyses prior to or after a computer match.[89] One reason why it was difficult to systematically prepare cost-benefit analyses was the lack of an accepted methodology for determining what should be included as costs and benefits and how to quantify each. In 1984 the Department of Health and Human Services (HHS) Office of the Inspector General published a guide to computer matching to assist managers in conducting cost-benefit analyses, which categorized costs and benefits as both quantitative and qualitative.[90] All costs would vary according to the size of the record set as well as according to the complexity, quality, and compatibility of the records. Moreover, the cost of verifying a "hit" was the highest cost of most matches and the most difficult to compute. An independent cost-benefit analysis conducted at the state level concluded that benefits outweighed costs in well-functioning matching programs.[91] In 1986 the OTA found "no firm evidence . . . to determine the costs and benefits of computer matching and to document claims made by OMB, the inspectors general, and others that computer matching is cost effective."[92] In 1986 the General Accounting Office published a report on the costs and benefits of computer matching,[93] concluding that all cost-benefit reports reviewed contained deficiencies, including use of inappropriate benefit measurements, no discounting of the present value of future revenues, incomplete reports, and more analysis of benefits than of costs.

The Computer Matching and Privacy Protection Act (CMPPA) that Senators Cohen and Levin had introduced during the 99th Congress (s. 2756) was reintroduced during the 100th Congress (s. 496). It required agencies to develop matching agreements that specified the purpose, justification, and legal authority for the match; procedures for verifying records and providing security; and procedures for notifying individuals that their records were to be matched. The CMPPA also established a new institutional mechanism, the Data Integrity Boards, to provide a check on the discretion of program managers. These boards, which the CMPPA required all federal agencies engaging in computer matching to create, had authority to approve or reject matching agreements. The concept was borrowed from the Defense Department, which had established a Defense Privacy Board for agency implementation of the Privacy Act of 1974. Despite the lack of evidence proving cost-effectiveness, the proposed CMPPA was silent on the question of cost-benefit analyses, agencies having argued against the inclusion of cost-benefit requirements.

After one day of hearings, the CMPPA was approved with the unanimous support of the nine members of the Subcommittee on Oversight of Government Management and was subsequently approved without dissent by the Governmental Affairs Committee. In introducing it to the full Senate in May 1987, Senator Levin noted that the bill "has also managed to satisfy a host of Government and private groups whose positions on computer matching range from violently opposed to violently in favor."[94] Although he did not elaborate on the composition of the two groups, those in favor of computer matching included federal agencies, especially the OMB and the inspectors general, while those opposed were the ACLU and the ABA. Senator Levin referred to the bill as "successfully balancing competing concerns for efficiency, privacy and fairness."[95] Senator William Roth (R-Del.), the chair of the full committee and the only other senator to speak about the bill, noted that the budget deficit made it necessary to reduce spending and that computer matching could "help to eliminate program mismanagement, fraud, and abuse."[96] The Senate unanimously approved the CMPPA.

A month later, the House Subcommittee on Government Information, Justice, and Agriculture of the Committee on Government Operations held one day of hearings on the CMPPA, which had just passed the Senate (s. 496). In his opening statement, Representative English commented that the bill "does not appear to be especially controversial. . . . It appears to have support from those on all sides of the issue."[97] However, privacy advocates believed that the CMPPA was something of a mixed blessing. For the first time, computer matching was regulated, which reflected both an acknowledgment of the importance of technology and a concession to the necessity of limiting use of personal information for a purpose other than that for which it was collected. Although the Senate bill provided some procedural limitations and protections, privacy advocates had testified that more were necessary. For example, the ACLU suggested that matching agreements be published in the *Federal Register* prior to approval to allow for public comment, that cost-benefit analyses be required, that notice be accompanied by signed consent, that the act require human verification of all data, and that the Data Integrity Boards be given stronger and clearer oversight authority.[98] Ronald Plesser, testifying for the ABA, also supported the bill but cautioned that "the legislation does not, on certain points, go far enough."[99] The OMB and the PCIE, on the other side of the debate, also voiced support for the bill but differed in that they believed the bill went too far. The deputy director of the OMB, Joseph Wright, began his testimony by noting that "we have a large stake in this issue."[100] The OMB and the PCIE were opposed to including intra-agency matches and matches conducted by the inspectors general, requiring cost-benefit analyses, and expanding the role of the Data Integrity Boards.

Following the House hearings, the CMPPA was revised and introduced in the House (H.R. 4699). The House bill strengthened privacy protections somewhat. Language in the committee report reflected a concern that the CMPPA should not be construed "as supporting, encouraging, or directing the linkage of computers or the establishment of any type of national data bank that combines, merges or links information on individuals maintained in systems of records."[101] To this end, the revised CMPPA explicitly stated that nothing in the act itself authorized the computer matching of records not otherwise authorized by law. It also required cost-benefit analyses, noting that "without a specific legislative directive and enforcement mechanism, the matching bureaucracy will not conduct satisfactory cost-benefit studies."[102] But on the whole, the House bill was similar to the Senate bill in placing procedural requirements on agency matches while also permitting the use of matching in certain cases.

The full House considered the CMPPA on August 1, 1988, at which time the House bill was substituted for the Senate bill and passed. The House subcommittee hearing had been held in June 1987. Over a year had passed before the bill returned to the floor for approval. During that time, four staff members from the House and Senate committees, the OMB, and the ACLU had worked informally to craft a compromise. On September 20, the Senate concurred with the amended House version but added several amendments of its own. Senator Cohen described these as "modest changes" and claimed that the amended version struck "the proper balance between the legitimate needs of Government efficiency and personal privacy."[103] The two most important changes that the Senate made to the House version were to provide more flexibility in the notice requirements so that individualized notice would not be costly or burdensome to agencies and to reduce the amount of time agencies would have to wait to take an adverse action based on information from a computer match from sixty days to thirty days. Senators Cohen, Levin, and Glenn were the only senators to speak briefly about the issue on the floor; the bill was approved unanimously by voice vote. On October 3, the House concurred, and the CMPPA was passed with no floor discussion by a vote of 398 to 8, with eight Republicans voting against passage.

To some extent, the CMPPA represented an incremental change. The Privacy Act was viewed as a substantive limitation on what could be done with records; for example, it prohibited certain uses of records. Because technological advances had obliterated the notion of records, replacing them with database systems, the CMPPA established procedural limitations. Computer matching was legitimated by statute, but in keeping with the Privacy Act, procedural requirements were placed on the agencies and individual rights were given some protection. But as was true in the adoption of the Privacy Act, an argument based on individual privacy failed to provide a meaningful focus for policy formulation. Political support and interest were generated mainly by discussion of information practices, technological developments, and organizational needs. Questions of efficiency, procedures, and cost-benefit dominated. David Flaherty agrees that "the new law emphasizes due process and administrative goals, including analysis of costs and benefits, rather than concentrating on privacy and surveillance issues," but also notes that "this reflects a shrewd political assessment of how best to persuade Congress to act."[104] Such a political assessment illustrates the difficulties in using privacy as a goal of legislation.

Perhaps most importantly, legislation has established some agency-wide, although not governmentwide, oversight over agency matching activities. Until this time, the inspectors general, operating largely through the PCIE and the OMB, controlled agency matches. The OMB resisted the establishment of Data Integrity Boards and was able to delay their establishment because, as Representative Robert Wise (D-W.V.) noted in introducing a bill to extend the deadline by which agencies were to create Data Integrity Boards, the "OMB took longer than it should have to issue implementing regulations required by the Act."[105] As with the Privacy Act itself, the powers of the Data Integrity Boards are likely to depend on congressional oversight, either through the relevant subcommittees or through outside investigations. Analyses of the first several years of experience with the Data Integrity Boards suggest that more active and direct oversight by Congress is necessary.[106]

The Third Concern: Webs of Private and Public Records

Although privacy legislation received bipartisan support and the legislation that passed Congress did so by wide margins, it was not easy either to formulate effective policy in this area or to oversee the implementation of policy that existed. These difficulties did not result from lack of congressional interest; privacy was frequently the subject of congressional activity, especially at the subcommittee level. But the issue of privacy did not receive a steady groundswell of support among members of Congress. Instead, the conflicts between privacy values and organizational interests largely resulted in policy stalemate, with the passage of only two major pieces of compromise legislation.

The privacy value was consistently defined throughout the thirty years of legislative deliberations as the right to control information about oneself. The difficulty, however, was in determining how individuals could exercise such control. The Code of Fair Information Practices established certain principles to govern organizational use of information. It also protected individual rights by guaranteeing access to one's own records and correction of inaccurate or irrelevant information. These practices were viewed as a means of allowing individuals greater control and were incorporated into the Privacy Act of 1974. But, as oversight of the Privacy Act revealed, these rights were not easily exercised because the costs involved were high, including expenditures of time and money. The rights and the control existed on paper but not in reality.

Questions of effective individual control also dominated debates over computer matching and other reuses of personal information. In principle, information collected for one purpose could not be used for another purpose without the consent of the individual. But given the extensive use of computer matching and other routine exchanges of personal information, how could individuals meaningfully consent? One suggestion was to require agencies to notify individuals who were to be the subjects of matches by sending them postcards. Privacy advocates questioned whether this gave individuals any real control, however, and agency officials questioned the expense entailed. The proposal was dropped, and Data Integrity Boards were created in part to act as intermediaries between individuals and agencies and approve matching agreements.

Information privacy concerns have by no means disappeared from the public or congressional agenda. Congressional interest in credit information has spiraled since 1989, when a cover story in *Business Week* exposed how easy it was to gain access to sensitive credit files, including those of the vice president.[107] The Fair Credit Reporting Act (FCRA), on the books since 1970, was the first information privacy legislation in the United States. Privacy advocates and others have pointed out gaps and weaknesses in the FCRA since its passage, numerous congressional hearings have been held, and commissions have called for stronger rules and enforcement. But the credit-reporting industry and its powerful customers have been effective in thwarting legislation.[108] The scenario is all too familiar in the area of information privacy but is unusual because of the number of horror stories of abuses and the social status of the victims of credit-report abuses. One reporter commented, "A steady parade of witnesses has appeared on Capitol Hill over the past few years with tales of unresponsive or rude employees at the credit reporting agencies."[109] Reports of erroneous information in credit files are legendary. One instance that received a great deal of media attention involved 1,500 property owners in Norwich, Vermont, who were mislabeled by a credit-reporting agency as "tax deadbeats."

Current legislative proposals address the use of credit data in generating mailing lists, the question of responsibility for accuracy of information, the protection of consumer rights (including the distribution of free copies of credit reports to individuals on a yearly or biyearly basis), and new legal bases for bringing civil suits for damages. Privacy advocates have been working with consumer rights groups for passage of legislation and emphasize the consumer rights nature of the proposed protections more than privacy. The credit-reporting industry does not welcome legislation and has taken steps to weaken perceptions of a need for legislation. For example, Equifax stopped selling credit-report information to direct marketers and made available a toll-free telephone number for consumer questions; TRW announced in 1992 that it would give free copies of credit reports annually to all consumers requesting them. The executive vice president of the Associated Credit Bureaus was quoted as saying that the industry was "willing to work toward passage of a piece of legislation that meets the legitimate needs of consumers, while offering a vehicle for the industry to provide quality service."[110]

In early 1994, an amendment to the FCRA, the Consumer Reporting Reform Act of 1994 (H.R. 1015 and S. 793), seemed to be continuing on what has been described as a "torturous course toward enactment."[111] In 1992 consumer and privacy advocates lost almost every vote in the Banking Committee. One committee member, Al McCandless (R-Calif.), said "he was sympathetic to the consumer groups' concerns but argued that their requests would raise costs or be cumbersome or impossible to implement."[112] A bill to strengthen federal regulation of the credit-reporting industry was pulled from floor consideration in the House after the defeat of an amendment stipulating the deletion of language preempting state laws. Despite broad support, the bill's sponsors, Henry B. Gonzales (D-Tex.) and Esteban E. Torres (D-Calif.), had offered the amendment because about twenty states already had more stringent laws on their books. The credit-reporting industry, banks, and retailers lobbied to keep the preemption provision in the bill, arguing that the existence of a variety of state laws was too burdensome on the credit-reporting industry. As the 103d Congress was closing its deliberations in the summer of 1994, prospects for enactment appeared good. Both the House and Senate approved similar bills, requiring that low-cost biannual reports be made available to consumers, preempting state laws for several years, and eliminating a private right of action for reporting of erroneous information except in limited instances. The key difference involved limitations on the use of information from a credit report for direct-mail purposes. Senate and House members agreed to drop these provisions from both bills, making the bills identical and virtually ensuring passage in both houses. The House, as expected, passed the revised bill. But in the Senate, Phil Gramm (R-Tex.), who had opposed FCRA reform, prohibited the bill from coming to the floor for a vote, killing any chance for passage in the 103d Congress.

Access to public record information was also on the congressional agenda after several media reports on the misuse of motor vehicle information. In one instance, an antiabortion group obtained address information from the state Department of Motor Vehicles (DMV) by using the license plate of a car driven by a woman who entered a clinic where abortions were performed. The woman was outraged to receive a harassing letter from the group, especially since she had gone to the clinic not to have an abortion but to try unsuccessfully to save her pregnancy. In another instance, a California actress, Rebecca Shaeffer, was stalked and murdered by a man who obtained her home address from the DMV. The Driver's Privacy Protection Act (H.R. 3365 and S. 1589) was introduced in the 103d Congress by two newcomers to the privacy issue, Representative Jim Moran (D-Va.) and Senator Barbara Boxer (D-Calif.). The original House bill prohibited disclosure of personal information held by motor vehicle departments without authorization by the individual except in certain circumstances, including "in the normal course of business by legitimate business, in research activities, and in marketing activities (subject to specified limitations)."[113] The bill reflected a compromise between individual privacy and the interests of direct marketers; although direct marketing is considered a "legitimate business purpose," individuals would be able to "opt-out" of allowing motor vehicle information to be given to direct marketers. In an "opt-out" system, individuals are given the choice to restrict secondary uses of their personal information. The direct-marketing industry has opposed placing any restrictions on the use of public records, and some privacy advocates have preferred an "opt-in" method, whereby additional uses of personal information must be authorized by the individual involved.

After hearings and floor consideration in both houses, the Driver's Privacy Protection Act was incorporated into the Violent Crime Control and Law Enforcement Act of 1994. As revised, the legislation completely exempts law enforcement agencies, employers, the automotive industry, the government, and the insurance industry. The "opt-out" provision was also expanded; after an individual has been offered an opportunity to "opt-out" but does not do so, motor vehicle information can be released to anyone for any purpose. This is the first legislation restricting access to public record information. The media, direct marketers, and the information industry are concerned that similar restrictions may be proposed limiting the uses of other public databases, such as voter registration lists and real estate records. The value of access to such databases is enormous, as indicated by a comment by the chief economist at Dun and Bradstreet's: "It's so inexpensive to redistribute data that public data has in effect become a commodity with very low overhead."[114] Through computer and telecommunications systems, direct marketers, private investors, banks, law firms, and journalists can access detailed databases containing public record information for as little as $15 per search. A 1994 Supreme Court decision signals judicial support for restricting access to personal information in public records. In *U.S. Department of Defense v. Federal Labor Relations Authority*, the Court held that individuals have a "far from insignificant" privacy interest in their home address information, an interest that is not already compromised because that information is in the public domain.[115]

The biggest information privacy issue in the 1990s will probably involve medical information. The Clinton administration's commitment to health care reform suggests that the issue of information privacy may be given a high priority on the congressional agenda. The proposals for a health security card, universal access to health care, and further computerization and standardization of medical records all raise privacy issues. At the present time, surprisingly few state or federal laws protect the privacy of medical records. Medical records contain not only diagnostic and testing information about a patient but also may contain information about an individual's medical history, family history, financial situation, employment history, drug and alcohol use, and sexual orientation and practices. In 1977 the American Medical Records Association, in a position statement on confidentiality of patient health information, listed twelve broad categories of what it termed "social users" of medical information, including public health agencies, medical and social researchers, employers, social welfare programs, insurance companies, government agencies, educational institutions, law enforcement agencies, credit investigation agencies, licensing agencies, and the media.[116]

The issue of medical record privacy has been the subject of policy formulation for over twenty years. Following the report of the Privacy Protection Study Commission in 1977 and with support from the Carter administration, Congress gave serious attention to the issue of medical privacy. The policy problem was typically framed in terms of how to balance the individual's privacy interest in his or her own medical records with society's legitimate need for such information.[117] Hearings were held in both the House[118] and the Senate.[119] Testimony at the hearings reflected not only the many uses of medical information but also the complexity of the medical information environment, in which nurses, doctors, hospitals, insurance companies, medical researchers, and employers all play roles in the provision of medical care and/or the collection of medical information. Both House and Senate committees issued reports.[120] The House, in a postelection session, considered the Federal Privacy of Medical Information Act (H.R. 5935), which protected patient privacy by controlling the use and disclosure of medical information. It also allowed release of medical information to the Secret Service and intelligence agencies and gave the physician discretion to disclose medical information without consent if a patient was a danger to the community. The bill reflected compromises made in committee. During the floor debate, Representative Edward Boland (D-Mass.), chair of the House Select Committee on Intelligence, spoke against the bill, arguing that its provisions would restrict disclosure of mental health information to government agencies, even "when there is a clear national interest in requesting it."[121] By framing the issue in terms of national security interests compromised by privacy protections, Boland was successful in gaining House defeat of the bill. The Senate did not consider its bill. During the Reagan and Bush administrations, no serious congressional efforts were made to revisit the issue of medical privacy.

The Clinton administration's commitment to health care reform sparked a flurry of activity about medical records, computerization, and privacy. The Institute of Medicine (IOM) issued a report in 1991 concluding that computerization of records will improve patient care and lower health care costs. The IOM report pointed out a number of privacy issues raised by computerization, including the need for standards for the protection of computerized medical information and the potential for privacy invasion posed by the use of identification numbers for patient records.[122] A task force within the Department of Health and Human Services also reported that computerization of medical information held great potential for improving the quality and efficiency of health care delivery but raised concerns about privacy and confidentiality.[123] The OTA concluded that "Federal legislation is necessary to address issues of patient confidentiality and privacy."[124] Results of a public opinion survey of attitudes toward medical privacy revealed that "although the privacy of medical records may not be an issue to which the general public has given much thought, it has the potential to become a very important issue."[125] When asked to rate the importance of six issues involved in health care reform, respondents ranked "protecting the confidentiality of peoples' medical records" third. Protecting confidentiality was rated as more important than "providing health care insurance for those who don't have it today," "reducing paperwork burdens," and "providing better data for research."[126]

Again, the policy problem has been defined largely in terms of the individual's right to privacy in his or her medical records against the competing interests of society for access to that information and for an efficient and effective health care delivery system. Discussions of how to balance such competing interests have been repeated. At a conference on medical information privacy,[127] it was agreed that privacy protections were an essential part of any health care reform plan. Representative Pete Stark (D-Calif.) stated that although privacy was not a major issue in health care reform, it was "one on which we could get hung up."[128] Senator Patrick Leahy (D-Vt.), whose Subcommittee on Law and Technology had recently held hearings on the privacy of medical information, commented that "privacy is going to be the cornerstone" of any type of health care reform. Alan Westin described medical privacy concerns as a "time bomb waiting to go off"; if accounts of medical record abuses were publicized or if proposals received negative publicity, privacy could become a central part of the health care debate. Don Lewers of the American Medical Association agreed that privacy would be a key issue and would be difficult to resolve. Two longtime privacy advocates, Janlori

Goldman of the ACLU and Marc Rotenberg of the Computer Professionals for Social Responsibility (CPSR), both took the position that trying to "balance" privacy and access to health care was not the appropriate approach. Both argued that the goal should be to pursue both access to health care and protection of privacy.

Informal working groups associated with the House Subcommittee on Information, Justice, Transportation, and Agriculture developed the Fair Health Information Practices Act of 1994 (H.R. 4077), which was introduced by Representative Gary Condit (D-Calif.). The subcommittee held the first in a series of hearings in the fall of 1993 and later held three days of hearings on the proposed bill.[129] In the summer of 1994, the bill was added to the Health Security Act (H.R. 3600).[130] In the report accompanying the bill, the Committee on Government Operations commented on the significance in proposing a Code of Fair Information Practices bill rather than a privacy bill. It noted the broadness and vagueness of the word "privacy" and the fact that health records are not private papers of an individual but maintained by, and available to, many public and private organizations. The committee concluded that "fair information practices for health information can be provided even though absolute privacy cannot."[131]

The bill provided for the traditional rights of individuals to see and correct their own records; its provisions limiting disclosure of information and requiring individual consent were more thoroughly crafted and restrictive than other fair information codes. The proposed act stipulated that authorization forms meet eight requirements, including that they be separate from the forms for the approval of the provision of or payment for health care. The Committee on Government Operations sought to avoid "the fiction of informed consent for routine disclosures for treatment or payment,"[132] authorizing these disclosures only under specified conditions and prohibiting reuse of information unless disclosure requirements were strictly followed. Any organization or person in possession of protected health information is considered a "health information trustee" and is subject to the fair information practices.

The concept of fair information principles has provided the beginning point for most policy proposals. But the sensitivity of medical information, the fact that it affects all individuals in a similar fashion, and the scale of computerization and ease of information exchanges that are envisioned have also prompted proposals for federal policies that are more aggressive than a law that merely gives individuals new privacy rights over their medical information. The Clinton health care proposals call for a Code of Fair Information Practices, a Health Privacy Board, and enforcement procedures. The OTA report also proposed as a policy option the establishment of a commission to oversee the protection of health care data. The original Health Modernization and Security Act called for the creation of a Health Care Data Panel with responsibility for adopting standards for electronic exchange of health care information and privacy and confidentiality requirements.[133] Most studies suggest that technological protections for privacy should be designed as part of a national computerized health care system.[134]

The question of what number to use on a health security card illustrates some of the likely difficulties in developing legislation. Some groups, such as the HHS task force, recommend the use of the social security number as the personal identifier on a health security card. New numbers would not need to be issued, and people would not have to remember yet another numerical identifier. In the 1993 Health Information Privacy Survey, a clear majority of respondents (67 percent) favored using the social security number, rather than a new number, as their identifier for health care.[135] But some groups fear that such additional use of the social security number signifies its status as a universal identification number. In the past, the public and members of Congress have been very suspicious of authorizing new uses for the social security number. A recent illustration involves a proposal by Senator Alan Simpson (R-Wyo.) in the 1990 Immigration Act for the creation of a forgery-proof driver's license that could be used by employers to detect illegal aliens.[136] The license was to include a "biometric" component, such as a fingerprint, and a social security number. In conference committee, the inclusion of the social security number on the card was dropped because of opposition from ethnic groups and the ACLU, both of which argued that this might be the first step toward a national identification card.

These debates about the privacy of credit information, marketing information, and medical information echo the earlier difficulties in formulating policy to protect information privacy. Despite media coverage and numerous accounts of problems with credit reports, the attempt to strengthen the FCRA has been blocked by effective industry lobbying. Concerns about individual privacy have been framed in terms of fairness in consumer relationships, which are largely controlled by the industry. Talk of health care reform has placed concerns about the privacy of medical information high on the policy agenda. In this debate, privacy is defined primarily in terms of fair information principles — giving individuals rights — and balancing competing interests. The difficulties in using such a definition as the goal of legislation are recognized by congressional committees. Attempts are being made to craft legislation that relies less on individual initiative and more on substantive requirements imposed on organizations. But the history of information privacy legislation suggests that as the policy process proceeds, privacy and fair information principles will become less prominent as symbols and goals of legislation. Concerns about organizational needs, efficiency of operations, and cost-effectiveness will become more important. Without aggressive action by privacy advocates and support from other players[137] in the health care debate, privacy concerns are likely to be compromised.

Chapter 5

Communication Privacy: Transmitting Our Messages

People have always been interested in the conversations of others, whether out of simple curiosity, jealousy, or a legitimate need to know what others are planning. At the same time, people having conversations generally assume that their exchanges are private. In the case of communication privacy, technological changes have expanded both the means by which we communicate — including telegraph, telephone, shortwave radio, electronic mail, and video conference — and the means by which someone can listen in on those communications — including wiretaps, bugs, parabolic microphones, and lasers. As the communications media have become more varied, so have the means to overhear those communications.

The primary policy tension in the area of privacy and communications has been between the privacy rights of individuals and the needs of law enforcement to conduct investigations. Somewhat less important in the policy debates have been concerns about eavesdropping by gossipers, business competitors, and jealous spouses. Instead, privacy, effective law enforcement, and crime — especially bootlegging, gambling, loan-sharking, and narcotics trafficking — have been the recurring themes since the turn of the century.[1] Enforcement of Prohibition in the 1920s, concern with organized crime in the 1950s and early 1960s, civil rights marches and Vietnam War protests in the 1960s and 1970s, and the drug war of the 1980s each provoked an increase in law enforcement wiretapping, court cases challenging the surveillance, media coverage and public interest, congressional hearings, and, only occasionally, legislation.

The Fourth Amendment provides the definition and meaning of communication privacy in stating that "the right of the people to be secure in their persons, houses, papers, and effects, against unreasonable searches and seizures, shall not be violated, and no Warrants shall issue, but upon probable cause, supported by Oath or affirmation, and particularly describing the place to be searched and the persons or things to be seized."

Because communication privacy issues are framed as constitutional issues, the courts have been involved in policy making. But the parameters of Fourth Amendment protection are not clear-cut. Are communications covered under "persons, houses, papers, and effects"? Is electronic surveillance an "unreasonable search and seizure"? In responding to defendants' challenges to evidence obtained through surveillance, the courts have offered answers to these questions and in doing so have been important actors in defining communication privacy issues. The courts, however, have not always had the last word and at times have called upon Congress for clarification and legislation.

Civil liberties groups and the legal profession in general have been active members of the policy community in the area of communication privacy, as have law enforcement officials at both the federal and state level. Telephone companies have also been major players, since their cooperation is needed in order to install telephone taps. Providers of new communication technologies — such as electronic mail, cellular phones, and database services — have been increasingly active due to their concern that consumers will not use a communications medium that can not ensure private communications.

The Early Years

In preelectronic times, in order to listen to another person's conversation, the listener had to be physically close enough to overhear what was being said. The word "eavesdrop" literally reflected this fact, meaning, according to Sir William Blackstone in his *Commentaries on the Laws of England* (1765–69), to "listen under walls or window, or the eaves of a house, to hearken after discourse, and thereupon to frame slanderous and mischievous tales."[2] In colonial New England, although eavesdroppers did threaten the privacy of the home, David Flaherty reports, "such offenders were not often prosecuted, since the matter could be handled in a more practical and perhaps more satisfying manner by the person who discovered the culprit."[3] At that time, eavesdropping was viewed primarily as a nuisance rather than as a calculated or official threat to privacy.

As technology made it possible to conduct communications in a physically private space and to send communications by wire, people assumed their communications had a level of privacy that often did not exist. Soon after the telegraph and telephone were invented, public officials and private parties learned how to tap into those communications. In fact, the first patent for a telephone scrambler, a device used to thwart the efforts of telephone tappers, was issued in 1881, only five years after the telephone was patented.[4] The ease of wiretapping and the value of the information that could be learned in effect dictated that tapping would occur. During the Civil War, the Union and Confederate armies tapped each other's telegraph communications to ascertain battle plans and troop movements. Rival press organizations tapped each other's wire communications in order to be the first to report major news items. Wiretapping was also used for personal financial gain. In the mid-1800s, several Western Union operators and a Wall Street broker intercepted messages concerning financial matters and substituted false information for their own investment purposes. During World War I, Congress, as part of federal regulation of the telephone system during the war emergency, prohibited the tapping of or interference with telephone and telegraph messages "without authority." The purpose of this legislation was not to protect the content of the communications or the privacy of the callers but rather to protect "the government and the property of the telephone and telegraph companies while under governmental control."[5] This legislation went out of effect in 1919 after the war emergency ended.

Privacy of communications did not become a public issue until the 1920s. More than twenty-five states had made wiretapping a crime by 1927, and the attorney general prohibited wiretapping by the Department of Justice, including the Bureau of Investigation (the predecessor of the Federal Bureau of Investigation [FBI]). Nevertheless, wiretapping was being used at the federal and state levels. Although the Department of Treasury, responsible for enforcing Prohibition, was officially opposed to wiretapping, its agents continued to wiretap in their investigations. The Department of Justice used wiretapping in Attorney General Palmer's investigations and deportation of aliens with radical political views.[6] At the same time, the telephones of some members of Congress had reportedly been wiretapped. Both stories got the attention of Congress and the public.

The constitutionality of the Treasury Department's use of wiretapping came before the Supreme Court in 1928 in *Olmstead v. United States*.[7] Roy Olmstead was a Seattle bootlegger who had been convicted, largely based on evidence gained by federal agents through a telephone wiretap, of violating federal Prohibition laws. Although wiretapping was prohibited under Washington state law, Washington did not deny the admissibility of illegally obtained evidence. On this basis, the federal trial judge ruled that the wiretap evidence was admissible in court. Olmstead appealed his conviction on constitutional grounds, claiming that the wiretap evidence should not have been admitted. The appeals court, by a 2 to 1 vote, upheld the conviction, ruling that wiretapping did not violate either the Fourth Amendment or the Fifth Amendment because no trespass or taking of physical possessions occurred. In its opinion, the appeals court did not differentiate between evidence obtained through a wiretap and evidence that was accidentally overheard or seen; since the latter was admissible, so was the former. The dissenting justice argued that wiretapping was different: "A person using the telegraph or telephone is not broadcasting to the world. His conversation is sealed from the public as completely as the nature of the instrumentalities employed will permit." He also argued that the purpose of the Fourth and Fifth amendments was not the protection of property but the "protection of the individual in his liberty and in the privacies of life."[8]

The Supreme Court agreed to review the appeals court decision and, in a 5–4 opinion, ruled that neither the Fourth Amendment nor the Fifth Amendment provided protection against wiretapping because no physical trespass and hence no "search" was involved and no "seizure" of tangible material took place. This case is probably most remembered for its dissenting opinions. In a short dissent, Justice Oliver Wendell Holmes termed wiretapping a "dirty business" and commented that, although a prohibition on wiretapping might restrict police investigations, "I think it a less evil that some criminals should escape than that the Government should play an ignoble part."[9] In an often quoted dissent, Justice Louis Brandeis, one of the coauthors of the 1890 *Harvard Law Review* article on privacy, argued that the Fourth Amendment protected individual privacy and warned against the "progress of science in furnishing the Government with means of espionage."[10]

Public and press reaction to the *Olmstead* decision was largely critical. The *New York Times*, for example, editorialized that "Prohibition, having bred crimes innumerable, has succeeded in making Government the instigator, abettor and accomplice of crime. It has now made universal snooping possible."[11] Once wiretapping had been ruled constitutional, those opposed to wiretapping moved the policy debate to the executive and Congress, as had been anticipated during the Court review. Chief Justice William Taft, in the majority opinion, recognized the possibility of congressional action, stating that "Congress may of course protect the secrecy of telephone messages by making them, when intercepted, inadmissible in evidence in federal criminal trials, by direct legislation, and thus depart from the common law of evidence."[12] Likewise, the solicitor general in his brief to the Court had argued that if wiretapping was "deemed an objectionable governmental practice, it may be regulated or forbidden by statute, or avoided by officers of the law."[13]

A number of bills were introduced in Congress to ban or regulate wiretapping.[14] The first step in developing congressional support for such bills was to determine the extent of wiretapping. In hearings, Congress learned that federal agencies were not following a uniform wiretap policy and that some agency heads believed that the privacy invasions posed by wiretapping were justified by law enforcement interests while other agency heads believed the privacy invasions were not justified. The Bureau of Prohibition in the Treasury Department did use wiretapping, while the Bureau of Investigation in the Justice Department did not. J. Edgar Hoover, in fact, testified: "We have a very definite rule in the bureau that any employee engaging in wiretapping will be dismissed from the service of the bureau. . . . While it may not be illegal, I think it is unethical, and it is not permitted under the regulations by the Attorney General."[15] When the Bureau of Prohibition was transferred to the Justice Department, the inconsistency in the practices of the two bureaus was reconciled when the attorney general issued a new policy in 1931 that allowed use of wiretapping only with permission of the bureau chief and the assistant attorney general in charge of the investigation. Under these new rules, Prohibition agents used wiretapping extensively while Bureau of Investigation agents used it infrequently.

Early congressional debates on wiretapping often reflected the larger social debate about the wisdom of alcohol prohibition. The policy conflict about wiretapping involved choosing between the idea of privacy and the interests of law enforcement in identifying bootleggers. Given this definition of the policy problem, views about privacy were affected by attitudes toward Prohibition. Those who supported Prohibition had little sympathy for suspected bootleggers whose privacy was being invaded by wiretaps. Despite repeated attempts to limit or proscribe wiretapping, there was not sufficient congressional support for passage. In the Seventy-first Congress, four bills were introduced to prohibit the use of wiretap evidence in federal courts.[16] In 1931 an amendment to the Justice Department's appropriation bill was introduced, preventing the department from spending money on wiretapping. The amendment was defeated but reintroduced. In the second round of hearings, the attorney general testified that his department's policy, which required the approval of two Justice Department officials, represented the best balance between law enforcement interests and individual rights. In discussing the criticisms of the *Olmstead* decision and the congressional attempt to regulate wiretapping, the attorney general pointed out that if the *Olmstead* case had involved the kidnapping of a young girl, "there would have been an overwhelming volume of approval by the people and the press of the country when the opinion was handed down. The disapproval that was expressed in some quarters I have always felt was affected very largely by people's attitudes on prohibition."[17] During that Congress, four more bills were introduced to prohibit wiretapping by federal employees and to prevent the use of wiretap evidence in federal courts.[18] In 1933, largely as a result of opposition to Prohibition, Congress banned the spending of funds for wiretapping, but only in Prohibition cases and only where the wiretap information was to be used as evidence in court.

After the end of Prohibition, federal and state authorities continued to wiretap, but wiretapping became less of a public and congressional concern. When Congress considered general communications policy in the early 1930s, questions of wiretapping and privacy of communications were not raised explicitly. In 1933 hearings commenced on major legislation to amend and update the Radio Act of 1927. In congressional debates, no discussion of wiretapping took place in committee hearings or on the floor. However, section 605 of the resulting Communications Act of 1934 took language from the Radio Act of 1927, which had in turn borrowed language from 1912 legislation providing that "no person not being authorized by the sender shall intercept any communication and divulge . . . the contents." The purpose of the earlier legislation was to protect the integrity of the communication system. The congressional intent in section 605 apparently was not to change the law but to recodify existing law. Use of wiretapping increased after 1934, accompanied by criticism in the press and among members of Congress. Alan Westin reports that "while bills to outlaw or regulate wiretapping were debated in Congress steadily (as they had been periodically since 1928), Congress passed no legislation and eavesdroppers listened to conversations unmolested."[19]

Despite the apparent legislative intent of the Communications Act of 1934, several defendants, convicted of illegally smuggling liquor on the basis of evidence gained through a wiretap, argued that section 605 made the divulgence of information discovered through wiretapping illegal and that thus the evidence was inadmissible in federal court. The trial judge and appeals court rejected this argument, but in a somewhat surprising decision in *Nardone v. United States*, the Supreme Court accepted the defendants' reasoning in 1937.[20] In part, the Court's decision, and its reversal of *Olmstead*, can be explained by a change in Court personnel; the three remaining *Olmstead* dissenters — Justices Louis Brandeis, Pierce Butler, and Harlan F. Stone — were joined by four new members — Charles Evans Hughes, Owen Roberts, Benjamin Cardozo, and Hugo Black. The Court's 1937 ruling meant a retrial for Nardone and the other defendants, in which the prosecution was prohibited from using the wiretap evidence. They were convicted a second time and again appealed the conviction on the grounds that evidence resulting from investigatory leads obtained through wiretaps was also inadmissible. The Court accepted this interpretation of section 605.[21]

Because there was no congressional record supporting the Court's interpretation of section 605, the decision was criticized as "judicial legislation."[22] A number of bills were introduced in Congress to allow wiretapping with certain procedural protections, especially in cases involving organized crime and national security. Bills allowing wiretapping with the prior approval of department heads passed both houses in 1938, but the session ended before the conference committee could resolve a difference in the two bills resulting from the fact that the House bill explicitly criminalized unauthorized wiretapping by government officials. The next year, a similar bill was introduced but opposed by the Justice Department. J. Edgar Hoover acknowledged that wiretaps were "from time to time of limited value in the criminal investigative field."[23] He feared, however, that legislation authorizing wiretaps would lead to overuse of wiretaps by law enforcement agents. Opposition to wiretapping grew after the Senate Interstate Commerce Committee's 1940 investigation of wiretapping found abuses and recommended legislation restricting the use of wiretapping.[24] At the same time, the attorney general banned the use of wiretapping by the Department of Justice and categorized it as an "unethical tactic" in the FBI manual.[25]

As national security matters grew in importance with the intensification of the war in Europe, the focus of the debate about wiretapping shifted from constitutional issues and law enforcement interests to national security concerns. In 1940 President Franklin Roosevelt authorized the use of wiretaps, when approved by the attorney general on a case-by-case basis, in investigations of those suspected of engaging in subversive activities. J. Edgar Hoover reversed his position because of national security concerns and condoned the use of wiretapping, with supervision and only for serious crimes, acknowledging that wiretapping "as an investigative function is of considerable importance."[26] During and after World War II, federal agencies actively used electronic surveillance.[27]

Congressional hearings on wiretapping continued but with a focus on developing, at the request of the Justice Department, a list of legitimate uses of wiretaps, for example, for purposes of national defense, including investigations of treason, espionage, and seditious conspiracy, or for purposes of law enforcement investigations of felonies. But there was disagreement among the executive agencies concerning which crimes to include on the list, as well as opposition to wiretapping in general, and Congress did not pass legislation.

In the 1950s, congressional hearings were held once again on a number of bills that permitted wiretapping for specific crimes or under certain conditions and that authorized the use of the resulting information as evidence in court. However, law enforcement officials and civil liberties advocates could not agree on a list of crimes or a procedure that satisfied each group's concerns. For example, civil liberties supporters favored requiring a court order before a wiretap could be installed, whereas law enforcement officials thought the attorney general should have the authority to sanction wiretaps. The list of witnesses at a 1953 congressional hearing reveals the division of opinion on the wiretap controversy. Civil liberties, labor, and liberal groups — including the American Civil Liberties Union (ACLU), Americans for Democratic Action, the American Jewish Congress, the American Federation of Labor, and various state bar associations — supported a limited list of crimes for which wiretaps could be used and a requirement for a court order. Law enforcement groups — including the International Association of Chiefs of Police, the National Association of County and Prosecuting Attorneys, the Department of Justice, the military, and various district attorneys — advocated more discretion for law enforcement use of wiretaps.[28] During this time, wiretapping technology was often demonstrated at hearings, such as playing a recording of phone calls from a congressional office. Westin describes the public response as a "mixture of technological fascination and civic alarm."[29] Given the anti-Communist climate and the McCarthy hearings, fears of wiretapping for political purposes were intense. The proposed wiretap legislation became entangled in the debate about loyalty and security, and the two sides in the conflict failed to reach an agreement. Alan Westin's summary of the situation aptly characterizes what occurred: "Though Congress was obviously aroused in the mid-1950s, gave the issue an enormous amount of committee attention and floor debate, and tried to frame a responsible statute that would bring order out of legal chaos, Congress simply could not take positive action."[30] (See appendix B for selected congressional activity on communication privacy, 1958–86.)

During this early period of policy debates about wiretapping, Congress was unable to balance privacy and law enforcement interests and craft a policy acceptable to both sides. Following the Supreme Court's ruling in *Olmstead*, Congress was given an opportunity to legislate. The Court, by ruling that wiretapping was not a violation of the Fourth Amendment, had not constrained legislative options; consequently, Congress could choose to agree and allow wholesale wiretapping, to disagree and ban wiretapping completely, or to partly agree and partly disagree and allow wiretapping under specific circumstances. The public was attentive to this issue and largely supported some legislative regulation of wiretapping. Moreover, federal agencies were divided about the merits and ethics of wiretapping. Under these circumstances, the stage was set for Congress to legislate policy. Through its Appropriations and Judiciary committees, Congress did hold hearings on numerous bills and conduct floor debates on several of these, but it failed to pass any legislation.

When the Court shifted policy attention by ruling in *Nardone* that wiretapping was a violation of section 605 of the Communications Act, Congress again was given an opportunity to act. The Court did not constrain the policy choices of Congress by ruling on the constitutionality of wiretapping but instead based its decision on statutory interpretation. The Court's statutory interpretation was widely regarded as differing from legislative intent, thus challenging Congress to reply and increasing public support for congressional action. Again, bills were introduced and hearings were held, but no legislation was passed. The onset of World War II and the growth of national security concerns changed the nature of congressional debates; politically and practically it was harder to argue that wiretapping should be banned, but it was difficult to specify the circumstances under which it should be used. Additionally, law enforcement opposition to a ban on wiretapping had strengthened, as reflected in J. Edgar Hoover's shift in support of wiretapping.

In both the post-*Olmstead* and post-*Nardone* policy formulation, a trend has developed that continues to the present. Congress does not find it easy to balance individuals' right to privacy against either law enforcement interests or national security interests. In analyzing congressional activity during this time period, Walter Murphy concluded that "Congress has been locked on dead center."[31] In the wiretap debates, privacy was defined in terms of Fourth Amendment protections against unreasonable searches and seizures. When the Court ruled in *Olmstead* that wire-tapping was not a search or seizure under the Fourth Amendment, it made the job of privacy advocates more difficult by taking away the constitutional basis. The early policy emphasis on the legal aspects of communication privacy narrowed the policy community concerned about wiretapping and restricted the forums for policy discussion to the courts and congressional hearings. Prohibition, national security, and internal security were the major reasons for the use of wiretapping, and each had some congressional and public support. Although the public and members of Congress might have abhorred the possibility of wholesale wiretapping, executive agencies offered justifications for their use of wiretapping. Moreover, it was difficult to arouse opposition to wiretapping when the individuals being wiretapped were suspected of wrongdoing. No crisis or compelling need motivated Congress to set policy since in the absence of a congressional decision, privacy advocates and law enforcement interests each got something they wanted — wiretapping could be used in investigations, but, based on Court decisions, the information gained through wiretaps could not be divulged and used in federal court as evidence.

The Court Establishes Policy and Congress Acquiesces

Pressure on Congress to pass legislation intensified in the 1960s. Continuing the trend of the 1950s, legislation was introduced to either ban wiretapping or to permit wiretapping under certain circumstances. The legal community became more vocal and increased pressure on Congress; new evidence of abuses of wiretapping were revealed at the state and federal levels; and public support for restrictions on wiretapping grew. In a 1952 *Columbia Law Review* article, Alan Westin argued that the "present stalemate" was "intolerable" and criticized Congress for its inaction: "To expect the Supreme Court to use the existing statute to find a solution is to confuse the function of the Court with that of Congress."[32] He suggested a statutory scheme specifying which law enforcement officers could wiretap[33] and for which crimes[34] and establishing a court procedure through which wiretaps would be authorized.[35] Information from unauthorized wiretaps would be inadmissible in court. Because of the difficulties in catching a wiretapper in action, possession of wiretapping equipment would be an offense. The Federal Communications Commission (FCC) would have some enforcement power.

The Pennsylvania Bar Association, convinced that the "time has arrived . . . for a nationwide fact-finding study of wiretapping practices, laws, devices, and techniques,"[36] sponsored a wiretapping study, appointing Samuel Dash as director and Robert Knowlton, a law professor at Rutgers University and an opponent of wiretapping, as associate director. Their report documented extensive official and private wiretapping and revealed the ineffectiveness of state statutes. In most states, they found it difficult to obtain accurate information about the number and purposes of official wiretaps. For example, their investigation revealed over 2,000 wiretaps in the state of New York, whereas the New York Central Investigation Bureau reported about 180. They also concluded that the official figure of 338 police wiretaps in New York City for the year 1952 was "hardly credible."[37]

The Dash study also brought attention to the role telephone companies played in wiretapping. Telephone company cooperation was necessary in identifying the correct line to tap. In some places, such as New Orleans, where state law allowed wiretaps and did not require a court order, little wiretapping occurred because the telephone company refused to cooperate in order to preserve the public's confidence in the privacy of telephone conversations.[38] In all states, investigators found that many wiretappers, official and private, were former telephone company employees, and in some states, phone company employees participated in illegal wiretaps for a price.

In 1964 public and congressional attention shifted to hearings on federal wiretapping held by Senator Edward V. Long's (D-Mich.) Subcommittee on Administrative Practice and Procedure.[39] These hearings did not focus on the legal issues or individual rights' infringements but instead concentrated on obtaining empirical evidence on the use of wiretapping by federal agencies. The Long subcommittee began its investigation with a study of electronic surveillance equipment approved for federal agency purchase and held hearings at which manufacturers demonstrated their products. It then examined the actual practices of federal agencies, including the Treasury Department, the Food and Drug Administration, the Postal Service, and the FBI. The report documented more wiretapping and surveillance than expected. The media covered the hearings extensively and intensified pressure on Congress to take action. Senator Long also worked to keep this issue on the public and congressional agendas by reporting daily in the *Congressional Record* what he termed his "Big Brother item for today"[40] and by publication in 1967 of his book, *The Intruders: The Invasion of Privacy by Government and Industry*, which was written for a general audience.[41]

After receiving the evidence from the Dash study and the Long investigations, public support for legislation restricting the use of wiretaps increased. Alan Westin reviewed newspaper editorials in over 170 papers from 1958 to 1963 and found that the great majority supported court-ordered wiretapping for a limited number of crimes and a prohibition on private wiretapping.[42] In 1964 two books — Vance Packard's *The Naked Society* and Myron Brenton's *The Privacy Invaders* — documented in layperson's terms the abuses of wiretapping and the privacy questions posed by wiretapping. Public attention was further heightened by a number of investigative reports, including ABC's "Big Brother Is Listening" and NBC's "The Big Ear."

The executive branch faced conflicting pressures. In 1961 Attorney General Robert Kennedy, as part of his attack on organized crime, sent a proposal to Congress to allow court-ordered wiretapping for certain crimes, including murder, kidnapping, gambling, narcotics trafficking, and extortion. National security wiretapping would not require a court order but would require the attorney general's authorization. In hearings before the Permanent Subcommittee on Investigations of the Senate Committee on Government Operations, chaired by Senator John L. McClellan (D-Alaska), debate centered on the list of crimes for which wiretapping could be authorized. A major concern of some senators was that the list would be endlessly expanded. Additionally, some senators remained opposed to any authorization of wiretapping. A similar bill was reintroduced in 1963, but no legislation resulted.[43] The Johnson administration continued the Kennedy administration's attack on organized crime and established a Commission on Law Enforcement and the Administration of Justice. At the same time, President Lyndon Johnson defended the Long subcommittee investigation against charges that it was damaging his efforts against organized crime. He also announced in 1965 a ban on wiretapping by federal agencies, except in national security cases where the approval of the attorney general had been secured.

The pivotal year in the development of wiretapping policy was 1967, during which the issue was the subject of the report of a presidential commission, statements from the president, two Supreme Court decisions, and congressional hearings. The question of how to balance individual privacy and the needs of law enforcement took central stage, and the scales tipped in favor of law enforcement. The President's Commission on Law Enforcement and the Administration of Justice recommended legislation "granting carefully circumscribed authority for electronic surveillance to law enforcement authorities."[44] The commission detailed the difficulties of obtaining evidence against organized crime because of its hierarchical structure, which insulated leaders from direct police investigation. The commission stated: "To maintain their insulation . . . the leaders . . . avoid direct communication with the workers. All commands, information, complaints, and money flow back and forth through" buffers.[45] The value of electronic surveillance in penetrating these buffers was recognized, as was the threat it posed to privacy. But only a minority of the commission members believed that giving law enforcement officials the authority to wiretap struck a "balance against the interests of privacy."[46]

After the release of the report of the president's commission, the policy focus shifted from the excesses of wiretapping and privacy concerns to the value of electronic surveillance in investigations of organized crime. A blanket prohibition on wiretapping unequivocally recognized privacy as a value. Once the policy debate moved to a consideration of the instances in which wiretapping could be justified, privacy concerns receded as the interests in wiretapping asserted themselves, and even dominated, policy discussions.

In 1967 the Supreme Court reentered the policy debates by handing down two important decisions. In *Berger v. New York*,[47] the Court declared the New York wiretapping statute unconstitutional because it did not provide for adequate judicial supervision. The Court ruled that the statute was not specific enough in describing the crimes for which wiretapping was authorized, the place to be searched, or the persons or things to be seized to meet Fourth Amendment requirements. Additionally, there were no limitations to ensure that the search did not become a general search, no requirements that the police return to court to show what had been seized, and no notice to persons whose privacy was invaded. The Court did not specifically rule that wiretapping was unconstitutional but pointed out the rules and procedures that should be taken into account in designing a statute that would meet constitutional requirements.

In *Katz v. United States*, the Court explicitly overturned *Olmstead* and ruled that wiretapping constituted a search under the Fourth Amendment. At issue in *Katz* was the legality of an FBI bugging device that was attached to the outside of a telephone booth in order to monitor conversations about gambling operations. Katz argued that the telephone booth was a constitutionally protected area, and the government argued "with equal vigor that it was not."[48] The Court, in a majority opinion by Justice Potter Stewart, concluded that this debate about "constitutionally protected areas" deflected attention from the real issue because "the Fourth

Amendment protects people not places,"[49] and therefore physical trespass was not required before the Fourth Amendment came into play. The telephone bug violated privacy and constituted a search and seizure under the Fourth Amendment: "The Government's activities in electronically listening to and recording the petitioner's words violated the privacy upon which he justifiably relied while using the telephone booth and thus constituted a 'search and seizure' within the meaning of the Fourth Amendment. The fact that the electronic device employed to achieve that end did not happen to penetrate the wall of the booth can have no constitutional significance."[50] The next question, then, was whether this search and seizure was "unreasonable" under the Fourth Amendment. After reviewing the actions of the FBI agents, the Court concluded that although they had acted "with restraint,"[51] it was self-imposed, without judicial oversight, and "searches conducted outside the judicial process, without prior approval by judge or magistrate, are per se unreasonable under the Fourth Amendment."[52] Justice John Harlan, in a concurring opinion, developed a general formula consisting of two conditions to determine whether an investigative technique conflicts with the Fourth Amendment: "first that a person have exhibited an actual (subjective) expectation of privacy and, second, that the expectation be one that society is prepared to recognize as 'reasonable.' "[53] Later courts have used this as a test to determine whether an individual has a "reasonable expectation of privacy."[54]

The Supreme Court's decisions restricting wiretapping under the Fourth Amendment, the report of the president's commission, and growing concern about crime brought the wiretapping issue to a prominent position on the congressional agenda. In 1967 bills were introduced in both the House and Senate permitting national security wiretapping by presidential order and court-ordered wiretapping for certain crimes.[55] In the Senate, hearings were held before the Subcommittee on Criminal Laws and Procedures of the Senate Committee on the Judiciary. At these hearings, Professor Robert Blakey, who was working on an American Bar Association (ABA) project on electronic surveillance, testified that since in organized crime the criminal is often known but the crimes are not, "it is necessary to subject the known criminals to surveillance, that is, to monitor their activities. It is necessary to identify their criminal and noncriminal associates; and their areas of operation, both legal and illegal. Strategic intelligence attempts to paint this broad, overall picture of the criminal's activities in order that an investigator can ultimately move in with a specific criminal investigation and prosecution."[56] In the

House, hearings were also held before a subcommittee of the Judiciary Committee.

At the same time, Senate and House committees were also holding hearings on privacy. The Subcommittee on Administrative Practice and Procedure of the Senate Judiciary Committee, chaired by Senator Edward Long, had compiled a record of privacy intrusions resulting in part from wiretapping. The hearings of the Special Subcommittee on the Invasion of Privacy of the House Committee on Government Operations, chaired by Representative Cornelius E. Gallagher (D-N.J.), had compiled a similar record. As a result of these privacy inquiries, bills were introduced in the House and Senate to prohibit wiretapping without the consent of one of the parties except in national security cases.[57] President Johnson supported this ban in his 1967 State of the Union message: "We should protect what Justice Brandeis called the 'right most valued by civilized men' — the right of privacy. We should outlaw all wire-tapping — public and private — wherever and whenever it occurs, except when the security of the nation is at stake — and only then with the strictest safeguards. We should exercise the full reach of our Constitutional powers to outlaw 'bugging' and 'snooping.' "[58] The ban on wiretapping was also supported by Ramsey Clark, the attorney general. After the Court decisions in *Berger* and *Katz*, the interests in permitting wiretapping under certain circumstances and with judicial checks were stronger than those supporting privacy. The Senate and House bills authorizing eavesdropping received more congressional attention.

In 1968 Congress passed the Omnibus Crime Control and Safe Streets Act, Title III of which allowed the interception of wire and oral communications under certain conditions and circumstances. In order to both protect privacy and allow for the legitimate needs of law enforcement, Title III specified crimes for which a court order could be requested and established procedural requirements for law enforcement, including obtaining a court order approved by a high-ranking prosecutor; proving that probable cause existed for believing that a crime had been committed, that the target of the surveillance was involved, and that evidence would be obtained through the surveillance; certifying that other investigative procedures would be ineffective; and describing how the surveillance effort would be minimized. If an application met these requirements, a judge could approve the court order for thirty days with a possible extension. At the close of the surveillance, notice was to be given to the people affected, unless the judge decided to postpone the notice. Illegally obtained evidence could not be used in any official proceedings.

A suit for damages could be brought for illegal surveillance, although a good faith defense was permitted, thus weakening the possibility of winning such a suit. Additionally, the manufacture, distribution, possession, and advertising of devices for electronic surveillance for private use were prohibited.

The content of Title III borrowed heavily from previous policy proposals, including the 1952 Westin law review article, the ABA standards of 1967, and the Supreme Court's decisions in *Katz* and *Berger*. What was important was that members of Congress and other interested groups were finally able to agree on what Alan Westin termed "the great compromise of 1968."[59] A number of reasons have been offered for why this compromise occurred at this time. Herman Schwartz attributed it to the 1968 assassination of Robert F. Kennedy: "Although it is usually difficult to point to one factor as decisive, particularly after 40 crowded years, it does seem that the key factor was the assassination of Robert F. Kennedy. Many of those including the writer, who were close to events, are convinced that it was that single event which overwhelmed opposition in the House, where it was thought the legislation would continue being bottled up."[60] In a 1969 *Michigan Law Review* article, Schwartz also pointed to "long standing Southern resentment toward the Court and . . . popular anxiety about lawlessness."[61] Richard Harris, in a 1968 *New Yorker* article, took an even stronger view, stating that "all those who voted against it, and most of those who didn't vote at all [believed] the bill was a piece of demagoguery, devised out of malevolence and enacted in hysteria."[62]

Robert Blakey, author of an ABA report on electronic surveillance and one of the key architects of the House bill, disputed the Schwartz and Harris analyses as "myth, particularly among those who opposed Title III."[63] He attributed passage to the forty years of legislative debate and the Court's rulings in *Katz* and *Berger*. Although he acknowledged that the House passed legislation following the assassinations of Martin Luther King, Jr., and Robert Kennedy, he argued that "at least in the Senate, Title III was the product of a lengthy and fair debate, in which amendments were offered and accepted or defeated by a majority vote. A motion to strike the entire title, for example, failed by a vote of 68 to 12. Supporters of the motion included Senators Hart of Michigan and Kennedy of Massachusetts. Opponents included Senators Bayh, Brooke, Ervin, Muskie, and Percy."[64] Civil liberties groups were clearly reluctant to support Title III. The *Katz* decision, by bringing electronic surveillance under Fourth Amendment protection, worked in their favor. On the other hand, the crusade against organized crime, the Kennedy and King assassinations, and the *Berger* decision's specification of procedures that the Court thought necessary for legitimate wiretapping worked in favor of those who were pushing legislation and helped break the stalemate of forty years.

Title III has been described as "a compromise of . . . opposing views"[65] between those who advocated a total ban on wiretapping because of its implications for individual privacy and those who opposed placing any restrictions on wiretapping for fear of tying the hands of law enforcement officials. An examination of the treatment of the idea of privacy and the power of interests, especially law enforcement interests, helps to explain the balance that was achieved. In policy debates, privacy interests were rarely analyzed, except by the Supreme Court. The involvement of civil liberties groups in discussions about the process and procedures of wiretapping indicates that they knew the likelihood of a total ban was slim and, politically and practically, realized they needed to be a part of the process of balancing privacy and law enforcement interests. But an examination of the privacy value to be protected was reduced to legal details.

The policy goal was not as much to protect privacy as it was to authorize wiretapping without permitting it to become indiscriminate. Once the policy question became what circumstances and procedures could warrant wiretapping, the dynamics of policy discussions turned from questions of principle to those of interests. Agreeing upon a list of crimes for which wiretapping might be appropriate was difficult and relied on law enforcement judgments about the usefulness of wiretapping. Similarly, the issue of what kind of authorization—the attorney general's or the court's—and what kinds of procedures should be required was less a privacy issue than a due process question. Questions about the relationship between federal and state laws and the constraints Congress should place on state authorities turned on questions of federalism rather than privacy. A reading of the history of legislative, executive, and judicial policy making in this area suggests that the real policy formulation consisted of crafting answers to these questions that would satisfy those in the middle. A concern about privacy provoked policy debates but did not determine the outcome of those debates.

Political Surveillance and Congressional Oversight

Once Title III passed, civil liberties groups and members of Congress who were concerned about privacy and suspicious of wiretapping continued to follow the issue and to press for oversight of federal agency use of electronic surveillance. Title III itself provided for continual congressional oversight by requiring annual reports of federal and state court-ordered wiretapping and bugging. Senator Sam Ervin, a key civil liberties advocate, commented in the foreword to a book on Title III: "The mere fact of passing a law never resolves a controversy as fierce as this one. The enactment of the eavesdropping legislation was only a watershed in the continuing debate, reconsideration and revision."[66]

In the aftermath of Watergate and its revelations of unauthorized and politically motivated surveillance, congressional and public interest in wiretapping was renewed. The House Subcommittee on Courts, Civil Liberties, and the Administration of Justice held hearings on ten bills that were introduced to place additional restrictions on wiretapping. Robert Kastenmeier, chair of the subcommittee, identified a "trend toward privacy invasions" and acknowledged the need to "reassert the right of the individual to be free of Government surveillance,"[67] while at the same time recognizing the "needs of investigative agencies for the best techniques available in the fight against organized crime and in the protection of national security."[68] After recessing its inquiry in order to conduct President Richard Nixon's impeachment hearings and the confirmation hearings for Vice President Nelson Rockefeller, the Kastenmeier subcommittee held nine more days of hearings on electronic surveillance. In his opening comments, Representative Kastenmeier referred to the "plethora of revelations" about intrusions of surveillance and intelligence gathering into the private lives of many citizens and the need "to learn what is happening and develop legislative remedies."[69]

Congressional interest was high, as reflected by the introduction of more than a dozen bills on the issue of surveillance with over seventy House sponsors. One of these bills, also introduced in the Senate by Senator Charles McC. Mathias (D-Md.), was the Bill of Rights Procedures Act, which was intended to reinforce Fourth Amendment protections by requiring any federal agent to obtain a court order, based upon probable cause, before conducting any form of surveillance on a private citizen. Surveillance was defined broadly to include "bugging, wiretapping and all other forms of electronic eavesdropping, opening of mail, entering of dwellings, and the inspection or procurement of the records of telephone, bank, credit, medical or other private transactions."[70] Many members of the House Republican Task Force on Privacy, a group of thirteen representatives chaired by Congressman Barry Goldwater, Jr., supported the bill and reported that they were "deeply disturbed by the increasing evidence of unregulated, clandestine government surveillance based solely on administrative or executive authority. . . . The various abuses of discretionary authority in the conduct of surveillance provide ample evidence that current safeguards do not work. Procedures allowing the executive branch to determine whether a surveillance activity is proper or not pose certain conflict of interest questions."[71]

Although this round of congressional hearings began with a concern about privacy, the themes of due process and accountability became more important in the aftermath of Watergate. The accountability of executive agencies and the need to monitor the activities of the prosecutor of a case were emphasized. In testimony, Senator Mathias argued that a requirement that federal agents report surveillance activities directly to Congress, as specified in the Bill of Rights Procedures Act, "means that there is a clear line of accountability. We know who has acted, who requested the wiretap, who ratified the request, and when the tap went on."[72]

The theme of accountability raised the question of the differences in executive control over domestic and national security matters—a question that had complicated the debate enormously from the beginning. Although it was generally acknowledged that surveillance used for national security purposes posed different issues than surveillance used for law enforcement, the Watergate excesses that had been committed under the shield of national security made clear the need for some court or congressional oversight. Time and space do not permit analysis of congressional debate on electronic surveillance for national security purposes, but the result of that debate was the Foreign Intelligence Surveillance Act of 1978, which established legal standards and procedures for the use of electronic surveillance to collect foreign intelligence and counterintelligence within the United States.[73] It created the Foreign Intelligence Surveillance Court, composed of seven federal district judges, to review and approve surveillance of persons in the United States.

In 1974 Congress amended Title III to establish the National Commission for the Review of Federal and State Laws Relating to Wiretapping and Electronic Surveillance. The commission membership reflected the divisions that appeared earlier in the debates over Title III. Senator McClellan, who was the key sponsor of Title III, was a member, as was Representative Kastenmeier, a civil liberties proponent. Similarly, both Robert Blakey and Alan Westin were members, and Herman Schwartz served as a consulting attorney. In its 1976 report, the majority of commission members "reaffirmed the finding of Congress in 1968 . . . that electronic surveillance is an indispensable aid to law enforcement in obtaining evidence of crimes committed by organized criminals."[74] They also agreed with the earlier congressional decision that wiretapping should occur only with authorization and only for certain crimes.

Four of the fifteen members,[75] however, disagreed "with this broad general approval of court-authorized wiretapping" and argued that "court-authorized surveillance had been used successfully in a limited number of cases, and has resulted in the conviction of only a few upper-echelon crime figures; more frequently, however, court-authorized surveillance has proven to be costly and generally unproductive, has served to discourage the use of other investigative techniques, and, even under the authorization and supervision of a court, has resulted in substantial invasions of individual privacy."[76] Alan Westin, one of the four in the minority, was critical of the commission for not reviewing wiretapping authorized as a "national security" measure but actually used for domestic purposes. He commented that, especially given the Watergate revelations that occurred during the time of the commission's study, the jurisdictional restrictions of the commission "gave our entire life as a Commission a strangely dream-like quality."[77]

The effectiveness of wiretaps and the technology of wiretapping dominated the commission's deliberations; privacy as an issue received less thorough consideration. In general, the commission concluded that Title III's procedural requirements had "effectively minimized the invasion of individual privacy in electronic surveillance investigations by law enforcement officers."[78] Privacy was again defined primarily in legal terms, with an emphasis on the procedural requirements of Title III that were designed to meet Fourth Amendment standards. There was no new analysis of privacy interests, although the commission had considered contracting for a public opinion survey to gauge public perceptions of wiretapping. The commission ultimately decided against conducting a survey. Westin accounted for this decision as follows: "The major reasons for this action were that the public wasn't really well informed about wiretapping anyway and its reactions would not be 'helpful'; that 'the Watergate thing' would skew any sampling of American public opinion; and — most important of all — we were a body of experts in law and criminal justice whose informed judgments were what mattered, not what 'a public opinion poll would say.'"[79] Westin was critical of this decision because it restricted the commission to "the customary field-investigation and law-revision-commission approach"[80] rather than broadening its purview and examining the public's changing views of privacy and law enforcement needs. Westin's concerns were realized in Robert Blakey's statement of concurrence with the commission's report; Blakey's discussion of privacy is primarily a legal review of Fourth Amendment development in which he urges the Court to give more guidance on the criteria for the "reasonable expectation of privacy" test. He argues that the fact that technology is involved does not mean that civil liberties are threatened. Instead, the threat to civil liberties comes from the abuse of the technology. If "technology merely augments practices not now thought to go too far, the technology itself presents no new issue."[81] Although a number of bills were introduced after release of the report, including several reflecting the views of the dissenters, and hearings were held, Congress took no action on Title III.

Technological Change and Policy Change

Due to the imminent arrival of the symbolically important year of 1984 and because technological changes appeared to be threatening the protections offered by Title III, technology took center stage in debates about wiretapping in the early 1980s. At the same time, the site of policy formulation shifted from commissions and the courts to Congress. Representative Kastenmeier's subcommittee held a series of hearings entitled "1984 — Civil Liberties and the National Security State." Privacy, technology, and surveillance were primary topics at these hearings.[82] In the Senate, a subcommittee of the Committee on the Judiciary, chaired by Senator Mathias, also held hearings on communication privacy.[83] The Kastenmeier subcommittee, along with the Senate Committee on Governmental Affairs, requested the Office of Technology Assessment (OTA) to undertake a study of developments in communication and surveillance technologies, federal agency uses of surveillance technologies, and the implications of these uses for civil liberties and congressional oversight.

Following these congressional hearings and during the course of the OTA study, policy debates focused on a number of gaps in the protections offered by Title III. Title III covered the "aural acquisition" of "wire and oral" communications that were carried over common carrier communications facilities. Technological innovations in communications threatened the protections offered by Title III in three ways. First, phone conversations were often transmitted in digital form, thus raising some question about whether the interception of such conversations was an "aural acquisition." Additionally, data communications between computers and electronic mail communications took place only in digital form, with no possibility of any meaningful "aural acquisition." A second technological change that narrowed the protections offered by Title III concerned the specification of "wire and oral" communications in the statute. Increasingly, communications were being transmitted through new media, including radio, microwave, satellite, and fiber optics, which apparently were not covered by Title III. The third change that narrowed Title III protections involved the limitation to common carrier communications. With the divestiture of AT&T and technological innovations in switching and transmission, it became easy to set up a private telecommunication system that served a specific business or group of customers. An individual or business could also lease dedicated lines from a telephone company, establish a local area network (LAN), or purchase a private branch exchange (PBX). In addition, some argued that the breakup of AT&T might exclude the regional holding companies from the category of common carrier engaged in interstate commerce as defined by Title III and thus remove these companies from Title III coverage.[84]

These gaps were raised in several court cases, but court decisions resulted in a patchwork of protections. The Ninth Circuit Court held that Title III protects any communication that is transmitted in part by wire. The court ruled that a telephone call from a mobile telephone to a landline telephone — which uses wire transmission — is protected by Title III, but that a phone call from a mobile telephone to another mobile telephone is not. The court itself characterized this as "an absurd result" but one required by the statute.[85] In general, the courts seemed reluctant to engage in judicial policy making in this area, instead applying Title III rather narrowly. For example, the courts did not expand the scope of Title III to cover digital or data communications. The Supreme Court held that, to be covered by Title III, a communication must be capable of being overheard.[86] The Fourth Circuit Court similarly ruled that nonaural communications were not protected by Title III.[87] Courts also seemed hesitant to expand the Fourth Amendment "expectation of privacy" to cover new communication devices. The highest state courts in both Kansas and Rhode Island ruled that the user of a cordless telephone did not have a Fourth Amendment "expectation of privacy" and that interception of such communication did not violate Title III.[88]

Even though court rulings gave the executive some freedom to use wiretaps without going through the Title III procedures, the Justice Department used a cautious approach. The department did not want to take the chance that evidence gained without a Title III warrant would later be ruled inadmissible in court. Therefore, the safer position was to obtain the Title III warrant when in doubt to ensure that there would not be any question of the admissibility of evidence.[89] But this position imposed additional, and possibly unnecessary, burdens on law enforcement officials. It was, therefore, in the interest of the department to secure legislative clarification concerning whether Title III covered new forms of electronic communication.

In 1984 and 1985 groups and individuals that were affected by or concerned about the gaps in Title III protections met both formally and informally to clarify the issues, discuss policy options, and begin to develop a consensus on what should be done. The ACLU established a Privacy and Technology Project, headed by Jerry Berman, the ACLU's legislative counsel. The goal of the ACLU project was to develop policy options to deal with privacy problems posed by new communication and computer technologies. By establishing this project, the ACLU took on a leadership role in forming a coalition to work for legislation. As part of this effort, the ACLU and the Public Interest Computer Association (PICA) held two consultations in 1984 and 1985 that were attended by privacy interests, technology experts, business groups, and congressional staff. The group reached three conclusions: that Title III's prohibition on the interception of "aural" communications was out of date; that the law should protect the "contents" of private communications regardless of the form or means of communication; and that legal protections for privacy would be illusory if limited to messages transmitted over common carrier networks.[90]

During the same time period, the OTA began its study of the civil liberties and congressional oversight issues posed by the government's use of new communication and information technologies. The advisory panel for the study included four prominent privacy advocates: Jerry Berman of the ACLU; David Flaherty of the University of Western Ontario; George Trubow of the John Marshall Law School; and Alan Westin of Columbia University. In addition, technology experts and business representatives also sat on the panel. As part of its research effort, the OTA held a workshop in 1985 at which privacy advocates, Justice Department and other executive branch officials, and prosecutors and defense attorneys discussed the gaps in Title III and the effects of various policy options. At the OTA workshop and the ACLU/PICA meetings, privacy issues were framed as legal and constitutional questions; the privacy examinations paralleled the discussions leading to the adoption of Title III. Those participants who did not have a law degree or had not taken a recent course in constitutional law often felt excluded from the discussions. Law en-

Figure 5.1
Summary of Findings of 1985 OTA Report on Electronic Surveillance

The contents of phone conversations that are transmitted in digital form or calls made on cellular or cordless phones are not clearly protected by existing statutes.

Data communications between computers and digital transmission of video and graphic images are not protected by existing statutes.

Existing law offers little protection for electronic mail messages, which can be intercepted at many stages: at the terminal of the sender, while being transmitted, in the electronic mailbox of the receiver, when printed into hardcopy, and while retained in the files of the electronic mail company.

Legislated policy on electronic physical surveillance (e.g., pagers and beepers) and electronic visual surveillance (e.g., closed-circuit television and concealed cameras) is ambiguous or nonexistent.

Legislated policy on database surveillance (e.g., monitoring of transactions on computerized record systems and data communication linkages) is unclear.

There is no immediate technological answer to protection against most electronic surveillance, although there are emerging techniques to protect communication systems from misuse or eavesdropping (e.g., low-cost data encryption).

Source: Office of Technology Assessment, *Federal Government Information Technology: Electronic Surveillance and Civil Liberties*, OTA-CIT-293 (Washington, D.C.: Government Printing Office, 1985), p. 4.

forcement officials were most concerned about the burden that would be imposed on investigations if Title III were expanded to encompass all electronic communications.

In October 1985, at hearings held by the Kastenmeier subcommittee, the OTA released its report, *Electronic Surveillance and Civil Liberties*. (See figure 5.1 for a summary of the findings.) The OTA study provided the subcommittee with what Representative Kastenmeier termed "the intellectual groundwork for legislative solutions."[91] By this time in the policy process, there was virtually no disagreement about the problems that were identified in the OTA report. Indeed, almost all of the other witnesses testifying before the subcommittee used the OTA report as their point of departure.

At the congressional hearings, it was generally agreed that Title III needed to be updated. The principle of protecting individual privacy was deemed important; the policy questions became whether all forms of new communications should, or could, receive similar legal protections and what benefits law enforcement gained by tapping into new electronic communications. For example, it is very easy to intercept communications over cordless phones. The FCC therefore required manufacturers of cordless phones to warn customers that the privacy of conversations conducted on cordless phones cannot be ensured. Law enforcement officials reported that drug dealers use cordless phones and electronic beepers to set up meetings. In a Rhode Island case, a drug dealer used a cordless phone for his business communications. Unknown to him, these conversations were broadcast over the AM airwaves and were heard by a boy whose mother informed the police. Without a court order, the police began to listen to the cordless phone conversations regarding drug transactions. On the basis of these conversations, the police gained enough evidence to arrest the drug dealer.[92]

Electronic mail, which was increasingly being used by businesses, also posed challenges. Justice Department officials testified that electronic mail was similar to regular mail and that the same search warrant procedures should apply. Their analysis was based on what they termed the "self-minimizing" character of electronic mail. James Knapp, the deputy assistant attorney general for the Criminal Division of the Justice Department, explained: "In a search warrant for electronic mail, you are talking about a search warrant for a specific communication. It is self-minimizing. It is a more commonly used investigative technique because search warrants for specific items of evidence, be it electronic mail, bank records or anything else, are self-minimizing."[93] Senator Mathias remained somewhat skeptical about how officials could extract a particular communication from "electronic mail, which is an ongoing process. The message is not a static object, like a piece of paper confined in an envelope that can be identified. These are bits and bytes."[94] Representatives of the electronic mail industry argued that electronic mail, because of its speed and interactive capabilities, was more often a substitute for the telephone, rather than a substitute for postal mail, and therefore should be given a comparable level of protection.[95]

Despite the apparent gaps in privacy protections posed by existing law, the Justice Department was initially reluctant to support changes in the "existing and well-understood statutory structure" of Title III.[96] In a letter to Representative Kastenmeier in May 1985, Mary Lawton, counsel for intelligence policy in the Justice Department, stated that since there were no "serious flaws in Title III or its implementation currently, . . . we believe the statutory structure should not be modified at this time."[97] She then went on for seventeen pages to detail the department's criticisms of the bill and of recommendations for action. Privacy concerns about new forms of electronic communications reawakened the Justice Department's opposition to interference with law enforcement interests. Much of the Justice Department's resistance to amending Title III can be accounted for by what Knapp termed the "additional procedural requirements and a tremendous burden" that Title III entails.[98]

In hearings before the Kastenmeier subcommittee in 1986, following an internal Justice Department review of the proposed legislation and discussions with House and Senate subcommittee staffs, James Knapp appeared more open to proposed legislation, stating that "there is new technology that is so similar to traditional telephonic communication that it belongs within the framework of Title III."[99] The department still maintained, however, that electronic mail and computer transmissions over wires should be covered by a new statute. Additionally, the Justice Department used the hearings as an opportunity to suggest changes in Title III procedures to make the statute "even more useful than the last 18 years have proven it to be."[100] The Justice Department was thus in a position to negotiate and could begin to work toward a consensus with the subcommittee staffs. The Justice Department's willingness to negotiate was partly the result of a suggestion from Representative William Moorhead, ranking minority member on the subcommittee, that the department meet with industry and congressional staff to discuss the issue and a letter from the president of the National Association of Manufacturers to Attorney General Edwin Meese emphasizing the importance of the bill to industry.[101]

On June 23, 1986, the Electronic Communications Privacy Act (ECPA) passed the House of Representatives on a voice vote without opposition. In introducing the bill for floor consideration, Representative Kastenmeier noted that it had "broad bipartisan support both inside and outside the Congress" and was supported by an "unusual . . . coalition of business, Government and civil liberties groups."[102] On October 1, the Senate passed an amended version of the House bill, which the House then ratified on October 2. The bill was signed by President Ronald Reagan on October 21 and became effective on January 20, 1987. The ECPA extends Title III protections to many new forms of "electronic communications," including electronic mail, cellular phones, computer transmissions of data or video, and voice or display paging devices. Cordless phones and tone-only paging devices were not brought under Title III protections, nor were communications for which privacy was not expected, such as amateur radio services and public safety radio systems. The ECPA increased penalties for the intentional or malicious interference with satellite transmissions but affirmed the right of satellite dish owners to receive unencrypted signals that are redistributed on facilities open to the public. The distinction between common carrier and private carrier communications was eliminated; any communications facilities that affect interstate or foreign commerce are covered by the ECPA. Additionally, the ECPA made some changes in Title III requirements that the Justice Department advocated, including expanding the list of felonies for which a wiretap order may be issued, increasing the number of Justice Department officials who may apply for a court order, and allowing wiretaps for an unspecified phone if evidence exists that the target of the wiretap is changing phones.[103]

Given the legal complexity surrounding Title III, the variety of new communication technologies and the rate of technological change in communications, the number of industries that would be affected by a new law, and the rate of change in the industry and market structure, it is somewhat remarkable that Congress passed the ECPA at all, much less in a relatively short period. Why did it take almost forty years to agree on Title III and just two years to reach agreement on the ECPA?

Most important in accounting for the speed of congressional action was industry support. Organizations that supported the final House bill represented all sectors of the communications and information industries, including the Electronic Mail Association, ADAPSO, the National Association of Broadcasters, the National Cable Television Association, the Videotext Industry Association, the Information Industry Association, the Direct Marketing Association, and the Associated Credit Bureaus. More general industry organizations that supported the bill included the National Association of Manufacturers and the U.S. Chamber of Commerce. Corporations supporting the bill included many Fortune 500 firms, such as AT&T and the Bell Operating Companies, General Electric, IBM, GTE, ITT, the three broadcast networks, Chase Manhattan Bank, TRW, and Equifax. Of the twenty-one organizations supporting the bill, the ACLU was the only nonindustry association.[104]

This industry support is not surprising given the fact that the manufacturers and providers of new communications products and services realized that if they could not ensure the privacy and security of their customers' communications, they would not be able to sell those products and services. Additionally, those businesses, especially banks and credit agencies, that were already dependent upon data communications had a very large interest in ensuring that such communications could not be intercepted. The idea of privacy was joined with industry interests, but industry interests, not privacy values, dominated the remaining policy debates. Once industry realized the implications of this bill, the policy goal shifted from "privacy" to the growth and competitiveness of the "electronic communications" industry. For example, in opening the first House subcommittee hearing, Representative Kastenmeier said: "The communications industry is sufficiently concerned about this issue to have begun the process of seeking *protective legislation*. This bill is, in large part, a response to these legitimate business concerns" (emphasis added).[105]

Of the fifteen witnesses appearing before the Kastenmeier subcommittee, ten were from the communications and information industries. Of forty-three letters or statements appended to the hearing record, twenty-nine were from industry and all spoke primarily to industry interests, not privacy values. A representative of the cellular telecommunications industry noted that "the growth of cellular and its contribution to economic development are closely tied to the legislation before this subcommittee today."[106] Michael Nugent, representing ADAPSO, stated that the proposed legislation was "necessary for the evolution of an information-based economy in society."[107] A representative of the paging and cellular telephone industry noted: "The absence of the law has, and I believe will continue to inhibit the growth of the industry, and inhibit the improvement in technology."[108]

Business representatives and business interests dominated the Senate subcommittee hearings as well. Representative Kastenmeier, in remarks before the Senate Subcommittee on Patents, Copyrights, and Trademarks on November 13, 1985, stated that "the adverse business consequence of inadequate protection for third-party records with respect to communications has led several industry groups to support — strongly support, I might add — the privacy provision of these bills."[109] At the same hearings, Senator Mathias, in questioning James Knapp about the Justice Department's position on protection of electronic mail, remarked: "You are putting a blight on an industry in its infancy if you are going to tell people that they should not have an expectation of privacy in the use of electronic mail."[110] Michael Nugent, speaking for ADAPSO, again stated that the proposed bill was "necessary for the evolution of an information-based economy."[111] Philip Walker, representing the Electronic Mail Association, stated that the lack of clear standards for the disclosure of electronic mail information "retards not only the growth of our industry, but the productivity of the entire economy."[112] Even Jerry Berman of the

ACLU got on the bandwagon, remarking: "Many things are at stake here. First of all, on the one hand, I think the productivity and growth of whole new technologies and industries which could be adversely affected—on the other hand is citizens' privacy."[113]

More Changes—More of the Same

Any communication-transmission technology—be it copper wire, microwave, satellite, or fiber optics—is somewhat vulnerable to interception by another technological device. A pattern is repeated: advances in communication technologies both precipitate advances in interception technologies and create gaps in existing laws. In the policy debates about the privacy of communications, the focus has been on determining what level of protection against interception is appropriate for a particular form of communication. The Fourth Amendment protection of "persons, houses, papers, and effects against unreasonable searches and seizures" provided the context for discussion. Communication privacy became a Fourth Amendment concern. But the appropriate level of Fourth Amendment protection was not obvious. Resolution of the problem turned for the most part on legal arguments about expectations of privacy and about the correct preelectronic analogy for a new communication technology. These legal issues brought the legal community, especially constitutional scholars and civil liberties advocates, into the congressional policy processes. Commissions and panels of legal experts provided important forums in making recommendations to Congress. But defining communication privacy as a constitutional issue confined discussions of the policy problem to a narrow group of constitutional experts.

The law enforcement community figured prominently in these legal deliberations because it was the interest in detecting criminal behavior—bootlegging, treason, gambling, or drug trafficking, for example—that provoked the interception of communications. The FBI, state and local police, and federal and state prosecutors were generally united in opposition to limits on their ability to gain access to communications in a timely fashion. The conflict, however, was not simply between privacy interests and law enforcement interests. Those who owned and operated the communication systems were also interested in influencing communication policy. When electronic communication simply entailed telegraph communication through Western Electric or telephone communication over the AT&T network, the interests of the communication providers were accommodated rather easily. No competitive advantage could be gained by either withholding or giving access to law enforcement officials when they deemed it necessary to intercept communications. But with the breakup of AT&T and the proliferation of new communication providers, privacy of communications was no longer an issue that could be worked out on an informal basis between law enforcement officials and communication providers. Indeed, as we have seen, the providers of new communication technologies saw a decided economic advantage in being able to assure their customers that communications using their technologies would be protected against interception. This change in the policy community supporting privacy has made policy formulation in the years since 1984 very different from previous policy formulation.

Communication privacy issues have not disappeared. Given the pace of technological change and the commercial and governmental advantages offered by these changes, communication privacy issues are likely to multiply in the next several decades. One example is the development of personal communication services, for which the FCC plans to auction frequencies within the electromagnetic spectrum.[114] In these systems, phone numbers would be assigned not to phones but to persons, and a network of computers, satellites, and transmitters would determine where the person was and send the phone call or data communication to the nearest phone, computer, or fax machine. In order to receive messages, individuals would possibly have to wear a beeper-type device that signaled their location. The details of monitoring the location of individuals are still being worked out, but as one commentator has noted, "whichever methods are chosen will inevitably raise concerns about privacy and eavesdropping."[115]

New uses of telecommunications lines have also provoked privacy concerns. In 1991 Congress passed the Telemarketing Protections Act (PL 102-243) to restrict telemarketing calls, especially those made by auto-dialers that systematically call every number in a telephone exchange and play a prerecorded message. Senator Ernest Hollings (D-S.C.) called auto-dialers an "outrageous invasion" of people's homes and asserted that privacy rights outweigh concerns about the free speech of marketing companies.[116] Although President George Bush voiced objections to "regulating one of business's most potent and economical marketing tools,"[117] he signed the compromise measure, which gave the FCC the task of establishing procedures to ensure the privacy of consumers. Congress is also considering legislation to restrict direct marketers' use of information on consumers' calls to 800 and 900 numbers. In the 103d Congress, Representative Edward Markey (D-Mass.), chair of the House Subcommittee on Telecommunications and Finance, introduced the Telephone Consumer Privacy Protection Act of 1993 (H.R. 3432), which includes provisions for nationwide call-blocking for Caller ID and protection of information about calls to 800 and 900 numbers.

One of the communication priorities of the Clinton administration is the development of a national digitized information superhighway. The capabilities of fiber optics have made it possible to offer a broadband cable over which a variety of voice, data, and video services will be provided. Vice President Al Gore has described the government's role in the development of the information superhighway as "Referee. Facilitator. Envisioner. Definer," in contrast to the spectator role he described the government as playing in the Reagan and Bush administrations.[118] Questions about who would own and operate these new "information superhighways of the future" are being addressed in congressional committees, executive agencies, the FCC, state public utilities commissions, and corporate boardrooms. The economic stakes are enormous and the lobbying intense, particularly among telephone and cable companies, newspaper publishers, and the motion picture industry. Questions are also being asked about how rights and responsibilities would be allocated. For example, what are the free speech and free press implications of electronic bulletin boards and computer networks? Could the owners and operators of these systems act as gatekeepers, controlling which people gain access to the system and what kind of information is communicated through the system?

As information flows more freely and extensively through various systems without clear boundaries, privacy also becomes an issue. New groups and forums have convened to discuss these issues; not surprisingly, many of these groups communicate via networks such as the Whole Earth 'Lectronic Link (WELL). The Electronic Frontier Foundation (EFF) was established in 1990 by Mitchell Kapor (formerly of Lotus) and John Perry Barlow "to help civilize the electronic frontier" and to foster the creation of a national public network open to all information providers and accessible to all citizens. The fourth annual conference, entitled "Computers, Freedom, and Privacy," was held in 1994 and continued a discussion of a range of issues involving the structure, rights, and responsibilities of the new communications infrastructure.

One important issue involves the transparency of the system — how hard should it be to read others' messages, and who should establish the standards for encrypting the contents of communication? When voice communications are translated into bytes and bits and transmitted as data, often packaged with other data communications in the transmission stream, it is more difficult to intercept the contents of the communications with existing technology. The same problem occurs when communications are transmitted as pulses of light in fiber optic networks. The law enforcement and intelligence communities want to ensure their ability to tap into voice and data communications. In 1992 the Bush Justice Department proposed legislation that would require telephone companies to modify network technology to ensure wiretapping capability and would give the FCC the authority to permit phone companies to pass the costs of retooling the network to consumers. Privacy and civil liberties advocates opposed this plan. The alliance between civil liberties groups and industry groups that had gained passage of the ECPA again lobbied against law enforcement interests. And once again the debate was not framed in terms of privacy versus law enforcement but in terms of technological progress versus law enforcement.

A 1992 exchange of articles on the editorial page of the *New York Times* best illustrates the contours of the policy debate. William Sessions, then director of the FBI, wrote that "if digital technology is fully introduced with insufficient attention to public safety, the effectiveness of law enforcement officers will be greatly impaired."[119] He did not mention privacy but instead addressed the issue of the costs that the private sector would bear in the development of technical solutions that would meet the needs of law enforcement — a cost that "would not be so substantial as to outweigh the consequences of an inability of law enforcement to act." Janlori Goldman, the director of the Privacy and Technology Project at the ACLU, countered that it was "wrongheaded and dangerous to require industry to put surveillance first by slowing innovation and retarding efficiency."[120] She also noted that no real evidence had been brought forward proving that the FBI could not execute wiretaps without some modification of the communications network. Her article was similar to Sessions's in that it did not mention privacy. In an article critical of the FBI's position, William Safire asserted that ultimately the point of the debate was "not to stop the march of progress, not to take tools from counterspies, but to preserve business and personal privacy."[121] Congress did not support the Bush proposal to require manufacturers of communication devices to provide a "trapdoor" for law enforcement surveillance.

Technological changes have now made it possible for individuals to ensure their own privacy by encrypting, or coding, their communications so that only the legitimate receiver of the communication, who has the key, can read or hear the message. But the National Security Agency

(NSA) is opposed to giving individuals and corporations the power to encrypt their own messages for fear that its ability to listen in on communications will be compromised. Export licenses for certain encryption codes were denied during the Bush administration, which not only curtailed privacy protections but also, as the ACLU's Janlori Goldman pointed out, inhibited "the private sector's development and use of the technology."[122]

This debate did not disappear with the change of administrations. The Clinton administration has proposed an encryption scheme that involves the use of an electronic circuit, the Clipper chip, that can scramble phone conversations; two government agencies would hold the keys for decoding.[123] Law enforcement officials would be required to present search warrants to both agencies before they could decode conversations. Citing privacy, security, and competitiveness concerns, the computer and telecommunications industries and civil liberties groups, as well as some cryptographers, have been critical of the Clinton proposal.[124] The industry concerns are likely to dominate this debate. A coalition of businesses, including Apple Computer, IBM, and Lotus, has been formed to lobby against the Clipper chip. They are concerned that technology equipped with the Clipper chip will not sell in other countries, that the government is stifling commercial encryption, and that U.S. businesses and consumers are not likely to trust a security system that is managed by the government. After a Commerce Department review, the Clinton administration announced in February 1994 that it would encourage the use of the Clipper chip and continue to impose export restrictions on encryption devices. Additionally, government officials indicated that the Clinton administration would support an FBI proposal requiring telecommunications firms to guarantee law enforcement's capability to wiretap.[125]

Congressional hearings were held on the administration's proposal, and a bill incorporating this proposal, the Digital Telephony and Privacy Improvement Act of 1994, was introduced.[126] The FBI actively lobbied for the legislation; privacy advocates, especially the ACLU and the Electronic Privacy Information Center, were opposed to the bill. Industry representatives, particularly from the Bell Operating Companies, initially were opposed but agreed to the legislation after inclusion of provisions authorizing that $500 million be available to cover the costs of changing telecommunications networks to facilitate the use of law enforcement wiretaps. In the last week of the 103d Congress, this legislation was approved by both houses.

Communication technologies are not the only cause of new communication privacy concerns. New uses of communication systems also pose privacy issues. Intelligent Transportation Systems (ITS), formerly Intelligent Vehicular Highway Systems (IVHS), serve as a good example. Although the purpose of the ITS may be the smooth and efficient flow of traffic, the systems are in essence information and communications networks supported by sophisticated computer and telecommunication technologies. Proponents of the ITS believe these technologies can rationalize vehicle transportation by informing drivers about congestion and weather and by planning routes that would minimize travel time and balance road usage. In order to support the ITS, "real-time" information will be monitored about where cars, and possibly drivers and passengers, are at any given time. The systems will also provide "historical" information about where vehicles, and the individuals in them, have been and "future-time" information about where they are going.

The information that would be generated in an ITS environment would be of interest primarily to law enforcement authorities and commercial marketers. Law enforcement monitoring of vehicle movement in the past has been expensive and risky. Access to "real-time" or "future-time" ITS would lower these costs. Commercial marketers who are interested in developing profiles of individual habits, patterns, and life-styles regard information resulting from the ITS as a key component of an individual profile that has not been easily documented before. Such transportation-related information will not only be of interest to companies in the travel sector (for example, hotels, conference centers, and car rental companies) but will also be of interest to any commercial group that wants to develop profiles of individuals for marketing purposes.

Two broad types of privacy issues are relevant to the development and implementation of the ITS. Privacy issues associated with the disclosure of "historical information," where someone has been, are likely to be regarded as information privacy issues. The second privacy issue involves "real-time" and "future-time" information — where someone is and where he or she will be going. These are classic surveillance and communication privacy issues. Some very interesting Fourth Amendment issues would be raised if government officials sought access to ITS information. Although it is not clear that individual travel information contained in the ITS would be considered one's "papers or effects," Fourth Amendment issues are likely to be debated. If ITS information systems operate in a fashion similar to electronic mail — in that a driver electronically sends travel information to another part of the system and then a response is electronically sent back to the driver — then they may be covered by the Electronic Communications Privacy Act.

For the fiscal year 1994, Congress appropriated $218 million for ITS research, development, and testing. Both the Bush and Clinton administrations have supported ITS initiatives. Businesses, including many that have not traditionally been involved in transportation, regard the ITS as a growth area, with some estimating that ITS products will exceed $200 billion in sales within the next fifteen years.[127] ITS America, which describes itself as a nonprofit educational and scientific society encouraging the development and deployment of advanced surface transportation systems and is designated by the Department of Transportation as a federal advisory committee, has established a Legal Issues Committee Privacy Task Group to consider appropriate safeguards and guidelines for the control and use of ITS information. Industry advocates recognize that privacy issues will affect consumer receptivity to the ITS and that self-regulation to protect privacy will be more advantageous to their interests than federal or state regulation.

In new efforts to ensure communication privacy, the scenario that occurred during the course of formulating the ECPA seems likely to be repeated. Concerns defined in terms of privacy have been raised both for the information superhighway and for the ITS; law enforcement would like to be able to access information in both systems. But as the policy process continues, the conflict will not be seen as one between privacy and law enforcement. Instead, business interests will complement privacy concerns and privacy will be replaced by the interest in competitiveness. Although privacy may be protected, it will not be because the value of privacy dominated the debate but because privacy was instrumental to business interests.

Chapter 6

Psychological Privacy: Evaluating Our Thoughts

Determining whether another person is telling the truth is a daily concern for most people. It is also a constant concern for employers, educators, retailers, and law enforcement or national security investigators. In these contexts, supervisors or investigators need to know as accurately as possible whether the people they deal with are being honest. A number of techniques are available to determine whether an individual is telling the truth, ranging from torture and intimidation to knowledge about the individual's character and past behavior to trust of one's own intuition. The polygraph, or lie detector, is a technique that some claim can detect deception. But others regard the polygraph as a form of "20th century witch-craft,"[1] as "strip searches of the mind,"[2] or as "mental wire-tapping."[3]

The primary policy tension in the area of privacy and polygraphs has been between the privacy of the individual's thoughts and beliefs and the interests of employers, government agencies, and others in determining whether an individual is being truthful. A number of traditional privacy concerns are raised by polygraph tests. The intrusiveness of the machine — the fact that subjects are strapped to a chair with electrodes and wires connecting them to a machine and recording their bodies' responses — raises privacy concerns. The invasiveness and relevance of the questions asked during the test are likewise of concern; for example, in 1964 Representative Cornelius Gallagher (D-N.J.) reported that a number of members of Congress had received complaints about "humiliating" and improper questioning about their sexual activities as part of polygraph testing for federal employment.[4] Moreover, privacy concerns about maintaining control over access to information about oneself are raised in the use of polygraphs because people divulge information about themselves that they may not want to divulge or that they may not know they are revealing. Polygraph tests also involve an information privacy question if test results are disclosed to third parties without the individual's permission.

Despite the powerful images evoked by the invasiveness of polygraphs, the public aversion to being strapped to a machine that detects lies, and the reversal of the principle "innocent until proven guilty," privacy concerns have not provided a consistent or compelling focus for policy debates. In the almost thirty years of congressional debates about the polygraph, the issue has been defined in a variety of ways, including as a matter of personal privacy, censorship of individuals, the validity and reliability of the tests, and the protection of employee rights. The policy community concerned about this issue changed with the different issue definitions, and as the issue definition changed, privacy advocates did not remain at the center of the policy community. Initially, civil liberties groups and privacy advocates who lobbied for legislation were met with resistance from the well-organized polygraph industry and its business and government customers. As the polygraph issue raised more general questions about the invasiveness of personality tests, test developers and test users resisted legislation. Next, the debate shifted to the use of the polygraph to detect subversives in the government, and government agencies and the intelligence community joined in efforts against legislation. When the accuracy of the polygraph was identified as the issue, the scientific community, especially through the American Medical Association and the American Psychological Association, became major players in the policy debates. With the definition of the polygraph as an issue of employment opportunity, the unions became actively involved as members of the policy community.

Because technical and scientific issues figured prominently in congressional debates, an understanding of how the polygraph works provides an important context for the policy discussion.

Theory and Practice of Lie Detection

In the early 1920s, William Marston, a psychologist and lawyer, claimed that he had identified a specific physiological lie response and had invented a machine, which he called the "lie detector," that would detect this response. Marston believed that an increase in blood pressure occurred when someone was being deceptive. Shortly thereafter, John Larson, a forensic psychiatrist, developed a "polygraph" machine that measured blood pressure, pulse, and respiratory changes during questioning. One of his colleagues refined the machine to also check for changes in galvanic skin response.[5]

The polygraph machine itself has changed very little since the 1930s. The subject is hooked up to a number of instruments: two belts — pneumograph tubes—around the stomach and chest measure the rate and depth of respiration; two electrodes on the ends of the subject's fingers measure sweating responses—the electrodermal or galvanic skin response; and a blood pressure cuff—the sphygmomanometer—measures cardiovascular activity. Some machines also monitor muscular flexing that could distort blood pressure readings, and other machines require a specific type of chair. Various measurement devices then spew out data in graph form reflecting the individual's physical responses to questions. The machine itself does not automatically identify a response as a lie or the truth; instead, the data have to be interpreted by the polygraph examiner.

One theory behind the polygraph or lie detector is that lying is accompanied by conflict, which leads to fear or anxiety, resulting in physiological change. These assumptions—that lying leads to a certain emotional reaction and that the emotional reaction is accompanied by certain measurable changes in the body—have been widely questioned by academic psychologists and physiologists.[6] An alternative theory is that the polygraph measures fear of detection rather than deception itself and assumes that a person who fears detection will produce a physiological response when responding to a question deceptively.[7] Despite various challenges to the theory behind polygraphy, polygraph schools—the Reid College of Lie Detection and the Keeler Polygraph Institute—and polygraph textbooks exist.[8] In the early 1980s, the lie detector industry was, as David Lykken points out, "a big business, one of the most important branches of applied psychology both in dollar volume and, especially, in its social consequences."[9] Additionally, an organized association of professional polygraphers has presented a unified front against criticism or legislative proposals.

Several methods and techniques of polygraphy are utilized.[10] The "relevant/irrelevant" or R/I technique, originally formulated by Larson, uses a mixture of questions that are irrelevant to the purpose of the investigation and questions that are relevant. This technique is based on the theory that if an individual is lying in response to the relevant questions, the physiological response will be different from the response to the irrelevant questions. If the individual is telling the truth, the responses to the relevant and irrelevant questions will be similar.[11]

Another popular technique is the "control question test" (CQT), which includes control questions, certain answers to which are assumed to be "lies." For example, examiners using this technique assume that anyone who answers "no" to the question "did you ever hurt someone?" is lying. The responses to the control questions are then compared to the responses to the relevant questions, with the theory being that a person who responds more strongly to a "known lie" control question than to a relevant question is being truthful. The CQT assumes that individuals will not know which are the relevant questions and which are the control questions. If individuals know which questions are more important, they may be able to control their responses and invalidate the test.[12]

A third technique is the "concealed information test," in which questions are asked that only a guilty subject could answer correctly. After asking a sequence of questions about a detail of the events being investigated—the color of a stolen car, for example—the test then measures the "peak of tension" associated with the responses. Knowledge of concealed information can also be determined through a "guilty knowledge test," which asks about specific details in a multiple-choice format.[13]

In each of the polygraph test techniques, the role of the polygraph examiner is crucial, both in convincing the "subject" or "respondent"[14] of the ability of the polygraph to detect lying and in interpreting the graph of responses to the questions asked. Most polygraph exams begin with a pretest session, lasting from twenty to ninety minutes, in which the examiner informs the person of his or her legal rights and consent procedures and explains how the machine works, what questions will be asked, and what form the responses should take. As part of the pretest, many polygraph examiners use a card test to convince the subject that the machine can detect lying. In the card test, the subject picks a card and the examiner asks a range of questions about the card to which the subject is instructed to answer "no." The subject is then shown the polygraph responses, which indicate when he or she was lying about the card selected. The purpose of this exercise is to convince the subject that the polygraph can detect lying and to establish a professional, or nonhostile, relationship between the subject and the examiner. Whether the subject believes the machine to be "infallible" is also inferred to be an indication of the subject's guilt or innocence. As two polygraphers note, "This belief that the innocent have in the accuracy of the lie-detector, and that they will be exonerated, is usually shown by their attitude. This attitude is one of genuine confidence in both the machine and the examiner. Because of this confidence they regard the examination as an experience they will want to relate to their family and friends."[15]

Following the actual polygraph test, the examiner interprets the responses. Because of the important role that the examiner plays in evaluating the results, Lykken maintains that most polygraph tests "are interrogations, not tests. They are semistandardized methods of clinical observation in which the examiner has the opportunity to collect relevant data."[16] The polygraph does not eliminate human bias or human error. Even lie detector proponents acknowledge that if one polygraph examiner is asked to evaluate polygraph results done by another examiner, the second examiner may arrive at a different conclusion because of the importance of the subject's behavior and the exam conditions in making a "diagnosis" about the subject.[17] The leading polygraph advocates suggest that polygraph examiners — many of whom have prior law enforcement experience — should undergo several months of training, but critics regard this as insufficient given the crucial role examiners play. An additional concern is that polygraphers are motivated to serve their clients by finding cases of deception; hence, biases in interpreting polygraph results may occur.[18]

As will be discussed shortly, much doubt has been cast on whether any scientific evidence exists that the polygraph actually works. But some critics maintain that the primary issue is not its scientific accuracy but its effectiveness in eliciting confessions; in this sense, then, it works even if it serves primarily as a stage prop. Jerome Skolnick points out that "through the creation of an atmosphere of examiner omniscience key information may be extracted from the subject which he might have withheld had he not been strapped to a 'scientific-looking' electronic apparatus."[19] Lykken similarly speaks to this capacity in quite compelling, but also critical, terms: "To sum up, polygraph interrogation in the hands of a skillful examiner is a powerful cathartic (emetic?), an effective inducer of confessions. Its confessionary influence may be most effective with the naive and gullible or, among criminals, with the less experienced, less hardened types. In preemployment or other screening applications, it appears that the majority of ordinary citizens may be led to make damaging admissions in this secular confessional."[20] Polygraph proponents also acknowledge the "practical utility" of the instruments, tests, and procedures the polygraph employs "in inducing confessions from guilty individuals."[21]

Despite questions about the effectiveness of the polygraph, it has been used in a number of settings — criminal investigations, courtrooms, military and intelligence inquiries, and personnel offices — and has generated a great deal of policy debate on a number of policy issues. In addition to privacy concerns, two issues — the legal admissibility of polygraph evidence and the accuracy of polygraph results — have been especially important.

Legal admissibility. In general, federal and state courts do not admit as evidence in a criminal trial polygraph results or the testimony of a polygraph examiner. This legal position was first stated in 1923 in *Frye v. United States*. The Court of Appeals for the District of Columbia rejected a criminal defendant's attempt to introduce the results of a systolic blood-pressure deception test, an early form of the polygraph. In reaching this decision, a unanimous court stated: "Just when a scientific principle or discovery crosses the line between the experimental and demonstrable states is difficult to define. Somewhere in this twilight zone the evidential force of the principle must be recognized, and while courts will go a long way in admitting expert testimony deduced from a well-recognized scientific principle or discovery, the thing from which the deduction is made must be sufficiently established to have gained general acceptance in the particular field in which it belongs."[22] The court went on to rule that the deception test in question "had not yet gained such standing and scientific recognition among physiological and psychological authorities" to warrant its admission as expert testimony. This decision has not been overruled, even after over sixty years of development of the polygraph technique and experience with the polygraph, and the Supreme Court has not accepted a case involving admissibility of polygraph evidence. The *Frye* ruling still provides the legal precedent on admissibility of polygraph evidence; in general, such evidence is not admitted because it has not gained the scientific recognition necessary to classify it as expert testimony.

Some state and federal courts, however, have admitted polygraph evidence, but with fairly stringent regulations or limitations. Usually both parties must agree, before the polygraph is administered, that the results of the test will be admitted as evidence. Additionally, many courts require that the polygraph examiner have a particular background or training, that the examiner be available for cross-examination, that the polygraph exam follow a certain procedure, and that there be evidence of the scientific basis for the test.[23]

Scientific accuracy. In determining the accuracy of a test or procedure, two standards are used: reliability and validity. The reliability of a test means that the test consistently measures the same properties. In other words, if an individual takes two polygraph tests, the second test will yield the same results as the first, regardless of who scores the test. The question of the reliability of the polygraph is complicated by the important role the examiner plays in interpreting the machine's data.

The validity of a test involves the appropriateness of inferences that can be drawn from the test. A valid test is one that measures what it is intended to measure. The polygraph is intended to measure deception and truthfulness; its validity relies on its accuracy in detecting deception and truthfulness. The handbook *Standards for Educational and Psychological Testing* regards validity as "the most important consideration in test evaluation. The concept refers to the appropriateness, meaningfulness, and usefulness of the specific inferences made from test scores. . . . The inferences regarding uses of a test are validated, not the test itself."[24] The inferences from a test used in preemployment or employment screening involve probable job behavior.[25]

In psychometric theory, validity has three dimensions: content validity, construct validity, and criterion validity.[26] In order to determine whether a test measures what it is intended to measure, validation strategies should include evidence from each category. Evidence of content validity "demonstrates the degree to which the sample of items, tasks, or questions on a test are representative of some defined universe or domain of content."[27] For example, ability tests should be made of up items that measure ability, and workplace tests should be related to job content.

Evidence of construct validity demonstrates that the test in fact adequately measures the underlying traits it is designed to assess; in the case of the polygraph, the traits would be deception and truthfulness. Construct validity requires that a test be based on some theory or conceptual model. When the validity of a test used for personnel decisions is based on construct-related evidence, the *Standards for Educational and Psychological Testing* requires that two links be established: "First, there should be evidence for the validity of the test as a measure of the construct, and second, there should be evidence for the validity of the construct as a determinant of major factors of job performance."[28]

Evidence of criterion validity demonstrates that the test predicts the behavior that it says it will predict. From a practical standpoint, criterion validity is the central component of a validity analysis. But in the absence of construct validity evidence, it is difficult to determine to what extent criterion validity data can be generalized.[29]

Polygraphs Become a Public Issue

Although press reports critical of polygraph use in the public and private sectors date back to the early 1950s, it was not until 1963, when the Department of Defense proposed using lie detectors to find the source of "leaks" of sensitive information to news reporters, that Congress took up the issue. The chair of the House Committee on Government Operations asked his Subcommittee on Foreign Operations and Government Information, chaired by John Moss (D-Calif.), to investigate the federal government's use of polygraphs. The subcommittee found that federal agencies had conducted almost 12,000 polygraph exams in 1963, not including polygraphs administered by the National Security Agency (NSA) and the Central Intelligence Agency (CIA). At this early stage of the policy debate, doubt was quickly cast on the theory and accuracy of the polygraph. The subcommittee concluded that there was no such thing as a "lie detector," that no scientific evidence supported the theory behind the polygraph, and that there was insufficient evidence to support the accuracy of the polygraph.[30] The subcommittee also concluded that polygraphs force individuals to incriminate themselves and that the exam cannot be considered voluntary if the individual does not want to take it.

The subcommittee report did not develop the privacy issues involved. Representative Gallagher, who had first called for a congressional investigation and then had been critical of the subcommittee for not being aggressive, attached "additional views" to the subcommittee report, arguing that polygraphs were a "blatant invasion of privacy." He argued, as would be argued again later but never successfully, that even if polygraphs were 100 percent accurate, they would still invade privacy because they search individuals' minds and seize their thoughts: "In my opinion, lie detector tests constitute an insidious search of the human mind and are a breach of the most fundamental of human rights. They provide a vehicle of excursion into the most private recesses of the human mind. Even if the polygraph testing was trustworthy, there is still no possible justification for such 'mental wire-tapping.' I believe the lie detector test under any compulsion is a violation of the fourth amendment to the Constitution."[31] Although this view was held by many privacy advocates, the courts did not accept the argument that polygraphs violated the Fourth Amendment protection against unreasonable searches and seizures. The leap from seizures of things to seizures of thoughts that the individual divulged in answering questions was not one that was made easily in constitutional reasoning.

The Moss subcommittee recommended that polygraphs be used only in the most serious national security and criminal cases and that procedural safeguards be imposed. It also recommended the establishment of an interagency polygraph committee, including representatives from the Department of Defense, the CIA, the Department of Justice, the Office of Science and Technology, and the Bureau of the Budget. The interagency committee considered both the accuracy of polygraphs and the privacy invasions they posed and reached a similar conclusion to that of the Moss subcommittee: "Use of the polygraph in the executive branch should be

generally prohibited, and permitted only in special national security operations and in certain specified criminal cases."[32] The general policy of the
federal government[33] was to restrict the use of polygraphs and to regulate
the procedures involved in conducting polygraph exams and the training
and supervision of polygraph examiners.[34] The staff of the Moss subcommittee had assisted the interagency committee in drafting the regulations
but had advocated more restrictions and broader coverage.[35]

While federal agencies deliberated about the use of the polygraph by
the federal government, two committees — Senator Sam Ervin's Subcommittee on Constitutional Rights of the Judiciary Committee and Representative Cornelius Gallagher's Special Subcommittee on Invasion of Privacy of the Committee on Government Operations — began hearings
about psychological testing and privacy, hearings that also raised issues
about the polygraph and framed the policy debate in terms of privacy.
Emphasizing the invasiveness of test questions, Senator Ervin stated that
"there are certain areas of our personal life and habits which the Government should not inquire about in its routine employment procedures"
and that "clearly, the Government should not send out an investigator to
peer through an employee's or applicant's bedroom window. Neither
should the Government ask, through subtle psychological questioning,
what a person does and thinks after he draws the curtains."[36] Senator
Ervin acknowledged the existence of questions about the reliability and
validity of the tests but argued that the privacy issues were separate from
such concerns — that even if the tests passed scientific standards, they
should still be required to respect an individual's privacy. Congressional
investigations focused on the types of questions asked and their relevance
to making a judgment about an individual for a job or promotion. Some
questions asked about sexual practices and attitudes, religious beliefs, or
feelings about family members. Representative Gallagher stated that "the
thread of voyeurism runs through too many of the cases that have come to
my attention regarding the use of the lie detector."[37]

The concern with personality testing that initiated the 1964–65 hearings came mostly from those on the right of the political spectrum —
partly stemming from concern over tests being given to schoolchildren —
but quickly picked up support from those in the middle and on the left.
The psychological community was significantly interested in the congressional investigations. *American Psychologist*, the journal of the American
Psychological Association (APA), dedicated a special issue to the topic of
testing and public policy in order "to inform APA membership as fully as

possible of the nature of the current attacks on psychological testing and selection procedures."[38]

In testimony before Gallagher's Special Subcommittee on the Invasion of Privacy, no consensus was reached as to whether privacy issues or reliability issues presented the key policy problem. John Macy, chair of the Civil Service Commission, restated the need for a ban on federal agencies' use of personality tests and inventories as selection methods. Macy supported this ban not because of the privacy issues raised by the questions but because of the lack of research regarding the effectiveness of testing and standards for professional use and interpretation. The president of the American Federation of Government Employees did, however, base his opposition to personality tests on the argument that they infringed on the right to privacy and violated the Fourth and Fifth amendments, and he referred to "the indignity of questioning of an extremely personal character."[39]

One conclusion of the various congressional hearings and agency investigations was that the use of the polygraph for employment-related purposes was increasing. Initially, the polygraph had been used primarily as a tool for police investigations in solving specific crimes. But by the mid-1960s, nearly 90 percent of polygraph tests were being used by government and business for personnel purposes. In testimony before Ervin's Subcommittee on Constitutional Rights, one industrial psychologist accounted for this increase as follows: "Personality testing is useful to industry not because it is scientifically valid nor because it represents enlightened human relations procedures. All of our experiences with personality tests in industry indicate that industries are interested only in quickie procedures of looking at people. . . . The reason industry is interested in these procedures, we believe, is that the managements of the large industries have found in testing procedures, perhaps unwittingly, various techniques to crystallize and strengthen management authority over those individual workers and unions."[40] Westin reported that "hundreds of leading companies" were using the polygraph and that one polygraph expert reported that over 30,000 businesses — including banks, mail-order companies, hotels, and department stores — were using the polygraph for personnel analysis.[41] He also found that in corporate use of the polygraph for personnel selection or evaluation of employee satisfaction, "the overwhelming trend is to impose sanctions upon those who will not consent to take the tests."[42]

The hearings of the Moss, Gallagher, and Ervin subcommittees brought to the public's attention the growth in the use of the polygraph by business and government, the invasiveness of some of the questions asked during polygraph and personality tests, and doubts about the reliability of conclusions based on individuals' responses to these exams. The hearings were successful in making psychological testing a public issue, in beginning to define it as a public problem, and in informing test developers and government and business users that a problem existed. A question remained, however, concerning the nature of the policy problem.

Privacy, in terms of both the invasiveness of questions and the intrusiveness of the technology, was an obvious issue and was considered in all debates. Despite rhetorical support, however, privacy was not compelling as a policy goal. The ethical implications of probing an individual's psychological state were not thoroughly explored; although polygraphs were seen by some as a form of search and seizure, and therefore prohibited by the Fourth Amendment, or as a form of self-incrimination, and therefore prohibited by the Fifth Amendment, no case law supported these positions. Users of polygraphs believed them to be helpful in making judgments; regardless of any privacy invasions, polygraphs served a practical purpose. Critics of polygraphs adopted the users' terms of debate, and the debate shifted to the question of reliability. Reliability issues were easier to grasp, discuss, and support with evidence than privacy issues.

The Search for Problem Definition

In 1974 a subcommittee of the House Committee on Government Operations revisited the issue of polygraph use by federal agencies[43] and the staff of the Senate Judiciary Committee's Subcommittee on Constitutional Rights revisited the issue of privacy, polygraphs, and employment.[44] The House subcommittee found that agency use had decreased since the mid-1960s. In 1973 almost 7,000 polygraph exams were conducted by federal agencies, including over 3,000 by the NSA; in comparison, almost 20,000 were conducted in 1963, not including those administered by the NSA and the CIA. The subcommittee also found little additional evidence of the validity of the polygraph. The Senate subcommittee revealed that an estimated 300,000 individuals, in both the public and private sectors, were given polygraph exams in 1974.[45] In 1976 the House Government Operations Committee reiterated its 1965 finding that "there is no 'lie detector'" but framed its conclusion not in terms of privacy but in terms of accuracy: "The nature of research undertaken, both federally and privately funded, and the results therefrom, have done little to persuade the committee that polygraphs . . . have demonstrated either their validity or reliability in differentiating between truth and deception, other than possibly in a laboratory situation."[46] A majority of the committee members recommended a total ban on use of polygraphs by all agencies and for all purposes because of the questions about validity and because the "inherent chilling effect on individuals subjected to such examination clearly outweighs any purported benefit to the investigative function of the agency."[47] Thirteen committee members recommended limited federal agency use of polygraphs.

Privacy reentered the polygraph debate in 1977 with the release of the report of the Privacy Protection Study Commission (PPSC). In its discussion of privacy rights and employment, the PPSC concluded that the polygraph should be proscribed because of its intrusiveness. The PPSC pointed out that, although the validity of the polygraph was the focus of much of the debate, from a privacy protection perspective the fact that the polygraph "deprives individuals of any control over divulging information about themselves" was the paramount concern.[48] It recommended that Congress pass a law forbidding employers to subject applicants or employees to polygraphs or any other truth-verification equipment. It also recommended a ban on the manufacture and sale of these devices.

In the years immediately following the release of the PPSC report, a great deal of congressional debate about the polygraph took place. Three different committees held hearings, and each defined somewhat differently the problem posed by polygraph use. In 1977 and 1978 the Senate Judiciary Committee's Subcommittee on the Constitution held four days of hearings on the Polygraph Control and Civil Liberties Protection Act.[49] The bill (s. 1845), introduced by Senator Birch Bayh (D-Ind.), followed the recommendations of the PPSC and banned the use of polygraph tests by private sector employers and government agencies. Civil liberties advocates and union representatives testified that such a prohibition was necessary to protect the constitutional rights of employees and job applicants. Users of polygraphs, such as employers in retailing and trucking, and the polygraph industry were opposed to the ban because of their belief that the polygraph helped reduce employee theft. A similar bill (H.R. 9335) was introduced in the House by Representative Edward I. Koch (D-N.Y.), a member of the PPSC. In 1979 the House Permanent Select Committee on Intelligence's Subcommittee on Oversight entered the polygraph debate and held hearings on preemployment security clearance procedures. The subcommittee concluded that research on the accuracy of the polygraph in screening job applicants was insufficient and recom-

mended that the director of the CIA conduct a study on polygraph validity for preemployment screening.[50] The primary focus of this subcommittee was the scientific validity of the polygraph. Also in 1979 the House
Subcommittee on Labor-Management Relations of the Committee on
Education and Labor held six days of hearings entitled "Pressures in
Today's Workplace."[51] In this subcommittee, the definition of the problems caused by the polygraph and other screening techniques was related
to workplace stress. Although these hearings reflect congressional concern about polygraphs, the concern was fragmented and there was no
consensus as to the policy problem or appropriate legislative action. (See
appendix C for a summary of congressional activity concerning psychological privacy, 1974–80.)

Focus on Polygraph Accuracy: Increased Use and More Studies

The Reagan administration proposed more extensive use of polygraphs. Although there was congressional and public criticism of these
proposals, most debate occurred in the intelligence agencies and the executive branch. The terms of debate emphasized the reliability questions
and the circumstances under which the polygraph should be used. In
1982 a Department of Defense panel reviewing personnel security procedures recommended wider use of the polygraph for security screenings
and for reinvestigations of clearance. In order to implement these recommendations, revisions of a Department of Defense directive were required.[52] Additionally, in 1983 President Reagan issued a National Security Decision Directive (NSDD-84) authorizing broader use of the
polygraph. These executive actions sparked congressional and public debate, including several series of congressional hearings, General Accounting Office studies, and a request to the Office of Technology Assessment
(OTA) by the House Committee on Government Operations to study the
scientific validity of the polygraph. The Justice Department announced
the administration's new polygraph policy, which authorized the use of
the polygraph by all federal agencies for the purposes proposed by the
Department of Defense, including random polygraph examinations of
those with access to highly sensitive information and denial of access to
information for those refusing to take a polygraph.

In November 1983 the OTA issued its report, which concluded that
"the available research evidence does not establish the scientific validity
of the polygraph test for personnel security screening."[53] The OTA also
declared that it was not possible to establish an overall measure for or

general judgment about the validity of polygraph testing because of the complexity of the polygraph examination itself and because of its different applications. For example, although the OTA found that the validity of the polygraph had not been established for personnel security screening, it did find that there was "meaningful scientific evidence" of "qualified" polygraph validity for investigations of specific criminal incidents.[54] The scope of the OTA study did not extend to privacy and ethical issues raised by the use of the polygraph, although at an OTA workshop on the subject, some participants argued that the OTA should undertake an analysis of privacy and other ethical issues.

From a public policy perspective, one of the most important findings of the OTA study was that when the polygraph was used for screening purposes, there was an increased chance of identifying "false positives," that is, incorrectly labeling innocent people as deceptive. The main reason for this is that within the population being tested the number of deceptive or guilty people, referred to as the base rate, is generally quite low. If, for example, 1 out of 1,000 employees was guilty and the polygraph was 95 percent valid, then the 1 guilty person would be identified along with 49 innocent persons, or false positives. Even if the polygraph was 99 percent valid, 9 innocent persons for every guilty person would be identified.

In 1984 Representative Jack Brooks (D-Tex.) introduced the Federal Polygraph Limitation and Anti-Censorship Act (H.R. 4681), which was referred to the Committee on Post Office and Civil Service and then sequentially referred to the Committee on the Judiciary's Subcommittee on Civil and Constitutional Rights.[55] The bill was in direct response to President Reagan's directive and the proposed revisions in the Department of Defense directive; it banned the imposition of prepublication review requirements by federal agencies and restricted the use of the polygraph to cases involving alleged criminal conduct. The CIA and the NSA were exempt from the restrictions. The Subcommittee on the Civil Service held hearings and received testimony from a number of groups, including the OTA, journalists and publishers, unions, federal agencies, and civil liberties advocates. The full committee sent the bill to the floor, noting that it was "concerned about the reliability of polygraph exams" and that it believed "they constitute a serious breach of personal privacy."[56]

Following this action, the House Judiciary Committee's Subcommittee on Civil and Constitutional Rights held hearings. Representative Patricia Schroeder (D-Colo.) summarized the action of her committee, expressing her concern that "polygraphs falsely label honest people as liars and liars as honest. Their main value is that they scare people into confessing."[57]

But Representative James Sensenbrenner (R-Wis.) cautioned against hasty action in "such a tremendously complicated area with so many competing values."[58] Most of the hearing focused on the prepublication review requirements, with testimony from a number of constitutional scholars, the American Civil Liberties Union (ACLU), and the Center for National Security Studies about the chilling effect such requirements would have. The little attention that the polygraph received focused not on privacy concerns but on the purposes for which the polygraph was used and the manner in which it was used. Witnesses from the Justice Department argued that the Federal Bureau of Investigation (FBI) should be given more discretionary authority in the use of the polygraph for preemployment screening and employment reviews because of its national security and intelligence responsibilities. They testified that in 1983 the polygraph was used in 166 situations that would be prohibited by the proposed bill. The FBI argued that although that number was small, the "benefit derived was extremely great," and that the FBI's polygraph use was "subject to stringent internal controls which include high level review and approval, strict guidelines, and annual audits."[59]

In addition to these hearings in subcommittees of the Committee on Post Office and Civil Service and the Committee on the Judiciary, a subcommittee of the House Committee on Armed Services also held hearings on the Federal Polygraph Limitation and Anti-Censorship Act.[60] Because of objections from Congress, the polygraph provisions of the president's directive were not put into place, although an experimental program of polygraph testing for security clearances was implemented.[61]

Refocus on Employment Opportunities: Legislative Results

Beginning in 1985, the focus of the polygraph debate shifted from the polygraph's use by the federal government and concerns about national security to its use in employment, especially in the private sector. The impetus for this shift came from the unions. Although union interest in polygraphs dated back to the 1950s, the increased use of polygraphs in employment screening provoked renewed concern, and union representatives approached Representative Pat Williams (D-Mont.) with an outline of the problem. Williams was a member of the Education and Labor Committee, with a strong labor record and a heavily unionized constituency. In hearings, Representative Williams commented that employee polygraph testing had been treated as "a constitutional issue, a privacy issue, a civil rights issue" but that it was "first and foremost in my mind a jobs issue, an employment opportunities issue."[62]

Two bills were introduced in the House prohibiting the use of polygraphs by employers, one emphasizing employment opportunities and the other, privacy. The bill introduced by Representative Williams, the Polygraph Protection Act of 1985 (H.R. 1524), prohibited the use of polygraphs by employers because they could result in "the denial of employment opportunities." Representative Stewart McKinney (R-Conn.) introduced the Polygraph Control and Privacy Protection Act of 1985 (H.R. 1924), declaring that polygraphs presented "an invasion of privacy." In hearings, Representative McKinney noted that Representative Ed Koch had passed this bill on to him when Koch left the House to become mayor of New York City and that he had been "struggling with it ever since, and it is hard enough to get this body to listen to it."[63]

Both bills were referred to the Committee on Education and Labor, and the Subcommittee on Employment Opportunities held hearings in July and September of 1985. In opening the hearings, Representative Matthew Martinez (D-Calif.), chair of the subcommittee, described the legitimacy of the use of polygraphs in employment as involving a balance between the interests of employers and employees. He also linked the privacy and reliability issues, implying that if the tests were reliable, no privacy issues were involved: "The right to privacy and due process dictates that we must carefully scrutinize the validity and effectiveness of the polygraph, and we must scrupulously protect the employee's right to fair employment opportunities. On the other hand, we must consider the interests of the employer. Employers also have the right to protect their business interests."[64] Representative Steve Gunderson (R-Wis.) added that although he believed "the evidence is very convincing that polygraphs are not always accurate,"[65] he questioned whether the federal government should prohibit businesses from using polygraphs. The hearings focused on three issues: the use of the polygraph in the private sector, the privacy and due process issues raised by the polygraph, and the accuracy of the polygraph.

Many witnesses referred to the widespread and increasing use of the polygraph. The number of over 1 million polygraph tests administered by private businesses annually was widely quoted. Examples of polygraph use both for preemployment screening and for identifying dishonest employees were numerous. Representative McKinney, for example, cited Gimbels, Saks Fifth Avenue, Marshall Fields, K-Mart, Chase Manhattan

Bank, Chemical Bank, Day's Inn, Arby's, and Pizza Hut as "major lie detector users."[66] Many witnesses referred to a 1978 survey of 400 major U.S. corporations that found that 20 percent of all respondents and half of the retailers and banks used polygraphs.[67] At the 1984 annual meeting of the American Polygraph Association, the figure of 2.3 million polygraph tests a year was cited as the most accurate estimate. Complaints to the ACLU about the use of polygraphs indicated that the type of job categories for which the polygraph was being used was expanding from entry-level positions to management positions.[68]

The impact of the use of polygraphs on employees' rights was also a major topic at the hearings, although the discussion was somewhat vague and often consisted of anecdotal evidence of individuals who had been harmed by the use of the polygraph. Representative McKinney, in responding to a question from Representative Gunderson about why the federal government should intervene, explained that the polygraph was an "invasion of someone's civil rights, which is the right to privacy, which is probably one of the most important rights we are assured under our Bill of Rights in our Constitution."[69] Norma Rollins, testifying for the ACLU, referred to polygraph tests as "inherently abusive, degrading, and humiliating"[70] and commented that part of the problem with the tests was the personal and private nature of the areas subject to questioning: "In fact, employment polygraph tests might well be characterized as strip searches of the mind, probing for hints of guilty knowledge, personal weaknesses, undetected misdeeds, bad habits, and attitudes. In both content and technique, polygraph tests violate personal privacy as most people understand that illusive concept."[71] In this sense, the polygraph was seen as violating the sphere of privacy and also as forcing people to reveal things about themselves without realizing it and against their will, thus violating the privilege against self-incrimination. Another theme was that the polygraph reversed the traditional American tenet that a person was "innocent until proven guilty." Many witnesses argued that the way the polygraph was used in employment settings meant that if employees "failed" the test they were regarded as guilty without further investigation and denied a job or promotion.

In discussing the accuracy of the polygraph, almost every witness referred to the findings of the 1983 OTA report. Given the lack of evidence as to the validity of polygraphs, the question then was why businesses used them. Generally, it was acknowledged that it was out of concern with hiring and retaining honest employees. Representative Pat Williams spoke in quite strong language of the efforts of the polygraph industry in marketing its product: "Even well-meaning employers . . . have I think been duped into believing that the polygraph is an acceptable, fast, cheap and easy method of checking the employment applications or controlling employee theft. The polygraph may be a dreaded machine to American workers, but to their employers it is simply a tool of convenience."[72] Witnesses from unions also attributed much of the increasing use of polygraphs to concern with internal theft but questioned whether the polygraph was the solution, citing not only problems with validity, privacy, coercion, and intimidation but also a National Institute of Justice study that concluded that "applying the law enforcement model to theft does not work very well. For example, assessing previous theft activity outside the work setting by using polygraph exams has little relevance to future workplace behavior."[73]

In response to the various criticisms of the polygraph, polygraphers and business users testified against the ban, citing questions about the methodology used in the OTA study and the impact a prohibition would have on industry. The interests of employers in protecting their assets and in hiring honest employees received much attention. For example, J. Kirk Barefoot, a past president of the American Polygraph Association, testified that "H.R. 1524 would adversely impact on hundreds of thousands of companies across the United States which depend on polygraph screening to maintain acceptable profit margins so that they may remain in business. If polygraph screening were to be denied to these companies many of them would eventually be forced out of business due to the higher theft rates by employees. Those which would not be forced out of business would simply have to raise the price of their products, which would impact on all of us as consumers."[74] Representatives of the National Association of Chain Drug Stores, as well as a security consultant and a retail jeweler, spoke of problems with internal, or employee, theft and of the utility of the proper use of the polygraph. They, as well as the American Polygraph Association, supported a substitute bill, H.R. 1792, sponsored by Representative Butler Derrick (D-S.C.), that would govern and regulate, rather than ban, polygraph testing in the workplace.

At the time of these congressional hearings, press attention was also popularizing the issue, especially the accuracy problems and the physical intrusiveness of the polygraph device. The television series *60 Minutes* featured a segment on the polygraph. A Philadelphia evening news show reported on an experiment using the polygraph to determine who stole a camera. One former polygrapher, a policeman from Oklahoma who had testified before Congress on the inaccuracy of the polygraph, traveled around the country to explain how to beat the polygraph test.

The Subcommittee on Employment Opportunities approved an amended version of H.R. 1524 prohibiting the use of lie detectors by employers involved in interstate commerce, except for certain national security functions. The full committee approved the bill for floor consideration. In discussing the need for legislation, the committee defined the polygraph issue as "primarily an employment opportunities issue."[75] In reviewing legislation in this area, the report stated: "Congress has been interested in the lie-detector test issue for more than 20 years. For the past seven Congresses, 35 separate bills have been introduced concerning the use of these devices. The majority of this legislation has been introduced in the House. Fourteen of the 35 bills supported regulation of the industry. The remaining 21 bills completely banned or partially banned the use of the lie detectors in the private workforce."[76]

Five committee members dissented from the committee report, stating that the bill established a more restrictive standard for the private sector, preempted state law, was unnecessary, and imposed an added burden on businesses. The dissenters suggested that at a minimum the bill should be amended on the floor to exempt industries that were vulnerable to employee theft.[77] Representative Steve Gunderson agreed that certain industries should be exempt from the ban on polygraph use.[78] On March 12, the House — with bipartisan support and by a vote of 236 to 173 — passed an amended version of H.R. 1524, which exempted from the ban on polygraph use a number of businesses in areas affecting national security or public health, including the drug industry, security services, public utilities, child care facilities, and nursing homes. The exemptions to the ban reflected industry's success in ensuring that its interests were recognized.

In April 1986 the Senate Committee on Labor and Human Resources held hearings on the Polygraph Protection Act of 1985, which was similar to the original House bill in prohibiting the use of polygraphs by employees involved in or affecting interstate commerce. The bill was introduced by Senators Orrin Hatch (R-Utah) and Edward Kennedy (D-Mass.), indicating bipartisan support and leadership for passage. In opening the hearings, Senator Hatch stated that, despite problems with the validity of the polygraph, "each day Americans are being branded by the 15-minute polygraph special, by ignorant and malicious examiners, and by employers who use the lie detector as a cover for improper acts."[79] Questions about polygraph use, effects on privacy and due process, and validity were addressed in the Senate hearings as they had been in the House, but two additional issues played a more decisive role in Senate deliberations.

The first was that of the appropriateness of federal government regulation of polygraph use. Senator Strom Thurmond (R-S.C.) argued that polygraph regulation should be left to state governments, thirty-one of which had enacted legislation regulating the use of the polygraph. The Justice Department testified that it "vigorously opposes federalizing the law in this area," which it viewed as "symptomatic of the persistent tendency of government officials in Washington — well meaning officials — to act as if only we can fully understand and remedy the problems confronting 240 million Americans."[80] In arguing in support of federal legislation, Representative Pat Williams pointed out that "state regulation has been perceived as the seal of approval on the gadget, and has thus resulted in the explosive rise to 2 million tests in the past 10 years."[81]

The second important issue in the Senate debates was the question of which industries should be exempted from the ban on the use of the polygraph. Senator Hatch commented that since the bill was introduced, "we have had almost everyone who uses the lie detector test come to us and try to justify their utilization of it."[82] A number of senators questioned whether any industries should be exempted. In justifying the House bill, Representative Williams said that although he supported a total ban, he did not believe it would pass either the House or Senate and that "we should be political realists."[83] He estimated that the House version would prohibit about 90 percent of current employment uses of the polygraph.

In September the committee favorably reported s. 1815.[84] With respect to the federalism issue, it concluded that Congress had preempted state labor law in a number of areas, that polygraph testing was within the purview of federal law, and that state laws had not been effective in stopping or curtailing polygraph abuse. As for industry interests, the committee maintained that industry's concerns were not sufficient to override the problems with polygraph testing, including abuses of the exam process, the inclusion of inappropriate questions, and the question of validity. No further action was taken by the Senate before the adjournment of the Ninety-ninth Congress.

In February 1987 Representative Pat Williams again introduced the Employee Polygraph Protection Act (H.R. 1212), which was similar to his previous bill in that it prohibited the use of polygraphs by private sector employers involved in interstate commerce, exempting only national defense and FBI contractors. The bill had 181 cosponsors and was backed by bipartisan support. Hearings were held in March and April by the Subcommittee on Employment Opportunities. The Justice Department reiterated its opposition to "federalizing the law in this area"[85] and, in answer to a question from Representative Gunderson, said that the department would recommend that the president veto the bill if Congress passed it.[86] A number of private sector employers and associations — including Orkin Pest Control, the Association of American Railroads, the vending machine industry, food retailers and wholesalers, the National Retail Merchants Association, and the National Tire Dealers and Retreaders Association — opposed the ban on polygraph use. Many of these groups, along with the American Polygraph Association, supported a substitute bill, H.R. 1536, introduced by Representatives Bill Young (R-Fla.) and George Darden (D-Ga.), which would establish federal standards for polygraph examiners. The ACLU and a number of unions — including the Hotel Employees and Restaurant Employees International Union; the International Brotherhood of Electrical Workers; the Retail, Wholesale, and Department Store Union; and the Service Employees International Union — voiced support for the ban.

Three other groups testified in support of a ban on the use of the polygraph by private sector employers. The American Medical Association opposed the use of the polygraph in employment because of the lack of evidence of the validity of the polygraph in personnel screening. On behalf of the association, John F. Beary testified that the polygraph was merely "an excitement detector" and that "the most important point to make is that there is no such machine as a lie detector, and there may never be. The theory is without scientific foundation."[87] Also citing problems with the validity of the polygraph, the APA testified that it supported the prohibition on private employers' use of the polygraph for personnel screening. It cited as a major problem the large number of false positives, or misidentification of honest people as deceptive. The APA also argued against exemptions for certain industries because of the consequences of misidentifying individuals in such settings and because dishonest people may be motivated to manipulate the tests.[88]

Another group to testify in support of the polygraph ban raised the issue of the test's discriminatory impact. The Legal Action Center, a public-interest law firm, testified that evidence existed that polygraph tests tend to discriminate against certain racial and ethnic groups and identified two factors contributing to this discrimination. First, "there is research evidence of ethnic differences in physiological reactivity to stress that may affect the polygraph's validity when it is used on different groups," and second, "the subjective nature of the tests creates extensive opportunities for conscious or unconscious biases and cultural stereotypes to affect decisions made by polygraph examiners."[89] Although recognition of the discriminatory impact of the polygraph did not gain any new congressional supporters for the polygraph bill, it did add ammunition to the arguments for a ban on the use of the polygraph in employment.

In June the Committee on Education and Labor approved the bill by a vote of 25 to 9. Four of the dissenters to the committee's report termed the bill "a hypocritical response to a problem that does not exist" and reasoned that "employers who use polygraphs also regard them as very accurate. They would not pay for them if they did not."[90] They also noted that polygraphs were no less accurate than other personnel investigations, such as interviews and background checks. Representatives Gunderson and Marge Roukema (R-N.J.) supported an alternative bill that would prohibit the use of the polygraph for preemployment screening but allow it to be used to investigate employee theft or crime. A number of the dissenters supported H.R. 1536, sponsored by Representatives Young and Darden, which would establish federal guidelines for examiners.[91] The full House passed H.R. 1212 on November 4, 1987, by a vote of 254 to 158. Two industries were exempted from the ban.

In December Senators Kennedy and Hatch introduced the Polygraph Protection Act of 1987 (S. 1904), and the Committee on Labor and Human Resources held a hearing on June 19, 1987.[92] This bill prohibited the use of the "least accurate yet more widely used lie-detector tests"[93] in preemployment and employment screenings that were not conducted as part of specific investigations into loss or injury. The bill prohibited questions about "religious beliefs or affiliations, racial matters, sexual behavior, political beliefs and affiliations, beliefs or opinions regarding unions or labor organizations."[94] It required that polygraph exams be at least ninety minutes long and that polygraphers be licensed. A number of business associations that had opposed H.R. 1212 came out in support of S. 1904, including those representing railroads, banks, convenience stores, grocery stores, retail establishments, restaurants, and securities. The committee, by a vote of 13 to 3, favorably reported the bill on February 3, 1988. The three dissenters — Senators Dan Quayle (R-Ind.), Strom Thurmond, and Thad Cochran (R-Miss.) — voiced concerns about the intrusion of federal law into the employment relationship and issues of federalism.

On March 1 the Senate began three days of debate on the Polygraph Protection Act of 1987. Floor debate included the filing of over 120 amendments, many of which were nongermane, and a cloture vote. The primary issues on the floor were those that had been debated in committee. Several senators spoke of the inconsistency of banning polygraph use in the private sector while allowing its use by the federal government. In response, Senator Kennedy pointed out that the typical preemployment polygraph in the private sector lasted fifteen minutes and cost $15 to $25, while the cost of a government polygraph was $800. He noted that the number of polygraphs administered was increasing, having doubled in four years to the figure of 2 million in the current year.[95] The other issue in floor debate was the question of whether the federal government should legislate in this area or leave responsibility with the states. For example, Senator Quayle stated: "I agree that the polygraph may lead to unfair decisions—but I do not agree that Federal law is the answer to all mistakes that are made."[96]

Senators opposed to the bill argued that it would make it more difficult for employers to make wise decisions about prospective employees, especially in areas such as day care. A list of employers opposed to the bill was read into the record; interestingly, it did not include day care operators but primarily employers in the restaurant, jewelry, and retail fields. On the Senate floor, there appeared to be some disagreement about the administration's position. Senator Thurmond noted that he had received a letter from the assistant attorney general expressing strong opposition to the bill.[97] The following day, Senator Quayle indicated that the administration had been lobbied by organized labor and civil liberties groups and stated: "A veto is not going to happen. This administration does not have the backbone at this time to veto this bill."[98] On March 3, the Senate passed the bill by a vote of 69 to 27, with only one Democrat (Bob Graham of Florida) voting against it.

A conference committee met to iron out the differences in the, by now, quite different bills that had passed the two houses. However, basically the same House and Senate committee members and staff had been working together quite closely for four years on this issue; the level of trust in each other that they had built simplified the conference negotiations.[99] The conference committee compromise was approved unanimously on May 17.

On June 1 the full House adopted the conference committee report by a vote of 251 to 120. The Senate added its approval by a vote of 68 to 24 on June 9. Although the Reagan administration initially had been opposed to the legislation, concessions had been made during conference at the request of Labor Secretary Ann Dore McLaughlin, and President

Reagan signed the Employee Polygraph Protection Act into law on June 27, 1988. Its passage was seen as "the first major piece of legislation backed by organized labor to be enacted in the 100th Congress."[100]

From Psychological Privacy to Biological Privacy

Two themes ran throughout the thirty-year debate about polygraphs — privacy and accuracy. Privacy became, however, a subtext of the congressional deliberations, while questions about reliability and validity provided the major story line. Difficulties in conceptualizing privacy and the influence of interests threatened by restrictions on the use of the polygraph once again help account for the long process of policy formulation.

The privacy questions raised by the polygraph were not narrowly focused. Instead, privacy provided a rubric under which a range of related issues were discussed. One aspect of privacy — the most central privacy concern according to some groups, such as the ACLU — was that the polygraph entailed the revelation of an individual's thoughts and beliefs without the individual's knowledge of what information was being released or understanding of the effects of the revelations. A second aspect of privacy involved the intrusiveness of the machine; being strapped and wired were regarded as invasions of one's bodily integrity. The invasiveness and irrelevance of questions asked during the course of the polygraph test constituted a third privacy issue, especially in the 1960s. Additionally, an information privacy issue was raised because the test results were likely to become part of an individual's file and could be disclosed to others.

These privacy issues were arrayed against a number of competing interests. The polygraph industry itself, albeit rather small in the context of the entire economy, was organized and politically aware of efforts to restrict the polygraph's use. Its interests were complemented by the concerns of polygraph users, including government agencies, especially the intelligence community and the Justice Department, and businesses that used the polygraph to screen for employment or for investigatory purposes. They argued that their need to detect people who were dishonest was served by the polygraph, even if it was not perfectly accurate in scientific terms. As the threat of legislation became more likely, users of the polygraph became more actively involved in the policy debates. They also utilized arguments about the appropriate use of federal power in an area of employment law to score additional points.

Issues about psychological privacy have not been eliminated by the

Employee Polygraph Protection Act. Many employers who had been using polygraphs replaced them with written integrity, or honesty, tests. The use of such tests dates back to the mid-1920s. After the prohibition of most private sector use of polygraphs, the publishers of integrity tests aggressively marketed their products as a means of detecting employees who are likely to steal or engage in "counterproductive" behavior. In the late-1980s, over forty integrity tests were offered by over twenty test publishers. In a 1984 review of integrity testing, Paul Sackett and Michael Harris surveyed more than 1,000 retailers about the types of psychological tests used for entry-level selection and identified twenty-four tests.[101] A 1989 survey found over forty integrity tests, thirty-four of which were used primarily in preemployment screening.[102]

Integrity tests are based on the theoretical assumption that an individual's attitudes toward theft and admissions of prior behavior are good predictors of future behavior. Integrity tests measure a number of honesty-related attitudes and admissions of dishonesty-related behaviors. Typical questions might include the following: How often do you tell the truth? Do you think you are too honest to take something that is not yours? Do you think taking small items home from work is stealing? What percentage of the people you know are so honest that they would not steal at all? Do you think some people have a good reason to steal? How often have you overcharged someone for your own gain? How many people do you like? How often do you blush? Do you ever feel guilty?

In 1989 the House Committee on Education and Labor asked the OTA to examine the research on integrity tests and to identify public policy issues raised by the use of integrity tests for preemployment screening. The integrity-testing industry had lobbied the OTA heavily, arguing that the tests were valid and reliable. One reporter described the industry efforts as follows: "Led by a coalition of disgruntled testing firms, supporters of the exams have been frantically goading government researchers and congressional aides for 15 months to postpone and alter the study."[103] The industry not only lobbied the OTA but also members of Congress on the Technology Assessment Board who had the responsibility of overseeing the work of the agency. The chief of staff of a member of the board commented that the board had encountered "lobbying by people who are complaining about the report at a level [of intensity] I've never seen before."[104]

As in the polygraph debate, most of the controversy focused on questions of validity and reliability. Again, privacy and validity were seen as at least partly related. Psychologists maintain that in order to protect the privacy of the individual, the information requested must be relevant to the stated purpose of the test.[105] Most psychologists agree that to ensure that an individual's right to privacy is not violated, "there must be valid psychological reasons for having the particular information sought in making the assessment."[106] The privacy questions raised by the use of integrity tests were similar to those raised concerning the polygraph. Although the integrity-test procedure was not intrusive, test questions could be perceived as invasive. Test publishers, however, claimed that subjects were asked whether they resented answering the questions and that most reported they did not. But respondents who have an interest in "passing" the test and being hired may not be entirely candid in reporting their views. As with the polygraph, individuals may not know how answers are being interpreted and may unknowingly reveal information about themselves that they do not want to reveal. Also relevant are information privacy questions regarding the exchanges and uses of test results.

The integrity-testing industry was described as being "in a furor over the pending release of a government study that they fear could demolish their products."[107] In an effort to avoid legislative action by instituting industry self-regulation, the Association of Personnel Test Publishers developed model guidelines for preemployment integrity-testing programs.[108] At a hearing of Pat Williams's Subcommittee on Employment Opportunities, the OTA testified that sufficient research did not exist to support the assertion that these tests could reliably predict dishonest behavior in the workplace.[109] The OTA also found that the possibility of errors in test results, of a discriminatory impact, and of violations of privacy raised important public policy issues pertaining to the use of integrity tests.

The release of the OTA report and the congressional hearing did not resolve the controversy over integrity tests. A task force of the APA also evaluated more than thirty integrity tests and concluded that despite its "reservations about honesty testing," it did not believe that such testing should be prohibited because this would only lead to other forms of preemployment screening that could be "less scientific and controllable."[110] It did, however, make recommendations for improving honesty tests. Although use of integrity tests continues in many sectors, numerous studies conclude that businesses should be cautious in basing judgments about potential employees on the results of these tests.[111]

The traditional notion of psychological privacy is being challenged most intensely by advances in biotechnology, especially genetic testing and genetic mapping. Currently, the Human Genome Project, which is jointly directed by the National Institutes of Health and the Department of Energy, represents an effort to determine the location and chemical sequence of all genes.[112] The medical and scientific advances that this project may make possible are enormous, but controversies have also arisen about potential adverse or unanticipated consequences. The Human Genome Project is developing the ability to map human genes and thus provide detailed information about biologically determined features of individuals. The "human genome" contains the basic material from which the human being develops; it is a complete recipe for a human being. As of 1990, the location of almost 2,000 genes had been mapped on the chromosomes. In 1988 the National Research Council predicted that the mapping project would be completed in fifteen years.[113]

Some observers see the next logical step as the creation of a database containing information about the genetic makeup of millions of people. Some speculate that genetic information on individuals will be contained in bar codes, facilitating its storage and exchange. Because of the importance of the ethical, legal, and social implications of this project — and because resolution of these issues is critical to the ultimate success of the project — Congress and the project coordinators have agreed that at least 3 percent of the budget for the Human Genome Project should be allocated to the study of ethical, legal, and social issues. This amounts to several million dollars a year. Many of the ethical, legal, and social concerns raised by genetic testing and screening, especially in employment and insurance decisions,[114] are being defined initially in terms of individual privacy.

Genetic testing is more comprehensive and detailed than polygraphs or integrity tests in terms of the information that is revealed. It is a form of "biological surveillance" that yields information about the likely course of one's physical and psychological development. Genetic testing would therefore appear to be a greater invasion of one's privacy because of the type of information it reveals. But the technique itself is not intrusive, and no invasive questions are asked. Despite these differences, genetic-testing issues have already been placed on the congressional agenda as privacy issues. The Human Genome Privacy Act, introduced by Representative John Conyers (D-Mich.) in 1990, would give individuals a right to privacy in the federal sector with respect to information about their genetic makeup and would prohibit employment, insurance, and education discrimination based upon genetic tests. The Fair Health Information Practices guidelines of the proposed Health Security Act (H.R. 4077) protect information about genetic characteristics if it was generated or obtained in connection with receiving health care or paying for health care.[115]

As was true with polygraphs and integrity tests, some have questioned the validity and relevance of information resulting from genetic testing. But these issues gain importance when discussed in relation to genetic testing. In an article in *Business and Professional Ethics Journal*, Ray Moseley et al. suggest that six discrete scenarios can occur as a result of genetic screening; the person screened

1. is *certain* to get X (or "already has it, subclinically").
2. is at some *explicitly specified risk* of getting X.
3. is at *increased, but unspecified, risk* of getting X.
4. will get or is at elevated risk of getting X *if medical/preventive measures are not taken.*
5. will get or is at elevated risk of getting X *if personal lifestyle behavioral changes are not initiated.*
6. will get or is at elevated risk of getting X *if exposed to some disease vector*, e.g., chemicals in the workplace, radiation, infectious agents.[116]

General questions about the validity and relevance of genetic tests would not be appropriate considering this complexity. Instead, validity and relevance issues regarding genetic tests would need to be debated and resolved for each of these scenarios. No test can be perfect. Questions of what level and what kinds of misclassifications (false positives or false negatives) to tolerate also need to be resolved.[117]

In a 1983 report on genetic screening in the workplace, the OTA found that few large firms in the United States were using genetic screening in personnel selection. Out of 366 respondents to a 1982 OTA survey, only 8 reported that they were currently doing any type of genetic tests, 17 had done so in the past, and 59 had plans to do so in the future.[118] In 1989 the OTA conducted a follow-up survey and found that 13 percent of the health officers from Fortune 500 companies responding to the survey reported that their companies had used some type of genetic monitoring or screening, either currently or in the past.[119] Twelve health officers reported that genetic monitoring or screening was currently conducted; in the 1982 survey, six health officers reported such activities. In 1989 the Northwestern National Life Insurance Company surveyed 400 firms and found that 15 percent planned by the year 2000 to test the genetic status of potential employees and their dependents before making employment decisions.[120]

Although the current use of genetic testing is not widespread, rising employer health insurance costs and the decreasing cost and increasing scientific value of genetic testing are creating more incentives for employer use of genetic tests. Larry Gostin, the executive director of the American Society of Law and Medicine, argues that "if the marketplace is the only restraint on this technology's proliferation, decreased prices and demonstrated cost-benefit advantages will make widespread adoption inevitable."[121]

In determining the policy questions raised by the use of genetic testing, it is helpful to consider the purposes for which genetic testing is likely to be conducted. The 1990 OTA report distinguishes between genetic monitoring and genetic screening. Genetic monitoring involves the periodic use of genetic testing on current workers to determine genetic changes that may be attributed to the effects of exposure to certain products or procedures, primarily exposure to toxic substances. But non-work-related factors (for example, personal habits, age, and environment) can also cause changes in genetic material. Genetic monitoring, then, does extend beyond work-related activities in its surveillance. Genetic screening entails the evaluation of the genetic makeup of an employee or potential employee to determine the individual's likely inherited, or genetically based, characteristics. Genetic screening can be used either to determine susceptibility to certain diseases that may be work related or caused by occupational factors or to determine the general health of an employee or potential employee.

Arguably, both types of genetic tests could provide benefits for workers. Genetic monitoring could be used to enhance the safety of work conditions or to change the working conditions of individual workers who exhibit signs of risk. Genetic screening could be used to ensure that workers are provided appropriate working conditions; workers who are susceptible to a specific risk would be placed in an environment that would not be hazardous to them. Genetic screening could also be used to promote health awareness programs, thus decreasing employers' health care costs.

At the same time, both types of genetic tests pose policy questions concerning the rights of workers and the interests of employers. Genetic screening to determine general health conditions — because it is administered to current employees and potential employees and because it is not necessarily work related — is often viewed as raising more serious policy questions. However, because genetic monitoring can also detect non-work-related chromosomal changes, its use raises significant policy questions as well. Primarily, these questions involve possible discrimination on the basis of genetic information,[122] confidentiality questions concerning third-party use of information and ownership of genetic test results, and worker privacy interests in being able to control employer access to information about them.

Congressional efforts to restrict the use of polygraphs and integrity tests because of their effects on privacy were not successful. If this history is instructive, it would indicate that privacy will provide a weak defense against the use of genetic tests in making employment and insurance decisions. Instead, it is likely that the debate will focus on validity and reliability and the pressure will be to use the new technologies of genetic screening in a variety of settings.

Chapter 7

Congress, Privacy, and Policy Decisions

In each of the policy areas examined in the previous three chapters, issues were placed on the congressional agenda in response to technological changes perceived as threatening privacy. In all three instances, the issues were on the congressional agenda for years, if not decades, before Congress passed legislation. In the area of information privacy, legislation was proposed in the early 1970s, a weakened law was passed in 1974, and the law was amended in 1988. In the case of communication privacy, legislation specifically restricting wiretapping was not passed until 1968; various amendments were proposed as early as 1974 but there was no major change in the law until 1986, when the issue and politics in general assumed a different emphasis. In the case of psychological privacy, legislation was proposed in the early 1960s, the issue was redefined in the late 1970s, and a law was passed in 1988.

What explains passage of these pieces of legislation? Why did it take Congress years, if not decades, to respond to perceived privacy invasions that had provoked press interest and some degree of public interest? Why was each case defined as balancing an individual interest in privacy versus a societal interest? Why were privacy advocates placed on the defensive, bearing the burden of proving that a particular activity invaded privacy? And perhaps most importantly, as Congress debated these issues, why did the focus on the value of privacy fade, to be replaced by the concerns of those whose particular interests would be jeopardized by the protection of privacy interests? In other words, why did the importance of privacy not carry more weight in the normal legislative process?

In chapter 1, ideas, interests, the policy community, and policy entrepreneurs were introduced as factors important in modern congressional policy making. In later chapters, the role each of these played in the course of policy making for a particular privacy issue was explored. It is now time to compare the dynamics of these factors for the three areas of privacy and technology and to make some judgments about why Congress acted as it did, and at the time it did, on these issues.

The Role of Ideas

Within the public policy literature, the importance of issue definition is well established. Indeed, how a policy issue is defined is critical to the ultimate resolution of that issue and to understanding the policy process. But issue definition is not predetermined or fixed. Issues are not self-defined. Rather a policy problem often has numerous, sometimes conflicting, components. Issue definition is itself a political decision. As John Kingdon points out, "There are great political stakes in problem definition. Some are helped and others are hurt, depending on how problems get defined."[1]

In these three cases, the initial policy issue was defined as one of "privacy." With this definition, supporters of legislation had what was apparently a good symbol with broad public appeal, providing benefits to dispersed interests. But in each case, protecting privacy involved costs to fairly defined interests — government agencies, law enforcement and intelligence officials, and employers. These interests were therefore concerned about redefining the issue from the idea of privacy to another idea, such as efficiency, crime control, or honesty and productivity in the workplace. In the process, the politics of interests dominated; the idea of "privacy" made it relatively easy to move from an emphasis on an idea to the politics of interests. This analysis of privacy and technology policy illustrates that the power of ideas in the policy process is dependent on the character of the idea. An ill-conceived or ambiguous idea can open the door to interest-group politics.

In each of the policy areas examined in this book, the idea of privacy provides the initial definition of the policy problem, and concern with privacy gets the issue on the congressional and public agendas. But privacy does not appear to account for the formulation of policy; legislation is not designed to protect a broad general interest in privacy at the expense of well-organized special interests, as was the case with deregulation and tax reform.[2] Do these areas of privacy and technology policy, then, fit the new "politics of ideas" model outlined in chapter 1? And if they do not, why? As was discussed in chapter 1, the literature on the politics of ideas suggests several conditions under which ideas might play a central role in policy making: the existence of an exogenous factor precipitating change, the presence of symbols or slogans, and the existence of latent public interest. These conditions are present in the cases of privacy and technology but do not lead to a politics of ideas.

In these cases, change was precipitated by the exogenous factor of technological advancement. Computerization of records was a catalyst in getting the issue of information privacy on the policy agenda in the 1960s. The development of computerized exchanges of personal information leading to a de facto national database put the issue back on the policy agenda in the 1980s. The invention of the telephone and the subsequent invention of methods of wiretapping brought the issue of communication privacy to the public's attention in the 1920s. The development and growing use of new communication technologies in the 1980s brought new attention to this issue. The polygraph was a technological device that brought the controversy over psychological privacy to the congressional agenda in the 1960s, and its increased use and questions about its accuracy and validity kept it on the agenda.

In each case, technological change established a new arena of conflict and brought together a group of players who previously had not interacted. For example, in the case of communication privacy, technological changes in the 1980s brought new players — the providers of new services, manufacturers of new equipment, and users — into an existing policy community, composed primarily of law enforcement officials and civil liberties groups. Following the breakup of AT&T and deregulation of the communications industry, providers of new communications equipment and services — such as electronic mail, cellular phones, and database service providers — became increasingly active, concerned that consumers would not use a communications media that did not provide private communications. Similarly, in information privacy, the early debates about computerization of records brought civil liberties advocates and computer specialists together. Subsequent debates about computer matching brought in management and efficiency specialists. And in the area of psychological privacy, the use of the polygraph brought together civil liberties groups, psychologists, and unions. But in none of these cases did privacy provide the central idea around which the new players aligned themselves.

The presence of symbols and slogans by which ideas can be popularized is also an important condition for a politics of ideas. In these cases of privacy and technology, the concept of "privacy" elicited symbols strongly identified with American culture; "Big Brother," "1984," and "Clockwork Orange" were all terms that were symbolically relevant in getting these issues on the public agenda and in defining the nature of the public problem. Policy issues about which a "good story" can be told and which are relatively visible are more open to influence by a politics of ideas. Steven Kelman suggests that the "media's choice of topics for coverage also testifies to the strength of the public spirit ideal."[3] Most media coverage developed the theme of individual privacy at risk because of new technologies. Privacy and technology are issues to which the print and electronic media are attuned, partly because they affect news gathering and reporting and perhaps more importantly because anecdotal reports of privacy invasions provide interesting stories. Press reports retained an emphasis on privacy even when the dynamics of the policy debate had shifted from privacy. The symbolism of privacy was important in the public arena.

The third, and related, condition thought important to the realization of a politics of ideas is the existence of a latent public interest that can be mobilized about the issue. As the review of the public opinion surveys in chapter 3 demonstrates, there is latent public interest in privacy and technology. But concern about threats to personal privacy from new technologies does not generally translate into public pressure on policy makers to take actions to curb technological developments and to protect privacy. Privacy in the abstract is important to people. But privacy in concrete situations is also valued. When privacy is contrasted with other social or personal interests, survey results indicate that people still regard privacy as important.

Each of the three conditions thought to be important in making possible a politics of ideas is present in the areas of privacy and technology policy examined in this book. Technological changes raise new issues, privacy elicits powerful symbols, and latent public concern about privacy exists. But these conditions did not result in policy making that conformed to the model of a politics of ideas. Analysis of the congressional politics of privacy and technology issues suggests that the character of the idea is critical in enabling a politics of ideas to be realized. This analysis of the formulation of privacy policy, in which ideas did not play a central role but might have, suggests that the character of the idea itself may determine whether ideas play a central role. Although this conclusion may seem obvious, most of the empirical support for a politics of ideas comes from cases in which ideas did play a role in policy making. But not all ideas will provoke or generate a politics of ideas.

Privacy as an idea has not had a powerful influence on policy making. This is true for the cases of computerized databases, electronic communications, and polygraph testing. In the case of information privacy, fair information principles replaced privacy in policy discourse; in communication privacy, industry competitiveness replaced privacy; and in psychological privacy, employment opportunities replaced privacy. The policy discussions began with privacy but ended up recasting the idea of privacy into something similar, as in the case of information privacy, or into something quite different, as in the case of communication privacy. The policy discourse changed, privacy as an idea becoming less important in that discourse.

The primary reason for the weakness of privacy as an idea is that privacy frames the policy debate in terms of individual rights — the right of the individual to control access to himself or herself, including personal information, communications, and thoughts. This elicits two dimensions of policy debate. First, privacy is viewed narrowly in terms of "individual utility"; individuals consider whether they have experienced privacy invasions and at what costs. If they have not been personally affected in a negative way, then the problem is not salient for them and they disengage from the debate. In chapter 8, we will examine the implications of this tendency. The second dimension of debate emphasizes the "rights" component of privacy claims. A right to privacy, as well as other individual rights, is not absolute. Instead, privacy competes with other individual rights and social interests. The result is a politics of competing rights or a politics of balancing individual rights and social interests. As Deborah Stone notes, "When groups seriously call for a right to something, they must go beyond slogan mongering and try to establish a formal legal rule to define the right."[4] It has been difficult, however, to establish such a rule to define privacy.

Privacy has a rich, if somewhat confused, legal tradition. Much of the policy debate that did focus on the idea of privacy got bogged down in disputes about whether or not prior court rulings indicated that individuals had a Fourth Amendment "expectation of privacy," due process protection for "liberty" that encompassed privacy interests, or Fifth Amendment protection against self-incrimination. In each of the privacy and technology areas examined in this book, a legal and constitutional history constrained the meaning of privacy and made it a weak basis for policy definition. In these areas, Congress was not writing on a blank slate or devising a new principle. Instead, privacy proponents were trying to place these issues into an established legal niche; this niche, however, did not lend itself to new development, especially where technological change was involved.

In dealing with these issues, privacy advocates and members of Congress struggled to work within the constraints imposed by prior judicial decisions; they attempted to identify preelectronic analogies and to reason from these to the correct constitutional interpretation of the issue. In information privacy debates, the question was what was covered by the Fourth Amendment protections of "persons, houses, papers, and effects." Are computerized records held by another party an individual's "papers," or do they belong to the government agency, bank, or credit card company? Based on the Supreme Court's ruling in *United States v. Miller*,[5] records that are held by a third party and used by that party for administrative purposes are considered the property of the third party. Under such circumstances, the individual does not have an assertable Fourth Amendment privacy interest in those records. Although the *Miller* decision applied to records held by a bank, its logic would also apply to records held by the government.

The scope of computer matches also raised Fourth Amendment questions. Computer matches are general electronic searches of millions of records. Under the Fourth Amendment, searches must not be overly inclusive; no "fishing expeditions" or "dragnet investigations" are allowed. Yet in computer matches, many people who have not engaged in fraud or are not actually suspected of criminal activity are subject to the computer search. This raises questions about the presumption of innocence, as reflected in Fourth and Fifth Amendment case law. If matches are considered a Fourth Amendment search,[6] then some limitations on the breadth of the match and/or justifications for a match would be necessary and procedural safeguards would be required. But if the records belong to a third party, then the individual has no Fourth Amendment "expectation of privacy" in them.

Communication privacy is largely defined in terms of the Fourth Amendment. Are communications covered under "persons, houses, papers, and effects"? Is electronic surveillance an "unreasonable search and seizure"? The courts, in responding to defendants' challenges to evidence that was obtained through surveillance, offered tentative answers to these questions but were hesitant to engage in judicial policy making or to be the engine powering privacy rights in an electronic environment. This legal constraint is perhaps most apparent concerning the issue of wiretapping. In the late 1920s, the Supreme Court ruled that wiretapping did not constitute a search or seizure because there was no trespass, thus no Fourth Amendment prohibition against wiretapping. Congress could have established a statutory prohibition or restriction of wiretapping, but the lack of Fourth Amendment protection was used as an argument against establishing statutory protection. In the 1980s, legal issues still dominated much of the congressional debate, raising questions about the appropriate level of protection for a new communication technology in terms of the appropriate preelectronic analogy. For example, regarding electronic mail, Justice Department officials argued that regular mail was the correct analogy and that the search warrant requirements for mail, which have lower standards than Title III, should apply. The electronic mail industry argued that because of its speed and interactive capabilities, electronic mail was used more often as a substitute for phone communications rather than for postal communications and that there should be a comparable level of protection.

Similarly, in polygraph policy formulation, much time was devoted to the debate about whether the polygraph violated the Fifth Amendment prohibition on self-incrimination — or if one's consent, in order to get a job or dispel doubts about one's innocence, meant that one had waived that protection — and whether the use of the polygraph test, in effect, was based on the presumption that one was guilty until proven innocent. Fourth Amendment questions were also raised concerning whether such psychological surveillance constituted a search and seizure of an individual's thoughts. But the courts were unwilling to extend the Fourth Amendment to cover polygraph tests. In terms of both the Fourth and Fifth Amendment, the fact that the individual consented in some fashion to the polygraph exam weakened the argument for a constitutional violation.

Limitations imposed by prior court rulings continue to constrain policy formulation in the area of privacy. A good example is the tension between the First Amendment protections afforded commercial speech and privacy invasions resulting from the sale of mailing lists and from telephone solicitations. Direct-marketing firms argue that corporations have First Amendment rights and that the sale of customer lists is a form of speech and is therefore protected from government regulation by the First Amendment.[7] Legislation requiring direct-marketing firms to use telephone preference services, which allow individuals to indicate whether they want to receive telemarketing calls at their homes, might be interpreted as barring an entire class of callers because of the content of their messages, thus raising First Amendment objections. Industry self-regulation, through the voluntary adoption of guidelines or preference lists, would not raise First Amendment concerns. First Amendment issues also would not be raised if regulation was directed clearly at conduct rather than speech. For example, regulation of automated calls as a category or class of calls regardless of their purpose or content would not raise First Amendment concerns. Regulating the times at which unsolicited calls could be made also would not raise First Amendment concerns if the times were reasonable.[8] But the web of prior First Amendment decisions, especially with regards to commercial speech, does have to be taken into account when formulating policy on uses of lists of individuals' addresses, phone numbers, and/or buying habits.

The Role of Interests

In the introduction to *The Power of Public Ideas*, Robert Reich suggests that in some cases "to disregard . . . ideas is to miss the essential story."[9] But in these areas of privacy and technology policy, interests are the essential story. Although initial policy definition and agenda setting were framed in terms of the idea of privacy and laws were proposed to protect privacy, the idea of privacy was less important in the passage of legislation. Instead, interests dominated policy formulation and adoption. In each policy area, a new technology, or application of a technology, precipitated social, economic, or governmental changes that generated a pattern of interests that had not existed before. As the technology-precipitated changes became apparent, groups and organizations that stood to derive benefits from those changes realized that their interests were threatened by proposals to protect privacy. In response, they sought to define their interests and to develop support for their position. In doing so, they were able to redefine the policy issue from one of "privacy" to one more amenable to their concerns.

As the analysis moves here from ideas to interests, it is important to note the difficulties in distinguishing between ideas and interests. How can one be sure that ideas are not just a smokescreen for institutional or personal interests and that those interests are not actually driving policy? How can one distinguish between the *idea* of economic competitiveness, tax fairness, or privacy and an *interest* in economic competitiveness, tax fairness, or privacy? And if ideas and interests are complementary, does the idea or the interest possess causal power? As Mark Moore points out: "It would be foolish to deny that the success of an idea is related to the play of interests."[10]

The varying influence of ideas apparently falls along a continuum. Ideas could change preferences that are based upon interests, in this case, actually overcoming interests. This would clearly be an instance in which a politics of ideas explains the policy outcome. Ideas might also cause or initiate the formation of a new coalition, but once the coalition is formed, either a politics of interests or a politics of ideas could dominate decision making. If a politics of interests dominates, then the effect of ideas is somewhat minimal. Ideas would not be directly influencing policy but fostering the formation of new coalitions in which interest-group politics operates. But if ideas dominate the new coalition, then ideas do have an independent effect. At the extreme end of the continuum would be those cases in which interests cause the formation of a policy position or coalition and ideas are used to argue in support of that position. In these cases, interests dominate and ideas represent more rhetoric than political reality.

Recognizing that ideas and interests work together helps us understand the policy dynamics that occurred in these three cases. The idea of privacy as the state of "being let alone" appears synonymous with self-interest; it does not elicit broader values. This individualistic idea of privacy does not *add* to self-interest; it merely restates it. But the ideas of government efficiency, effective law enforcement, and an honest work force provide a higher-order, or broader, rationale for the narrow self-interests of government bureaucrats, law enforcement officials, and employers. As Jane Mansbridge points out, dual streams exist in American political thinking — one stream promoting self- or individual interest and the other, public interest.[11] These two streams are not necessarily conflicting but complementary or mutually supportive. Arguments for privacy have relied primarily on the former — "accommodation to self-interest" — while those seeking to restrict or weaken proposals to protect individual privacy have tapped into both streams — "commitment to the public good" and "accommodation to self-interest." Those opposing privacy policy benefit from two sources of support, while those concerned about privacy rely on one — individual self-interest.

If privacy is framed as an individual interest, then it primarily elicits self-interest as a political motivator; it does not as easily tap into ideas that coincide with a public purpose or a broader meaning. Steve Kelman points out that "to win the consent of others, political arguments must be expressed in terms broader than the self-interest of the individual or the group making the claim."[12] But arguments for privacy have not successfully transcended self-interest. In the cases of communication and psychological privacy, where privacy advocates aligned with other interests, the other interests drew on the commitment to the public good. The competitiveness of new telecommunications industries was presented as an issue of economic growth and global competitiveness. Employment opportunities drew not on individual self-interest alone but on broad-based concerns related to employment that were shared with other people in similar situations. In the case of information privacy, in which privacy advocates had no other allies, the balancing involved in establishing fair information principles was framed in terms of the individual interest in privacy versus organizational and public interests.

In the areas of privacy and technology policy examined in this book, those opposed to privacy redefined the issue in terms of another idea — government efficiency, effective law enforcement, and honesty and productivity in the work force. These ideas drew upon both self-interest and public interest. They can be viewed as expressions of a broad public interest, but they are also ideas that serve the particular interests of particular groups. The question then becomes how to distinguish the influence of ideas from the influence of interests in these debates.

Ideas and interests both motivated those opposed to privacy, but this analysis of congressional policy formulation and adoption would suggest that interests were more important. If the policy debate had been framed in terms of ideas, broad appeals and broad-based interest would have supported the ideas. Instead, in these cases, the ideas were used to shield interests — the interests of federal agencies in restricting outside control of their operations, the interests of law enforcement in retaining discretion in their investigations, and the interests of employers in being able to screen potential employees in whatever ways possible. In these cases, those articulating the opposing "idea" were those who would have borne the heaviest costs if privacy legislation had been passed. The opposing idea also offered something of a smokescreen. In all three cases, no evidence existed that the technology being used actually fulfilled the idea put forth: that computer matches enhanced efficiency, that wiretaps caught criminals, or that polygraphs identified dishonest employees. But by being able to muster the support of both ideas and interests, those whose interests benefited from the use of new technologies were able to control the political debate.

A review of the arguments offered in congressional debates supports the suggestion that self-interest, more than a commitment to public ideas, explains the actions of those opposed to privacy protections. Those opposed to privacy did not adopt that position because of their dedication to another public idea but because privacy protections would affect their self-interest by imposing costs on them.

Information privacy. Although computerization of databases generated concerns about the privacy of information contained in the databases, computerization provided organizations with a tool of immense potential. Computerization, especially when linked to telecommunication systems, increases an organization's resources because it increases exponentially the information-processing capabilities of an organization. Computers improve information processing by virtue of their storage capacity, their speed in retrieving data, their ability to manipulate information, and their facility for transmitting information. Computerized information systems reduce the costs of processing information, especially in terms of time and personnel, and increase the value of the information itself. Complex programs involving the manipulation of huge quantities of information can be performed as easily as routine procedures. With computers, not only is more extensive use of the information itself possible, but also new information is created through sorting, comparing, and integrating data.

The capability of computerized information systems to bring about more overt manipulations of people and attitudes, leading to social engineering, was noted in the early 1960s: "The computer provides two prerequisites for the development of effective social engineering. First, only the computer can process fast enough the enormous amounts of data needed to know what the existing states of social and economic affairs are. . . . In the second place, the computer will let the social scientist manipulate enough variables and enough circumstances in sufficiently complex ways to invent subtle models about the behavior of man and his instincts."[13] Computerized information systems make it possible for organizations to be more efficiently administered and to offer better services. At the same time, organizations could become less accountable and controllable.

Policy makers were aware of this tension between organizations that recognized the great benefits to be gained from computerization and privacy advocates who feared the intended and unintended consequences of technological advances. For example, Senator Sam Ervin argued that the new computer technology "extends and unifies official power to make inquiries, conduct investigations, and to take note of the thoughts, habits and behavior of individuals."[14] In 1973 a report of the Department of Health, Education, and Welfare concluded that "the net effect of computerization is that it is becoming much easier for record-keeping systems to affect people than for people to affect record-keeping systems."[15] Similarly, the Privacy Protection Study Commission concluded in 1977 that the "growth in society's record-keeping capability threatens to upset existing power balances between individuals and organizations, and between government and the rest of society."[16]

By the 1980s, two generations of advances in information technology had resulted in phenomenal changes in the record-keeping environment of the federal government.[17] Information was no longer merely stored and retrieved by computer but was also routinely collected on computer tapes, used by agencies in computer form, exchanged with or disclosed to regional offices or other agencies in computer form, and manipulated and analyzed using sophisticated computer software. Microcomputers were widely used in the federal government, vastly increasing the potential points of access to personal record systems and the creation of numerous new decentralized record systems. Computer matching, front-end verification, and computer profiling were becoming routine in many federal programs. The widespread use of telecommunications for the direct linking of separate databases led to what the Office of Technology Assessment (OTA) termed the creation of a de facto national database with the social security number being used as a de facto national identifier.

Given the benefits that computerization and telecommunications bring to record keeping, it is not surprising that federal agencies have lobbied against policies that restrict their use of computers in personal information handling. As we saw in chapter 3, federal agencies—through the Ford administration and through the Office of Management and Budget (OMB)—were actively opposed to the proposed Privacy Act and were successful in thwarting the establishment of a Federal Privacy Board. After the act was passed, federal agencies, again working with and through the OMB, worked to undercut the effectiveness of the act by urging a broad interpretation of the "routine use" provision, which allows disclosures without the consent of the individual "for a purpose which is compatible with the purpose for which it was collected."[18] The broad interpretation that was incorporated into the OMB computer-matching guidelines facilitated the use of computer matching.

Since the late 1970s, concern about the size and efficiency of the federal government and the increase in the federal deficit made management a policy priority. This was reflected during the Reagan administration in the establishment of a number of executive bodies with an emphasis on management: the President's Council on Integrity and Efficiency, to enhance interagency efforts to reduce fraud and waste; the President's Council on Management Improvement, to advise the president; and the President's Private Sector Survey on Cost Control (the so-called Grace Commission), to study management problems in government. All these bodies advocated the use of computer and communication technology to enhance the efficiency of the federal government and particularly the use of computer matching as a technique to detect fraud, waste, and abuse. Representatives from these bodies were active in congressional policy making and extolled the benefits of computer matching, often, as discussed in chapter 4, without hard data on costs and benefits.

Federal agencies, with the support of Democratic and Republican presidents, viewed legislation to protect the privacy rights of individuals as a restriction on the use of computer and telecommunication technologies to enhance the efficiency of their operations. Rather than challenging the idea of privacy, federal agencies placed greater emphasis on the idea of government efficiency and their interests in improving efficiency. To some extent, this represents a conflict between ideas — the idea of privacy versus the idea of efficiency. But the commitment to efficiency was derived not solely from a public commitment to good government but also from the interest of federal agencies in maintaining control over their own information-processing systems.

Communication privacy. From the time that electronic surveillance became a technological possibility, law enforcement officials emphasized its importance as a method of detecting illegal activities. Their support for this method wavered little during the over sixty years of policy debate. From a law enforcement and investigative standpoint, the potential benefits offered by electronic surveillance are substantial and include the accumulation of more accurate and complete information on suspects, the possible reduction in time and manpower required for case investigations, and the expansion of options for preventing and deterring crime.

The discussions in the 1960s and 1970s about the use of electronic surveillance in organized crime investigations best exemplify the importance that law enforcement placed on electronic surveillance. The 1967 report of the President's Commission on Law Enforcement and the Administration of Justice detailed many difficulties that the hierarchical structure of organized crime posed to traditional law enforcement investigations. The commission stated: "To maintain their insulation . . . the leaders . . . avoid direct communication with the workers. All commands, information, complaints, and money flow back and forth through" buffers.[19] Electronic surveillance was an important technique in penetrating these buffers. Robert Blakey, the author of an American Bar Association (ABA) report on electronic surveillance, made the same argument before congressional hearings in 1967: in organized crime, the criminal is often known but the crimes are not, and surveillance of known criminals is necessary to identify their criminal behavior and their associates.[20]

Although strong arguments in support of electronic surveillance have been offered, hard data confirming its benefits have been less forthcoming. As with computer matches, the debate about the effectiveness of electronic surveillance has two sides. Herman Schwartz has argued that government use of electronic surveillance results in very few convictions, that the costs have been understated, and that the social costs have not been taken into account and outweigh the benefits.[21] In support, he cited 1970 figures indicating that federal eavesdropping on 10,260 people and 147,780 conversations produced 48 convictions and 613 arrests. Law enforcement has responded to such criticisms by pointing out that arrests are not the only indication of the effectiveness of electronic surveillance and that such surveillance is generally part of an ongoing investigation and often produces important leads concerning other criminal activity.

Data on the number of electronic surveillance devices being used in law enforcement activities have never been easy to collect. The Dash study in the late 1950s found it difficult to obtain accurate information about the number and purposes of official wiretaps. For example, the investigation revealed that over 2,000 wiretaps had been performed in New York, whereas the New York Central Investigation Bureau reported about 180 for the same time period.[22] The Long subcommittee in the mid-1960s also concentrated on obtaining empirical evidence about federal agency surveillance activities and found more wiretapping and other surveillance than was expected.[23] Since passage of Title III in 1968, statistics on government use of some electronic surveillance techniques, primarily telephone wiretaps and hidden microphones, have been collected and published by the Administrative Office of the U.S. Courts. During the discussions of the Electronic Communications Privacy Act of 1986 (ECPA), the 1984 figures were widely quoted—federal and state judges approved 801 out of 802 requests for authorization of electronic surveillance.[24] In general, electronic surveillance had been used primarily in narcotics and gambling cases; in 1974 more gambling cases than narcotics cases were investigated using electronic surveillance, and in 1984 the order was reversed. The reported costs of electronic surveillance increased dramatically, from about $8,000 each in 1974 to about $45,000 in 1984. In 1984 approximately 25 percent of the intercepted communications were reported to be incriminating in nature; 2,393 persons were arrested as a result of electronic surveillance, and about 27 percent were convicted.[25]

Until the late 1960s, law enforcement officials were successful in blocking legislative attempts, supported by civil liberties groups, to restrict the use of wiretaps by limiting the crimes for which electronic surveillance could be used or by establishing procedures for the use of electronic surveillance. It was not until the *Katz* decision of 1967, ruling that wiretaps were prohibited by the Fourth Amendment, that law enforcement officials had an incentive to compromise with civil liberties groups in crafting legislation. In discussions and hearings on the Electronic Communications Privacy Act of 1986, the Justice Department spoke on behalf of the law enforcement community, originally opposing any changes in Title III. In a letter to Representative Robert Kastenmeier in 1985, the counsel for intelligence policy in the Department of Justice stated that since there were no "serious flaws in Title III or its implementation currently . . . we believe the statutory structure should not be modified at this time."[26] The Justice Department preferred that problems arising from the use of new technologies be addressed through departmental policy rather than legislative action. It was not until it became clear that the administration supported the bill because of industry interest that the Justice Department weakened its opposition and seriously worked with congressional committees in fashioning legislation; the resulting legislation also brought changes that advantaged law enforcement interests.

Psychological privacy. Since the early twentieth century, employers have been using numerous tests to assist them in making personnel decisions. Observers have suggested that the pressures on employers to select employees more carefully have increased due to specialization of job categories, high rates of employee turnover, concerns about worker productivity, workplace theft, increased liability and insurance costs, and drug and alcohol use on the job.[27] As a result, employers are interested in examining many facets of employees', or potential employees', lives, including their honesty, indebtedness, prior convictions, drug and alcohol use, health, dependability, education, skills, and family history. Employers use a variety of personnel screening techniques, such as background checks, especially into criminal history[28] and credit records, reference checks, ability tests, blood and urine tests,[29] handwriting analysis, and face-to-face interviews.

Until passage of the Employee Polygraph Protection Act of 1988, polygraphs were a major method of screening potential employees as well as evaluating current employees. Proposals to ban or restrict the use of the polygraph threatened the interests of the many private sector employers who had come to rely on the polygraph as part of routine employment screening. Many businesses argued that the increase in employee theft made it necessary for them to use the polygraph as a screening device in their endeavors to hire "honest" employees. There was a widespread perception that employee theft was on the rise, despite difficulties in arriving at an accurate figure of employee theft.[30] A figure quoted often in discussions of theft in the workplace was $40 billion annually,[31] which is the American Management Association's 1975 estimate of the financial impact of eleven nonviolent crimes against business.[32] Of the crimes studied, the association estimated that actual employee pilferage accounted for between $5 and $10 billion. In another attempt to gather empirical data on the scope of employee theft, Richard Hollinger and John Clark, in a study funded by the National Institute of Justice, surveyed over 9,000 employees in the retail, hospital, and manufacturing sectors.[33] Based on responses to a self-report questionnaire, they found that 35.1 percent of employees in the retail sector, 33.3 percent in the hospital sector, and 28.4 percent in the manufacturing sector reported some involvement in property theft. An earlier survey of ninety-eight retail employees found that 50 percent reported taking merchandise without paying for it; however, 33 percent of those said that the value of the merchandise was less than one dollar.[34]

In addition to problems with defining and measuring employee theft, there is also debate about the causes of employee theft and, consequently, about the effectiveness of tests such as the polygraph in either identifying or reducing employee theft. In 1976 the National Council on Crime and Delinquency proposed and found evidence supporting three hypotheses for explaining employee theft:[35] that an employee is predisposed to crime and, given an opportunity, will steal from an employer; that psychological or economic pressures cause an employee to steal; and that an employee who is dissatisfied with certain aspects of the work environment such as pay and promotions will engage in theft. Hollinger and Clark's review of prior studies of employee theft and their own employee survey led them to conclude that the work environment, including informal rules and social control processes, was important in explaining the amount and type of deviant employee behavior. Their data supported the hypothesis that the disgruntled employee was involved in more theft: "Specifically, where the integrity, fairness and ethical quality of the organization were questioned, we found more theft. Where the supervisory personnel were perceived as unhelpful, incompetent and unconcerned, we again detected higher theft."[36] Their survey also revealed that younger employees engage in more theft, which was explained not by a general propensity to be dishonest but by their "lesser stakes in conformity" and "lesser social risk."[37] Employees who have the most freedom and access to assets and materials were also more heavily involved in theft.

Despite difficulties in defining, measuring, and accounting for employee theft, a widespread perception existed that employee theft was growing and was a legitimate problem for employers. Within this environment, the polygraph test was seen as an important method employers used to identify people who were prone to or engaged in dishonest behavior and to convey the message to employees and prospective employees that dishonest behavior was not tolerated. Employers who used the polygraph were vocal in congressional hearings. For example, a spokesperson for the National Association of Chain Drug Stores testified that "corporate drugstores are experiencing approximately $480 million in losses due to employee pilferage" and that the internal and external losses had nearly reached "the limit most of our companies can tolerate."[38] Polygraph advocates went on to extol the merits of the polygraph examination as an important tool in identifying security risks. In the 1987 hearings, the list of organizations on record as opposed to legislation restricting employers' use of the polygraph had grown; it now included the National Association of Showroom Merchandisers, the National Automatic Merchandising Association, the National Grocers Association, the National Mass Retailing Institute, the National Retail Merchants Association, the National Tire Dealers and Retreaders Association, the National Wholesale Druggists' Association, and the Securities Industry Association.

In debates about information privacy, communication privacy, and psychological privacy, the groups and organizations who benefited from new technologies realized they would be disadvantaged by privacy protections. In opposing legislation, they defined their interests in terms of ideas with broad public support — government efficiency, effective law enforcement, and honesty and productivity in the work force. Although these groups and organizations were able to call upon public ideas to support their interests, their remarks to congressional committees frequently revealed that their real motivation was concern for their particular interests and the burdens that privacy protections would place on those interests. Indeed, when questions arose about the actual benefits that resulted from new technological applications such as computer matching and wiretapping, it became apparent that the public ideas were used most often to mask a lack of empirical support for the claims groups and organizations were making.

The Role of the Policy Community

In each of the three areas of privacy and technology policy, the development of a policy community that supported passage of legislation and monitored implementation and evaluation was critical in mobilizing support and keeping the issue on the congressional agenda. That such policy communities or issue networks exist in a number of policy areas and exert considerable influence over policy making in those areas is not disputed. What is somewhat less well understood is how these communities develop. In the case of privacy and technology, by the late 1970s an identifiable policy community existed. By looking back at the 1960s, it is possible to find the genesis of the policy community and then to trace its development and changes.

The Social Science Research Council's mid-1960s proposal to establish a National Data Center provided the first congressional opportunity to discuss and debate privacy issues. The hearings of the Senate Subcommittee on Administrative Practice and Procedure, chaired by Senator Edward Long, drew upon a number of people who eventually became members of a privacy community. Arthur R. Miller, at that time a law professor at the University of Michigan, testified about the effects of computers on individual privacy. He later wrote in the preface to his 1971 book *The Assault on Privacy*: "Since that first appearance before a congressional subcommittee I have slowly been devoured by the issue."[39] The hearings of Senator Long's Subcommittee on Administrative Practice and Procedure in March and June 1966, of Representative Cornelius Gallagher's Special Subcommittee on Invasion of Privacy in July 1966, and of Senator Sam Ervin's Subcommittee on Constitutional Rights in 1971 provided the first public forums for an incipient privacy community. Congressional hearings are the product of much behind-the-scenes work by congressional staff, interest-group members, academic researchers, and journalists. In this case, a number of people were important sources of ideas and support, including Marcia MacNaughton and John Davidson, members of the Ervin subcommittee staff; Alan Westin, who was in the process of completing his book *Privacy and Freedom*; Hope Eastman, acting director of the American Civil Liberty Union's (ACLU) Washington, D.C., office; and Arthur Miller. The perspectives of these individuals emphasized the constitutional rights and civil liberties aspects of the changes precipitated by new technologies. This perspective, however, was not solely an individual rights perspective but also stressed the need for accountability in government operations.

Computer specialists concerned about security also joined the privacy policy community in the late 1960s, especially in the area of information privacy. Privacy and security were viewed as two sides of the same coin, with the interest in individual privacy seen as compatible with the interest in system integrity that was of concern to computer system users and managers. A secure computer system was thought to be one that would limit the misuse of personal information. Willis Ware of the RAND Corporation was chair of the HEW's Secretary's Advisory Committee on Automated Data Systems, which developed the Code of Fair Information Practices. Lewis Branscomb, an IBM vice president and chief scientist, testified on privacy and data security issues. Alan Westin and Michael Baker received funding from the Russell Sage Foundation in 1968 to conduct a study for the National Academy of Sciences on computers, record keeping, and privacy.

The Westin and Baker study brought several individuals into the privacy community, many of whom are still active. Lance Hoffman, then an assistant professor of electrical engineering and computer sciences at the University of California at Berkeley, was a staff associate of the project; he is now a professor at George Washington University and was chair of the Second Annual Conference on Computers, Freedom, and Privacy held in Washington, D.C., in March 1992. Robert Belair, a student at Columbia University Law School, was a research assistant for the Westin and Baker study and continues to be an active member of the privacy community as a Washington, D.C., attorney. Kenneth Laudon, then a graduate student at Columbia studying with Alan Westin, participated in site visits and later worked on the OTA study on criminal history records and authored *Dossier Society*.

Many of these individuals testified at congressional hearings prior to the passage of the Privacy Act, most notably, Alan Westin, Arthur Miller, Hope Eastman, and John Shattuck of the ACLU. The hearings also provided an opportunity for new individuals to take more active roles in the privacy community. For example, testifying at the 1971 and 1974 hearings of Ervin's Subcommittee on Constitutional Rights was Christopher Pyle, a former captain in army intelligence and a doctoral student working with Alan Westin at Columbia University. Pyle brought attention to the army's surveillance of civilian political activity in the United States, which he traced to the year 1965 — "the year of the Watts riots, the 'black power' movement, and the establishment of the Army Intelligence Command."[40] For the June 1974 joint Senate hearings,[41] G. Russell Pipe, formerly an aide to Representative Barry M. Goldwater, Jr., who chaired the Republican Privacy Task Force, submitted a statement for the record supporting the Senate bill (s. 3418). He went on to establish and edit *Transnational Data Reports*, a publication that reports on information policies and practices throughout the world.

Discussion and passage of the Privacy Act of 1974 served as a catalyst of media interest. A few journalists, such as David Burnham of the *New York Times*, developed an ongoing interest in privacy issues and followed congressional activity in the area. Burnham became active in the privacy community and authored *The Rise of the Computer State*. Additionally, the editors of two specialized newsletters on the issue of privacy, Robert Ellis Smith of *Privacy Journal*, founded in 1974, and Evan Hendricks of *Privacy Times*, begun in 1981, provided sustained coverage of privacy issues and facilitated the maintenance and growth of the privacy community.

The establishment of the Privacy Protection Study Commission (PPSC) in 1976 provided a forum where the privacy community could meet, energized those who identified with the issue, and brought several new people into the policy community. Although the focus of the commission's study was on records, it looked broadly at a range of types of record keeping — in education, medicine, the credit industry, and government — and at a range of privacy issues, including the polygraph. The vice chair of the PPSC was Willis Ware from the RAND Corporation, who was formerly head of the HEW advisory committee. Carole Parsons, who had played a key role in writing the report of the HEW advisory committee, was executive director. Two House members with privacy interests — Barry Goldwater, who headed the Republican Task Force on Privacy, and Edward Koch, who was active in polygraph issues as well as information privacy issues — were also on the PPSC. Alan Westin served as a special consultant, and James Rule and Russell Pipe also served as consultants.

In addition, the PPSC brought together a number of new individuals who later continued to be active in the privacy community. Ronald Plesser served as general counsel for the commission and later organized the ABA's efforts in the early 1980s on behalf of privacy; he currently often lobbies for those interested in getting access to information but has also retained ties to the privacy community in the United States and internationally. Fred Weingarten was a professional staff member of the PPSC on detail from the National Science Foundation; he went on to become program director of the Communications and Information Technology Program at the OTA during the time that the agency conducted a number of studies on a range of privacy and technology issues. Arthur Bushkin was a

PPSC project manager responsible for assessing the Privacy Act and later participated in the privacy initiative in the Carter administration. Lois Alexander was on detail from the Social Security Administration and was a project manager for research and statistics.

In the late 1970s, the OTA began a study of the societal impact of national information systems that was requested by the Senate and House Judiciary committees and the House Post Office and Civil Service Committee. As part of this assessment, the OTA established an advisory panel for its reports on national information systems[42] and electronic message systems.[43] Members of the panel included a number of people who had been actively involved in information privacy issues before — Arthur Miller, Russell Pipe, James Rule, Willis Ware, and Alan Westin. Lance Hoffman served as a member of a special advisory panel on information technology. As part of the assessment, the OTA also established an advisory panel for its report on computerized criminal history systems.[44] This panel was chaired by Arthur Miller and included as members other recognized members of the information privacy community: Jerry Berman, legislative counsel for the ACLU; Lance Hoffman; Christopher Pyle; and James Rule. Marcia MacNaughton served as director of the criminal history systems study from October 1978 to July 1980, and Kenneth Laudon was a contractor for the study.

The symbolically important year of 1984 provided a focus for the general privacy community. The ABA, the ACLU, and the Public Interest Computer Association (PICA) worked together to sponsor a series of meetings, which were funded primarily by the Benton Foundation. Ron Plesser and George Trubow represented the ABA; John Shattuck and Jerry Berman represented the ACLU. The PICA was largely the creation of Marc Rotenberg, then an intern with the ACLU's Privacy and Technology Project and later head of the Washington, D.C., office of the Computer Professionals for Social Responsibility (CPSR). These conferences not only provided a forum where members of the privacy community could meet and discuss legislative proposals and strategies but also broadened the focus of the privacy community. Until then, the general privacy community had largely concentrated its attention on information privacy, a perspective that had drawn them into most privacy issues up to that time because information and records were a component of other privacy issues such as psychological testing and polygraphs. With the merging of computer and telecommunication technologies in the 1980s, the general privacy community moved actively into the area of communication privacy.

An international dimension was added to the privacy community in the 1980s. International issues had entered policy discussions in the 1970s when private sector firms lobbied against their inclusion in the Privacy Act in part because of concerns about the "free flow of information" and "transborder data flows." Individuals with international concerns had not been identified with the privacy community, with the exception of Russell Pipe, who monitored privacy developments in other countries as head of the Transnational Data Reporting Service. In the 1980s, as criticisms of the Privacy Act and its implementation mounted, interest in the European model of data protection, with oversight by an advisory or regulatory body, grew in the United States. David Flaherty, a former student of Alan Westin's who had written a book on privacy in colonial times and was a professor at the University of Western Ontario conducting research on privacy regulation in a number of countries, testified at House hearings in 1984 about the need for such a body in the United States. Flaherty became an active member of the privacy community in this country as well as internationally and serves as the information and privacy commissioner in the province of British Columbia, Canada.

In the mid-1980s, the OTA began a study on the civil liberties and congressional oversight implications of federal agency use of new information technologies. This study provided another opportunity for the privacy community to become formally involved in policy formulation. Members of the advisory panel included several members of the privacy community: Jerry Berman of the ACLU; David Flaherty; George Trubow, director of the Center for Information Technology and Privacy Law at the John Marshall Law School; and Alan Westin. Additionally, two workshops on privacy issues were held, one on electronic record systems and the other on electronic surveillance. Participants in the workshop on electronic record systems included two longtime members of the privacy community, Robert Belair and James Rule. Two federal agency representatives at the workshop — William Cavaney of the Defense Privacy Board and Robert Veeder of the Office of Information and Regulatory Affairs at the OMB — had also been actively involved in the privacy community following passage of the Privacy Act of 1974. The workshop on electronic surveillance also attracted a number of members of the privacy community, including Gary Marx, Ronald Plesser, Christopher Pyle, and James Rule.

The privacy community has been relatively stable in its perspective and strategy for over twenty-five years, reflecting shared values, shared concerns, and shared problem definition. It has been nonhierarchical and open in its membership, easily integrating new members. Within the privacy community, individuals assume a variety of roles, including advocate, expert, and facilitator. The ACLU has been and continues to be the most prominent advocate. Since the 1960s, it has maintained an active interest in privacy and technology issues; organized itself, both at the national and state level, around privacy; and devoted financial and personnel resources to privacy issues. Alan Westin was the creator and first chair of the ACLU Privacy Committee. In the Washington, D.C., office, three individuals — John Shattuck, legislative director from 1980 to 1984; Jerry Berman, legislative director and head of the Privacy and Technology Project from 1984 to 1988; and Janlori Goldman, head of the Privacy and Technology Project from 1988 to 1993 — were not only privacy advocates but also were instrumental in building a policy community. In 1988 Jerry Berman left the ACLU to work on policy issues for the Electronic Frontier Foundation (EFF), and in 1993 Janlori Goldman brought the Privacy and Technology Project to the EFF. Berman and Goldman formed a new organization, the Center for Democracy and Technology, in 1995. Since the 1980s, the CPSR, through the activities of Marc Rotenberg, has also been an important advocate of privacy interests, gaining the support of both technology users and some providers of computer and communication technologies and services. In 1994 Rotenberg formed a new organization, the Electronic Privacy Information Center.

Prior to the passage of legislation and the accumulation of records of the uses of new technologies and their effects on privacy, no "experts" on privacy existed. During this period, advocates were the key actors. However, over time several of these actors became recognized experts on legal issues, implementation strategies, and likely effects of new technologies. A number of academics who wrote about privacy in the 1960s and were instrumental in getting privacy and technology issues on the public agenda and then in testifying and crafting policy alternatives have become privacy experts. Most notable of this group is Alan Westin; Arthur Miller and James Rule are also important. Several lawyers are recognized as privacy experts, especially Ronald Plesser and Robert Belair. A number of computer scientists, such as Willis Ware and Lance Hoffman, are regarded as privacy and security experts. Knowledge of the international scene has enabled some people to play the role of privacy expert, especially David Flaherty and Russell Pipe. The establishment of a group of privacy experts has brought stability and continuity to the issue, as well as a certain amount of legitimacy and credibility.

Several members of the press have played important roles in facilitating the development of a privacy community and in keeping privacy initiatives on the public agenda. The newsletters of Evan Hendricks and Robert Ellis Smith are very important in reaching the community concerned about privacy. Within the daily press, David Burnham was an important player during the time that he was a reporter for the *New York Times*. In addition, John Markoff of the *New York Times* and Michael Miller of the *Wall Street Journal* have been important in reporting on privacy issues.

Congressional staff members have also been important members of the policy community and have helped to facilitate the development of new policy initiatives and to provide opportunities for bringing the privacy community together. Most important among these have been Robert Gellman of the House Information, Justice, Transportation, and Agriculture Subcommittee of the Committee on Government Operations; James Dempsey of the Subcommittee on Constitutional Rights of the House Judiciary Committee; John Podesta, Anne Harkins, and Cathy Russell of the Senate Law and Technology Subcommittee of the Judiciary Committee; Mary Gerwin of the Subcommittee on Oversight of Government Management of the Senate Committee on Governmental Affairs; David Beier and Deborah Leavy of the Subcommittee on Courts, Civil Liberties, and the Administration of Justice of the House Judiciary Committee; and Steve Metalitz of the Subcommittee on Patents, Copyrights, and Trademarks of the Senate Committee on the Judiciary.

Within the privacy community, personal relationships are critical; the policy network is cemented by interpersonal relationships rather than by institutional links. Congressional hearings, OTA studies, executive agency committees, and privately funded workshops and conferences provide important opportunities for the privacy community to meet, discuss ideas and policy proposals, and attract new members. Concerned that a focal point for their ongoing activities and interests was missing, several members of the privacy community established the U.S. Privacy Council in 1991. The council was formed at a conference entitled "Computers, Freedom, and Privacy" in March 1991, which brought new people into the privacy community and energized existing members. In the early 1990s, two other organizations brought new groups and individuals into the privacy community. The Center for Social and Legal Research, headed by Alan Westin, started a monthly newsletter, *Privacy and American Business*, to inform the business community about privacy-related issues and to develop a dialogue about common business interests in privacy. In 1994 the first annual Conference on Privacy and American

Business was held in Washington, D.C. The international dimension of several privacy issues, as well as the similarities among privacy problems that different countries confront, generated the formation of Privacy International by Australian Simon Davies. It publishes the quarterly newsletter, *International Privacy Bulletin*.

Realization of the importance of coalitions is the result of experiences in passing legislation. By trial and error, the privacy community has learned the importance of building coalitions with other groups that have related interests in promoting legislation that protects privacy. Over the thirty or so years of policy making covered in this book, somewhat different groups have worked together to protect information privacy, communication privacy, and psychological privacy. These groups exhibit many of the characteristics of what Paul Sabatier terms "advocacy coalitions," which are composed of "people from a variety of positions (elected and agency officials, interest group leaders, researchers) who share a particular belief system — i.e., a set of basic values, causal assumptions, and problem perceptions — and who show a non-trivial degree of coordinated activity over time."[45]

In the case of information privacy, especially government collection and use of personal information, privacy advocates were the core of the advocacy coalition, working almost alone for passage of legislation and monitoring implementation of legislation. No other group or interest aligned itself directly with the information privacy community. Good-government groups — such as Common Cause, the OMB Watch, and the Public Interest Research Group — often worked on the periphery of the information privacy community and served on advisory boards or testified in support of information privacy legislation, but these groups were already largely overextended. In general, the executive branch was opposed to privacy legislation; therefore, an advocacy coalition between the privacy community and federal agencies could not be forged. However, in formulating and later implementing the Privacy Act of 1974, some federal agency officials — including John Fanning and Hugh O'Neill at HEW, William Cavaney at the Department of Defense, and Lois Alexander at the Social Security Administration — were interested in privacy and played a role in generating some agency interest in the issue. A few people at the OMB also cared about privacy and acted as advocates within the OMB and facilitators between the agencies and the privacy community. In the 1980s, welfare rights organizations were concerned about computer matching, but instead of joining in an advocacy coalition for passage of federal legislation, they worked through the courts and at the state level.

In information privacy issues, the narrow privacy community was oftentimes strengthened by outside events. In almost all cases in which
Congress did pass legislation (see figure 4.2 for a brief summary), a critical event focused attention on the issue and opened the "policy window"[46] for serious policy formulation and adoption. For example, the
1974 Privacy Act was in part a response to the misuses of government
information that were revealed during the Watergate scandal; the 1978
Right to Financial Privacy Act was a response to the Supreme Court's
1976 ruling in *United States v. Miller* that bank records were the property
of banks and that individuals have no property interest in those records;
the current attempt to strengthen the 1970 Fair Credit Reporting Act can
be attributed to the *Business Week* report that one of its reporters easily
gained access to the credit history of the vice president; and the adoption
of the 1988 Video Privacy Protection Act followed a Washington, D.C.,
paper's publication of a list of the videotapes rented by Robert Bork, then
a nominee for the Supreme Court.

In the case of communication privacy, the politics leading to passage of
Title III of the Omnibus Crime Control and Safe Streets Act do not reflect
any strong alliances between privacy advocates and other groups. Labor
was opposed to wiretapping and aligned itself with privacy interests, but
the community was largely dominated by civil liberties advocates and
constitutional scholars. The executive branch, especially law enforcement
and national security agencies, was opposed to legislation. There were
few natural allies for the privacy community to reach. At that time, the
wire telecommunications network was a monopoly controlled by AT&T.
Some AT&T executives, such as William Caming, recognized that ensuring the privacy of the AT&T network was in AT&T's interest as well as in
the interests of privacy advocates. But AT&T generally had been able to
deal directly with government officials in voicing its interests and concerns about privacy.

By the 1980s, with the breakup of AT&T and the introduction of new
communication providers, industry interests in providing privacy in communication services had changed. Jerry Berman of the ACLU realized that
the new communication providers were potential allies in supporting a
revision of Title III and that their support could be critical in winning
passage of a new law. After passage of the ECPA, he was quoted as saying
that he realized legislation "would never get off the ground until we got a
new coalition. As long as privacy groups were just talking to each other,
nothing was going to happen. We thought business could be convinced
[to get involved] if we could show them it was in their own economic

interest."[47] In an effort to build a coalition with industry, the ACLU held two conferences in June 1984 and January 1985. As we saw in chapter 5, these conferences were successful in bringing on board a number of important industry groups, such as the Electronic Mail Association and ADAPSO. In a law review article examining the passage of the ECPA, the bill's primary sponsor, Representative Robert Kastenmeier, and his two chief aides, Deborah Leavy and David Beier, noted that when the ECPA was first introduced, it had little chance of passage because it furthered privacy and civil liberties interests at the expense of law enforcement interests. They argued that "the extra ingredient that enabled the bill to pass was the strong support of the business community, including both providers and users of new communications technologies."[48]

In 1991 the Justice Department proposed that the Comprehensive Counter-Terrorism Act (s. 266; later revised as s. 1241) include a provision that would require communication providers to furnish a "trapdoor" to facilitate government eavesdropping. Section 2201 of that bill stated: "It is the sense of Congress that providers of electronic communications services and manufacturers of electronic communications services equipment shall ensure that communications systems permit the government to obtain the plain-text contents of voice, data, and other communications when appropriately authorized by law." In response, the industry-privacy coalition reemerged to lobby against the requirement. A conference was held in June 1991 on cryptography and privacy,[49] sponsored by the CPSR, the Electronic Frontier Foundation, and RSA Data Security. RSA had initiated the meeting because of its concern that the proposed requirement would compromise its efforts to market an encryption technique that gave those initiating communications, by voice or data, control over the security of their messages.[50] The privacy-industry coalition was successful in gaining the removal of the Justice Department proposal from the final omnibus anticrime legislation that passed Congress.

In the area of psychological privacy, the advocacy coalition that was successful in passing the Employee Polygraph Protection Act of 1988 was quite broad based, including groups that had come on board over an extended time period. Part of the reason for the slowness in bringing about legislative action was the lack of strong leadership within the coalition. The ACLU had been concerned about this issue since the 1960s. Its activities concerning polygraphs, however, were not integrated into its Privacy and Technology Project at the Washington, D.C., office but were directed largely from the New York City office. The American Psychological Association (APA) had also been concerned about polygraphs and privacy since the 1960s but sought to prevent criticisms of the polygraph from becoming criticisms of psychological testing in general. The APA was rather cautious in its activities and was not inclined to adopt a leadership role in opposing the polygraph. From a scientific perspective, a number of people were critical of the validity or accuracy of the polygraph and their voices were heard often throughout the 1970s and early 1980s. But, again, they were unlikely to become leaders in an advocacy coalition. It was not until the unions became actively involved in the mid-1980s that opposition to the polygraph coalesced. Their leadership and the focus of the opposition on employment opportunities provided the sustained momentum necessary for passage of legislation. As we saw in chapter 6, the Employee Polygraph Protection Act was the only legislation backed by organized labor that was enacted in the 100th Congress. A somewhat similar coalition of union leaders and privacy advocates, again primarily from the New York ACLU, has continued to work on issues of employee monitoring and privacy.

In general, the privacy community has not only grown in size during the last twenty-five years but has also learned the importance of building broader coalitions in order to effect legislative change. This strategy, which was first consciously applied to lobbying efforts for the ECPA, is now viewed among many in the privacy community as the way to get legislation passed. This strategy is reflected in the successful efforts to delete requirements damaging to privacy interests from the anticrime bill and, perhaps more importantly, in the current attempt to amend the Fair Credit Reporting Act. The ACLU has taken a leadership role in forging a coalition of consumer groups — including the National Consumers Union, the Consumers Federation of America, and the Public Interest Research Group — and industry representatives who will work together in lobbying Congress.

Members of the privacy community recognize that pursuing a strategy of forming coalitions may involve dangers, especially the possibility that privacy interests will be diluted by compromises. To some extent, the debate is between "purists" and "pragmatists," with the pragmatists arguing for the necessity of forming coalitions if legislation is the goal. Most members of the privacy community, at this time, are comfortable, though cautious, about the coalition strategy. The continued success of this strategy hinges on the perceived strength of privacy interests. With public opinion polls reflecting great public concern about privacy, especially involving consumer issues, the privacy community is in an advantageous position in forming coalitions and in advocating a central place for privacy values within those coalitions.

The Role of Policy Entrepreneurs

In the areas of privacy and technology policy examined in this book, constituency pressure, or an "electoral connection,"[51] does not provide an explanation for why a member of Congress chooses to champion privacy issues. The question remains, therefore, as to why some members of Congress — such as Senators William Cohen, Sam Ervin, Orrin Hatch, Edward Kennedy, Patrick Leahy, and Charles Mathias and Representatives Don Edwards, Glenn English, Cornelius Gallagher, Robert Kastenmeier, Edward Koch, and Pat Williams — adopted leadership positions on privacy-related issues. The answer is not simple; instead, a number of factors affect members' behavior.

Discussions with members and staff and an analysis of legislative histories suggest that a member is brought to privacy issues not because of a commitment to the importance of the value of privacy but because the privacy issues are related to broader issue areas with which a particular member identifies. Senator Ervin, chair of the Constitutional Rights Subcommittee of the Judiciary Committee and an important leader in early policy formulation involving both computerized databases and polygraphs, had a deep personal concern for protecting constitutional rights and pointed out many due process problems associated with computerized databases and polygraphs. Indeed, Senator Ervin reportedly resisted categorizing these concerns as "privacy" issues, preferring instead to emphasize due process; he argued that individuals had the right to know the uses of information about themselves and to be able to respond to interpretations of that information. Somewhat similarly, other members of Judiciary Committee subcommittees — Senator Russell Long, chair of the Administrative Practice and Procedure Subcommittee, and Robert Kastenmeier, chair of the Subcommittee on Courts, Civil Liberties, and the Administration of Justice — were opposed to the arbitrary use of the police power of government and approached privacy issues from that perspective. McCarthy era excesses and fear of the creation of a "national security state" were important factors in attracting Representative Kastenmeier to the issue of surveillance and privacy. Senator Cohen approached privacy and computer matching as an issue of the accountability of government agencies in dealing with citizens. The polygraph issue was ultimately resolved when key labor supporters, especially Representative Williams and Senator Kennedy, brought their perspective of employee rights to the abuses generated by the use of lie detectors.

It is not privacy per se that fuels the interest of a member of Congress in a particular privacy and technology issue but the fact that the privacy value fits within a broader conceptual or policy framework with which a member is comfortable. Within the confines of their subcommittee or committee jurisdiction, members of Congress do regard a commitment to privacy as "good public policy," although they do not see it as enhancing reelection or influence within the chamber, to use Richard Fenno's terms.[52] But members do not identify themselves with privacy issues in general. For example, those members interested in passage of the Electronic Communications Privacy Act were not active in congressional debates on polygraph legislation or computer-matching legislation and vice versa. As one staff member commented, "There is not a necessary carry over among issues on the basis of privacy." The fragmentation of interest in privacy was not as apparent in the early 1960s when privacy issues were first placed on the public agenda. At that time, several general hearings were held on privacy invasions. By the 1980s, congressional interest in privacy had fragmented.

This fragmentation is explained in large part by the committee and subcommittee structure of the modern Congress. One of the factors that influences members' choice of committee assignments is their intellectual or substantive policy interests. Committee jurisdictions provide an opportunity for a member of Congress to develop interest in and leadership for privacy-related issues, but those jurisdictions also place limitations on a member's interests. For example, in the mid-1980s, Representative Don Edwards, as chair of the Judiciary Committee's Civil and Constitutional Rights Subcommittee, conducted oversight hearings on privacy and criminal justice records. At the same time, Representative Kastenmeier, as chair of the Judiciary Committee's Subcommittee on Courts, Civil Liberties, and the Administration of Justice, was working for passage of the ECPA, and Representative Robert Wise, as chair of the Government Information, Justice, and Agriculture Subcommittee of the Committee on Government Operations, was conducting hearings on public opinion surveys about privacy and current changes in organizational information practices. Also, Representative Williams, as chair of the Subcommittee on Employment Opportunities of the House Education and Labor Committee, was working on the Employee Polygraph Protection Act. These four members did not directly discuss the common elements in their legislative and oversight endeavors—although their staffs did communicate, especially the Judiciary Committee's subcommittee staffs. Nor did they directly solicit each other's support for the bills they had introduced. Nor did these members testify or offer statements in support of the privacy-related initiatives of their House or full-committee colleagues. Senate and House colleagues with jurisdiction over an issue worked more closely together and offered statements or testimony in support of legislation in the other chamber.

As in other policy areas, some element of committee or subcommittee rivalry exists in the privacy area. The desire to protect committee and/or subcommittee jurisdictions led some committees to hold hearings or take some action out of fear that the issue might be redefined away from them. For example, in the 1960s and 1970s, jurisdictional infighting occurred between the Senate Judiciary and Governmental Affairs committees regarding who had primary ownership of the issue. According to Morris Ogul, fierce jockeying for control of the issue of personality testing also took place between Senator Ervin's Subcommittee on Constitutional Rights and Representative Gallagher's Special Subcommittee on the Invasion of Privacy. Ogul reported that an attempt to coordinate the two committees' activities failed: the subcommittees "tried to resolve their problems in terms of scheduling hearings and so forth by having one staff meeting. It broke up into a debate as to who got there first, and whose issue it was. It was not fruitful to continue these discussions because these problems simply could not be solved. So what happened was that each committee went its own way and held hearings from different foci about the same time."[53]

Jurisdictional questions continue in some areas because the connection between civil liberties and organizational practices is inherently of interest to the Judiciary committees as well as to committees with substantive jurisdiction over those areas. But this sharing of interest does not have to develop into rivalry. Representative Kastenmeier, for example, pointed out that he was pleased to have other committees, such as the Banking and Currency Committee, handle issues such as credit privacy, because those committees were not as likely to encounter ideological issues that surfaced when the primary focus was civil liberties.

In all three areas of privacy and technology policy, staff members played an important role in initiating interest in the issue and then, and perhaps more importantly, in keeping it alive across Congresses and changes in committee and subcommittee leadership and membership. This is especially true in the area of government information, where the key staff person on the House subcommittee, Robert Gellman, has been with the subcommittee since 1977, through four different subcommittee chairs — Richardson Preyer, Robert Wise, Glenn English, and Gary Condit. Much of the privacy work of that subcommittee can be described as "staff driven." On the other subcommittees, more active synergy appears to exist between the staff and members of Congress. Members and staff work together collectively and reenergize each other periodically on privacy issues. A pattern that Ogul observed on the Special Subcommittee on the Invasion of Privacy appears to be fairly typical: staff members reflected Representative Gallagher's "energy and concern with invasion of privacy and, in some cases, even prodded the chair into greater activity concerning invasion of privacy."[54]

In general, staff members develop a real concern about the privacy interest — they begin to care about the issue — and become involved in the privacy community and in forming advocacy coalitions. Although members of Congress do not deal directly with one another on different privacy issues, their staffs are likely to do so. Interaction occurs frequently between the staffs of the Judiciary and Government Operations committees in both houses. Staff members concerned with workplace privacy issues from the Education and Labor committees are not as likely to look to the Judiciary or Government Operations committees for support or advice but may consult staff of the civil service committees, who have dealt with similar issues in the federal workplace.

Member interest, committee or subcommittee jurisdiction, and a willing staff set the stage for a member to exercise leadership on a privacy issue, but a link outside the chamber is necessary to push a member to adopt a leadership role and become a policy entrepreneur for passage of legislation. This link is supplied most often by evidence of the very real effect of technological changes on people. Anecdotal accounts of how people's livelihood or family were affected by revelations of personal details about their lives have been very important in getting the attention of members of Congress. Senator Ervin initially got involved in the privacy area because of the thousands of complaints that he, as committee chair, got on a range of issues, including polygraphs, background checks, and census questions. These complaints led him to convene hearings in 1968 and to question such activities within federal agencies. As a result of these hearings, Elliot Richardson, as secretary of HEW, established the advisory committee that developed the Code of Fair Information Practices.

Similarly, Representative Gallagher became interested in the use of polygraphs because of the case of a seventeen-year-old girl who "was subjected to humiliating questions about sexual matters when she applied for a job with the National Security Agency as a typist."[55] For Senator Cohen, computer matches of bank records in Massachusetts illustrated the threats to privacy posed by computer matching and the scale of the potential problem. Senator Barbara Boxer's interest in introducing the Driver's Privacy Protection Act of 1993 was provoked by the murder of actress Rebecca Schaeffer by someone who had stalked her using information from motor vehicle files. On the same issue, Representative James Moran's interest was generated by an antiabortion group's use of motor vehicle records to target victims.

In organizing hearings on privacy issues, congressional staff always try to find individuals who have been adversely affected by information use, wiretaps, or polygraphs. These real-life experiences have been critical in making the issue real to members of Congress. In reflecting on his experience as an advocate for privacy legislation, Alan Westin also makes this point: "When I write an article or testify before Congress, if I can describe one or several such real cases of mistreatment or abuse, real people whose situations are compelling and will stand up under close scrutiny, that is worth oceans of passionate rhetoric in affecting policy-makers.... I think one reason for the failure of Congress to pass a federal medical privacy law was that the committees did not come up with real-world cases and vignettes of people whose privacy interests as patients had been abused."[56] It is interesting that in the 1990s debate about medical privacy, a member of Congress, Representative Nydia Velazquez (D-N.Y.), whose health records had been leaked during a political campaign, stepped forward to testify at a congressional hearing and provide a powerful real-life story for her colleagues.

The human element frequently focuses the attention of committee and subcommittee members on the issue and commits them to take action. But the human element is not always available or necessarily attractive. In some cases, those whose privacy was invaded by polygraphs, wiretaps, or computer matches were bootleggers, drug dealers, liars, or welfare cheats. Another difficulty with developing support and leadership was that, especially in cases involving computer matching or wiretapping, the subjects often did not know they were "victims" or that their privacy had been invaded in some way. It was therefore harder to find credible witnesses for those hearings. David Flaherty notes that part of the difficulty in achieving legislative success is that it is "very difficult to demonstrate need in the commonsense way that Congress requires. This is the particular bane of the sectoral approach to data protection, since it is so hard to document the necessary horror stories without holding full-scale investigations of a particular sector."[57]

Although anecdotal accounts of privacy invasions may not provide the best empirical basis for policy formulation, they not only influence members of Congress to take leadership positions on privacy issues but also generate press interest in privacy and technology. The public does not vote on the basis of these issues, but people are attuned to them and the press considers them "newsworthy." Technology gives the issue an element of being "new and different"; the real or potential horror stories of privacy invasions give it a human-interest angle. The press, then, is likely to cover these issues when Congress holds hearings or debates legislation. And its coverage is likely to take the perspective of the individual against the technology. Morris Ogul reported that all three members of the Special Subcommittee on the Invasion of Privacy "received much publicity, many requests to address groups, and other political bonuses from their work on the subcommittee."[58] This was also the case for members of Congress active on privacy issues in the 1970s and 1980s.

The visibility and symbolism of the privacy issue and the press interest sustain member interest and attention. For a member of Congress, as Ogul notes, "here was a series of visible, emotionally charged issues that provided psychic payoffs, if not concrete ones, from much of the attentive public."[59] These advantages also result in policy payoffs, as demonstrated by the relatively quick passage of the Video Privacy Protection Act following the release and publication of Robert Bork's video rentals. Although anecdotal accounts may become less compelling during the course of the policy process, they get the public's attention and often provide the stimulus for congressional hearings and introduction of legislation. A good example is the policy interest that resulted after a pregnant woman who had been seen entering a clinic where abortions were performed was harassed by an antiabortion group, which had gotten her address through the Department of Motor Vehicles. Congressional hearings and the introduction of a bill to restrict access to motor vehicle records quickly followed press reports of this incident.

A related factor that may motivate a member of Congress to advocate privacy issues is that these issues are unlikely to provoke opposition from other members of Congress or from future electoral challengers. The results of public opinion surveys demonstrate that the "potential preferences," to use Douglas Arnold's term,[60] of constituents are proprivacy. Although leadership on privacy issues is not likely to have a direct electoral connection, it is an issue for which electoral opposition is unlikely and which can be used to a legislator's electoral advantage. A legislator's proprivacy vote is unlikely to generate constituency criticism. As one of the members of the Special Subcommittee on Invasion of Privacy stated, "There are surely no political minuses in this committee work."[61] But an antiprivacy vote, or one that could be interpreted as opposing individual rights, could be used against a legislator by proprivacy interest groups or future electoral challengers. This is one reason why groups opposed to privacy-related issues are so interested in redefining them; they have to be redefined so that members can vote against them without worrying about the "potential privacy preferences" of their constituents.

Congressional leadership for much of the policy making on issues of privacy and technology thus appears to follow a different pattern from the "policy entrepreneurship" model that explains congressional passage of most reform legislation of the 1970s.[62] In James Q. Wilson's model of "entrepreneurial politics," a skilled entrepreneur "can mobilize latent public sentiment . . . put the opponents of the plan publicly on the defensive . . . and associate the legislation with widely shared values."[63] During the early course of policy making for these issues, several members of Congress, most notably Senator Ervin and Representatives Gallagher and Long, acted as policy entrepreneurs in getting privacy issues on the public agenda and played the roles that Wilson outlines. In the 1970s and 1980s, however, congressional leadership patterns were less closely aligned with the model Wilson outlined. For privacy-related issues, congressional leaders could not mobilize latent public sentiment, did not put opponents publicly on the defensive, and, in general, weakened the legislation's association with the value of privacy.

In the areas of privacy and technology policy, the leadership model is closer to the newer style of entrepreneurship identified by Burdett Loomis, whereby politicians "chair subcommittees and enter the increasingly important 'middle management' that is central to running the contemporary Congress."[64] As Loomis points out, few policy entrepreneurs "push for the acceptance of a truly new idea. Rather, they tend to endorse, repackage, or resurrect concepts and ideas that either come from the outside (for example, academia) or have previously circulated within the Congress. Policy entrepreneurs are often both patient and persistent as they reshape policy solutions to fit emerging political conditions."[65] In these cases of privacy and technology policy, persistence was critical to passage of legislation.

Congressional leaders played the role of policy brokers within Congress more than that of policy advocates mobilizing popular sentiments and putting the opponents on the defensive. This occurred, in part, because of leaders' political calculations that the interests opposed to privacy protections could not easily be put on the defensive — indeed, those supporting privacy were the ones put on the defensive. This parallels the conclusion that was reached earlier in discussing the role of ideas: on issues of privacy and technology, members of Congress cannot easily adopt roles that fit the traditional policy entrepreneur model but instead are constrained by the politics that the concept of privacy elicits.

Conclusion

In each area of privacy and technology policy examined here, similar scenarios occur. Policy proposals to protect privacy were initiated by members of Congress who served as chairs of committees or subcommittees with relevant jurisdiction. The executive branch — including both federal agencies and the president — opposed the policy initiatives. The courts might have played a more active role but chose to leave policy resolution to the elected branches. Public opinion supported protection of privacy but was not politically aware of proposed legislation or politically mobilized to advocate privacy. And political parties offered no active support or opposition, privacy issues being basically nonissues from a partisan perspective. Given this general scenario, it is not at all surprising that these issues were on the congressional agenda for years, if not decades, before Congress passed legislation. What is more surprising is that legislation did pass and in two of the three areas was subsequently amended to address changing technologies. The analysis presented here suggests why it has been so difficult to pass legislation to protect privacy and offers some insights into how political support can be mobilized for the formulation of policy to protect privacy.

The idea of privacy provided a weak basis for the formulation of public policy. This does not mean that ideas are unimportant in the policy process or that privacy is not an important value but merely that the presence of an idea is not enough to ensure policy resolution. Not every idea will succeed in bringing about policy initiatives. Deregulation and tax fairness as ideas worked; privacy did not. This analysis suggests that the legal and philosophical tradition of the idea of privacy constrained policy based on this idea. The definition of privacy as an individual right hampered policy formulation both because policy discussion often became dominated by lawyers debating the relevance of certain legal precedents and because it entailed the balancing of an individual right to privacy against other competing rights and values.

Once this occurred, policy formulation focused not on the idea or value of privacy but on how to balance competing interests. Opponents of privacy legislation did not attack privacy as an idea or value but instead emphasized the importance of a competing idea. In each of these cases, the competing idea had broad appeal — efficiency of government operations, law enforcement and national security, and reduction of theft and fraud in the workplace. The competing idea also supported the interests of those whose activities would be curtailed by privacy protections. In addition, the technological innovation that threatened privacy made it easier to achieve each of these goals. Once the policy debate focused on competing ideas and interests, those who perceived themselves as being adversely affected by privacy protections — government agencies, the law enforcement community, and employers — mobilized their resources. At this point, privacy was likely to lose.

Privacy advocates were most successful in achieving privacy legislation when they reached beyond the privacy policy communities to form advocacy coalitions with other groups. This was the case with the passage of the Electronic Communications Privacy Act and the Employee Polygraph Protection Act. In both of these cases, however, privacy became a secondary goal in policy formulation while protection of new industries and employment opportunities became of primary concern. This did not necessarily mean that privacy lost out or that privacy advocates were forced to make unattractive compromises. Instead, the privacy value was compatible with the other interest. In the case of efforts to reform government information practices, in which the formation of an advocacy coalition did not occur, privacy goals were weakened because of the need to compromise with efficiency interests. Increasingly, privacy advocates recognize the value of the strategy of forming advocacy coalitions and are using it in current attempts to amend the Fair Credit Reporting Act and to develop legislation to prevent threats to privacy by the information superhighway.

Because of the lack of public outrage about privacy invasions and electoral mobilization around privacy issues, privacy concerns were not high priorities for most members of Congress. But congressional leadership on issues for which there is no clear electoral support is essential if legislation is to pass. In these three cases, leadership came from members who chaired the subcommittees with relevant jurisdiction. They became active on these privacy issues not because of a previous interest in privacy but because the threat to privacy fit within a broader conceptual or policy framework with which the members identified. Once a member of Congress had a policy hook for the issue, staff interest and support were important in establishing ties to the privacy community and in sustaining the interest of the legislator.

The important conclusion to be drawn from this analysis of congressional policy making is that privacy as an idea or value did not provide the engine for policy change or the basis for political mobilization. Yet public opinion polls indicate that Americans do care about privacy and want to protect privacy in the face of technological change. Privacy is important to people. At the same time, privacy does not provide a meaning that sustains its importance through the policy process. It is not that privacy is unimportant, but that our current conception of privacy furnishes too narrow a basis from which to formulate public policy. The next chapter analyzes why privacy does not provide a good basis from which to develop policies and suggests an expanded understanding of the value of privacy, one that takes into account privacy's broader social importance.

Chapter 8

Privacy and the Common Good: Implications for Public Policy

Although privacy initially defined the policy issues discussed in this book, interests that benefited from uses of new technologies and invasions of privacy were able to redefine the issues. If a concerned policy community and congressional leadership had not existed, the legislation discussed in this book would not have been adopted; when legislation was adopted, however, it was far weaker than privacy advocates wanted. Does the course of legislative policy making mean that privacy is not important or valued in today's society? Survey data and anecdotal evidence indicate that privacy is increasingly important. The fact that privacy received broad public support but did not operate in public discourse in such a way as to elicit legislative interest in its protection presents something of a quandary. When a value fails to sustain legislative interest, there is a danger that it will disappear or be rendered meaningless on our political landscape. Indeed, some have heralded the death of privacy, generally placing the blame on technologies that threaten privacy.[1] By viewing these congressional debates through the lens of values, a different explanation is suggested. Privacy may be close to extinction, but not because of technology or lack of public concern; the reason may be a failure to conceptualize privacy in a way that sustains public interest and support.

The philosophical basis of privacy policy overemphasizes the importance of privacy to the individual and fails to recognize the broader social importance of privacy. This emphasis on privacy as an individual right or an individual interest provides a weak basis for formulating policy to protect privacy. When privacy is defined as an individual right, policy formulation entails a balancing of the individual right to privacy against a competing interest or right. In general, the competing interest is recognized as a social interest. For example, the police interest in law enforcement, the government interest in detecting fraud, and an employer's interest in securing an honest work force are discussed and defined as societal interests. It is also assumed that the individual has a stake in these societal interests. As a result, privacy has been on the defensive, with those alleging a privacy invasion bearing the burden of proving that a certain activity does indeed invade privacy and that the "social" benefit to be gained from the privacy invasion is less important than the individual harm incurred.

Once one recognizes the sources and effects of modern threats to "individual" privacy, the notion that privacy should be considered from a social perspective rather than solely from an individual perspective becomes apparent. Database surveillance, electronic eavesdropping, and polygraph testing are generally not techniques that individuals use in relation to other individuals. These techniques do not primarily affect individuals' relationships of friendship, love, and trust. Instead, these threats come from private and governmental organizations—the police, welfare agencies, credit agencies, banks, and employers—and affect all individuals' relationships to these organizations and all individuals' ability to get a job, credit, or insurance. In modern society, then, privacy pertains to relations between individuals and corporate or government organizations as well as to relations among individuals. When these organizations are part of the public realm, privacy concerns cross the boundary between public and private.

I argue that privacy is not only of value to the individual as an individual but also to society in general, and I suggest three bases for a social importance of privacy. The first two are normative bases that were identified in some of the earlier writing on privacy but have been overshadowed by an emphasis on the importance of privacy to the individual. A reconsideration of these social bases is especially important in light of the policy experiences that resulted from focusing on the importance of privacy to the individual. Privacy is a *common value* in that all individuals value some degree of privacy and have some common perceptions about privacy. Privacy is also a *public value* in that it has value not just to the individual as an individual or to all individuals in common but also to the democratic political system. The third basis for the social importance of privacy is derived from the theoretical literature in economics. Privacy is rapidly becoming a *collective value* in that technology and market forces are making it hard for any one person to have privacy without all persons having a similar minimum level of privacy.

It may be that *all* individual interests or rights are important to both individuals and society. But in the case of privacy, its importance to society has not been pursued while its importance to the individual has received much attention. Therefore, I have attempted to make explicit the social importance of privacy. My goal here is to reconsider the social or public importance of privacy, to introduce a conceptual framework for thinking about the social importance of privacy, and to discuss why the recognition of the social importance of privacy has implications for current policy debates involving privacy.

Most interests could be conceived as both individual interests and social interests. For example, "the *individual* interest in communicating one's ideas to others may also be stated as a *societal* interest in a diverse marketplace of ideas. Time, place, and manner limitations on expressive behavior may be based on a *governmental* interest in public safety or a *private* interest in unencumbered access to public facilities" (emphasis in original).[2] In previous discussions of privacy, however, more attention has been paid to the individual interest in privacy than to a societal or governmental interest. In charting the ways in which the importance of privacy might be conceived in broader terms, the point is not to denigrate privacy's importance to the individual but to explore a conceptual framework for privacy's social importance. Rethinking the importance of privacy in this way will change the definition of policy problems involving privacy and technology and provide a more convincing argument for formulating policy to protect privacy. But first I analyze why an emphasis on privacy as an individual interest and right has been a weak basis from which to formulate policy to protect privacy. This analysis establishes the importance of considering privacy from a broader social perspective.

Individual Privacy and Public Policy

As discussed in chapter 2, most legal and philosophical writing about privacy stresses the policy goal of protecting privacy because of its importance to the individual.[3] Generally, the importance of privacy is rooted in traditional liberal thinking—privacy inheres in the individual as an individual and is important to the individual for self-development or for the establishment of intimate or human relationships. Given that the philosophical justification for privacy rests largely on its importance to the individual as an individual, policy discussions about protecting privacy focus on the goal of protecting an individual value or interest. The result has been an emphasis on an atomistic individual and the legal protection of his or her rights.

But, as illustrated in congressional attempts to protect privacy, defining privacy primarily in terms of its importance to the individual and in terms of an individual right has served as a weak basis for public policy. There are three explanations for the weakness of individual privacy as a policy goal: it emphasizes the negative value of privacy; it establishes a conflict between the individual and society; and it fails to take into account the importance of large social and economic organizations.

Negative value. As was discussed in chapter 2, American legal and philosophical thinking on privacy as a specific value and right takes as its point of departure Samuel Warren and Louis Brandeis's 1890 *Harvard Law Review* article, in which they defined a "right to privacy" as the "the right to be let alone."[4] The Warren and Brandeis right to privacy was very much an individual right and a right from social intrusion. The view of privacy as the "right to be let alone" draws attention to the possible reasons why an individual might want to be let alone. Other than for the establishment of intimate relationships and the development of autonomy, the reason offered most often is to "hide" things the individual does not want known. In policy discussions, those opposed to privacy protections easily raise suspicions about the reasons individuals want privacy. Two possibilities seem to follow from these suspicions. First, if an individual does not have anything to hide, then privacy would not be of value to him or her. Second, if the individual does have something to hide, the question is whether it should remain private or whether others need to know about it. This second possibility has brought much attention to what is sometimes referred to as the "pathology of privacy." H. W. Arndt, for example, writes: "The cult of privacy rests on an individualist conception of society, not merely in the innocent and beneficial sense of a society in which the welfare of individuals is conceived as the end of all social organization, but in the more specific sense of 'each for himself and the devil take the hindmost.' "[5] Many legal and philosophical scholars recognize that privacy may be used to conceal antisocial behavior.[6]

Policy difficulties that result from viewing privacy as a negative value can be seen in Richard Posner's analysis of privacy. Posner turns Alan Westin's definition of an individual's right to privacy "as the right to control the flow of information about himself" into "a right to misrepresent one's character" and notes that "others have a legitimate interest in unmasking this misrepresentation."[7] Posner takes issue with Warren and Brandeis's view that people want to be let alone; rather, he argues that they want "to manipulate the world around them by selective disclosure of facts about themselves."[8] This gives support to Posner's view that the information privacy right should not be given to the "possessor of guilty secrets"[9] if "secrecy would reduce the social product by misleading others."[10] The privacy right, then, would turn on the content or quality of the information one wishes to withhold. But Posner also goes on to say that the "case for protecting business privacy is stronger, in general, than that for protecting individual privacy," because "secrecy is an important method of appropriating social benefits to the entrepreneur who creates them, while in private life it is more likely to conceal legitimately discrediting or deceiving facts."[11] Posner argues that business privacy is of greater value because the benefits to the entrepreneur are regarded as "social" while the value of individual privacy is not only individual rather than social but also assumed to be used largely for negative purposes.

In order to gain supporters for privacy protections, this negative conception of privacy must be overcome. Most often, privacy advocates have relied upon anecdotal accounts to belie the assumption that people are using privacy to hide adverse things about themselves. Real-life witnesses who are believable and respectable can move policy discussions past the negative view of privacy. But the cases of congressional policy making examined here suggest that the use of anecdotes in policy making has limitations. Anecdotes are most powerful in getting issues on the congressional agenda; as the policy process proceeds, however, those opposed to privacy protections have the opportunity to raise questions about whether the anecdotes are isolated occurrences. When it comes to formulating general principles and regulations, discussion inevitably moves from particular cases to general situations, and those opposed to privacy protections often have the most to say about general concerns. Government bureaucrats, law enforcement officials, and employers are experts on the general practices and needs of their organizations; privacy advocates are therefore cast as having a narrower focus. Another limitation of relying on anecdotal accounts is that it may be hard to identify people whose privacy has been invaded — for example, in cases of computer matching or wiretapping — and it may be difficult to convince people to make their privacy invasions public — for example, in misuses of medical information.

Conflict with "society." In much of the philosophical and legal literature on privacy, a conflict is established between the individual and society. Alan Westin, in his seminal work *Privacy and Freedom*, views privacy and social participation as competing desires and sees each individual establishing a balance between the two that is best for that individual. Although the norms of society may set some parameters on that balance, basically it is a "personal adjustment process."[12] Thus, each individual establishes a unique balance between privacy and social participation.

Charles Fried likewise analyzes privacy primarily in terms of its importance to the individual rather than to society. For him, privacy signifies the mutual respect between individuals in a society but is not an essential ingredient of a society of individuals.[13] In other words, the importance of privacy is in forming the basis of personal relationships between individuals, not in forming a society of individuals or in forming relationships with organizations.

The more privacy is identified with the individual's ability to withdraw from society or establish a boundary between himself or herself and society, the more privacy is viewed as an impediment to the functioning of society. Spiros Simitis makes a similar point: "Far from being considered a constitutive element of a democratic society, privacy appears as a tolerated contradiction, the implications of which must be continuously reconsidered."[14] As we saw in congressional debates about privacy, the philosophical thinking about privacy that establishes a tension between the individual and society often moves policy debate into a discussion of how privacy conflicts with social interests such as government efficiency, law enforcement, and an honest work force. Not only is the conflict cast as one between the individual and society, but because the other interests are defined as social interests, they can draw upon both self-interest and public interest in mobilizing support.

The view of privacy as being in conflict with society is reflected in this statement by Barrington Moore: "Privacy cannot be the dominant value in any society. Man has to live in society, and social concerns have to take precedence."[15] Although one could dispute the view that social concerns must take precedence, my quarrel is with the common notion that social concerns and privacy values are antithetical. Not only has this assumption not been adequately or critically explored, but framing debate in terms of an individual interest in competition with a social interest does not make for fruitful discussions of social issues. As John Dewey pointed out: "One of the obstructions in the path is the seemingly engrained notion that the first and last problem which must be solved is the relation of the individual and the social: — or that the outstanding question is to determine the relative merits of individualism and collective or of some compromise between them. In fact, both words, individual and social, are hopelessly ambiguous, and the ambiguity will never cease as long as we think in terms of an antithesis."[16] Framing privacy as a conflict between the individual and society is not only philosophically difficult, as Dewey suggested, but is also somewhat simplistic. People are both public and private, they operate in both contexts, and they see both as important.

The two spheres are not necessarily contradictory or in conflict; instead, a dynamic relationship exists between the two. A simple dichotomy between the individual and society, or private and public, fails to take into account the modern reality that people operate in a range of contexts that can be more or less public or private.

One suggestion for resolving conflicts between the individual and society has been that community interests should take precedence over individual interests. Amitai Etzioni and others advocate a communitarian movement, because "the pendulum has swung too far toward the radical individualistic pole" and a "judicious mix of self-interest, self-expression, and commitment to the commons—of rights *and* responsibilities" is needed.[17] But if privacy continues to be valued primarily for its importance to the individual or for reasons of self-interest, then the community or communitarian values will be viewed as restraints on privacy, as reasons to restrict the area of privacy rather than as a basis for a shared interest in privacy. Privacy is more likely to be regarded as one of the individual rights or demands that must be curbed rather than as part of the commons.[18] Proposals to introduce community as a space between public and private do not appear to resolve questions about privacy's conflict with society but raise new questions about defining "common."[19]

Failure to acknowledge social organizations. Related to this antithetical view of the individual and society is the absence of an examination of the constituent parts of society. In much of the philosophical writing about privacy, the components of society are not identified; only the individual and the society are recognized. What elements make up "society" and whether the interests of these elements are indeed "social" are not critically explored. For example, the omission of large social and economic organizations from the individual-society dichotomy presents a serious problem when discussing privacy and technology. In both the philosophical literature and policy discussions, such organizations are assumed to operate as part of society, and their interests are considered social interests. But there is no serious analysis of the nature of social organizations.

As we saw in chapter 2, the philosophical literature does not confront situations in which privacy is threatened by the activities of large organizations. For Charles Fried, the collection of information by third parties—in his example, by the state—was problematic because of its effect on intimate relationships. He was not concerned about the effect of third-party collection of information on the relationship between the individual and the third party. Although James Rachels similarly argued that privacy is important because it allows people to maintain differ-ent social relationships, his example of such relationships was group therapy rather than the new relationship between a credit agency and a consumer.[20]

This lack of acknowledgment of social organizations and the role they play in the latter twentieth century relegates privacy to not only a narrow sphere but also one that may be obsolete. John Dewey quotes Woodrow Wilson as saying in *The New Freedom*: "Yesterday and ever since history began, men were related to one another as individuals. . . . Today, the everyday relationships of men are largely with great impersonal concerns, with organizations, not with other individuals. Now this is nothing short of a new social age, a new age of human relationships, a new stage-setting for the drama of life."[21] Dewey goes on to say that this "indicates the enormous ineptitude of the individualist philosophy to meet the needs and direct the factors of the new age."[22] This is especially true in relation to the information-gathering practices of credit agencies, insurance com-panies, and tax departments.

As one European commentator pointed out, an "enormous imbalance of power between the isolated individual and the great data collection organizations" exists, and "under these conditions, it is a pure illusion to speak of 'control.' Indeed, the fact of insisting exclusively on means of individual control can in fact be an alibi on the part of a public power wishing to avoid the new problems brought about by the development of enormous personal data files, seeking refuge in an illusory exaltation of the powers of the individual, who will thus find himself alone to run a game in which he can only be the loser."[23] A definition of privacy as the right of the individual to control access to himself or herself, in effect, rests upon an "exaltation of the powers of the individual." It also explains the failure to examine the interests of the organizations collecting and using personal information; instead, the individual is given the means to mediate his or her relationship with the organization. By placing the burden on the individual, there is less need to evaluate whether organiza-tional interests are indeed social interests or whether individual privacy interests could be conceived as social interests.

Most critics of the current American approach to information privacy protection point to this imbalance. Spiros Simitis notes the "chimerical nature" of the assumption that the individual can exert control in the cur-rent information- and technology-intensive environment: "The process of consent is no more than a 'mystification' that ignores the long-standing experience that the value of a regulatory doctrine such as 'informed consent' depends entirely on the social and economic context of the individual activity."[24] Similarly, Oscar Gandy points out that the individual's power over the organization "is almost always insignificant in comparison with the power brought to bear when the organization chooses to withhold goods or services unless the information is provided."[25]

In the areas of communication privacy and psychological privacy, the problem definition moved from privacy — or lack of individual control over access to communications and/or to thoughts and beliefs — to the reasons why organizations were trying to obtain access. As this occurred, policy proposals focused less on giving individuals rights and more on regulating organizations — through requiring court orders for wiretaps in the case of communication privacy and through prohibiting private sector use of the polygraph in the case of psychological privacy. In both of these cases, the policy problem moved from privacy. When the focus was on privacy, policy solutions were not forthcoming; by changing the policy focus, the goals of privacy advocates may have been protected.

The question therefore becomes why the focus must move from privacy in order for effective policy solutions to be considered. If the way to protect privacy interests is to transform them into something else and eliminate privacy from the policy discourse, will privacy as a value be ultimately lost or forgotten? Because privacy has been viewed as an individual interest, because it has been conceptualized as a means of hiding something, and because the organizational interests threatening privacy have not been questioned, privacy has not generated public interest. The conceptualization of privacy has instead narrowed political support and policy options.

The Social Importance of Privacy

Is privacy only important to the individual for his or her self-development, or is it also of social importance? I argue that privacy's importance does not stop with the individual and that a recognition of the social importance of privacy will clear a path for more serious policy discourse about privacy and for the formulation of more effective public policy to protect privacy. In doing this, I confront a fundamental difficulty within liberal political thought. Does "society" consist of the sum or aggregation of individuals, or does a more organic component to society exist? Political philosophers have been struggling with this question for centuries, and I cannot attempt to answer it here. Instead, I take the position that part of the liberal tradition overemphasizes the atomistic nature of the individual and the separateness and conflict that isolate individuals. As will be seen, notions of commonality also can be found in the liberal tradition.

Privacy has value beyond its usefulness in helping the individual maintain his or her dignity or develop personal relationships. Most privacy scholars emphasize that the individual is better off if privacy exists; I argue that society is better off as well when privacy exists. I maintain that privacy serves not just individual interests but also common, public, and collective purposes. If privacy became less important to one individual in one particular context, or even to several individuals in several contexts, it would still be important as a value because it serves other crucial functions beyond those that it performs for a particular individual.[26] Even if the individual interests in privacy became less compelling, social interests in privacy might remain. As was discussed in chapter 2, social interests in privacy have been alluded to but not fully developed. I suggest that three concepts provide bases for discussing a more explicitly social importance for privacy — privacy as a common value, privacy as a public value, and privacy as a collective value. The first two concepts are derived from normative theory, while the latter is derived from economic theory; the styles of analysis, therefore, are different, with the first two being conceptual and the third more technical.

Common value. Some rights, which protect individual interests, are regarded as so fundamental that all individuals in common have a similar interest in them. This is true not only for the traditional liberal interests in self-preservation and property but also for a host of other interests that people may define differently. For example, although different people exercise the right to free conscience differently, believe in different things, and belong to different religions, all individuals have a common interest in this right. The same is arguably true for privacy. Even though people may define their right to privacy in somewhat different terms, draw different lines to divide the public and the private spheres, and vary in their sensitivity about what is known about them, they all have a common interest in a right to privacy. In much the same way that people of different religious beliefs have a common interest in a right to free conscience, people of different privacy beliefs or preferences have a common interest in a right to privacy. In both instances, prior to making the individual decision or choice about what to believe or where to draw a privacy boundary, individuals recognize the importance or need to develop their religious preferences and privacy boundaries. This step provides a common core that establishes space for individual choices about what to believe or what should remain private. More importantly, the common core also gives social importance to the freedom of conscience and privacy.

Philosophical and empirical arguments can be made to support the claim that privacy is a common value. William Galston's and Stephen Macedo's responses to communitarian critiques of liberalism help establish the theoretical argument. Galston argues that there are "liberal purposes" that "define what the members of a liberal community must have in common" and provide "the unity that undergirds liberal diversity."[27] He believes that the virtue of tolerance is necessary to the maintenance of social diversity.[28] Similarly, Stephen Macedo presents "the notion of liberalism as a public morality"[29] and argues that "the enforcement of liberal freedoms is not a way of supplanting the value of community, it is a way of constituting a community that is valuable."[30] He speaks of the liberal idea of "social pluralism," which recognizes disagreement about "goals, lifestyles and religious beliefs."[31]

In examining privacy in this context, parallels can be drawn to John Stuart Mill's discussion of the value of individuality: "In proportion to the development of his individuality, each person becomes more valuable to himself, and is therefore capable of being more valuable to others. . . . When there is more life in the units there is more in the mass which is composed of them."[32] For Mill, the private sphere of the individual was important not only in individual development but also in producing the type of public sphere or society that Mill envisioned. A similar utilitarian argument for the importance of privacy is made by Ruth Gavison, who sees privacy as important in "the promotion of liberty, autonomy, selfhood and human relations, and furthering the existence of a free society."[33] She recognizes the importance of privacy both to the individual and to society: "We desire a society in which individuals can grow, maintain their mental health and autonomy, create and maintain human relations, and lead meaningful lives. . . . Some privacy is necessary to enable the individual to do these things, and privacy may therefore both indicate the existence of and contribute to a more pluralistic, tolerant society."[34] Thus, privacy is important, as liberty was for Mill, because it enables the development of the type of individual that forms the basis of a certain type of society.

Both tolerance and social pluralism acknowledge that individuals will display differences, not just because these differences are important to them but also because differences are part of the fabric of society. Differences contribute to the whole, not just the individual parts. Privacy — or the ability to control access to oneself — could also be a "liberal purpose," a means of providing "unity that undergirds liberal diversity." Without privacy, it would be more difficult, as Ruth Gavison points out, to develop diversity and social pluralism. But this makes the importance of privacy dependent upon, or a result of, the importance of tolerance or social pluralism. The possibility that individuals have a common interest in privacy beyond its importance to social diversity needs to be explored.

John Dewey's discussion of the distinction between the private and public spheres helps to further this theoretical argument. Dewey claims that the source of a "public" is "the perception of consequences which are projected in important ways beyond the persons and associations directly concerned in them."[35] The perception of the consequences of activity creates a common interest, or "concern on the part of each in the joint action and in the contribution of each of its members to it. Then there exists something truly social and not merely associative."[36] Michael Walzer, although a critic of liberalism, provides another way of looking at privacy within a common social context rather than from the perspective of an atomistic individual. He writes: "The goal that liberalism sets for the art of separation — every person within his or her own circle — is literally unattainable. The individual who stands wholly outside institutions and relationships and enters into them only when he or she chooses and as he or she chooses: this individual does not exist and cannot exist in any conceivable social world."[37] He goes on to argue that in the modern world the goal is not the "freedom of the solitary individual" but "institutional integrity."[38]

The concepts of common perceptions and institutional relationships are relevant to the issues of information privacy. Some people question the need for, or legitimacy of, the privacy of personal affairs by referring to the example of the typical small town of the past, in which everyone knew almost everything about everyone else. They argue that residents of such a town did not complain of a lack of "privacy." But the analogy between a small town of the past and the information practices of a modern organization is somewhat specious. In a small town, every individual knew every other individual within a social context; they did not know isolated data about the person. Moreover, the knowledge was reciprocal; they knew about others, and others knew about them. Common perceptions existed. In contrast, in the late twentieth century, parts of every individual's life are recorded in a number of computerized databases and exchanged with other organizations. Access to these bits of information gives, at best, a fragmented picture of an individual; the individual is not seen in a social context, no reciprocity exists, and no common perceptions are recognized.

The question then is whether the consequences of exchanges of personal information by credit agencies, government bureaucracies, and direct-mail marketers do create some common perceptions among individuals that lead to common interests in privacy. As we saw in chapter 3, survey data support the claim that there are common perceptions about privacy. From the 1970s to 1990, general concern about threats to personal privacy from technology increased. The privacy Americans voice concern about in these surveys is not privacy in relationships involving intimacy, friendship, and trust, but privacy within the context of their relationships with institutions. People seem to believe that the privacy of their personal or human relationships is not endangered. But since the mid-1970s, Americans have increasingly expressed concern about their knowledge of and control over how organizations are using information. The privacy people express concern about is not abstract but derived from real circumstances with immediate consequences. In addition to common perceptions about privacy concerns, survey data indicate common perceptions about the need for government action in this area, with 65 percent of respondents in 1990 supporting the establishment of some institutional mechanism to protect privacy and 79 percent agreeing that privacy would be included as a fundamental right if the Declaration of Independence were rewritten.

The survey data give evidence that people are concerned about their privacy in relation to corporate and government organizations, that they share this concern in quite large numbers, and that their perceptions of the problem are held in common. These empirical data support the claim that privacy is a common value. The individual privacy preferences that are revealed in public opinion surveys do not merely reflect the sum of individual preferences for privacy but also reflect the more general importance of privacy as a common value. In arguing that privacy is a common value, I am not simply stating that people agree that privacy is a value. People do not merely have individual idiosyncratic preferences about privacy but also have a shared meaning for privacy, although they might apply that meaning somewhat differently in their own lives. They have common perceptions about the value. Survey responses do not reflect individualistic, unique desires to withdraw from society. Instead, they reflect a common understanding of the impact of societal changes. A prior commitment is made to an overarching concept of privacy from which we derive the meaning of privacy in particular circumstances.

Public value. Privacy has value not just to individuals as individuals or to all individuals in common but also to the democratic political system. In legal and philosophical writing, as well as in policy discussions, a public value of privacy has been acknowledged as being important to the exercise or fulfillment of other values. Privacy has been regarded as an instrumental value, having value not as an end in itself but as a means of achieving other ends. For example, a public value of privacy can be derived from the public value of freedom of speech. Thomas Emerson recognizes that privacy has a social importance but primarily in its relationship to freedom of expression:[39] "In its social impact a system of privacy is vital to the working of the democratic process. Democracy assumes that the individual citizen will actively and independently participate in making decisions and in operating the institutions of society. An individual is capable of such a role only if he can at some points separate himself from the pressures and conformities of collective life."[40] A number of Supreme Court cases have recognized a right to privacy as being important to the exercise of other rights. Since the 1950s, the Court has upheld, under the First Amendment and the due process clause, a series of privacy interests, such as "associational privacy,"[41] "political privacy,"[42] and the "right to anonymity in public expression."[43] In these cases, the Court did not view privacy as an independent right but saw privacy as important in furthering the values protected by the First Amendment.

Another basis for a public value of privacy can be found in the liberal belief in limited government, or more specifically, in restrictions on the arbitrary and capricious use of power. A public value of privacy derives not only from its protection of the individual as an individual but also from its usefulness as a restraint on the government or on the use of power. In thinking of privacy as establishing boundaries for the exercise of power, it is instructive to refer to John Stuart Mill's discussion of the "struggle between liberty and authority." His concept of "civil, or social, liberty" involves not the rights of individuals but "the nature and limits of the power which can be legitimately exercised by society over the individual."[44] His emphasis is not on the rights of individuals but on limitations on the exercise of power. Privacy in this sense is not important just to individual liberty but also to civil or social liberty because it helps establish the boundaries for the exercise of power.

Support for this interpretation of a public value of privacy can be found in a number of Fourth Amendment cases on the prohibition of unreasonable searches and seizures. For example, in the cases involving the exclusionary rule, the Court clearly viewed the Fourth Amendment as serving a public purpose in providing procedural safeguards on the use of government power. Justice Felix Frankfurter, writing for the majority in *Wolf v. Colorado*, noted that "the security of one's privacy against arbitrary intrusion by the police — which is at the core of the Fourth Amendment — is basic to a free society."[45] Similarly, in wiretapping cases, the Fourth Amendment is regarded as serving a public interest in protecting individuals against unjustifiable intrusions by government agents.[46]

A public value of privacy, then, is derived from its importance to the exercise of rights that are regarded as essential to democracy, such as freedom of speech and association, and from its importance as a restraint on the arbitrary power of government. But does privacy itself have independent value to the political system? In policy debates, if privacy is reduced to, or becomes synonymous with, due process protections or is viewed as essential to free speech, industry competitiveness, or employment opportunities, then privacy's completeness may be overlooked. Does privacy provide something important in and of itself?

Hannah Arendt's discussion of the public and private realms offers some insights into an independent public value for privacy. She notes that privacy originally meant a deprivation of something, "the privative trait of privacy," for example, being deprived of entering the public realm, and later took on importance as an individual protection, "to shelter the intimate."[47] In order for the "common" to develop in the public realm, however, there must be the "simultaneous presence of innumerable perspectives and aspects in which the common world presents itself and for which no common measurement or denominator can ever be devised."[48] In order for the common to develop, the private realm is essential. If the private realm is destroyed, the public is destroyed as well because the human is destroyed. Arendt then points to the older, nonintimate, traits of privacy that are important to the development of the common public world; without initiative and a hiding place from being seen and heard, the public would become shallow. This is similar to Alexis de Tocqueville's distinction between *individualism*, or a preoccupation with self-interest and economic pursuit, which was associated with the isolation of the individual, and *individuality*, which was associated with the political exercise of public virtue in the company of others.[49]

Privacy may be essential to a democratic political system because some commonality among individuals is necessary to unite a political community and the development of commonality requires privacy. The more other people know about the details of one's personal life, communications, and thoughts, the more individual or unique one is considered and the more difficult it is to construct a "public" or Arendt's "community of one's peers." The more fragmented or differentiated people become, the harder it is to put them together in a society or body politic. In this way, privacy can be viewed as essential to John Rawls's "circumstances of justice," in which "mutually disinterested persons put forward conflicting claims to the division of social advantages under conditions of moderate scarcity."[50] As more is known about the uniqueness or distinctive characteristics of others, it becomes more difficult to find "mutually disinterested persons." In a related way, privacy is essential to the development of trust and accountability, which are basic to the development of a democratic political community. Oscar Gandy also makes this point: "The same technology that threatens the autonomy of the individual seems destined to frustrate attempts to reestablish community and shared responsibility because it destroys the essential components of trust and accountability."[51] The survey data that indicate a strong relationship between distrust in government and institutions and serious concerns about privacy give empirical support to this theoretical connection.

The privacy issues raised by direct-mail marketing and by the targeting of political messages take on new significance—a more public significance—when framed in this way. One could argue that the privacy invasions that occur in the targeting of political messages violate the integrity of the electoral process because they fragment the body politic.[52] This is similar to Carl Friedrich's view that the privacy of the secret ballot serves a public function. Relating the importance of privacy to the ability of constructing a public, and to the development of trust and accountability, would expand the list of public functions that privacy performs and might make clearer that privacy itself is an essential element to a good society.

Collective value. The concept of collective value used here is derived from the economists' concept of collective or public goods, which are those goods defined as indivisible or nonexcludable; no one member of society can enjoy the benefit of a collective good without others also benefiting.[53] Clean air and national defense are examples of public or collective goods. If a good is a collective good, then it will not be produced through the market or a market solution will result in a suboptimal supply of a collective good. The market is an inefficient mechanism for supplying collective goods. As mentioned above, two criteria are important in defining a collective good. First, collective goods cannot be easily divided. Second, collective goods are nonexcludable. Once the good is provided, people cannot be prevented from obtaining those goods or enjoying them. This gives rise to the problem of free riders — people who want to enjoy the good without paying for it. The question, then, is whether privacy can be considered a public good by either of these criteria.

Currently a number of policies and policy proposals treat privacy as a "private good" and allow people to buy back or establish the level of privacy that they wish. For example, when you subscribe to a magazine, you can indicate that you do not want your name and information about you incorporated in a mailing list and sold for direct-mail purposes. Similarly, one policy proposal concerning Caller ID is that individuals be given the ability to "block" the display of their numbers. Such examples suggest that you can indeed "divide" privacy into components and allow people to establish their own privacy level. But three factors limit the effectiveness of this individual or market-based solution for privacy: the interests of third-party record holders; the nonvoluntary nature of many record-keeping relationships; and computer and telecommunication technologies.

Vast quantities of personal information about individuals are now held by third-party organizations, including credit-reporting agencies, insurance companies, schools, employers, mail-order companies, hospitals, and video rental stores. In each case, the personal information becomes part of a record that is largely the property of the organization, not the individual.[54] The organization uses this information for its own administrative and marketing purposes, and it often sells that information to yet another organization. Information about people's transactions with one organization or one type of organization is valuable to other organizations. What results is a lucrative market in the sale, packaging, and resale of people's characteristics and transactions. Although people are often given an opportunity to remove themselves from this market, few people avail themselves of the opportunity, largely because they do not have adequate information about how this market operates or what its implications for privacy might be.[55] At the same time, it is not in the interests of the third-party record keepers to give people complete information about the market and its privacy implications because it would lower the value of their product if people denied organizations the ability to use personal information as a commodity. Additional evidence of the ineffectiveness of using a market solution may be seen in the reluctance of government agencies to notify individuals every time their records are matched and the reluctance of credit agencies to notify individuals every time their records are sent to another organization; in both cases, the organization maintains that the cost of such notification would be prohibitive.

Another element that gives privacy a collective, or indivisible, quality is that the nature of the relationships that generate records and information is changing. It is hard to define these relationships as truly voluntary. In some cases — as with tax records and social security records — one is required by law to be a part of the system — one cannot set the level of privacy that one desires; instead, some minimum level of privacy, or means to exercise privacy, is established as part of the relationship. In other systems, such as those involving credit records or bank records, the relationship might be regarded as somewhat voluntary, in that one can choose not to have a credit card or a bank account, but necessary enough that the government has intervened to legislate some level of privacy protection. As more record-generating relationships are regarded as necessary parts of modern life, the list of laws also grows, establishing a minimum level of privacy expectations for those relationships. The nonvoluntary nature of some relationships is complicated further because the individual is not technically a party, or the responsible party, in some relationships. For example, medical records that result from a transaction between a patient and a doctor are sent to a health insurance company for payment. But because the health insurance company has a relationship with the patient's employer, not directly with the patient, then employers can argue that they have legitimate interests in the content of those records.

These institutional-individual relationships are not just necessary for the individual to function in modern life, but are also necessary for the functioning of a modern economy and society. For example, if a large number of people opted out of the credit system, the consumer economy would slow down and be less efficient. If a number of people with health problems opted out of the health system because they did not believe their medical records received adequate protection, there would be spillover effects on everyone's health. If citizens refused to participate in the census, or misrepresented themselves in the census, the funding of major public programs and the apportionment of congressional districts would be affected.

The complexity and interrelatedness of the computer and communication infrastructure that underlies these record exchanges also make it more difficult to divide privacy. This may appear counterintuitive in that computer software makes it easier to program specific instructions into systems. But at the same time, the design of the overall communication or information system becomes more important in determining what is possible.[56] For example, when a representative of AT&T testified against federal legislation requiring telecommunication providers to offer blocking of the identification of the calling party, she suggested that privacy levels or possibilities must be part of the overall system design. The AT&T representative stated that "it is not technologically possible today to restrict presentation of the calling number on calls to 700, 800 or 900 services on a selective basis."[57] The level of privacy possible was dependent on the hardware and software of the communication system. Somewhat similarly, it is also difficult to isolate one record from a system of records and give that record a particular level of privacy. Error rates in credit-reporting systems and criminal justice systems are evidence of the problems of buying "effective" individual privacy without also monitoring or auditing the entire system for the level of record quality.

Privacy is becoming less an attribute of individuals and records and more an attribute of social relationships and information systems or communication systems. Discussions about an "information age" and communication systems as part of a national, and even global, "infrastructure" signal profound changes in both the role of information and the systems for processing information.[58] The design of information and communication systems and the rules governing organizational life determine the parameters of privacy. If this is the case, then some minimum level of privacy may be indivisible. As personal information becomes a valuable commodity for marketing purposes and as information and communication systems become more interconnected and complicated, it may become increasingly difficult to enable individuals to buy privacy, despite an increase in policy proposals to make this possible.

In *Nobody's Business*, Alida Brill also struggles with the issue of the broader importance of privacy. She recognizes that privacy "is dependent on the behavior of others" and that privacy "exists only when others let you have it — privacy is an accorded right."[59] She concludes: "Privacy may still be considered and fought for as an individual liberty, but as individuals acting alone we can no longer control and safeguard our privacy. Technology and life-styles have made privacy protection a very different endeavor."[60] Similarly, Spiros Simitis argues that "privacy considerations no longer arise out of particular individual problems; rather, they express conflicts affecting everyone."[61] Difficulties with protecting privacy, especially information privacy or data protection, are also acknowledged by Colin Bennett, who regards such protection as providing "an indivisible, public good; it applies to the whole society."[62] His interest is in explaining the difficulties with organizing individuals to provide such goods.[63] But privacy advocacy groups and experts exist and are integrated into the political system. The problems of organizing have been addressed; the difficulty remains with the basis of their argument for privacy. I argue here that if we did recognize the collective or public-good value of privacy, as well as the common and public value of privacy, those advocating privacy protections would have a stronger basis upon which to argue for its protection. It is to the specifics of this analysis that we now turn.

Policy Implications

In policy debates about privacy, it has generally been assumed, if not explicitly argued, that threats to privacy invade an individual interest and that privacy protections are individual rights. The above sections suggest that society (the collective) also has an interest in privacy. Instead of a conflict between an individual interest and a societal interest, the policy problem in fact involves a conflict between two societal interests — privacy and effective law enforcement, for example. I believe that turning the discussion around to emphasize the social importance of privacy will have important policy implications. The policy debates will be different if the policy issue involves the balancing of two societal interests. In turn, the policy outcomes may also be different.

Viewing privacy from this broader perspective of its importance to society generally rather than to individuals as individuals would change the definition of the policy problem, the terms of policy discourse, and the patterns of interest-group and congressional activity. Acknowledging that privacy is a common and public value would weaken the criticism that privacy is a negative value. Moreover, privacy advocates could then draw for support from the dual streams of "accommodation to self-interest" and "commitment to the public good."[64] Aligning privacy with societal interests would remove some of the difficult philosophical and policy issues involved in reconciling the balance between individual and society. Recognition that privacy has some features of a public or collective good would make clearer the institutional or organizational interests in personal information and the weaknesses of a market solution in providing privacy protection.

In order to support the argument that an appreciation of the social importance of privacy would change policy debates and may result in stronger policies supporting privacy, the next sections analyze a number of current privacy issues, suggest how the privacy interests might be viewed as being of broad social importance, and discuss the implications of such a view on policy formulation and adoption.

Information privacy. A common value in a right to privacy of personal information could be derived from reframing the right of information privacy as a social claim rather than an individual claim. Instead of defining privacy as the right of the individual to control information about and access to himself or herself, privacy would be defined as the right of a society to require institutions using personal information to do so in a manner that respects the shared interests in that information. Policy discussion would then focus both on how institutions are using information and on the common interests and concerns individuals have in that information. In congressional hearings, anecdotal accounts of privacy invasions would not represent isolated instances of individual problems but examples of common problems. Permitting individuals to know about, see, and correct information in their files, as is stipulated in the Code of Fair Information Practices, would be insufficient to address a social problem. In the United States, this code is rooted in a liberal notion of privacy in that it is up to the individual to monitor the use of information and to initiate legal action against an organization that is using information in ways contrary to the code. A recognition of the common interest in privacy would require more attention to customary standards that organizations should follow in handling personal information and would compel more active social monitoring of compliance with the code. Moreover, viewing privacy as a common value — as a social claim rather than an individual claim — would also shift the burden of proof. Rather than leaving it up to individuals to show damages or to prove willful intent on the part of the record keeper, the burden would be placed on the organization. The organization would be responsible for justifying the need for the information rather than the individual being responsible for justifying withholding the information.

In considering the policy implications of viewing information privacy as a public value, it is instructive to consider the different orientations of the definitions of freedom of information policies and privacy policies, which are often thought of as companion policies. Freedom of information legislation has been cast in terms of a right of *public* access to government records, while privacy has been framed in terms of a right of *individual* access to personal information in those records. But is it not possible to define privacy as a right of the public to access records about themselves? The concept of access is common to both policies, but is one type of access necessarily public and the other individual? In freedom of information policy, individual access, especially by reporters and researchers, is seen as serving some public good. In privacy policy, individual access is viewed as serving only the individual's good. But it could also be possible that in gaining access to information about themselves, individuals could discover and then place before the public information about how government agencies or credit bureaus are using personal information. In other words, an individual's use of his or her privacy rights could serve a public purpose in much the same way as an individual's use of freedom of information laws. Both privacy and freedom of information policies have a public value in that they open up organizational information practices to citizen oversight.

Viewing information privacy as a collective value would generate the most significant changes in the types of policy considered appropriate to protect privacy. If we consider privacy as a collective good, then the costs of considering each information privacy decision as an individual market transaction in which the individual establishes the level of privacy appropriate for that transaction are too high. As Meheroo Jussawalla and Chee-Wah Cheah similarly point out, the large number of "potential 'providers' of privacy invasions" makes it "too costly for a data subject to engage in private contracting with all those who might violate his privacy, [therefore] the collective enforcement of privacy rights appears warranted on grounds of economic efficiency."[65] The establishment of an agency to monitor and oversee personal information practices and to advise on new uses of personal information would be an appropriate mechanism to correct for market imperfections.

If privacy is, or is becoming, a collective or public good, the weaknesses of policy solutions that establish a property right in personal information or that allow one to waive one's privacy rights also would become clear. If one individual or a group of individuals waives privacy rights, the level of privacy for all individuals decreases because the value of privacy decreases. Similarly, proposals that allow an individual to "opt out" of mailing lists would not be sufficient. Instead, the baseline policy would be privacy protection and individuals might have the opportunity to "opt in" to programs in which their personal information was sold or used in additional ways. The choice between "opt-in" and "opt-out" approaches has significant implications. Direct-mail experience indicates that only about 20 percent of people make use of the "opt-out" option, that is, requesting that their information not be used for another purpose, while it is estimated that an "opt-in" option would result in only about 5 to 10 percent giving their consent for further uses of information.[66]

In the case of information privacy, arguments can be made, then, that the kinds of issues currently being debated raise privacy issues that involve not just individual interest but also social interests. The privacy issues raised by increased use of transactional information for marketing purposes and those generated by proposals for some form of national health care system are issues that are not just important to individuals as individuals but are also important to people in common; to the democratic system, because of the need to check the arbitrary use of power and because room for individuality is necessary to constitute a public; and to the collective, because some level of information privacy must become a part of the system of records since protecting one individual record no longer can provide effective privacy protection.

If information privacy concerns are of broader social importance, then additional support exists for an institutional mechanism to protect information privacy as is found in most European countries, Canada, and Australia. As was discussed in chapter 4, the need for such institutional oversight has been recognized since the 1970s and has been repeatedly proposed by study commissions and congressional committees. Scholars who have compared the American experience in implementing privacy protections to the experience of other countries have concluded that the lack of institutional oversight explains many shortcomings in American privacy protections.[67] Privacy advocates in the United States also recommend the establishment of such a commission.[68] Most of the arguments offered in support of establishing an American Privacy Commission or a Data Protection Commission emphasize the need to protect the individual right of privacy and address weaknesses in the current reliance on individual initiative and the legal barriers and high costs. But as Spiros Simitis points out, the establishment of a Data Protection Commission would also signal recognition that privacy is of broad societal value because the task or goal of such a commission would consist in "preventing both government and private institutions from overstepping the boundaries guaranteeing the democratic structure of society."[69]

A recognition that privacy is of broader social importance would lend additional support to these arguments and create an awareness of the public interest that is involved in privacy protection. If such a shift in focus occurred, privacy advocates would not have to overcome the suspicion that privacy is a "guilty person's privilege," would not have to justify why the "average" person would want privacy, and would not have to show how record-keeping practices invade individual privacy. Congressional hearings would not be dominated by the anecdotal accounts of individuals who have been harmed by privacy invasions and by the arguments of organizations that such witnesses represent the exception and not the rule.

Communication privacy. Computer and communication technologies continue to transform the structure and products of the communication system.[70] The early debate about Caller ID provides an example of the new types of services available and the kinds of privacy issues that will be raised. Caller ID is a service that displays the telephone number of the calling party to the person being called. Much of the controversy over this service has focused on privacy — the privacy of people with unlisted phone numbers who might not want their numbers displayed, the privacy of people calling hot lines, the privacy of doctors calling from their home phones. But this list of privacy concerns largely masks, once again, some of the broader organizational interests.[71] For example, the phone companies see great revenue potential in this new service since access to the phone numbers of the calling parties enhances the efficiency of direct-mail and telemarketing firms and makes phone numbers a commodity to be exchanged for value in the marketplace.[72] Policy discussions that focus on protecting individual privacy and individual rights underestimate the character of changes taking place in social organizations and relationships.

If the privacy issues raised by the construction of a new communication infrastructure are considered solely from the perspective of an individual interest in privacy, then privacy is likely to be overcome by corporate special interests — which in the short run may be compatible with the protection of individual privacy — or by the public interest in updating and making competitive the communication system. The question of whether there is a common, public, or collective value in protecting privacy in a new communication infrastructure is important to consider. The current debate about employers reading employees' electronic mail in the workplace is illustrative of the policy implications of viewing communication privacy as being of broad social importance as well as of individual importance. If electronic mail privacy is discussed with an emphasis on the importance of privacy to the individual, this leads to a discussion about employees versus employers and to a rather complicated legal area of balancing interests and rights. If electronic mail privacy is viewed with an emphasis on the social importance of privacy, the focus is on how society wants electronic mail to function. The traditional view of individual importance elicits the conflict between the individual and the organization; a recognition of the social importance of privacy leads to analysis of the optimum electronic mail system for both users and operators, or employees and employers. The policy focus is not on how to protect individual rights but on how to provide an effective social system. Privacy becomes important within that context, and its common and collective nature is acknowledged. As is true for other forms of communication, if some level of privacy is not protected, the overall use and effectiveness of the system is likely to be compromised.

The common value of privacy in communication is implicit in the distinction made between point-to-point communication and point-to-mass communication. Traditionally, some level of privacy has been protected in all forms of point-to-point communication — mail, telegraph, and telephone. If the new communication infrastructure will continue to provide possibilities for point-to-point communication, then it will need to provide privacy as well as security. Users of the system will need to know not only that the integrity of the overall system is protected but also that they have control over who has access to the messages they are sending. The common perception or expectation that privacy is an essential part of point-to-point communication is well established as part of our political, economic, and social culture. Without privacy protections, the new communication infrastructure would in effect be able to offer only point-to-mass communication. This would severely limit the use of the system and prohibit many competitive advantages that can be gained by a communication system. But it would also significantly limit the ways in which individuals could communicate and would change society in a fundamental way. A recognition of the common interest in, and perception about the importance of, privacy in point-to-point communication would give privacy importance not just for competitive reasons but also for common social reasons.

The public value of privacy in communication is reflected in the First Amendment protections afforded freedom of speech and press. It is also seen in the Communication Act of 1934, which viewed communication as an essential service or a basic need of organized society and deemed interception of the contents of communication a violation of the act. Because communication is an essential service or element of a democratic society and democratic political system, and because privacy is essential to communication, privacy's public value should be considered in constructing a new communication infrastructure and determining the rights and responsibilities involved. In this context, privacy interests are less likely to be considered of public importance in and of themselves but more likely to be considered important because of their relationship to

First Amendment interests. However, it is also likely that conflicts between First Amendment interests and privacy interests will occur, as illustrated in the current arguments of direct marketers that privacy protections may inhibit their freedom of speech and of reporters that privacy protections may inhibit freedom of the press. But the discussion of the public importance of privacy suggests that privacy's public value is not just derived from the First Amendment but that privacy of communications is also important to trust and accountability and to the possibility of constructing the body politic.

The notion that privacy is a collective good that cannot easily be divided for those who want privacy and those who do not is relevant to the concept of the new communication infrastructure as a system of technologies and rules. Although one may construct a system in which individuals could buy certain levels of privacy, at a minimum the possibility of privacy must be a part of the initial technological design and the rules for privacy must be established in advance and their implications must be clear. But a collective-good perspective would suggest that merely providing the possibility of privacy would not be sufficient. Some would select not to buy privacy protections, resulting in a suboptimal supply of privacy. Those who bought additional privacy might be regarded as suspicious. Making privacy protections dependent upon wealth might create classes of "privacy haves" and "privacy have-nots," which could affect other areas of social life. But perhaps most importantly, those who bought privacy might never feel certain that their privacy was truly protected, for example, that their encryption codes could not be broken. The debates about the Clipper chip illustrate that many privacy advocates are concerned about government control over encryption codes; but at the same time, they recognize that some basic level of encryption should be assured as part of the system. Because of the history of government wiretapping, privacy advocates at this time are more comfortable with the idea of encryption codes being supplied through the private sector. This perspective may change, however, if some individuals are unable to secure privacy protections due to the cost.

From these three perspectives, privacy can be seen as a common value in that it makes possible a type of communication people have common perceptions about, as a public value in that it is essential to the provision of an essential service and to the possibility of constructing a body politic, and as a collective value in that privacy — or at least a minimum level of privacy — is established as part of the technology or system rules. This would lead to the perception that communication privacy has social importance—that it is not solely an individual interest that is important in achieving relationships of trust and intimacy. Privacy claims as they relate to a new communication infrastructure are not only claims about the importance of privacy to individual relationships but a recognition that privacy is part of the fabric of society.

Psychological privacy. Although psychological testing generally involves potentially sensitive or intimate information and the procedures used affect the subject directly, congressional efforts at resolving psychological privacy issues have not been very successful. In the 1960s, congressional debate about personality tests did not result in legislation. When debate about the polygraph was framed as a privacy issue, legislation was not forthcoming. Replacement of polygraphs with written integrity or honesty tests and the lack of congressional action in response to these tests despite serious questions as to their validity attest to the continuing difficulties in resolving issues of psychological privacy when they are conceived as issues of individual privacy. The concept of psychological privacy as an individual right forms a surprisingly weak basis for legislation—surprising because one might assume that since these issues are more closely identified with the sphere of individuality, individual rights claims would be accepted. But this has not been the case, partly because policy questions are often raised in the employment context and partly because of the difficulties inherent in viewing the privacy claim as an individual claim.

An examination of the privacy issues raised by genetic screening and mapping reveals the individual and social interests involved in issues of individuality. Genetic information fundamentally entails individuality. Genetic variations account for many individual variations. One's genetic makeup is unique and is thought to offer explanations for behavior and attitudes. Two professors of ethics, John Fletcher and Dorothy Wertz, describe advances in genetic knowledge as creating a situation in which "human beings will be laid genetically bare and thereby rendered vulnerable."[73] It would thus seem that on this issue it would be difficult to develop common perceptions. But science does have its limitations, and these limitations make possible, if not necessary, common perceptions. In the foreseeable future, gene maps will not be able to predict most characteristics.[74] They will not yield information about the presence or absence of most major diseases (cancer or heart conditions) or particular conditions (psychological disorders or alcoholism).[75] Instead, genetic mapping will indicate predispositions. The realization of a genetic predisposition will depend on other genetic predispositions and on a host of environmental factors. Even in those cases in which genetic information yields a clear answer on the presence or absence of a disease or condition, medical science may not yet have a cure or treatment. People would have knowledge but not the power or wisdom necessary to act. In commenting on the discovery of genetic markers associated with breast cancer, Ellen Goodman points out the questions that could be raised: "What should a 24-year-old with an 85 percent chance of getting breast cancer do? Get a double mastectomy? Go on the drug tamoxifen? Have more frequent mammograms? Or fewer? . . . And by the way, when should a female in a high-risk family be tested? At 30, 17, 8 or in the womb? Is breast cancer such a dread disease that some parents would choose to abort a fetus with the gene? Will the men and women who carry this gene consider themselves too genetically flawed to reproduce? Will they blame themselves for the cancer of their children?"[76]

It is unlikely, certainly in the near future, that people will know their particular, self-interested privacy concerns about their genetic information. This lack of complete genetic information therefore results in the existence of John Rawls's "mutually disinterested persons."[77] Before scientific and technological advances make possible a complete genetic map, no individual will know his or her particular interest. John Fletcher and Dorothy Wertz note that "genetics is a great equalizer, and eventually, everyone will understand that they suffer from diseases and burdens having a strong to moderate genetic determinant."[78] Similarly, neuroscientist James Santiago Grisolia argues that our traditional concepts of individual diversity and commonality will need to be rethought since "our approximately 100,000 genes are mostly uniform, so that our genetic heritage binds us together more tightly than it divides us."[79] The privacy issues raised by genetic mapping or testing can be seen as important to all individuals in the same way. Hence these debates might begin with a recognition of the social importance of privacy because initially in the process of genetic mapping common or reciprocal interests in genetic privacy will exist.

Recent survey data support the existence of common perceptions. In a 1985 *Business Week*–Louis Harris survey, 89 percent of the respondents believed employers should not have the right to use genetic tests in making hiring decisions. Eighty-two percent responded that an employer's knowledge of a job applicant's likelihood of contracting a serious disease in the future was not an acceptable reason to reject that applicant. Sixty-five percent believed that employers should not be able to exclude employees or potential employees from certain jobs based upon the results of genetic tests indicating an employee's vulnerability to a heart attack or stroke because of stress. Seventy-nine percent believed that insurance companies would not be justified in refusing life or health insurance coverage based on the results of genetic tests. In general, this poll found that as long as genetic testing was not related to employment or insurance decisions, approximately 50 percent of respondents were willing to be tested for incurable or fatal diseases they might develop at some point in their lives.[80] A 1992 Louis Harris poll conducted for the March of Dimes found that respondents approved of the use of gene therapy to treat or cure genetic diseases but that 63 percent believed an employer should not know that someone is a carrier of a defective gene or has a genetic disease.[81]

In terms of genetic privacy's importance as a public value, consider its implications in the formation of Arendt's "community of one's peers." Knowledge of genetic information, even if that information does not give a complete and dependable picture of an individual, may make the notion of "peers" obsolete. Differences among individuals are likely to be emphasized rather than shared or common characteristics or circumstances. Within a democratic society, some level of equality among individuals is assumed. Genetic information, especially regarding intelligence, may lead to elitism, a hierarchy based upon genetic characteristics. Any possibility of eugenics challenges traditional democratic assumptions. As an article in the *U.S. News and World Report* concludes, "The most obvious danger is that genetic screening, like race, will provide one more excuse to divide the world up into superior and inferior, us and them."[82] A public value of genetic privacy therefore exists, which might necessitate total restrictions on certain genetic tests or on certain uses of genetic information.

Consideration of genetic privacy as a collective or public good also raises interesting questions. One scholar who has written extensively about the ethical issues posed by genetic testing notes that three levels of issues are raised by the human genome initiative: individual/family, societal, and species. Issues on the species level raise fundamental questions involving "the fact that powerful new technologies do not simply change what human beings can do, but also change the way humans think, especially about themselves."[83] Can some members of society have genetic privacy and others not? If policies allow people to buy levels of genetic privacy protection, it is likely that those who want a high level of genetic privacy will be perceived as trying to hide something. Genetic privacy would be seen as a "guilty man's privilege"[84] used to hide genetic weaknesses. If this occurred, the level and degree of genetic privacy would likely be lower than people would optimally prefer.

Speculation about the future of health insurance in an age of genetic mapping illustrates the collective-good component of genetic privacy. In a *New Republic* article in 1990, Robert Wright argues that laws establishing that DNA is private and that no one can gain access to genetic information without the individual's permission will not be sufficient.[85] He recognizes that if insurance companies offer discounts to people with "good" genes, those people will voluntarily divulge their genetic information and the cost of insurance for everyone else will rise. Even if the government prohibited people from revealing genetic information to insurance companies, they might indirectly disclose genetic information since they would not seek insurance coverage for diseases they know they are not likely to get. This scenario suggests that genetic privacy may not be in the interest of any particular individual but may only be in the collective interest.

Somewhat ironically, genetic testing and mapping, which many regard as having the potential to destroy our common notions of privacy and individuality, may instead be an issue that will facilitate a discussion of the social importance of privacy. Arguments can be made that genetic privacy is a common value, a public value, and a collective value. Given these values, the kinds of public policies that would be appropriate in protecting genetic privacy would involve government restrictions on the collection and use of certain kinds of genetic information in certain circumstances. This would result in a higher level of protection of individual privacy than would be likely if the goal was to protect only individual interests.

Conclusion

Privacy is a value that Americans have cherished for over two centuries and continue to believe is important. It is a value that has been threatened by technological changes since the mid-twentieth century. Technological changes expected by the turn of the century will continue to threaten privacy. But examination of policy processes that began with the goal of protecting privacy reveals a disjuncture between the importance of this value and the ability to protect it through the political process. I have argued that this occurs because our emphasis on privacy as an individual interest and right does not serve as a strong basis upon which to develop policy to protect privacy.

My purpose has not been to clarify or simplify the concept of privacy but instead to argue that we need to consider its importance from a broader social or public perspective rather than looking at it exclusively from the individual's perspective. The beginnings of an acknowledgment of privacy's social importance can be found in the philosophical and legal scholarship on privacy. But most authors turn privacy inward and develop its importance to individual self-development and the establishment of human relationships. Our thinking on privacy now needs to turn outward, to its importance to social, political, and economic relationships — rather than solely to personal relationships — and to our common or public life more generally.

Developing an understanding of the social importance of privacy is critical not just in gaining philosophical clarity about privacy but also because our emphasis on privacy as an individual right has largely offered a weak basis for formulating policy to protect privacy. In policy debates about the marketing of consumer information, the surveillance of criminal suspects, and the testing of job applicants, the primary policy question does not involve what type of individual we want but what type of society we want, including concerns about the relationships between individuals and social/political/economic organizations and the powers these organizations have. If these social goals are the relevant policy goals, an understanding of privacy's importance to society is likewise relevant.

The problems that have been identified here regarding the conceptualization of privacy as a value and as a goal of public policy are problems that generally occur within liberal interest-group pluralism. Within pluralism, difficulties exist in conceptualizing the public interest in shared terms; instead, the public interest is viewed as the outcome of the policy-making process or the sum of interest-group demands. These "ethical limitations of pluralism"[86] reduce values and principles to interests in large part because of the lack of development of other normative criteria in American political thinking. When this occurs, values that draw their support from the importance to the individual are particularly threatened if the competing interest is one that derives support from both particular interests and public interests. As Jane Mansbridge suggests, being able to draw upon the dual streams of "accommodation to self-interest" and "commitment to the public good"[87] provides a firmer basis than drawing upon self-interest alone. In policy debates about privacy, the interests competing against privacy were able to draw upon both of these streams. Privacy advocates relied primarily on the "self-interest" stream because much of the legal and philosophical support for privacy rested on its importance to the individual.

Yet privacy serves not just individual interests but also common, public, and collective interests. Privacy can be considered one of James Madison's "permanent and aggregate interests of the community."[88] Common perceptions about the importance of privacy and common ways of thinking and talking about privacy exist. A recognition of this shared context provides the basis for a different calculation of the importance of privacy. Instead of being derived from an aggregation of individual preferences, privacy's importance derives from a sense of connection and mutuality. In congressional policy debate, the common foundations of privacy have not provided a basis for public policy. But common foundations do exist. A recognition of these common foundations would change the nature of the policy debate, possibly resulting in the adoption of stronger public policy protecting privacy.

Appendixes

Appendix A:
Selected Congressional Activity Concerning Information Privacy, 1965–1988

YEAR	LOCATION	ACTIVITY
1965	House Committee on Government Operations; Special Subcommittee on Invasion of Privacy	Special Inquiry on Invasions of Privacy; hearings, June 2–4, 7, 23, Sept. 23
1965–66	Senate Committee on the Judiciary; Subcommittee on Administrative Practice and Procedure	Invasions of Privacy; hearings, Feb. 18, 23–24, Mar. 2–3, Apr. 13, 27–29, May 5–6, June 7, July 13–15, 19–21, 27, Aug. 9, Oct. 18–20, 1965, Feb. 2–4, Mar. 23, 29–30, June 7–9, 14, 16, 1966
1966	House Committee on Government Operations; Special Subcommittee on Invasion of Privacy	The Computer and Invasion of Privacy; hearings, July 26–28
1967	Senate Committee on the Judiciary; Subcommittee on Administrative Practice and Procedure	Computer Privacy; hearings, Mar. 14–15
1967	Senate Committee on the Judiciary; Subcommittee on Administrative Practice and Procedure	Government Dossier (Survey of Information Contained in Government Files); committee print, Nov.
1969	Senate Committee on the Judiciary; Subcommittee on Constitutional Rights	Privacy, the Census, and Federal Questionnaires; hearings, Apr. 24–25, May 2, July 1
1971	Senate Committee on the Judiciary; Subcommittee on Constitutional Rights	Federal Data Banks, Computers, and the Bill of Rights; hearings, Feb. 24–25, Mar. 2, 4, 9–11, 15, 17
1972	House Committee on Government Operations; Subcommittee on Foreign Operations and Government Information	Sale or Distribution of Mailing Lists by Federal Agencies; hearings, June 13, 15
1972	House Committee on Government Operations; Subcommittee on Foreign Operations and Government Information	Records Maintained by Government Agencies; hearings, June 22, 27
1973–74	House Committee on the Judiciary; Subcommittee on Civil and Constitutional Rights	Dissemination of Criminal Justice Information; hearings, July 26, Aug. 2, Sept. 26, Oct. 11, 1973, Feb. 26, 28, Mar. 5, 28, Apr. 3, 1974
1974	House Committee on Government Operations	Federal Information Systems and Plans, Implications and Issues; hearings, Jan. 29, 31, Feb. 5

YEAR	LOCATION	ACTIVITY
1974	House Committee on Government Operations; Subcommittee on Foreign Operations and Government Information	Access to Records; hearings, Feb. 19, 26, Apr. 30, May 16
1974	Senate Committee on the Judiciary; Subcommittee on Constitutional Rights	Criminal Justice Data Banks; hearings, Mar. 5–7, 12–14
1974	Senate Committee on Government Operations; Ad Hoc Subcommittee on Privacy and Information Systems; and Senate Committee on the Judiciary; Subcommittee on Constitutional Rights	Privacy — The Collection, Use, and Computerization of Personal Data; hearings, June 18–20
1974	Senate Committee on Government Operations	Protecting Individual Privacy in Federal Gathering, Use, and Disclosure of Information; report 93-1183, Sept. 26
1974	House Committee on Government Operations	Privacy Act of 1974 (H.R. 16373); report 93-1416, Oct. 2
1974	Senate floor	Consideration and passage of Privacy Act, Nov. 21
1974	House floor	Consideration and passage of Privacy Act, Dec. 11
1974	Senate floor	Concurrence with House amendments to Privacy Act, with additional amendments, Dec. 17
1974	House floor	Concurrence with Senate amendments to Privacy Act, Dec. 18
1974	Senate Committee on Government Operations and House Committee on Government Operations; Subcommittee on Government Information and Individual Rights	Legislative History of the Privacy Act of 1974
1974	Senate Committee on the Judiciary; Subcommittee on Constitutional Rights	Federal Data Banks and Constitutional Rights: A Study of Data Systems on Individuals Maintained by Agencies of the Federal Government; committee print
1975	House Committee on Government Operations and Senate Committee on Governmental Affairs	Privacy and Protection of Personal Information in Europe; committee print, Mar.
1975	House Committee on Government Operations; Subcommittee on Government Information and Individual Rights	Central Intelligence Agency Exemption in the Privacy Act of 1974; hearings, Mar. 5, June 25

YEAR	LOCATION	ACTIVITY
1975	Senate Committee on Finance; Subcommittee on Administration of the Internal Revenue Code	Federal Tax Return Privacy; hearings, Apr. 21, 28
1975	House Committee on Government Operations; Subcommittee on Government Information and Individual Rights	Implementation of the Privacy Act of 1974 — Data Banks; hearings, June 3
1975	Senate Committee on the Judiciary; Subcommittee on Constitutional Rights	Criminal Justice Information and Protection of the Privacy Act of 1975 (S. 2008); hearings, June 15–16
1975	House Committee on Banking, Finance, and Urban Affairs; Subcommittee on Financial Institutions, Supervision, Regulation, and Insurance	Bank Failures; Regulatory Reform; Financial Privacy; hearings, June 26, July 14–17, 21, 26
1975	House Committee on the Judiciary; Subcommittee on Civil and Constitutional Rights	Criminal Justice Information Control and Protection of the Privacy Act; hearings, July 14, 17, Sept. 5
1976	Senate Committee on Finance	Federal Tax Return Privacy; hearings, Jan. 23
1976	House Committee on Ways and Means	Confidentiality of Tax Return Information; hearings, Jan. 28
1976	Senate Committee on Banking, Housing, and Urban Affairs; Subcommittee on Financial Institutions	Right to Financial Privacy Act (S. 1343); hearings, June 16–17
1977	House Committee on Government Operations; Subcommittee on Government Information and Individual Rights	Final Report of the Privacy Protection Study Commission; hearings, July 12
1977	House Committee on Education and Labor; Subcommittee on Elementary, Secondary, and Vocational Education	Family Educational Rights and the Privacy Act of 1974; hearings, Aug. 2
1977	Senate Committee on Finance; Subcommittee on Health	Confidentiality of Medical Records; hearings, Sept. 15
1977	House Committee on Government Operations; Subcommittee on Government Information and Individual Rights	Privacy and Confidentiality: Report and Final Recommendations of the Commission on Federal Paperwork; hearings, Oct. 17
1978	Senate Committee on Banking, Housing, and Urban Affairs; Subcommittee on Financial Institutions	Electronic Funds Transfers and Financial Privacy; hearings, Apr. 18, 20, May 17

YEAR	LOCATION	ACTIVITY
1978	House Committee on Science, Space, and Technology; Subcommittee on Domestic and International Scientific Planning	Computers in Health Care; hearings, May 9–11
1978	House Committee on Government Operations; Subcommittee on Government Information and Individual Rights	Right to Privacy Proposals of the Privacy Protection Study Commission; hearings, May 23–24
1979	House Committee on Government Operations; Subcommittee on Government Information and Individual Rights	Privacy of Medical Records; hearings, Apr. 4, 9, 11, June 14, July 9, 14, Sept. 17
1979	House Select Committee on Intelligence; Subcommittee on Legislation	Impact of the Freedom of Information Act and the Privacy Act on Intelligence Activities; hearings, Apr. 5
1979	House Committee on Government Operations; Subcommittee on Government Information, Justice, and Agriculture	Public Reaction to Privacy Issues; hearings, June 6
1979	Senate Committee on Governmental Affairs	Legislation to Protect the Privacy of Medical Records; hearings, June 27, Aug. 3, Nov. 13
1979–80	House Committee on Government Operations; Subcommittee on Government Information and Individual Rights	Confidentiality of Insurance Records; hearings, Nov. 27, 1979, Mar. 3, 6, May 1, 22, 1980
1980	House Committee on Government Operations; Subcommittee on Government Information and Individual Rights	International Data Flow; hearings, Mar. 10, 13, 27, Apr. 21
1980	House Committee on Government Operations	Federal Privacy of Medical Information Act (H.R. 5935); report 96-832, Mar. 19
1980	House Committee on Ways and Means; Subcommittee on Health	Federal Privacy of Medical Information Act (H.R. 5935); hearings, Apr. 17
1980	Senate Committee on Labor and Human Resources	Labor Statistics Respondent Privacy Protection Act of 1980; hearings, July 23
1980	House Committee on Ways and Means; Subcommittee on Oversight	Review of Taxpayer Privacy Issues; hearings, July 30
1980	Senate Committee on Governmental Affairs	Privacy Act Amendments of 1979 (S. 503); report 96-935, Sept. 10
1980	House Committee on Interstate and Foreign Commerce	Securities Investor Protection—Right to Financial Privacy (H.R. 7939); report 96-1321, Sept. 16

YEAR	LOCATION	ACTIVITY
1981	House Committee on Government Operations	Privacy Act Amendments; report 97-147, June 16
1981	House Committee on Ways and Means; Subcommittee on Oversight	Taxpayer Privacy Issues; hearings, Dec. 14
1982	Senate Committee on Governmental Affairs; Subcommittee on Oversight of Government Management	Oversight of Computer Matching to Detect Fraud and Mismanagement in Government Programs; hearings, Dec. 15–16
1983	House Committee on Government Operations; Subcommittee on Government Information, Justice, and Agriculture	Oversight of Privacy Act of 1974; hearings, June 7–8
1983	House Committee on Government Operations	Who Cares about Privacy?: Oversight of the Privacy Act of 1974 by the OMB and Congress; report 98-455, Nov. 1
1984	House Committee on Government Operations; Subcommittee on Government Information, Justice, and Agriculture	Privacy and 1984: Public Opinions on Privacy Issues; hearings, Apr. 4
1984	Senate Committee on Governmental Affairs; Subcommittee on Oversight of Government Management	Computer Matching — Taxpayer Records; hearings, June 6
1984	House Committee on the Judiciary; Subcommittee on Civil and Constitutional Rights	Unauthorized Access to Individual Medical Records; hearings, Aug. 9
1986	Senate Committee on Governmental Affairs; Subcommittee on Oversight of Government Management	Computer Matching and Privacy Protection Act of 1986; hearings, Sept. 16
1987	Senate floor	Consideration and passage of Computer Matching and Privacy Protection Act of 1987 (s. 496), May 21
1987	House Committee on Government Operations; Subcommittee on Government Information, Justice, and Agriculture	Computer Matching and Privacy Protection Act of 1987; hearings, June 23
1988	House Committee on Government Operations	Computer Matching and Privacy Protection Act of 1988; report 100-802, July 27
1988	House floor	Consideration and passage of Computer Matching and Privacy Protection Act with amendment, Aug. 1

YEAR	LOCATION	ACTIVITY
1988	House Committee on the Judiciary; Subcommittee on Courts, Civil Liberties, and the Administration of Justice; and Senate Committee on the Judiciary; Subcommittee on Technology and the Law	Video Privacy Protection Act of 1988 (H.R. 4947 and S. 2361); hearings, Aug. 3
1988	Senate Committee on Governmental Affairs	Computer Matching and Privacy Protection Act of 1987 (S. 496); report 100-516, Sept. 15
1988	Senate floor	Concurrence in House amendment to Computer Matching and Privacy Protection Act, with additional amendment, Sept. 20
1988	House floor	Concurrence in Senate amendment to Computer Matching and Privacy Protection Act, Oct. 3
1988	Senate floor	Consideration and passage of Video Privacy Protection Act of 1988 (S. 2361), Oct. 14
1988	House floor	Consideration and passage of Video Privacy Protection Act of 1988 (H.R. 4947), Oct. 19
1988	Senate Committee on the Judiciary	Video Privacy Protection Act of 1988 (S. 2361); report 100-599, Oct. 21

Appendix B:
Selected Congressional Activity Concerning Communication Privacy, 1958–1986

YEAR	LOCATION	ACTIVITY
1958–59	Senate Committee on the Judiciary; Subcommittee on Constitutional Rights	Wiretapping, Eavesdropping, and the Bill of Rights; hearings, May 20, 22, 1958, July 9, 1959
1967	Senate Committee on the Judiciary; Subcommittee on Administrative Practice and Procedure	Right of Privacy Act of 1967; hearings, Mar. 20
1967	Senate Committee on the Judiciary; Subcommittee on Criminal Law and Procedures	Controlling Crime through More Effective Law Enforcement; hearings
1972	Senate Committee on the Judiciary; Subcommittee on Administrative Practice and Procedure	Warrantless Wiretapping; hearings, June 29
1974	House Committee on the Judiciary; Subcommittee on Courts, Civil Liberties, and the Administration of Justice	Wiretapping and Electronic Surveillance; hearings, Apr. 24, 26, 29
1975	House Committee on the Judiciary; Subcommittee on Courts, Civil Liberties, and the Administration of Justice	Surveillance; hearings, Feb. 6, 18, Mar. 4, 18, 21, May 22, June 26, July 25, Sept. 8
1975	Senate Committee on Commerce, Science, and Transportation; Special Subcommittee on Science, Technology, and Commerce; and Senate Committee on the Judiciary; Subcommittee on Constitutional Rights	Surveillance Technology; hearings, June 23, Sept. 9–10
1975–76	House Committee on Government Operations; Subcommittee on Government Information and Individual Rights	Interception of Nonverbal Communications by Federal Intelligence Agencies; hearings, Oct. 23, 1975, Feb. 25, Mar. 3, 10–11, 1976
1976	Senate Select Committee on Intelligence; Subcommittee on Intelligence and the Rights of Americans	Electronic Surveillance within the United States for Foreign Intelligence Purposes; hearings, June 29, July 1, Aug. 6, 10, 24
1976	Senate Committee on the Judiciary	Foreign Intelligence Surveillance Act of 1976; report 94-1035, July 15
1976	Senate Committee on the Judiciary; Subcommittee on Constitutional Rights	Surveillance Technology — 1976 Policy and Implications: An Analysis and Compendium of Materials; committee print, 1976

YEAR	LOCATION	ACTIVITY
1977	Senate Committee on the Judiciary; Subcommittee on Criminal Laws and Procedures	Foreign Intelligence Surveillance Act of 1977 (S. 1566); hearings, June 13–14
1977–78	Senate Select Committee on Intelligence; Subcommittee on Intelligence and the Rights of Americans	Foreign Intelligence Surveillance Act of 1978 (S. 1566); hearings, July 19, 21, 1977, Feb. 8, 24, 27, 1978
1978	House Committee on the Judiciary; Subcommittee on Courts, Civil Liberties, and the Administration of Justice	Foreign Intelligence Surveillance Act; hearings, June 22, 28–29
1978	House Committee on the Judiciary; Subcommittee on Courts, Civil Liberties, and the Administration of Justice	Bill of Rights Procedures Act (H.R. 214); hearings, July 13, 20
1979	Senate Committee on Commerce, Science, and Transportation; Subcommittee on Communications	Amendments to Communications Act of 1934; hearings, May 10–11, 16, June 5–7
1979	House Committee on Interstate and Foreign Commerce; Subcommittee on Communications	Communications Act of 1979 (H.R. 3333); hearings, June 6–7
1980	Senate Committee on the Judiciary; Subcommittee on Criminal Justice	Wiretap Amendments (S. 1717); hearings, Mar. 5
1981	House Committee on Science, Space, and Technology; Subcommittee on Science, Research, and Technology	Information and Telecommunications: An Overview of Issues, Technologies, and Applications; committee print, July
1983	House Committee on Science, Space, and Technology; Subcommittee on Transportation, Aviation, and Materials	Computer and Communications Security and Privacy; hearings, Sept. 26, Oct. 17, 24
1983	Senate Committee on Foreign Relations; Subcommittee on Arms Control, Oceans, International Operations, and Environment	International Communication and Information Policy; hearings, Oct. 19, 31
1983–84	House Committee on the Judiciary; Subcommittee on Courts, Civil Liberties, and the Administration of Justice	1984 — Civil Liberties and the National Security State; hearings, Nov. 2–3, 1983, Jan. 24, Apr. 5, Sept. 26, 1984
1984	House Committee on Government Operations; Subcommittee on Legislation and National Security	Federal Telecommunications Privacy Act of 1984 (H.R. 4620); hearings, Mar. 1
1984	House Committee on the Judiciary; Subcommittee on Criminal Justice	Nonconsensual Recording of Telephone Conversations; hearings, Mar. 8, Apr. 5

YEAR	LOCATION	ACTIVITY
1984	House Committee on Science, Space, and Technology; Subcommittee on Transportation, Aviation, and Materials	Computer and Communications Security and Privacy; committee print, Apr.
1984	House Committee on Government Operations	Federal Telecommunications Privacy Act of 1984 (H.R. 4620); report 98-815, May 31
1984	Senate Committee on the Judiciary; Subcommittee on Criminal Law	Tapping Wire or Oral Communications; hearings, June 13
1984	House Committee on Post Office and Civil Service; Subcommittee on Human Resources	Federal Telecommunications Privacy Act of 1984 (H.R. 4620); hearings, July 14
1984	House Committee on the Judiciary	Recording of Telephone Conversations by Federal Officers and Employees; report 98-905, July 25
1984	Senate Committee on the Judiciary; Subcommittee on Patents, Copyrights, and Trademarks	Oversight on Communications Privacy; hearings, Sept. 12
1984	House Committee on Science, Space, and Technology; Subcommittee on Transportation, Aviation, and Materials	Computer and Communications Security and Privacy; hearings, Sept. 24
1985	Senate Committee on the Judiciary; Subcommittee on Patents, Copyrights, and Trademarks	Electronic Communications Privacy; hearings, Nov. 13
1985–86	House Committee on the Judiciary; Subcommittee on Courts, Civil Liberties, and the Administration of Justice	Electronic Communications Privacy Act of 1985 (H.R. 3378); hearings, Sept. 26, Oct. 24, 1985, Jan. 30, Mar. 5, 1986
1986	House Committee on the Judiciary	Electronic Communications Privacy Act of 1986 (H.R. 4952); report 99-647, June 19
1986	House floor	Consideration and passage of H.R. 4952, June 23
1986	Senate floor	Consideration and passage of H.R. 4952 with amendment, Oct. 1
1986	House floor	Concurrence with Senate amendment to H.R. 4952, Oct. 2
1986	Senate Committee on the Judiciary	Electronic Communications Privacy Act of 1986 (S. 2575); report 99-541, Oct. 17

Appendix C:
Selected Congressional Activity Concerning Psychological Privacy,
1974–1988

YEAR	LOCATION	ACTIVITY
1974	House Committee on Government Operations; Subcommittee on Foreign Operations and Government Information	The Use of Polygraphs and Similar Devices by Federal Agencies; hearings, June 4–5
1974	Senate Committee on the Judiciary	Privacy, Polygraphs, and Employment; committee print, Nov.
1976	House Committee on Government Operations	The Use of Polygraphs and Similar Devices by Federal Agencies; report 94-795, Jan. 28
1977–78	Senate Committee on the Judiciary; Subcommittee on the Constitution	Polygraph Control and Civil Liberties Protection Act (s. 1845); hearings, Nov. 15–16, 1977, Sept. 19, 21, 1978
1979	House Select Committee on Intelligence; Subcommittee on Oversight	Preemployment Security Procedures of the Intelligence Agencies; hearings, May 16–17, 24, June 21
1979–80	House Committee on Education and Labor; Subcommittee on Labor-Management Relations	Pressures in Today's Workplace; hearings, Oct. 16–18, Dec. 4, 6, 15, 1979, Feb. 26–28, 1980
1980	House Committee on Education and Labor	Pressures in Today's Workplace; committee print, Dec.
1983	House Committee on Government Operations; Subcommittee on Legislation and National Security	Review of the President's National Security Decision Directive 84 and the Proposed DOD Directive on Polygraph Use; hearings, Oct. 19
1983	House Committee on Government Operations	Administration's Initiatives to Expand Polygraph Use and Impose Life Long Censorship on Thousands of Government Employees; report 98-578, Nov. 22
1983–84	House Committee on Post Office and Civil Service; Subcommittee on Civil Service	Presidential Directive on the Use of Polygraphs and Prepublication Review; hearings, Apr. 21, 28, 1983, Feb. 7, 1984
1984	House Committee on Post Office and Civil Service; Subcommittee on Civil Service	Federal Polygraph Limitations and Anti-Censorship Act of 1984; hearings, Feb. 29
1984	House Committee on Post Office and Civil Service	Federal Polygraph Limitation and Anti-Censorship Act of 1984 (H.R. 4681); report 98-961, Aug. 6 (part 1), Sept. 21 (part 2)

YEAR	LOCATION	ACTIVITY
1984	House Committee on Armed Services; Subcommittee on Investigations	Hearing on H.R. 4681, Relating to the Administration of Polygraph Examinations and Prepublication Review Requirements by Federal Agencies, Sept. 6
1984	House Committee on the Judiciary; Subcommittee on Civil and Constitutional Rights	Federal Polygraph Limitation and Anti-Censorship Act; hearings, Sept. 12
1984	House Committee on Armed Services	Full Committee Consideration of H.R. 4681, Relating to the Administration of Polygraph Examinations and Prepublication Review Requirements by Federal Agencies; hearings, Sept. 19
1985	Senate Committee on Governmental Affairs; Permanent Subcommittee on Investigations	Federal Government Security Clearance Programs; hearings, Apr. 16–18, 25
1985	House Committee on Education and Labor; Subcommittee on Employment Opportunities	Polygraphs in the Workplace: The Use of "Lie Detectors" in Hiring and Firing; hearings, July 30, Sept. 18
1985	House Committee on Education and Labor	Employee Polygraph Protection Act of 1985 (H.R. 1524); report 99-416, Dec. 5
1986	House floor	Consideration and passage of H.R. 1524, Mar. 12
1986	Senate Committee on Labor and Human Resources	Polygraph Protection Act of 1985; hearings, Apr. 23
1986	Senate Committee on Labor and Human Resources	Polygraph Protection Act of 1985 (S. 1815); report 99-447, Sept. 17
1987	House Committee on Education and Labor; Subcommittee on Employment Opportunities	Polygraph Testing in the Private Work Force; hearings, Mar. 5, Apr. 30
1987	Senate Committee on Labor and Human Resources	Polygraphs in the Workplace; hearings, June 19
1987	House Committee on Education and Labor	Employee Polygraph Protection Act of 1987 (H.R. 1212); report 100-208, July 9
1987	House floor	Consideration and passage of H.R. 1212, Nov. 4
1988	Senate Committee on Labor and Human Resources	Polygraph Protection Act of 1987 (S. 1904), report 100-284, Feb. 11
1988	Senate floor	Consideration of S. 1904, Mar. 1–3
1988	Senate floor	Passage of H.R. 1212 with an amendment and postponement of S. 1904, Mar. 3

YEAR	LOCATION	ACTIVITY
1988	Conference committee of House Committee on Education and Labor and Senate Committee on Labor and Human Resources	Appointed, Mar. 22
1988	House Committee on Education and Labor	Conference Report on H.R. 1212: "Employee Polygraph Protection Act of 1988," May 26
1988	House floor	Agreement to conference report on H.R. 1212, June 1
1988	Senate floor	Agreement to conference report on H.R. 1212, June 9

Notes

PREFACE

1. The question of the role ideas or values play in the policy-making process is of increasing interest to political scientists and policy scholars. The role the idea of privacy played in these cases will be analyzed in chapter 7. For background about the role of ideas and interests in policy making, see John W. Kingdon, "Ideas, Politics, and Public Policies" (paper presented at the annual meeting of the American Political Science Association, Washington, D.C., Sept. 1988); Robert B. Reich, ed., *The Power of Public Ideas* (Cambridge: Harvard University Press, 1990); and Jane J. Mansbridge, ed., *Beyond Self-Interest* (Chicago: University of Chicago Press, 1990).

2. Charles O. Jones, *An Introduction to the Study of Public Policy* (Monterey, Calif.: Brooks/Cole, 1984), p. 6.

3. Mary Ann Glendon, *Rights Talk: The Impoverishment of Political Discourse* (New York: Free Press, 1991), p. 12.

CHAPTER ONE

1. Jeffrey Rothfeder, "Is Nothing Private?," *Business Week*, Sept. 4, 1989, pp. 74–82.

2. *Olmstead v. United States*, 277 U.S. 438, 473–74 (1928).

3. Oscar H. Gandy, Jr., *The Panoptic Sort: A Political Economy of Personal Information* (Boulder: Westview Press, 1993), pp. 1–2. The term comes from Jeremy Bentham, whose "Panopticon" was a prison that enhanced the efficient surveillance of prisoners. Gandy points out: "It is critical to note that the purpose of the modern prison and of other panoptic systems that imitate its technology is not punishment, but transformation, rehabilitation, and correct training. The same may be said of the panoptic sort: It is not limited to identification, classification, and assessment, but includes the goal of normalizing behavior within categories" (ibid., p. 24).

4. Surveillance has been an important, and recurring, theme in the literature on privacy, even though it has not served as a goal for public policy in the United States. See Alan F. Westin, *Privacy and Freedom* (New York: Atheneum, 1967); James B. Rule, *Private Lives and Public Surveillance: Social Control in the Computer Age* (London: Allen Lane, 1973); David Burnham, *The Rise of the Computer State* (New York: Random House, 1983); Kenneth C. Laudon, *Dossier Society: Value Choices in the Design of National Information Systems* (New York: Columbia University Press, 1986); and David H. Flaherty, *Protecting Privacy in Surveillance Societies: The Federal Republic of Germany, Sweden, France, Canada, and the United States* (Chapel Hill: University of North Carolina Press, 1989).

5. Westin, *Privacy and Freedom*, p. 7.

6. Judith Jarvis Thomson, "The Right to Privacy," *Philosophy and Public Affairs* 4, no. 4 (Summer 1975): 295.

7. David M. O'Brien, *Privacy, Law, and Public Policy* (New York: Praeger, 1979), p. vii.

8. Julie Inness, *Privacy, Intimacy, and Isolation* (New York: Oxford University Press, 1992), p. 3.

9. Vincent J. Samar, *The Right to Privacy: Gays, Lesbians, and the Constitution* (Philadelphia: Temple University Press, 1991), p. 13.

10. Spiros Simitis, "Reviewing Privacy in an Information Society," *University of Pennsylvania Law Review* 135 (Mar. 1987): 708.

11. For a review of the different definitions of privacy that have appeared in legal and philosophical works, see W. A. Parent, "Recent Work on the Concept of Privacy," *American Philosophical Quarterly* 20, no. 4 (Oct. 1983): 341–55. Parent concludes that research on privacy is in "hopeless disarray" (ibid., p. 341). Important anthologies on privacy include J. Roland Pennock and John W. Chapman, eds., *Privacy*, Nomos Series 13, Yearbook of the American Society for Political and Legal Philosophy (New York: Atherton Press, 1971), and Ferdinand David Schoeman, ed., *Philosophical Dimensions of Privacy: An Anthology* (Cambridge: Cambridge University Press, 1984).

12. Isaiah Berlin, "Two Concepts of Liberty," in *Four Essays on Liberty* (London: Oxford University Press, 1969), pp. 118–72.

13. Samar, *The Right to Privacy*, p. 53.

14. For an analysis of the role rights play as resources in political action and rhetoric, see Stuart A. Scheingold, *The Politics of Rights: Lawyers, Public Policy, and Political Change* (New Haven: Yale University Press, 1974).

15. Inness, *Privacy, Intimacy, and Isolation*; Samar, *The Right to Privacy*.

16. Flaherty, *Protecting Privacy in Surveillance Societies*.

17. Colin J. Bennett, *Regulating Privacy: Data Protection and Public Policy in Europe and the United States* (Ithaca: Cornell University Press, 1992).

18. David F. Linowes, *Privacy in America: Is Your Private Life in the Public Eye?* (Urbana: University of Illinois Press, 1989).

19. Jeffrey Rothfeder, *Privacy for Sale: How Computerization Has Made Everyone's Private Life an Open Secret* (New York: Simon and Schuster, 1992).

20. H. Jeff Smith, *Managing Privacy: Information Technology and Corporate America* (Chapel Hill: University of North Carolina Press, 1994).

21. For summaries of congressional activity during this period, see James B. Rule et al., *The Politics of Privacy: Planning for Personal Data Systems as Powerful Technologies* (New York: Elsevier, 1980); U.S. Senate Committee on the Judiciary, Subcommittee on Constitutional Rights, *Federal Data Banks and Constitutional Rights: A Study of Data Systems on Individuals Maintained by Agencies of the U.S. Government*, 93d Cong., 2d sess. (Washington, D.C.: Government Printing Office, 1974); and U.S. Senate and House Committees on Government Operations, *Legislative History of the Privacy Act of 1974, s. 3418 (PL 93-579)*, 94th Cong., 2d sess. (Washington, D.C.: Government Printing Office, 1976).

22. These categories are derived from Alan Westin's classification in his seminal work, *Privacy and Freedom*. Westin speaks of data surveillance (information collection and processing), physical surveillance (listening and watching), and psychological surveillance (probing the mind).

23. The Radio Act of 1927, which had borrowed language from 1912 legislation, provided that "no person not being authorized by the sender shall intercept any communication and divulge . . . the contents." Section 605 of the Communication Act of 1934 adopted this language.

24. Langdon Winner, *Autonomous Technology: Technics-out-of-Control as a Theme in Political Thought* (Cambridge: MIT Press, 1977), p. 76.

25. Leslie A. White, *The Science of Culture: A Study of Man and Civilization* (New York: Farrar, Straus and Cudahy, 1949), p. 365.

26. John Kenneth Galbraith, *The New Industrial State* (Boston: Houghton Mifflin, 1971), p. 7.

27. Jacques Ellul, *The Technological Society*, translated by John Wilkinson (New York: Vintage Books, 1964).

28. Edward Glaser, "Information Technology: Power without Design, Thrust without Direction," in Conference Board, *Information Technology: Some Critical Implications for Decision Makers* (New York: Conference Board, 1971), p. 25.

29. Victor C. Ferkiss, *Technological Man: The Myth and the Reality* (New York: George Braziller, 1969), pp. 29–30.

30. Gandy, *The Panoptic Sort*, p. 36.

31. James R. Beniger, *The Control Revolution: Technological and Economic Origins of the Information Society* (Cambridge: Harvard University Press, 1986).

32. Neil Postman, *Technopoly: The Surrender of Culture to Technology* (New York: Knopf, 1992), p. 5.

33. Ibid., p. 18.

34. Winner, *Autonomous Technology*, p. 316.

35. Edward V. Long, *The Intruders: The Invasion of Privacy by Government and Industry* (New York: Praeger, 1967), p. 4.

36. Arthur R. Miller, *The Assault on Privacy: Computers, Data Banks, and Dossiers* (Ann Arbor: University of Michigan Press, 1971), p. 8.

37. Westin, *Privacy and Freedom*, p. 3.

38. Ibid., p. 67. Westin later wrote: "In *Privacy and Freedom*, I assumed a strong technological determinism. The data banks research [Alan F. Westin and Michael A. Baker, *Databanks in a Free Society: Computers, Record-Keeping, and Privacy*, report of the Project on Computer Databanks of the Computer Science and Engineering Board, National Academy of Sciences (New York: Quadrangle/New York Times Book Company, 1972)] made me move to a much more cautious and theoretically different approach." Alan F. Westin, "The Protection of Privacy in the Public and Private Sectors," in *Effective Social Science: Eight Cases in Economics, Political Science, and Sociology*, edited by Bernard Barber (New York: Russell Sage Foundation, 1987), p. 141.

39. In his important analysis of agenda setting and policy formulation, John W. Kingdon poses the question of why some ideas are accepted and others are not. See John W. Kingdon, *Agendas, Alternatives, and Public Policies* (Glenview, Ill.: Scott, Foresman, 1984).

40. Paul J. Quirk, "In Defense of the Politics of Ideas," *Journal of Politics* 50 (Feb. 1988): 31.

41. John W. Kingdon, "Ideas, Politics, and Public Policies" (paper presented at the

annual meeting of the American Political Science Association, Washington, D.C., Sept. 1988), p. 3.

42. Ibid., p. 6.

43. Martha Derthick and Paul J. Quirk, *The Politics of Deregulation* (Washington, D.C.: Brookings Institution, 1985).

44. Timothy J. Conlan, Margaret T. Wrightson, and David R. Beam, *Taxing Choices: The Politics of Tax Reform* (Washington, D.C.: Congressional Quarterly Press, 1990).

45. Peter H. Schuck, "The Politics of Rapid Legal Change: Immigration Policy in the 1980s" (paper presented at the annual research conference of the Association for Public Policy Analysis and Management, Bethesda, Md., Oct. 1991).

46. This argument is also presented in Priscilla M. Regan, "Ideas or Interests: Privacy in Electronic Communications," *Policy Studies Journal* 21, no. 3 (Autumn 1993): 450–69.

47. The scholarly literature on interest-group politics is extensive. Among the most important works are David B. Truman, *The Governmental Process: Political Interests and Public Opinion* (New York: Knopf, 1951); Earl Latham, *The Group Basis of Politics: A Study in Basing-Point Legislation* (Ithaca: Cornell University Press, 1952); Grant McConnell, *Private Power and American Democracy* (New York: Knopf, 1966); Theodore J. Lowi, *The End of Liberalism: Ideology, Policy, and the Crisis of Public Authority* (New York: W. W. Norton, 1969).

48. Robert B. Reich, ed., *The Power of Public Ideas* (Cambridge: Harvard University Press, 1990), p. 4.

49. Kingdon, *Agendas, Alternatives, and Public Policies*, pp. 122–28.

50. The literature on subgovernments and iron triangles is enormous. For a good critical review of the concept and earlier studies, see Daniel McCool, "Subgovernments as Determinants of Political Viability," *Political Science Quarterly* 105, no. 2 (Summer 1990): 269–93.

51. Hugh Heclo, "Issue Networks and the Executive Establishment," in *The New American Political System*, edited by Anthony King (Washington, D.C.: American Enterprise Institute, 1978), p. 102.

52. There is much current discussion distinguishing terms related to issue networks and policy communities. See, for example, R. A. W. Rhodes and David Marsh, "New Directions in the Study of Policy Networks," *European Journal of Political Research* 21, no. 2 (1992): 181–205; Grant Jordan and Klaus Schubert, "A Preliminary Ordering of Policy Network Labels," *European Journal of Political Research* 21, no. 2 (1992): 7–27; and Michael M. Atkinson and William D. Coleman, "Policy Networks, Policy Communities, and the Problem of Governance," *Governance* 5, no. 2 (1992): 154–80.

53. For a discussion of each of these alternative definitions, see Priscilla M. Regan, "Public Use of Private Information: A Comparison of Personal Information Policies in the United States and Britain" (Ph.D. diss., Cornell University, 1981), chap. 3.

54. Richard F. Fenno, *Congressmen in Committees* (Boston: Little Brown, 1973).

55. David R. Mayhew, *Congress: The Electoral Connection* (New Haven: Yale University Press, 1974); R. Douglas Arnold, *The Logic of Congressional Action* (New Haven: Yale University Press, 1990).

56. Kingdon, *Agendas, Alternatives, and Public Policies.*

57. James Madison, "Federalist Paper #10," in *The Federalist Papers* (New York: Mentor, 1961), p. 78.

CHAPTER TWO

1. Thomas E. McCollough, *The Moral Imagination and Public Life: Raising the Ethical Question* (Chatham, N.J.: Chatham House Publishers, 1991), p. 32.

2. Samuel D. Warren and Louis D. Brandeis, "The Right to Privacy," *Harvard Law Review* 4 (Dec. 1890): 195.

3. Ibid., p. 193. Warren and Brandeis attributed use of this phrase to Thomas M. Cooley, *A Treatise on the Law of Torts* (Chicago: Callaghan, 1888).

4. Warren and Brandeis, "The Right to Privacy," p. 197.

5. Ibid., p. 205.

6. Ibid., p. 196.

7. Ibid., p. 214.

8. William L. Prosser, "Privacy," *California Law Review* 48, no. 3 (Aug. 1960): 383–423; Edward J. Bloustein, "Privacy as an Aspect of Human Dignity — An Answer to Dean Prosser," *New York University Law Review* 39 (Dec. 1964): 962–1007, reprinted in Ferdinand David Schoeman, ed., *Philosophical Dimensions of Privacy: An Anthology* (Cambridge: Cambridge University Press, 1984), pp. 156–202.

9. Bloustein, "Privacy as an Aspect of Human Dignity," p. 158.

10. Ibid., p. 181.

11. Ibid., p. 191.

12. Ibid., p. 185.

13. Alan F. Westin, *Privacy and Freedom* (New York: Atheneum, 1967), p. 7.

14. Ibid., p. 368.

15. Ibid., pp. 24–25.

16. Ibid., p. 7.

17. Ibid., pp. 31–32.

18. Ibid., p. 42.

19. Ibid., p. 20.

20. Ibid.

21. Ibid., p. 39.

22. Charles Fried, "Privacy," *Yale Law Journal* 77, no. 3 (Jan. 1968): 475–93, reprinted in Schoeman, *Philosophical Dimensions of Privacy*, p. 219.

23. Ibid., p. 211.

24. Ibid., p. 212.

25. J. Roland Pennock and John W. Chapman, eds., *Privacy*, Nomos Series 13, Yearbook of the American Society for Political and Legal Philosophy (New York: Atherton Press, 1971), p. vii.

26. Ibid.

27. Carl J. Friedrich, "Secrecy versus Privacy: The Democratic Dilemma," in ibid., p. 115.

28. Ibid., p. 112.

29. Ibid., p. 107.

30. Ibid., pp. 115–16.

31. Ibid., p. 119.

32. Arnold Simmel, "Privacy Is Not an Isolated Freedom," in ibid., p. 71.

33. Ibid.

34. Ibid., p. 72.

35. Ibid., p. 86.

36. Ibid., p. 87.

37. Judith Jarvis Thomson, "The Right to Privacy," *Philosophy and Public Affairs* 4, no. 4 (Summer 1975): 303.

38. Thomas Scanlon, "Thomson on Privacy," *Philosophy and Public Affairs* 4, no. 4 (Summer 1975): 315.

39. Ibid.

40. Ibid., pp. 317–18.

41. Ibid., p. 322.

42. James Rachels, "Why Privacy Is Important," *Philosophy and Public Affairs* 4, no. 4 (Summer 1975): 323–33, reprinted in Schoeman, *Philosophical Dimensions of Privacy*, p. 292.

43. Ibid., p. 295.

44. Ibid., p. 297.

45. Robert Merton, *Social Theory and Social Structure* (1957), p. 375, cited in Westin, *Privacy and Freedom*, p. 58.

46. Julie Inness, *Privacy, Intimacy, and Isolation* (New York: Oxford University Press, 1992), p. 140.

47. Vincent J. Samar, *The Right to Privacy: Gays, Lesbians, and the Constitution* (Philadelphia: Temple University Press, 1991), p. 86.

48. Arthur R. Miller, *The Assault on Privacy: Computers, Data Banks, and Dossiers* (Ann Arbor: University of Michigan Press, 1971), pp. 211–16.

49. David M. O'Brien reaches a similar conclusion and presents a more complete discussion of the constitutional development of a right to privacy. See David M. O'Brien, *Privacy, Law, and Public Policy* (New York: Praeger, 1979).

50. Prosser, "Privacy," p. 386.

51. Prosser delineated the differences among these torts as follows: "Taking them in order — intrusion, disclosure, false light and appropriation — the first and second require the invasion of something secret, secluded or private pertaining to the plaintiff; the third and fourth do not. The second and third depend upon publicity, while the first does not, nor does the fourth, although it usually involves it. The third requires falsity or fiction; the other three do not. The fourth involves a use for the defendant's advantage, which is not true of the rest" (ibid., p. 407).

52. His analysis of the elements in a tort of privacy was adopted in the 1967 draft Second Restatement of the U.S. Law of Torts.

53. Harry Kalven, "Privacy in Tort Law — Were Warren and Brandeis Wrong?," *Law and Contemporary Problems* 31 (Spring 1966): 333.

54. For this argument, see Guy J. Sternal, "Informational Privacy and Public Records," *Pacific Law Journal* 8 (Jan. 1977): 25.

55. Kalven, "Privacy in Tort Law," p. 333.

56. This is discussed further in chapter 4. The Code of Fair Information Practices specifies the rights of individuals — to see, correct, and consent to disclosure — and the responsibilities of organizations — to keep accurate, complete, and timely records.

57. Westin, *Privacy and Freedom*, p. 324.

58. Miller, *Assault on Privacy*, p. 212.

59. James B. Rule, "My Mailbox Is Mine," *Wall Street Journal*, Aug. 15, 1990, p. A8.

60. *NAACP v. Alabama*, 357 U.S. 449 (1958).

61. *Watkins v. United States*, 354 U.S. 178 (1957); *Sweezy v. New Hampshire*, 354 U.S. 234 (1957).

62. *Talley v. California*, 362 U.S. 60 (1960).

63. Quoted in O'Brien, *Privacy, Law, and Public Policy*, p. 39.

64. 116 U.S. 616 (1886).

65. 277 U.S. 438 (1928).

66. Ibid.

67. Ibid., p. 478.

68. *Katz v. United States*, 389 U.S. 347, 350 (1967).

69. Ibid., p. 361.

70. First used by Justice Powell in *Couch v. United States*, 409 U.S. 322 (1973), in rejecting a Fourth Amendment objection to an Internal Revenue Service summons and later used by Powell in *United States v. Miller*, 425 U.S. 435 (1976).

71. 439 U.S. 128 (1978).

72. Peter Goldberger, "Consent, Expectation of Privacy, and the Meaning of 'Searches' in the Fourth Amendment," *Journal of Criminal Law and Criminology* 75, no. 2 (1984): 319–62; Gerald G. Ashdown, "The Fourth Amendment and the 'Legitimate Expectation of Privacy,'" *Vanderbilt Law Review* 34 (Oct. 1981): 1289–1345.

73. *United States v. Miller*, 425 U.S. 435, 442 (1976). In response to this decision, Congress passed the Financial Privacy Act of 1978 (PL 95-630), providing bank customers with some privacy regarding records held by banks and other financial institutions and mandating procedures whereby federal agencies can gain access to such records.

74. Ashdown, "The Fourth Amendment and the 'Legitimate Expectation of Privacy,'" p. 1321.

75. "Tracking *Katz*: Beepers, Privacy, and the Fourth Amendment," *Yale Law Journal* 86, no. 7 (June 1977): 1477.

76. O'Brien refers to these rationales respectively as the fox hunter's reason, the old woman's reason, and the hermit's reason. For his discussion, see O'Brien, *Privacy, Law, and Public Policy*, pp. 95–113.

77. *Schmerber v. California*, 384 U.S. 757 (1966).

78. *Couch v. United States*, 409 U.S. 322 (1973).

79. This concept was first articulated in *Shapiro v. United States*, 335 U.S. 1 (1948), and later clarified in *Grosso v. United States*, 390 U.S. 62 (1968).

80. Westin, *Privacy and Freedom*, p. 350.

81. William M. Beaney, "The Right to Privacy and American Law," *Law and Contemporary Problems* 31 (1966): 257.

82. 381 U.S. 479 (1965).

83. *Eisenstadt v. Baird*, 405 U.S. 438 (1972).

84. 410 U.S. 113 (1973).

85. 424 U.S. 693 (1976).

86. Ibid., p. 713.

87. 429 U.S. 589 (1977).

88. Ibid., pp. 599–600.

89. Ibid., p. 600.

90. 433 U.S. 425 (1977).

91. Ibid., p. 465.

92. Ibid., p. 457.

93. Ibid., p. 465.

94. Donald L. Horowitz, *The Courts and Social Policy* (Washington, D.C.: Brookings Institution, 1977), p. 23.

CHAPTER THREE

1. The two most complete and thorough treatments of this subject are David H. Flaherty, *Privacy in Colonial New England* (Charlottesville: University Press of Virginia, 1972), and David J. Seipp, *The Right to Privacy in American History*, Program on Information Resources Policy, Publication P-78-3 (Cambridge: Harvard University, 1978). This section is primarily based on the above works.

2. Edward J. Bloustein, "Privacy as an Aspect of Human Dignity — An Answer to Dean Prosser," *New York University Law Review* 39 (Dec. 1964): 984.

3. Flaherty, *Privacy in Colonial New England*, p. 85.

4. Alan F. Westin, *Privacy and Freedom* (New York: Atheneum, 1967), pp. 8–21.

5. Flaherty, *Privacy in Colonial New England*, p. 245.

6. Ibid., pp. 167–79.

7. Ibid., p. 175.

8. Ibid., chap. 7.

9. For a more extensive discussion, see ibid., chap. 4.

10. Seipp, *The Right to Privacy*, p. 11.

11. Quoted in ibid., p. 12.

12. 96 U.S. 727 (1878).

13. For a more extensive discussion, see Seipp, *The Right to Privacy*, pp. 42–54.

14. Ibid., p. 43.

15. Jesse Chickering to Senator John Davis, Boston, Jan. 20, 1849, in Sen. Misc. Doc. No. 64, 30th Cong., 2d sess., Mar. 3, 1849, pp. 21–22, cited in Seipp, *The Right to Privacy*, p. 19.

16. Ibid., p. 45.

17. Ibid., p. 53.

18. As reported in William H. Dutton and Robert G. Meadow, "Public Perspectives on Government Information Technology: A Review of Survey Research on Privacy, Civil Liberties, and the Democratic Process" (unpublished contractor report for the Office of Technology Assessment, 1985), p. 8.

19. In 1978, 76 percent agreed (Louis Harris and Associates and Alan F. Westin,

The Dimensions of Privacy: A National Opinion Research Survey of Attitudes toward Privacy [Stevens Point, Wis.: Sentry Insurance, 1979], table 1.4, p. 15). In 1990, 79 percent agreed (Louis Harris and Associates and Alan F. Westin, *The Equifax Report on Consumers in the Information Age* [Atlanta: Equifax, Inc., 1990], table 1.5, p. 7).

20. The results of these surveys are reported and analyzed in Herbert McClosky and Alida Brill, *Dimensions of Tolerance: What Americans Believe about Civil Liberties* (New York: Russell Sage Foundation, 1983). The Civil Liberties Survey used a national cross-sectional random sample of 1,993 adults as well as a sample of 1,891 community leaders and included about 400 questions. The Opinion and Values Survey involved a national cross-sectional sample of 938 respondents as well as samples of opinion elites and included about 350 questions.

21. Albert H. Cantril and Susan Davis Cantril, *Live and Let Live: American Public Opinion about Privacy at Home and at Work* (New York: American Civil Liberties Union Foundation, 1994). This survey involved in-person interviews with 993 people drawn from a representative cross section of the adult population. The interviews lasted 45–50 minutes and were conducted between November 13 and December 13, 1992.

22. Ibid., p. 7.

23. Most important among these are Louis Harris and Associates and Alan F. Westin, *Harris-Equifax Health Information Privacy Survey, 1993* (Atlanta: Equifax, Inc., 1993), *Harris-Equifax Consumer Privacy Survey, 1992* (Atlanta: Equifax, Inc., 1992), *Harris-Equifax Consumer Privacy Survey, 1991* (Atlanta: Equifax, Inc., 1991), *The Equifax Report on Consumers in the Information Age* (Atlanta: Equifax, Inc., 1990), and *The Dimensions of Privacy: A National Opinion Research Survey of Attitudes toward Privacy* (Stevens Point, Wis.: Sentry Insurance, 1979); and Louis Harris and Associates, *The Road after 1984: A Nationwide Survey of the Public and Its Leaders on the New Technology and Its Consequences for American Life* (conducted for Southern New England Telephone for presentation at the Eighth International Smithsonian Symposium, 1983).

24. Irving Crespi, *Public Opinion, Polls, and Democracy* (Boulder: Westview Press, 1989), pp. 39–40.

25. Oscar H. Gandy, Jr., *The Panoptic Sort: A Political Economy of Personal Information* (Boulder: Westview Press, 1993), p. 125.

26. James E. Katz and Annette R. Tassone, "Public Opinion Trends: Privacy and Information Technology," *Public Opinion Quarterly* 54, no. 1 (Spring 1990): 126 (n. 1).

27. Dutton and Meadow also make this point in "Public Perspectives on Government Information Technology," and "A Tolerance for Surveillance: American Public Opinion Concerning Privacy and Civil Liberties," in *Government Infostructures*, edited by Karen B. Levitan (New York: Greenwood Press, 1987), pp. 147–70.

28. Gandy, *The Panoptic Sort*, p. 127. For discussion of the problem of nonattitudes, see Herbert Asher, *Polling and the Public: What Every Citizen Should Know* (Washington, D.C.: Congressional Quarterly Press, 1992), pp. 21–37.

29. See Katz and Tassone, "Public Opinion Trends," p. 127 (n. 2).

30. The 1978 and 1983 surveys began with the preamble, "Now let me ask you about technology and privacy."

31. McClosky and Brill, *Dimensions of Tolerance*, table 5.2, p. 188.

32. Gandy, *The Panoptic Sort*, p. 127.

33. Cantril and Cantril, *Live and Let Live*, p. 5.

34. Ibid., pp. 55–65.

35. Ibid., p. 69.

36. Gandy, *The Panoptic Sort*, p. 135.

37. James E. Katz and Merton M. Hyman, "Dimensions of Concern over Telecommunications Privacy in the United States," *Information Society* 9, no. 2 (1993): 251–75.

38. Mary J. Culnan, "Consumer Attitudes toward Direct Mail, Privacy, and Name Removal: Implications for Direct Marketing" (paper presented at the Symposium on Consumer Privacy, Chicago/Midwest Direct Marketing Days, Chicago, Jan. 20, 1993), pp. 2–3. Culnan notes that in earlier empirical studies, "differences in attitudes toward information practices and demographic differences were assessed after classifying subjects according to their concern for privacy. This research is inappropriate for understanding privacy attitudes in the U.S. because the U.S. has adopted a highly targeted or sectoral approach to regulating privacy and fair information practices are often implemented voluntarily by individual organizations, or not at all" (ibid., p. 2).

39. Cantril and Cantril, *Live and Let Live*, p. 9.

40. Harris–Sentry Insurance, 1979, table 3.1, p. 33.

41. Cantril and Cantril, *Live and Let Live*, chart D, p. 24.

42. Harris–Sentry Insurance, 1979, table 3.2, p. 35.

43. Ibid.

44. Cantril and Cantril, *Live and Let Live*, p. 29.

45. Harris–Sentry Insurance, 1979, table 3.2, p. 35.

46. McClosky and Brill, *Dimensions of Tolerance*, table 5.2, p. 188.

47. Harris–Sentry Insurance, 1979, table 8.3, p. 69.

48. McClosky and Brill, *Dimensions of Tolerance*, table 5.2, p. 188.

49. Ibid.

50. Harris–Sentry Insurance, 1979, table 8.5, p. 70.

51. Harris-Equifax, 1990, table 2.6, p. 18.

52. Ibid., table 2.1, p. 11.

53. Harris–Sentry Insurance, 1979, table 2.2, p. 24.

54. Harris–Southern New England Telephone, 1983, table 1.3, p. 12.

55. Harris–Sentry Insurance, 1979, table 2.2, p. 24.

56. Harris–Southern New England Telephone, 1983, table 1.6, p. 16.

57. Ibid., table 1.7, pp. 17–18.

58. Ibid., table 1.2, p. 11.

59. Harris-Equifax, 1990, table 2.1, p. 11.

60. Harris-Equifax, 1991, table 6, p. 15.

61. Cantril and Cantril, *Live and Let Live*, table 2, p. 13.

62. Ibid., table 3, p. 14.

63. Gandy, *The Panoptic Sort*, p. 163. Gandy also found that "those who view more television estimate the extent of public concern about privacy to be higher than those who watch less" (ibid., p. 165).

64. See Katz and Tassone, "Public Opinion Trends," p. 134.

65. Crespi, *Public Opinion, Polls, and Democracy*, p. 66.

66. Harris-Equifax, 1990, table 2.3, p. 14.

67. Ibid., table 2.5, p. 16.

68. Harris-Equifax, 1993, table 4.2B, p. 49.

69. Ibid., table 4.3, p. 50.

70. Harris–Sentry Insurance, 1979, table 1.10, p. 20. In December 1978, 9 percent replied affirmatively to the question, "Do you believe that your telephone has ever been tapped or not?"; 12 percent had replied affirmatively in January 1978.

71. Harris-Equifax, 1991, table 4, p. 13.

72. Harris–Sentry Insurance, 1979, table 10.3, p. 84.

73. Roper Organization, *Roper Reports 82.6*, June 5–12, 1982, cited in Office of Technology Assessment, *Federal Government Information Technology: Electronic Record Systems and Individual Privacy*, OTA-CIT-296 (Washington, D.C.: Government Printing Office, 1986), pp. 28–29.

74. Harris–Southern New England Telephone, 1983, p. 41.

75. Included among the "privacy-intensive industries" are insurance, credit grantors, banks and thrifts, direct marketers, and human resources. Harris-Equifax, 1990.

76. Ibid., table 11.7, p. 106.

77. Harris-Equifax, 1993, table 10.1, p. 98.

78. Ibid., table 10.4, pp. 101, 97.

79. Ibid., tables 10.2–10.6, pp. 97–103.

80. Harris-Equifax, 1990, table 1.6, p. 8.

81. Ibid., pp. 4–5.

82. Harris-Equifax, 1993, pp. 27–28.

83. Harris-Equifax, 1990, p. xxvi.

84. Cantril and Cantril, *Live and Let Live*, p. 19.

85. Harris–Sentry Insurance, 1979, table 9.1, p. 76.

86. Harris–Southern New England Telephone, 1983, table 3.2, p. 43. The 1990 survey did not ask this question of the general public but only of executives in the "privacy-intensive industries" of insurance, credit grantors, banks and thrifts, direct marketers, and human resources. From 50 to 64 percent of these executives believed that the present use of computers was not an actual threat to privacy. For the three industries for which similar 1978 survey data is available, the percentage of executives who perceive use of computers as a threat has increased: insurance, from 33 percent in 1978 to 44 percent in 1990; credit grantors, from 29 percent in 1978 to 35 percent in 1990; and banks and thrifts, from 22 percent in 1978 to 45 percent in 1990. Harris-Equifax, 1990, p. 83.

87. Harris-Equifax, 1992, table 3, p. 17.

88. Ibid., table 5, p. 19.

89. Ibid., table 4, p. 18.

90. Ibid., table 7, p. 21; Harris-Equifax, 1993, p. 31.

91. Harris–Southern New England Telephone, 1983, table 3.3, p. 44.

92. Harris-Equifax, 1993, table 1.7, p. 32.

93. Harris-Equifax, 1992, table 6, p. 20.

94. Harris-Equifax, 1990, p. 23.

95. Ibid., table 3.2, p. 27.

96. Ibid., table 3.3, p. 28.

97. Ibid., table 7.2, p. 69.

98. Ibid., table 7.4, p. 70.

99. Ibid., table 8.1, p. 79.

100. Ibid., table 8.2, p. 80.

101. Harris-Equifax, 1992, table 14, p. 31.

102. Demographic variables included region, sex, age, locality size, employment status, education, father's education, and income. See Cantril and Cantril, *Live and Let Live*, chap. 4, for the results of the multiple regression analyses for these variables.

103. Nondemographic variables included support for "traditional" civil liberties (assembly, speech, expression, religion, no unreasonable search); intensity of religious beliefs and practices; other values and views including alienation from public officials, confidence in big corporations, views on the government's role in helping the poor, confidence in the country, and perceptions of opportunities for minorities and the gap between rich and poor; perceived trends for self and country; political leanings; individual differences in self-esteem, tolerance of ambiguity, and independence of judgment; news interest and political involvement; and past experience. See ibid., chap. 5, for results of multiple regression analyses for these variables.

104. Ibid., pp. vi–vii, 137–38.

105. Harris-Equifax, 1991, p. 9.

106. Harris-Equifax, 1990, table 2.3, p. 14.

107. Harris-Equifax, 1991, table 11, p. 19.

108. Ibid., table 15, p. 21.

109. Ibid., table 14, p. 21.

110. Katz and Tassone, "Public Opinion Trends," p. 136.

111. Ibid., p. 137.

112. Harris-Equifax, 1992, p. 24.

CHAPTER FOUR

1. See chapter 2 for a discussion of the common law protections for privacy.

2. Arthur R. Miller, *The Assault on Privacy: Computers, Data Banks, and Dossiers* (Ann Arbor: University of Michigan Press, 1971), p. 189.

3. Ibid.

4. Virtually every other Western democracy that has passed privacy or data protection legislation has established an agency or commissioner with advisory or regulatory powers. For analyses of the workings of these bodies and background on the support for the need for one in the United States, see Colin J. Bennett, *Regulating Privacy: Data Protection and Public Policy in Europe and the United States* (Ithaca: Cornell University Press, 1992), and David H. Flaherty, *Protecting Privacy in Surveillance Societies: The Federal Republic of Germany, Sweden, France, Canada, and the United States* (Chapel Hill: University of North Carolina Press, 1989).

5. U.S. House Committee on Government Operations, Special Subcommittee on Invasion of Privacy, *The Computer and Invasion of Privacy: Hearings*, 89th Cong., 2d sess., July 26–28, 1966.

6. U.S. Senate Committee on the Judiciary, Subcommittee on Administrative Practice and Procedure, *Invasions of Privacy (Government Agencies): Hearings*, 89th Cong., 2d sess., part 5, Mar. 23–30, June 7–9, 14, 16, 1966. The subcommittee held a series of hearings on privacy issues related to government agencies: part 1, Feb. 18, 23–24, Mar. 2–3, 1965; part 2, Apr. 13, 27–29, May 5–6, June 7, 1965; part 3, July 13–15, 19–21, 27, Aug. 9, 1965; part 4, Oct. 18–20, 1965, Feb. 2–4, 1966; and part 5, Mar. 23–30, June 7–9, 14, 16, 1966.

7. The subcommittee existed from 1964 to 1968 and had three members: Gallagher as chair, Benjamin Rosenthal (D-N.Y.), and Frank Horton (R-N.Y.). In an analysis of the work of this subcommittee, Morris S. Ogul concludes that although his framework for evaluating congressional oversight leads to the expectation that this subcommittee would have a low potential for oversight, the Special Subcommittee on Invasion of Privacy provided substantial oversight. See Morris S. Ogul, *Congress Oversees the Bureaucracy: Studies in Legislative Supervision* (Pittsburgh: University of Pittsburgh Press, 1976).

8. U.S. House Committee, *Computer and Invasion of Privacy*, p. 2.

9. Ogul, *Congress Oversees the Bureaucracy*, p. 114.

10. Ibid.

11. U.S. Senate Committee on the Judiciary, Subcommittee on Administrative Practice and Procedure, *Government Dossier (Survey of Information Contained in Government Files)*, 90th Cong., 1st sess., 1967, table 4B, pp. 26–27.

12. Ibid., p. 8.

13. Quoted in "Privacy and Efficient Government: Proposals for a National Data Center," *Harvard Law Review* 82 (Dec. 1968): 404.

14. U.S. Senate Committee on the Judiciary, Subcommittee on Administrative Practice and Procedure, *Computer Privacy: Hearings*, 90th Cong., 1st sess., Mar. 14–15, 1967.

15. U.S. Senate Committee on the Judiciary, Subcommittee on Constitutional Rights, *Federal Data Banks, Computers, and the Bill of Rights: Hearings*, 92d Cong., 1st sess., Feb. 23–25, Mar. 2–4, 9–11, 15, 17, 1971.

16. Ibid., p. 1.

17. Ibid., p. xxxvii.

18. U.S. Department of Health, Education, and Welfare, Secretary's Advisory Committee on Automated Personal Data Systems, *Records, Computers, and the Rights of Citizens* (Washington, D.C.: Government Printing Office, 1973).

19. Alan F. Westin and Michael A. Baker, *Databanks in a Free Society: Computers, Record-Keeping, and Privacy*, report of the Project on Computer Databanks of the Computer Science and Engineering Board, National Academy of Sciences (New York: Quadrangle/New York Times Book Company, 1972), p. 392.

20. U.S. Department of Health, Education, and Welfare, *Records, Computers, and the Rights of Citizens*, p. 12.

21. Ibid., pp. 37–38.

22. In July 1972, the Younger Committee in Britain recommended "principles for handling personal information" that are very similar to those of the HEW committee (Great Britain, Home Office, *Report of the Committee on Privacy*, Cmnd. 5012

[London: HMSO, 1972]). Colin Bennett concludes that it is "impossible to judge which came first or how one influenced the other" (*Regulating Privacy*, p. 99).

23. U.S. Senate Committee on Government Operations, Ad Hoc Subcommittee on Privacy and Information Systems, and Committee on the Judiciary, Subcommittee on Constitutional Rights, *Privacy—The Collection, Use, and Computerization of Personal Data: Joint Hearings*, 93d Cong., 2d sess., June 18–20, 1974.

24. The other four bills were s. 2633, introduced by Senators Ervin, Bayh, Goldwater, Kennedy, and Mathias, which covered only federal personal information systems and those state and local systems funded by the federal government and gave oversight and registration authority to the General Accounting Office; s. 2542, introduced by Senator Bayh, which covered only federal government records and provided for a Federal Privacy Board; s. 2810, introduced by Senator Goldwater, which covered all public information systems and private systems that were supported by federal funds; and s. 3116, introduced by Senator Hatfield, which prohibited the sale or distribution of certain personal information.

25. U.S. House Committee on Government Operations, *Privacy Act of 1974*, 93d Cong., 2d sess., 1974, report 93-1416.

26. U.S. Senate Committee, *Privacy*, pp. 515, 450–51.

27. Ibid., p. 75.

28. U.S. Senate Committee, *Federal Data Banks*, p. 19.

29. Ibid., p. 713.

30. U.S. Department of Health, Education, and Welfare, *Records, Computers, and the Rights of Citizens*, p. 43.

31. U.S. Senate Committee, *Privacy*, p. 444.

32. Ibid., p. 480.

33. Ibid., p. 667.

34. U.S. Senate Committee on Government Operations, *Protecting Individual Privacy in Federal Gathering, Use, and Disclosure of Information*, 93d Cong., 2d sess., 1974, report 93-1183, p. 26.

35. Ibid.

36. Ibid., pp. 23–24.

37. *Congressional Record* (Nov. 21, 1974), 93d Cong., 2d sess., vol. 120, pt. 162:H10962.

38. Senate floor debates, reprinted in U.S. Senate and House Committees on Government Operations, *Legislative History of the Privacy Act of 1974, s. 3418 (PL 93-579)*, 94th Cong., 2d sess. (Washington, D.C.: Government Printing Office, 1976), p. 775.

39. Ibid., p. 803.

40. Ibid., p. 899.

41. Ibid., pp. 908–19.

42. Ibid., p. 905.

43. Ibid., p. 884.

44. Ibid., p. 883. It is important to point out that the House began its floor debate on November 20, 1974, the same day that it overrode President Ford's veto of amendments to strengthen the Freedom of Information Act.

45. Ibid., p. 770.

46. Colin Bennett reports that "an ad hoc meeting was arranged late one night in Senator Ervin's private office. The four principal sponsors — Senators Ervin and Percy and Congressmen Moorhead and Ehrlenborn — were present as were their counsels. All knew that any one of them could veto the whole idea; all knew that the President endorsed the House version" (*Regulating Privacy*, p. 73).

47. Senator Ervin, Senate floor debates, Nov. 21, 1974, U.S. Senate and House Committees, *Legislative History of the Privacy Act of 1974*, p. 775.

48. *Privacy Act of 1974*, 93d Cong., 2d sess. (Dec. 31, 1974), PL 93-570, sec. 5b.

49. See Privacy Protection Study Commission, *Personal Privacy in an Information Society* (Washington, D.C.: Government Printing Office, 1977), pp. 621–38, for a schedule of hearings.

50. Francis M. Gregory, Jr., and Wright H. Andrews, "The Privacy Debate — Business Must Be Seen and Heard," *Data Management*, Aug. 1975, p. 36.

51. Privacy Protection Study Commission, *Personal Privacy*, p. 21.

52. Ibid.

53. Ibid., p. 29.

54. Ibid., p. 3.

55. Ibid., p. 32.

56. Ibid., p. 36.

57. Ibid.

58. Ibid., p. 37.

59. William G. Dearhammer, "Lessons to Learn from the Privacy Report," *Credit and Financial Management*, Mar. 1978, p. 24.

60. Trudy Hayden, "The Privacy Commission Report: A National Privacy Program," *Privacy Report*, Feb. 1978, p. 1.

61. For a thorough discussion of the development of Project Match and the controversies it raised among federal agencies, see Jake Kirchner, "Privacy — A History of Computer Matching in the Federal Government," *Computerworld*, Dec. 14, 1981, pp. 1–16.

62. Laura B. Weiss, "Government Steps Up Use of Computer Matching to Find Fraud in Programs," *Congressional Quarterly Weekly Report*, Feb. 26, 1983, p. 432.

63. Section 3b of the Privacy Act establishes the conditions under which an agency can disclose personal information to another party without the prior consent of the individual. One of these conditions for disclosure is that the information be intended for "routine use," defined as "the use of such record for a purpose which is compatible with the purpose for which it was collected" (3[a] [7]). All routine uses are to be published in the *Federal Register*, including "the categories of users and the purpose of such use" (3[e] [4] [D]).

64. Office of Management and Budget, "Guidance to Agencies on Conducting Automated Matching Programs" (effective Mar. 30, 1979), *Federal Register* 44, no. 76 (Apr. 18, 1979): 23138–42.

65. For further discussion, see John Shattuck, "Computer Matching Is a Serious Threat to Individual Rights," *Communication of the ACM* 27, no. 36 (June 1984): 538–41.

66. *Jaffess v. Secretary HEW*, 393 F. Supp. 626 (S.D. N.Y. 1975).

67. Kenneth James Langan, "Computer Matching Programs: A Threat to Privacy?," *Columbia Journal of Law and Social Problems* 15, no. 2 (1979): 158–59.

68. If the purpose of a match is to produce evidence that someone has defrauded the government, then a computer match could be regarded as a search under the Fourth Amendment. But if the purpose of a match is to detect and correct errors, then a match would probably not be regarded as a search under the Fourth Amendment.

69. Office of Technology Assessment, *A Preliminary Analysis of the IRS Tax Administration System*, OTA-TCI-43 (Washington, D.C.: Government Printing Office, 1977); *A Preliminary Assessment of the National Crime Information Center and the Computerized Criminal History System*, OTA-I-80 (Washington, D.C.: Government Printing Office, 1978); *Implications of Electronic Mail and Message Systems for the U.S. Postal Service*, OTA-CIT-183 (Washington, D.C.: Government Printing Office, 1982); *Selected Electronic Funds Transfer Issues: Privacy, Security, and Equity*, Background Paper (Washington, D.C.: Government Printing Office, 1982); and *An Assessment of Alternatives for a National Computerized Criminal History System*, OTA-CIT-161 (Washington, D.C.: Government Printing Office, 1982).

70. Office of Technology Assessment, *Computer-Based National Information Systems*, OTA-CIT-146 (Washington, D.C.: Government Printing Office, 1981), pp. 73–78.

71. U.S. Senate Committee on Governmental Affairs, Subcommittee on Oversight of Government Management, *Oversight of Computer Matching to Detect Fraud and Mismanagement in Government Programs*, 97th Cong., 2d sess., Dec. 15–16, 1982.

72. Ibid., p. 1.

73. U.S. House Committee on Government Operations, Subcommittee on Government Information, Justice, and Agriculture, *Oversight of the Privacy Act of 1974*, 98th Cong., 1st sess., June 7–8, 1983.

74. Ibid., p. 2. An earlier oversight hearing had actually been held, chaired by Representative Bella S. Abzug, before the Privacy Act went into effect. U.S. House Committee on Government Operations, Subcommittee on Government Information and Individual Rights, *Implementation of the Privacy Act of 1974 — Data Banks: Hearings*, 94th Cong., 1st sess., June 3, 1975.

75. For a complete list of these reports, see General Accounting Office, *Eligibility Verification and Privacy in Federal Benefit Programs: A Delicate Balance*, GAO/HRD-85-22 (Washington, D.C.: General Accounting Office, 1985), appendixes 4 and 5.

76. James B. Rule, *Private Lives and Public Surveillance: Social Control in the Computer Age* (London: Allen Lane, 1973), p. 28.

77. David Burnham, *The Rise of the Computer State* (New York: Random House, 1983), p. 39.

78. Gary T. Marx and Nancy Reichman, "Routinizing the Discovery of Secrets: Computers as Informants," *American Behavioral Scientist* 27, no. 4 (Mar./Apr. 1984): 425.

79. John Shattuck, "In the Shadow of *1984*: National Identification Systems, Computer-matching, and Privacy in the United States," *Hastings Law Journal* 35 (July 1984): 992.

80. U.S. House Committee on the Judiciary, Subcommittee on Courts, Civil Liber-

ties, and the Administration of Justice, *1984—Civil Liberties and the National Security State: Hearings*, 98th Cong., 1st and 2d sess., Nov. 2–3, 1983, Jan. 24, Apr. 5, Sept. 26, 1984.

81. U.S. Senate Committee on Governmental Affairs, Subcommittee on Oversight of Government Management, *Computer Matching—Taxpayer Records: Hearings*, 98th Cong., 2d sess., June 6, 1984.

82. U.S. House Committee on Government Operations, Subcommittee on Government Information, Justice, and Agriculture, *Privacy and 1984: Public Opinions on Privacy Issues: Hearings*, 98th Cong., 1st sess., Apr. 4, 1984. The same subcommittee had held hearings in 1979 when an earlier Harris survey, *The Dimensions of Privacy*, was released. See *Public Reaction to Privacy Issues: Hearings*, 96th Cong., 1st sess., June 6, 1979.

83. The purpose of the survey was to gather data on a number of topics including Privacy Act implementation; computer matching and front-end verification; third-party information and profiling; use of credit reports; and electronic records management and electronic mail. The survey was sent to 13 cabinet-level agencies and 20 selected subcabinet agencies; a total of 142 agency components provided information. Office of Technology Assessment, *Federal Government Information Technology: Electronic Record Systems and Individual Privacy*, OTA-CIT-296 (Washington, D.C.: Government Printing Office, 1986).

84. Ibid., pp. 4–6.

85. Ibid., p. 3.

86. See, for example, William C. Rempel, "Computers: Is Privacy the Loser?," *Los Angeles Times*, July 29, 1986, pp. 1, 10; Steve Levin, "Computers and Your Privacy," *Dallas Morning News*, Sept. 18, 1986, pp. C1, C2; Joseph E. Collins, "Computer Matching Draws Concern," *Data Management*, Dec. 1986, pp. 6, 8; Anne R. Field, " 'Big Brother Inc.' May Be Closer Than You Thought," *Business Week*, Feb. 9, 1987, pp. 84–86; Donald Harris, "A Matter of Privacy: Managing Personal Data in Company Computers," *Personnel*, Feb. 1987, pp. 34–43; and Bob Davis, "Abusive Computers: As Government Keeps More Tabs on People, False Accusations Rise," *Wall Street Journal*, Aug. 20, 1984, pp. 1, 12.

87. U.S. Senate Committee on Governmental Affairs, Subcommittee on Oversight of Government Management, *Computer Matching and Privacy Protection Act of 1986: Hearings*, 99th Cong., 2d sess., Sept. 16, 1986, p. 2.

88. Joseph Wright, OMB deputy director, OMB Circular 83-14; President's Private Sector Survey on Cost Control, *A Report to the President*, part 2, *Issue and Recommendation Summaries* (Washington, D.C., 1984), pp. 82–86; statement of former Department of Labor inspector general Thomas McBride, in U.S. Senate Committee, *Oversight of Computer Matching*, p. 19; Richard P. Kusserow, "Fighting Fraud, Waste, and Abuse," *Bureaucrat* 12 (Fall 1983): 23.

89. Office of Technology Assessment, *Federal Government Information Technology: Electronic Record Systems*, p. 50.

90. The HHS guide suggested that quantitative benefits include estimated savings and measures of grant reductions, collections, and corrections, while qualitative benefits include increased deterrence, improved eligibility determinations, enhanced public credibility, more effective referral services, and improved databases. Quantitative

costs include hardware and software requirements, computer-processing time, space, supplies, personnel managers, data-processing staff, clerical workers, hearings officers, fraud investigators, collections staff, attorneys, and training staff. Qualitative costs include reduced staff morale; heightened public concerns about "Big Brother"; increased political conflict; gamesmanship with numbers; operational inefficiencies; and diversion of resources. See U.S. Department of Health and Human Services, Office of the Inspector General, *Computer Matching in State Administered Benefit Programs* (Washington, D.C., 1984), p. 40.

91. In 1985 David H. Greenberg and Douglas A. Wolf constructed a cost-benefit framework for evaluating computer-matching programs implemented by state welfare agencies and applied it to four cases: Camden County, New Jersey; Mercer County, New Jersey; San Joaquin County, California; and the state of New Hampshire. They identified the following benefits: restitution of previous overpayments; savings from food stamp disqualifications; savings from benefit reductions and discontinuances (including prevention of future overpayments and administrative savings); and changes in behavior and attitudes (such as deterrent effects, improved client attitudes, higher staff morale, and better relations with the public). As costs, they listed personnel costs (including salaries and fringe benefits of at least the income-maintenance staff, the fraud-investigative staff, and the district attorney staff) and materials and facilities costs (including computers, word processors, forms, and general overhead). For their study, they selected sites with well-functioning matching programs. For each of these sites, they found it easier to obtain accurate and complete information on the costs of matches than on the benefits. They concluded that the benefits outweighed the costs by "substantial amounts" in each case. If computer matching was as effective nationally, they suggested, the savings in AFDC programs would be about 1 to 2 percent, but they cautioned that the savings would depend on how well the computer-matching programs were functioning. David H. Greenberg and Douglas A. Wolf, "Is Wage Matching Worth All the Trouble?," *Public Welfare* 43 (Winter 1985): 13–20.

92. Office of Technology Assessment, *Federal Government Information Technology: Electronic Record Systems*, p. 50.

93. General Accounting Office, *Computer Matching: Assessing Its Costs and Benefits*, GAO/PEMD-87-2 (Washington, D.C.: General Accounting Office, 1986).

94. *Congressional Record* (May 21, 1987), 100th Cong., 1st sess., vol. 133, pt. 10:S7041.

95. Ibid.

96. Ibid., p. S7042.

97. U.S. House Committee on Government Operations, Subcommittee on Government Information, Justice, and Agriculture, *Computer Matching and Privacy Protection Act of 1987: Hearings*, 100th Cong., 1st sess., June 23, 1987, p. 1.

98. Statement of Janlori Goldman, ACLU, in ibid., pp. 94–113.

99. Statement of Ronald L. Plesser, ABA, in ibid., p. 118.

100. Statement of Joseph R. Wright, OMB deputy director, and Richard P. Kusserow, HHS inspector general and PCIE vice chair, in ibid., p. 15.

101. U.S. House Committee on Government Operations, *Computer Matching and Privacy Protection Act of 1988*, 100th Cong., 2d sess., 1988, report 100-802, p. 21.

102. Ibid., p. 16.

103. *Congressional Record* (Sept. 20, 1988), 100th Cong., 2d sess., vol. 134, pt. 17:S13000.

104. Flaherty, *Protecting Privacy in Surveillance Societies*, p. 357.

105. Statement of Representative Bob Wise on the House floor, in *Congressional Record* (July 11, 1989), 101st Cong., 1st sess., vol. 135, pt. 91:H3562.

106. Priscilla M. Regan, "Data Integrity Boards: Institutional Innovation and Congressional Oversight," *Government Information Quarterly* 10, no. 4 (1993): 443–59; General Accounting Office, *Computer Matching: Quality of Decisions and Supporting Analyses Little Affected by 1988 Act*, GAO/PEMD-94-2 (Washington, D.C.: General Accounting Office, 1993).

107. Jeffrey Rothfeder, "Is Nothing Private?," *Business Week*, Sept. 4, 1989, pp. 74–82.

108. Rothfeder notes that in 1988 the three largest credit bureaus reported the following revenues and number of individual files: TRW, $335 million in revenues with 155 million individual files; TransUnion, $300 million in revenues with 155 million files; and Equifax, $259 million in revenues with 100 million files. Ibid., p. 81.

109. Albert B. Crenshaw, "Public Turns the Tables on Credit Bureaus," *Washington Post*, Nov. 1, 1991, p. F3.

110. Leonard Sloane, "Credit Reports: The Overhaul Rolls On," *New York Times*, Jan. 4, 1992, p. 48.

111. "Fair Credit Reporting Act Reform Legislation," *Privacy and American Business* 1, no. 2 (Jan./Feb. 1994): 8.

112. "Credit Reform Dies in House," *1992 Congressional Quarterly Almanac* (Washington, D.C.: Congressional Quarterly Press, 1993), p. 119.

113. *Driver's Privacy Protection Act of 1993*, 103d Cong., 1st sess., H.R. 3365.

114. Quoted in "Sellers of Government Data Thrive," *New York Times*, Dec. 26, 1991, p. D2.

115. No. 92-1223 (Feb. 23, 1994), pp. 12–14.

116. American Medical Records Association, "Confidentiality of Patient Health Information: A Position Statement of the American Medical Record Association" (1977), summarized in Robert M. Gellman, "Prescribing Privacy: The Uncertain Role of the Physician in the Protection of Patient Privacy," *North Carolina Law Review* 62, no. 2 (1984): 261–63. The American Medical Records Association changed its name to the American Health Information Management Association in October 1991.

117. Carole M. Cleaver, "Privacy Rights in Medical Records," *Fordham Urban Law Journal* 13, no. 1 (1984–85): 165–204.

118. U.S. House Committee on Government Operations, Subcommittee on Government Information and Individual Rights, *Privacy of Medical Records: Hearings on H.R. 2979 and H.R. 3444*, 96th Cong., 1st sess., 1979; U.S. House Committee on Ways and Means, Subcommittee on Health, *Federal Privacy of Medical Information Act: Hearings on H.R. 5935*, 96th Cong., 2d sess., 1980.

119. U.S. Senate Committee on Governmental Affairs, *Legislation to Protect the Privacy of Medical Records: Hearings on s. 503*, 96th Cong., 1st sess., 1979; U.S. Senate Committee on Finance, Subcommittee on Health, *Confidentiality of Medical Records: Hearings*, 95th Cong., 1st sess., 1977.

120. U.S. House, 96th Cong., 2d sess., 1980, report 832, and U.S. Senate, 96th Cong., 2d sess., 1980, report 96-935.

121. *Congressional Record* (Dec. 1, 1980), 96th Cong., 2d sess., vol. 126, pt. 23:H11370.

122. Institute of Medicine, *The Computer-Based Patient Record: An Essential Technology for Health Care*, edited by Richard S. Dick and Elaine B. Steen (Washington, D.C.: National Academy Press, 1991), and *Health Data in the Information Age: Use, Disclosure, and Privacy* (Washington, D.C.: National Academy Press, 1994).

123. U.S. Department of Health and Human Services, Work Group on Computerization of Patient Records, *Toward a National Health Information Infrastructure* (Washington, D.C., Apr. 1993).

124. Office of Technology Assessment, *Protecting Privacy in Computerized Medical Information*, OTA-TCT-576 (Washington, D.C.: Government Printing Office, 1993), p. 19. The report was requested by the Senate Subcommittee on Federal Services, Post Office, and Civil Service and the House Subcommittee on Government Information, Justice, and Agriculture.

125. Louis Harris and Associates and Alan F. Westin, *Harris-Equifax Health Information Privacy Survey, 1993* (Atlanta: Equifax, Inc., 1993). See chapter 3 for highlights of the survey results.

126. Ibid., table 8.1, p. 88.

127. "Medical Information Privacy: Health Care Reform and the American Public" (conference cosponsored by the American Health Information Management Association and Equifax, Inc., in cooperation with the U.S. Office of Consumer Affairs, Washington, D.C., Oct. 29, 1993).

128. In the 102d Congress, Representative Stark introduced the Prescription Drug Records Privacy Protection Act of 1992 (H.R. 5615), which was modeled on the Video Privacy Protection Act and would restrict the disclosure of pharmacy records and allow for a civil remedy for unauthorized disclosure. No action was taken on the bill.

129. Witnesses at the first hearing, which was held November 4, 1993, and was titled "Health Reform, Health Records, Computers, and Confidentiality," included representatives from the American Medical Records Association, the American Hospital Association, the American Health Information Management Association, Electronic Data Systems, and the ACLU. The three legislative hearings took place on April 20, May 4–5, 1994.

130. It became part 2, "Fair Health Information Practices," of subtitle B, "Administrative Simplification and Fair Health Information Practices."

131. U.S. House Committee on Government Operations, *Health Security Act of 1994*, 103d Cong., 2d sess., 1994, report 103-601, part 5, p. 83.

132. Ibid., p. 114.

133. This bill was developed by Senator Richard Bond (R-Mo.), Senator Donald Riegle, Jr. (D-Mich.), and Representative David Hobson (R-Ohio). The Health Care Data Panel would be composed of designees from the Departments of Health and Human Services, Defense, and Veterans Affairs as well as from the National Institute of Standards and Technology and the National Telecommunications and Information Administration.

134. For examples, see Office of Technology Assessment, *Protecting Privacy*; Institute of Medicine, *Computer-Based Patient Record*; and Sheri Alpert, "Smart Cards, Smarter Policy," *Hastings Center Report*, Nov.–Dec. 1993, pp. 13–23.

135. Alan Westin remarked at the Medical Information Privacy conference (Washington, D.C., Oct. 29, 1993) that the public preference for use of the social security number was not necessarily permanent and that acceptance of health care cards and numbers will depend on the level of confidence in the overall scheme to protect privacy.

136. "Sizable Boost in Immigration OK'd," *1990 Congressional Quarterly Almanac* (Washington, D.C.: Congressional Quarterly Press, 1991).

137. Such support may be furnished by primary care providers—doctors and nurses—whose interest in establishing the confidentiality of patient records and maintaining some control over them comes closest to the patient's interest in the privacy of those records. See Gellman, "Prescribing Privacy," for an analysis of the physician's role in protecting patient privacy.

CHAPTER FIVE

1. National security concerns have also been important but generally have been dealt with separately because of the need to restrict knowledge about the use and effectiveness of surveillance in this area. For example, the National Commission for the Review of Federal and State Laws Relating to Wiretapping and Electronic Surveillance (1976) explicitly decided not to review national security surveillance. In 1978 Congress legislated separately for this area in the Foreign Intelligence Surveillance Act (FISA). The politics of national security surveillance are generally similar to those of law enforcement surveillance with the substitution of the intelligence community for the law enforcement community and with greater regard for the need to restrict access to information about national security surveillance.

2. Sir William Blackstone, *Commentaries on the Laws of England*, 4:168, cited in National Commission for the Review of Federal and State Laws Relating to Wiretapping and Electronic Surveillance, *Electronic Surveillance* (Washington, D.C.: National Wiretap Commissions, 1976), p. 33.

3. David H. Flaherty, *Privacy in Colonial New England* (Charlottesville: University Press of Virginia, 1972), p. 89.

4. George O'Toole, *The Private Sector* (New York: W. W. Norton, 1978), p. 97.

5. Herman Schwartz, "Surveillance: Historical Policy Review," unpublished contractor report for the Office of Technology Assessment, 1984, p. 3.

6. Frank J. Donner, *The Age of Surveillance: The Aims and Methods of America's Political Intelligence System* (New York: Alfred A. Knopf, 1980), pp. 35–39. Part of the reason this official opposition to wiretapping coexisted with its use is that wiretapping can serve many purposes. Wiretaps provide background information about criminal organizations and plans. They help to identify criminals and crimes, which can then be investigated through more routine police work. The information gained through wiretaps may be used by the police for investigatory purposes. If information obtained through wiretapping does not become public, the use of a wiretap need not be revealed. As police and prosecutors have come to rely more on wiretap informa-

tion, it has become more difficult to suppress the acknowledgment of use of wiretaps from the court record.

7. 277 U.S. 438 (1928). For a complete history of this case, see Walter F. Murphy, *Wiretapping on Trial* (New York: Random House, 1965).

8. Quoted in Murphy, *Wiretapping on Trial*, p. 52.

9. *Olmstead v. United States*, 277 U.S. 438, 470 (1928).

10. Ibid., pp. 473–74.

11. "Government Lawbreakers," *New York Times*, June 6, 1928, p. 24, cited in Murphy, *Wiretapping on Trial*, p. 125.

12. *Olmstead v. United States*, 277 U.S. 438, 465–66 (1928).

13. "Brief of the United States," *Olmstead v. United States*, October Terms, 1927, p. 41, reprinted in *Landmark Briefs and Arguments of the Supreme Court of the United States: Constitutional Law*, edited by Philip B. Kurland and Gerhard Casper (Washington, D.C.: University Publications of America, 1975), p. 232.

14. For more complete reviews of congressional activity in the period 1930–67, see Murphy, *Wiretapping on Trial*, esp. chap. 9; Herman Schwartz, "Surveillance: Historical Policy Review" (unpublished contractor report for the Office of Technology Assessment, 1984); and Alan F. Westin, *Privacy and Freedom* (New York: Atheneum, 1967), esp. chap. 8, and "The Wire-Tapping Problem: An Analysis and a Legislative Proposal," *Columbia Law Review* 52, no. 2 (Feb. 1952): 165–208.

15. U.S. House Committee on Expenditures in the Executive Departments, *Hearings: Wiretapping in Law Enforcement*, 71st Cong., 3d sess., 1931, p. 26, cited in Murphy, *Wiretapping on Trial*, p. 129.

16. Westin, "Wire-Tapping Problem," p. 173.

17. U.S. House Subcommittee of the Committee on Appropriations, *Hearings on Department of Justice Appropriations Bill for 1933*, 72d Cong., 1st sess., 1932, p. 253, cited in Murphy, *Wiretapping on Trial*, pp. 131–32.

18. Westin, "Wire-Tapping Problem," p. 174.

19. Westin, *Privacy and Freedom*, p. 175. Westin also points out that "Congress was presented with a perfect opportunity to consider these problems [the problems of wiretapping in the investigations of crimes] in 1934, when it established federal rules for the radio, telephone, and telegraph industries. However, no reference was made to wiretapping in the committee hearings or floor debates, and no specific provision on police use of wiretapping was included among the new sections added to the Radio Act of 1927, on which the 1934 Federal Communication Act was based" (ibid.).

20. *Nardone v. United States*, 302 U.S. 379 (1937).

21. *Nardone v. United States*, 308 U.S. 338 (1939).

22. National Commission, *Electronic Surveillance*, p. 35.

23. Quoted in Murphy, *Wiretapping on Trial*, p. 135.

24. U.S. Senate Committee on Interstate Commerce, *Hearings before and Report of a Subcommittee of the Senate Committee on Interstate Commerce, Pursuant to Sen. Res. 224*, 76th Cong., 3d sess., 1940, cited in Westin, *Privacy and Freedom*, p. 176.

25. National Commission, *Electronic Surveillance*, p. 36.

26. U.S. House Committee on the Judiciary, *To Authorize Wiretapping: Hearings on H.R. 2266 and H.R. 3099*, 77th Cong., 1st sess., 1941, p. 112, cited in Murphy, *Wiretapping on Trial*, p. 137.

27. See Samuel Dash, Richard F. Schwartz, and Robert E. Knowlton, *The Eaves-droppers* (New Brunswick: Rutgers University Press, 1959), and Herman Schwartz, *Taps, Bugs, and Fooling the People* (New York: Field Foundation, 1977).

28. Westin, *Privacy and Freedom*, p. 181.

29. Ibid., p. 180.

30. Ibid., p. 183.

31. Murphy, *Wiretapping on Trial*, p. 157.

32. Westin, "Wire-Tapping Problem," p. 186.

33. Westin suggested that only federal enforcement officers and district attorneys should be able to wiretap. He argued that legislative committees and administrative agencies should be excluded because of inadequate due process safeguards for their procedures and that police departments should be excluded because of their record of abuses of wiretapping. Ibid., p. 202.

34. He suggested that, except in national security cases, wiretapping should be permitted only if human safety was at stake. As an alternative, he said that Congress might follow the model of the statute on searching the mail and list the crimes for which wiretapping was allowed. Westin believed that wiretapping should be permitted in cases involving national security; no court order would be required, but the attorney general or secretary of defense would have to authorize it. Ibid., pp. 203–5.

35. The court procedure Westin suggested would require demonstrating that a crime had been committed or was about to be committed, that there was a reasonable expectation that wiretapping would produce evidence essential to the solution of that crime, and that no other means were readily available. Wiretap authorization would be limited to sixty days and renewed for the same length of time. Ibid., p. 203.

36. Dash, Schwartz, and Knowlton, *Eavesdroppers*, p. 5.

37. Ibid., p. 68.

38. Ibid., p. 122.

39. U.S. Senate Committee on the Judiciary, Subcommittee on Administrative Practice and Procedure, *Invasions of Privacy (Government Agencies): Hearings*, 89th Cong., 1st sess., 1965.

40. Westin, *Privacy and Freedom*, p. 198.

41. Edward V. Long, *The Intruders: The Invasion of Privacy by Government and Industry* (New York: Praeger, 1967).

42. Westin, *Privacy and Freedom*, p. 424 (n. 93).

43. Edith J. Lapidus, *Eavesdropping on Trial* (Rochelle Park, N.J.: Hayden Book Company, 1974), p. 12.

44. President's Commission on Law Enforcement and the Administration of Justice, *The Challenge of Crime in a Free Society* (Washington, D.C.: Government Printing Office, 1967), p. 203.

45. Ibid., p. 193.

46. Ibid., p. 203.

47. 388 U.S. 41 (1967).

48. *Katz v. United States*, 389 U.S. 347, 351 (1967).

49. Ibid.

50. Ibid., p. 353.

51. Ibid., p. 356.

52. Ibid., p. 357.

53. Ibid., p. 361.

54. For the development of case law in this area, see, for example, Anthony G. Amsterdam, "Perspectives on the Fourth Amendment," *Minnesota Law Review* 58 (Jan. 1974): 349–439; Gerald G. Ashdown, "The Fourth Amendment and the 'Legitimate Expectation of Privacy,'" *Vanderbilt Law Review* 34 (Oct. 1981): 1289–1345; and Peter Goldberger, "Consent, Expectation of Privacy, and the Meaning of 'Searches' in the Fourth Amendment," *Journal of Criminal Law and Criminology* 75, no. 2 (1984): 319–62.

55. These bills were S. 675, introduced by Senator McClellan, and H.R. 10037, introduced by Representative William McCulloch (R-Ohio). S. 2050, later introduced by Roman L. Hruska (R-Nebr.), was identical to H.R. 10037. See Lapidus, *Eavesdropping on Trial*, pp. 12–13.

56. U.S. Senate Committee on the Judiciary, Subcommittee on Criminal Law and Procedures, *Controlling Crime through More Effective Law Enforcement: Hearings*, 90th Cong., 2d sess., 1967, pp. 957–58.

57. The Right of Privacy Act of 1967 (S. 928) was introduced by Senator Long, and a similar bill (H.R. 5386) was introduced by Representative Emanuel Celler (D-N.Y.). See ibid., p. 13.

58. Quoted in Westin, *Privacy and Freedom*, p. 206.

59. Alan F. Westin, "Separate Statement," in National Commission, *Electronic Surveillance*, p. 213.

60. Schwartz, "Surveillance," p. 27.

61. Herman Schwartz, "The Legitimation of Electronic Eavesdropping: The Politics of 'Law and Order,'" *Michigan Law Review* 67 (Jan. 1969): 455.

62. Richard Harris, "Annals of Legislation—The Turning Point," *New Yorker*, Dec. 14, 1968, p. 68.

63. G. Robert Blakey, "Concurrence," in National Commission, *Electronic Surveillance*, p. 189 (n. 7).

64. *Congressional Record* (May 22, 1968), 90th Cong., 2d sess., vol. 114, pt. 11, cited in ibid.

65. Ibid., p. xiii.

66. Sam Ervin, foreword to Lapidus, *Eavesdropping on Trial*.

67. U.S. House Committee on the Judiciary, Subcommittee on Courts, Civil Liberties, and the Administration of Justice, *Wiretapping and Electronic Surveillance: Hearings*, 93d Cong., 2d sess., Apr. 24, 26, 29, 1974, p. 1.

68. Ibid., p. 3.

69. U.S. House Committee on the Judiciary, Subcommittee on Courts, Civil Liberties, and the Administration of Justice, *Surveillance: Hearings*, 94th Cong., 1st sess., Feb. 6, 18, Mar. 4, 18, 21, May 22, June 26, July 25, Sept. 8, 1975, p. 1.

70. Joint statement of Senator Charles McC. Mathias and Congressman Charles A. Mosher, in ibid., p. 64.

71. House Republican Task Force on Privacy, *Report* (Aug. 1974), cited in ibid., p. 65.

72. Ibid., p. 67.

73. U.S. Senate Select Committee on Intelligence, Subcommittee on Intelligence and

the Rights of Americans, *Foreign Intelligence Surveillance Act of 1978: Hearings,* 95th Cong., 2d sess., July 19, 21, 1977, Feb. 8, 24, 27, 1978.

74. National Commission, *Electronic Surveillance,* p. xiii.

75. The minority report was offered by Senator James Abourezk, Representatives Robert W. Kastenmeier and John F. Seiberling, and Professor Alan F. Westin.

76. National Commission, *Electronic Surveillance,* p. xiii.

77. Westin, "Separate Statement," in ibid., p. 213.

78. Ibid., p. 11.

79. Ibid., p. 215.

80. Ibid.

81. Blakey, "Concurrence," in ibid., p. 205.

82. U.S. House Committee on the Judiciary, Subcommittee on Courts, Civil Liberties, and the Administration of Justice, *1984 — Civil Liberties and the National Security State: Hearings,* 98th Cong., 1st and 2d sess., Nov. 2–3, 1983, Jan. 24, Apr. 5, Sept. 26, 1984.

83. U.S. Senate Committee on the Judiciary, Subcommittee on Patents, Copyrights, and Trademarks, *Oversight on Communications Privacy: Hearings,* 98th Cong., 2d sess., Sept. 12, 1984.

84. Bruce E. Fein, "Regulating the Interception and Disclosure of Wire, Radio, and Oral Communication: A Case Study of Federal Statutory Antiquation," *Harvard Journal on Legislation* 22, no. 1 (Winter 1985): 69.

85. *United States v. Hall,* 488 F.2d 193 (1973).

86. *United States v. New York Telephone Company,* 434 U.S. 159 (1977).

87. *United States v. Seidlitz,* 589 F.2d 152 (1978).

88. *Kansas v. Howard,* 679 P.2d 197 (1984); *Rhode Island v. Delaurier,* 488 A.2d 688 (1985).

89. Although there was debate about whether Title III covered telephone conversations that were being transmitted in digital form, the Justice Department's position was that Title III concerned not the method by which communication was transmitted but the means used to acquire the information; since the government's interception was aural, Title III applied and the Justice Department required a Title III court order for wiretapping of all wire phone conversations, regardless of the method by which they were transmitted. For the interception of conversations on cordless phones, the Justice Department also required a Title III warrant despite the state court rulings that Title III did not apply. Similarly, the Justice Department required a Title III warrant for the interception of a telephone conversation over a mobile telephone because it was impossible to know in advance whether the receiver of the call would be using a landline phone and hence using telephone wires. See Office of Technology Assessment, *Federal Government Information Technology: Electronic Surveillance and Civil Liberties,* OTA-CIT-293 (Washington, D.C.: Government Printing Office, 1985), pp. 36–37.

90. Jerry J. Berman, "Prepared Statement on Behalf of the American Civil Liberties Union," in U.S. Senate Committee on the Judiciary, Subcommittee on Patents, Copyrights, and Trademarks, *Electronic Communication Privacy: Hearings,* 99th Cong., 1st sess., Nov. 13, 1985, pp. 130–31.

91. U.S. House Committee on the Judiciary, Subcommittee on Courts, Civil Liber-

ties, and the Administration of Justice, *Electronic Communications Privacy Act: Hearings*, 99th Cong., 1st and 2d sess., Sept. 26, Oct. 24, 1985, Jan. 30, Mar. 5, 1986, p. 41.

92. At his trial, the drug dealer argued that the evidence was inadmissible because the police had neglected to obtain a court order to listen to the telephone conversations. The judge ruled that a court order was not necessary in this instance because the conversations were not transmitted over wire and therefore did not come under the purview of Title III. *Rhode Island v. Delaurier*, 488 A.2d 688 (R.I. 1985).

93. U.S. Senate Committee, *Electronic Communication Privacy*, p. 77.

94. Ibid., p. 80.

95. Philip M. Walker, on behalf of the Electronic Mail Association, in ibid., p. 119.

96. Ibid., p. 45.

97. U.S. House Committee, *Electronic Communications Privacy Act*, p. 484.

98. Ibid., p. 70.

99. Ibid., p. 222.

100. Ibid., p. 240. These recommendations included expanding Title III to cover all felonies, authorizing the acting assistant attorney general in charge of the Criminal Division to sign a Title III warrant, and permitting the targeting of an individual rather than a particular phone line.

101. Nadine Cohodas, "Congress Races to Stay Ahead of Technology," *Congressional Quarterly Weekly Report*, May 31, 1986, pp. 1235–36.

102. *Congressional Record* (June 23, 1986), 99th Cong., 2d sess., vol. 132, pt. 11:H4045–46.

103. For analyses of the coverage of the law, see Russell S. Burnside, "The Electronic Communications Privacy Act of 1986: The Challenge of Applying Ambiguous Statutory Language to Intricate Telecommunication Technologies," *Rutgers Computer and Technology Law Journal* 13 (1987): 451–517; Robert L. Corn, "Tapping New Technologies: New Law Offers Easy Listening," *Nation* 243, no. 21 (Dec. 20, 1986): 696–97, and "The Odyssey of Federal Wiretapping Law: Beware of Meese Bearing Gifts," *Cato Policy Report* 9, no. 1 (Jan./Feb. 1987): 1; and Robert W. Kastenmeier, Deborah Leavy, and David Beier, "Communications Privacy: A Legislative Perspective," *Wisconsin Law Review*, July/Aug. 1989, pp. 715–37.

104. U.S. House Committee, *Electronic Communications Privacy Act*, p. 155.

105. Ibid., p. 2.

106. Philip J. Quigley, president and chief executive officer, PACTEL Mobile Company, in ibid., p. 29.

107. Ibid., p. 74.

108. John W. Stanton, chair, Telocator Network of America, and executive vice president, McCaw Communications Company, Inc., in ibid., p. 93.

109. U.S. Senate Committee, *Electronic Communication Privacy*, p. 33.

110. Ibid., p. 71.

111. Ibid., p. 100.

112. Ibid., p. 120.

113. Ibid., p. 125.

114. For a review of the issues and players, see Anthony Ramirez, "Mapping Out the Wireless-Phone Future," *New York Times*, Nov. 12, 1992, pp. A1, D6.

115. Anthony Ramirez, "Coming: Telephone Calls That Follow You Around," *New York Times*, Jan. 5, 1992, p. D1.

116. Edmund L. Andrews, "Telephone Autodialers under Fire," *New York Times*, Oct. 30, 1991, pp. D1, D24.

117. Cindy Skrzycki, "House Votes to Restrict Calls by Telemarketers," *Washington Post*, Nov. 19, 1991, p. B1.

118. Ken Auletta, "Under the Wire," *New Yorker*, Jan. 17, 1994, p. 49.

119. William S. Sessions, "Keeping an Ear on Crime," *New York Times*, Mar. 27, 1992, p. A35.

120. Janlori Goldman, "Why Cater to Luddites?," *New York Times*, Mar. 27, 1992, p. A35.

121. William Safire, "Foiling the Compu-Tappers," *New York Times*, May 11, 1992, p. A15.

122. Goldman, "Why Cater to Luddites?," p. A35.

123. The proposed encryption scheme employs key-escrow technology, which uses two integrated circuit chips, necessitating a key for each to decode the communications. The current federal standard, the Data Encryption Standard, uses a single key. Under the proposed scheme, the Clipper would be used for encrypting digital telephone signals and the Capstone would be used for encrypting data communications. See Ivars Peterson, "Encrypting Controversy," *Science News*, June 19, 1993, pp. 394–96.

124. Eliza Newlin Carney, "Clashing over Clipper," *National Journal*, Sept. 11, 1993, pp. 2184–87.

125. Edmund L. Andrews, "U.S. Plans to Push Computer Coding Police Can Read," *New York Times*, Feb. 5, 1994, pp. 1, 48; John Mintz and John Schwarts, "Clinton Backs Security Agencies on Computer Eavesdropping," *Washington Post*, Feb. 5, 1994, pp. A1, A8.

126. U.S. House Committee on Science, Space, and Technology, Subcommittee on Technology, Environment, and Aviation, *Communication and Computer Surveillance, Privacy, and Security: Hearings*, 103d Cong., 2d sess., May 3, 1994.

127. "Privacy Poses Test for IVHS Industry," *Privacy and American Business* 1, no. 2 (Jan./Feb. 1994): 2.

CHAPTER SIX

1. Senator Sam Ervin (D-N.C.), quoted in David Thoreson Lykken, *A Tremor in the Blood: Uses and Abuses of the Lie Detector* (New York: McGraw Hill, 1981), p. 183.

2. Statement of Norma Rollins, ACLU, in U.S. House Committee on Education and Labor, Subcommittee on Employment Opportunities, *Polygraphs in the Workplace: The Use of "Lie Detectors" in Hiring and Firing: Hearings*, 99th Cong., 1st sess., July 30, Sept. 18, 1985, p. 29.

3. Representative Cornelius Gallagher (D-N.J.), quoted in Alan F. Westin, *Privacy and Freedom* (New York: Atheneum, 1967), p. 233.

4. U.S. House Committee on Government Operations, Subcommittee on Foreign

Operations and Government Information, *Use of Polygraphs as "Lie Detectors" by the Federal Government: Hearings*, 88th Cong., 2d sess., 1964.

5. For summaries of the early history of polygraphy, see Lykken, *Tremor in the Blood*, chap. 3, and Jerome H. Skolnick, "Scientific Theory and Scientific Evidence: An Analysis of Lie-detection," *Yale Law Journal* 70, no. 5 (Apr. 1961): 696–99. For more detailed information, see John A. Larson, *Lying and Its Detection* (Chicago: University of Chicago Press, 1932), and William M. Marston, *The Lie Detector Test* (New York: Richard R. Smith, 1938).

6. For summaries of the criticisms, see Lykken, *Tremor in the Blood*, chap. 4, and Skolnick, "Scientific Theory and Scientific Evidence," pp. 699–703.

7. The 1983 OTA report on polygraphs refers to this as the "most commonly accepted theory at present" (Office of Technology Assessment, *Scientific Validity of Polygraph Testing: A Research Review and Evaluation*, OTA-TM-H-15 [Washington, D.C.: Government Printing Office, 1983], p. 6). Fred E. Inbau supports this view, stating that "fear of detection [operates] as the principal factor accounting for the physiological changes which constitute the symptoms of deception" (Fred E. Inbau, *Lie Detection and Criminal Interrogation* [Baltimore: Williams and Wilkins, 1948], p. 47).

8. John E. Reid and Fred E. Inbau, *Truth and Deception—The Polygraph Technique*, 3d ed. (Baltimore: Williams and Wilkins, 1977); Fred E. Inbau and John E. Reid, *Lie Detection and Criminal Interrogation* (Baltimore: Williams and Wilkens, 1953). Robert J. Ferguson and Chris Gugas, Sr., *Preemployment Polygraphy* (Springfield, Ill.: Charles C. Thomas, 1984), specifically addresses the use of the polygraph for preemployment screening.

9. Lykken, *Tremor in the Blood*, p. 4.

10. For a review of these methods, see Office of Technology Assessment, *Scientific Validity of Polygraph Testing*, pp. 17–23; Lykken, *Tremor in the Blood*, chaps. 7–13; and Gershon Ben-Shakhar and John J. Furedy, *Theories and Applications in the Detection of Deception* (New York: Springer-Verlag, 1990), chap. 2.

11. The 1983 OTA report on polygraphs summarizes a number of problems with the R/I technique. One problem is that because the intent of the relevant and irrelevant questions is transparent, both truthful and deceptive subjects are likely to give more truthful responses to the relevant questions. Another problem is that these questions are not usually reviewed beforehand with the individual and surprise or misunderstanding may trigger a truthful response. Office of Technology Assessment, *Scientific Validity of Polygraph Testing*, p. 17.

12. Ibid.,, p. 22.

13. For a comparison of this test to the control question test, see Ben-Shakhar and Furedy, *Theories and Applications in the Detection of Deception*, chap. 2. Ben-Shakhar and Furedy conclude that the guilty knowledge test is the only method "based on a sound rationale, whereas all the other methods suffer from serious logical and theoretical flaws" (ibid., p. 32). It is widely agreed, however, that the test is not useful for preemployment screening but only for investigations of specific incidents for which someone might have "guilty knowledge."

14. In the literature on polygraphy, the individual is always referred to as the "subject" or "respondent."

15. John E. Reid and Richard O. Arther, quoted in Skolnick, "Scientific Theory and Scientific Evidence," p. 705.

16. Lykken, *Tremor in the Blood*, p. 34.

17. Inbau and Reid, *Lie Detection and Criminal Interrogation*, p. 116.

18. Benjamin Kleinmuntz and Julian J. Szucko, "On the Fallibility of Lie Detection," *Law and Society Review* 17, no. 1 (1982): 97.

19. Skolnick, "Scientific Theory and Scientific Evidence," p. 714.

20. Lykken, *Tremor in the Blood*, p. 214.

21. Inbau, *Lie Detection and Criminal Interrogation*, p. 73.

22. *Frye v. United States*, 293 F. 1013 (D.C. Cir. 1923), cited in Bureau of National Affairs, *Polygraphs and Employment* (Washington, D.C.: Bureau of National Affairs, 1985), p. 28.

23. For a review of these cases, see Stanley Abrams, *A Polygraph Handbook for Attorneys* (Lexington, Mass.: Lexington Books, 1977), chap. 7; Bureau of National Affairs, *Polygraphs and Employment*, pp. 40–45; Andre A. Moenssens, Fred E. Inbau, and James E. Starrs, *Scientific Evidence in Criminal Cases* (Mineola, N.Y.: Foundation Press, 1986); and "Pinocchio's New Nose," *New York University Law Review* 48 (May 1973): 339–68.

24. American Educational Research Association, American Psychological Association, and National Council on Measurement in Education, *Standards for Educational and Psychological Testing* (Washington, D.C.: American Psychological Association, 1985), p. 9.

25. Society for Industrial and Organizational Psychology, *Principles for the Validation and Use of Personnel Selection Procedures*, 3d ed. (College Park, Md.: Society for Industrial and Organizational Psychology, 1987), p. 4.

26. For a more complete discussion, see Office of Technology Assessment, *The Use of Integrity Tests for Pre-Employment Screening*, OTA-SET-442 (Washington, D.C.: Government Printing Office, 1990).

27. American Educational Research Association, *Standards*, p. 10.

28. Ibid., p. 61.

29. Office of Technology Assessment, *Scientific Validity of Polygraph Testing*, p. 38.

30. U.S. House Committee on Government Operations, Subcommittee on Foreign Operations and Government Information, *Use of Polygraphs as "Lie Detectors" by the Federal Government*, 89th Cong., 1st sess., 1965, report 198.

31. Quoted in Westin, *Privacy and Freedom*, p. 233.

32. U.S. Civil Service Commission, letter to the president, July 29, 1966, quoted in Office of Technology Assessment, *Scientific Validity of Polygraph Testing*, p. 34.

33. Civil service regulations, which remained in effect through the 1980s, prohibited federal agency use of the polygraph for personnel screening, except for positions involving national security. The regulations established criteria for determining whether an agency had a highly sensitive mission. Agencies wishing to use the polygraph for personnel screening were required to meet certain conditions concerning the purposes for which the polygraph would be used and prior notification of the individual of the intent to use the polygraph and of the fact that refusal to consent to the polygraph would not be included in the personnel record. Approval to use the polygraph was granted only for one-year periods. See ibid.

34. U.S. Department of Defense, *Department of Defense Directive Number 5210.48: Conduct of Polygraph Examinations and the Selection, Training, and Supervision of DOD Polygraph Examiners* (Washington, D.C., July 13, 1965).

35. Westin, *Privacy and Freedom*, p. 234.

36. Senator Sam J. Ervin, Jr., "Why Senate Hearings on Psychological Tests in Government," *American Psychologist* 20, no. 11 (Nov. 1965): 880.

37. Quoted in Westin, *Privacy and Freedom*, p. 153.

38. Michael Amrine, "The 1965 Congressional Inquiry into Testing: A Commentary," *American Psychologist* 20, no. 11 (Nov. 1965): 859.

39. Testimony of John F. Griner, president, American Federation of Government Employees, before the Senate Subcommittee on Constitutional Rights, reprinted in ibid., p. 952.

40. Testimony of Karl U. Smith, professor of industrial psychology, University of Wisconsin, before the Senate Subcommittee on Constitutional Rights, reprinted in ibid., p. 910.

41. Westin, *Privacy and Freedom*, p. 148.

42. Ibid., p. 149.

43. U.S. House Committee on Government Operations, Subcommittee on Foreign Operations and Government Information, *The Use of Polygraphs and Similar Devices by Federal Agencies: Hearings before Subcommittee on Foreign Operations and Government Information*, 93d Cong., 2d sess., 1974.

44. U.S. Senate Committee on the Judiciary, Subcommittee on Constitutional Rights, *Privacy, Polygraphs, and Employment* (Washington, D.C.: Government Printing Office, 1974).

45. Ibid., p. 3.

46. U.S. House Committee on Government Operations, *The Use of Polygraphs and Similar Devices by Federal Agencies*, 94th Cong., 2d sess., 1976, cited in Office of Technology Assessment, *Scientific Validity of Polygraph Testing*, pp. 34–35.

47. Ibid.

48. Privacy Protection Study Commission, *Personal Privacy in an Information Society* (Washington, D.C.: Government Printing Office, 1977), p. 239.

49. U.S. Senate Committee on the Judiciary, Subcommittee on the Constitution, *Polygraph Control and Civil Liberties Protection Act: Hearings*, 95th Cong., 2d sess., Nov. 15–16, 1977, Sept. 19, 21, 1978.

50. U.S. House Select Committee on Intelligence, Subcommittee on Oversight, *Preemployment Security Procedures of the Intelligence Agencies: Hearings*, 96th Cong., 1st sess., May 16, 17, 24, June 21, 1979.

51. U.S. House Committee on Education and Labor, Subcommittee on Labor-Management Relations, *Pressures in Today's Workplace: Hearings*, 96th Cong., 1st and 2d sess., vols. 1–3, Oct. 16–18, Dec. 4, 6, 15, 1979, Feb. 26–27, 1980.

52. The 1975 revisions in DOD directive number 5210.48 authorized use of the polygraph at the DOD for various counterintelligence and intelligence purposes. The 1983 revisions proposed the authorization of use of the polygraph for screening personnel — civilians, military staff, and contractors — with access to highly classified information. The polygraph could be used in the initial screening for security clearance as well as in the determination of continuing eligibility. The proposed revisions

also provided that refusal to take a polygraph exam could result in adverse consequences, including denial of employment or assignment, denial or revocation of clearance, and reassignment. Office of Technology Assessment, *Scientific Validity of Polygraph Testing*, pp. 34–36.

53. Ibid., p. 4.

54. Ibid., p. 5.

55. The Committee on the Judiciary requested sequential referral because of the constitutional issues raised by both prepublication review and polygraph tests.

56. U.S. House Committee on Post Office and Civil Service, *Federal Polygraph Limitation and Anti-Censorship Act of 1984*, 98th Cong., 2d sess., 1984, report 98-961, p. 7.

57. U.S. House Committee on the Judiciary, Subcommittee on Civil and Constitutional Rights, *Federal Polygraph Limitation and Anti-Censorship Act: Hearings*, 98th Cong., 2d sess., Sept. 12, 1984, p. 2.

58. Ibid.

59. Statement of John Otto, executive assistant director of the FBI, Department of Justice, in ibid., p. 10.

60. U.S. House Committee on Armed Services, Subcommittee on Investigations, *Hearing on H.R. 4681, Relating to the Administration of Polygraph Examinations and Prepublication Review Requirements by Federal Agencies*, 98th Cong., 2d sess., Sept. 6, 1984, and Committee on Armed Services, *Full Committee Consideration of H.R. 4681, Relating to the Administration of Polygraph Examinations and Prepublication Review Requirements by Federal Agencies: Hearings*, 98th Cong., 2d sess., Sept. 19, 1984.

61. Bureau of National Affairs, *Polygraphs and Employment*, p. 18.

62. U.S. House Committee, *Polygraphs in the Workplace*, p. 17.

63. Ibid., p. 16.

64. Ibid., p. 1.

65. Ibid., p. 2.

66. Ibid., p. 3.

67. J. Belt and P. Holden, "Polygraph Usage among Major U.S. Corporations," *Personnel Journal* 57 (Fall 1978): 80.

68. U.S. House Committee, *Polygraphs in the Workplace*, p. 34.

69. Ibid., p. 15.

70. Ibid., p. 28.

71. Ibid., p. 29.

72. Ibid., p. 19.

73. Quoted by Robert F. Harbrant, president, Food and Allied Service Trades Department, AFL-CIO, in ibid., p. 45.

74. Ibid., p. 139.

75. U.S. House Committee on Education and Labor, *Employee Polygraph Protection Act of 1985*, 99th Cong., 1st sess., 1985, report 99-416, p. 6.

76. Ibid.

77. Bill Goodling, Marge Roukema, Steve Bartlett, Dick Armey, and Harris W. Fawell, "Dissenting Views on H.R. 1524," in ibid., pp. 15–17.

78. "Supplemental Views by the Honorable Steve Gunderson on H.R. 1524," in ibid., p. 19.

79. U.S. Senate Committee on Labor and Human Resources, *Polygraph Protection Act of 1985: Hearings*, 99th Cong., 2d sess., Apr. 23, 1986, p. 1.

80. Statement of Stephen J. Markman, assistant attorney general, Office of Legal Policy, Department of Justice, in ibid., p. 28.

81. Ibid., p. 17.

82. Ibid., p. 23.

83. Ibid.

84. U.S. Senate Committee on Labor and Human Resources, *The Polygraph Act of 1985*, 99th Cong., 2d sess., 1985, report 99-447.

85. Statement of Stephen J. Markman, assistant attorney general, Office of Legal Policy, Department of Justice, in U.S. House Committee on Education and Labor, Subcommittee on Employment Opportunities, *Polygraph Testing in the Private Work Force: Hearings*, 100th Cong., 1st sess., Mar. 5, Apr. 30, 1987, serial 100-23, p. 42.

86. Ibid., p. 76.

87. Statement of John F. Beary III, M.D., assistant dean for planning and development, Georgetown University School of Medicine, on behalf of the American Medical Association, in ibid., p. 51.

88. Statement of Edward S. Katkin, Ph.D., chair, Department of Psychology, State University of New York at Stonybrook, on behalf of the American Psychological Association, in ibid., p. 65.

89. Statement of Jon Bauer, staff attorney, Legal Action Center, New York, in ibid., p. 101.

90. Steve Bartlett, Dick Armey, Harris W. Fawell, and Cass Ballenger, "Minority Views on H.R. 1212," in U.S. House Committee on Education and Labor, *Employee Polygraph Protection Act*, 100th Cong., 1st sess., July 9, 1987, report 100-208, p. 15.

91. Bill Goodling, Steve Bartlett, Dick Armey, Harris W. Fawell, and Cass Ballenger, "Additional Views," in ibid., p. 21.

92. U.S. Senate Committee on Labor and Human Resources, *Polygraphs in the Workplace: Hearings*, 100th Cong., 1st sess., June 19, 1987.

93. U.S. Senate Committee on Labor and Human Resources, *Polygraph Protection Act of 1987*, 100th Cong., 2d sess., Feb. 11, 1988, report 100-284, p. 39.

94. Ibid., p. 40.

95. *Congressional Record* (Mar. 2, 1988), 100th Cong., 2d sess., vol. 134, pt. 2:S1702–3.

96. Ibid., p. S1699.

97. Ibid., p. S1688.

98. Ibid. (Mar. 3, 1988), p. S1796.

99. The conference committee agreed to the following:
—It defined not a lie detector test but the device itself, including mechanical or electrical devices but not chemical, written, or oral tests.
—It retained exemptions for federal, state, and local governments and provided exemptions for private intelligence contractors.
—It authorized exemptions for employers in businesses involving private security services and controlled substances but not nuclear power facilities.

— It allowed use of the polygraph, but not other lie detector devices, in specific investigations of economic loss or injury to an employer's business.

— It agreed that the refusal to take a polygraph test or the results of a polygraph test may not serve as the sole basis for an adverse employment action and that employees must be informed of their rights when taking an exam.

100. "Congress Clears Lie-Detector Ban," *Congressional Quarterly Weekly Report*, June 11, 1988, p. 1630.

101. Paul R. Sackett and Michael M. Harris, "Honesty Testing for Personnel Selection: A Review and Critique," *Personnel Psychology* 37 (Summer 1984): 221–45.

102. R. Michael O'Bannon, Linda A. Goldinger, and Gavin S. Appleby, *Honesty and Integrity Testing: A Practical Guide* (Atlanta: Applied Information Resources, 1989), p. 8.

103. Gilbert Fuchsberg, "Integrity-Test Firms Fear Report Card by Congress," *Wall Street Journal*, Sept. 20, 1990, pp. B1, B5.

104. Tom McNamara, chief of staff of Representative Don Sundquist's (R-Tenn.) office, quoted in ibid.

105. Anne Anastasi, "The Use of Personal Assessment in Industry: Methodological and Interpretive Problems," in *Personality Assessment in Organizations*, edited by H. John Bernardin and David A. Bownas (New York: Praeger, 1985), pp. 7–10.

106. James Neal Butcher, "Personality Assessment in Industry: Theoretical Issues and Illustrations," in ibid., p. 281.

107. Fuchsberg, "Integrity-Test Firms Fear Report Card by Congress."

108. John W. Jones, David Arnold, and William G. Harris, "Introduction to the Model Guidelines for Preemployment Integrity Testing," *Journal of Business and Psychology* 4 (Summer 1990): 525–32.

109. Office of Technology Assessment, *Use of Integrity Tests*, p. 10.

110. "Honest Tests: The Defense Rests," *Training* 28 (May 1991): 12.

111. Carolyn Wiley and Docia L. Rudley, "Managerial Issues and Responsibilities in the Use of Integrity Tests," *Labor Law Journal* 42 (Mar. 1991): 152–59; Elliot D. Larson, "How Good Are Integrity Tests?," *Personnel Journal* 71 (Apr. 1992): 35–36.

112. A growing literature is developing in this area. For background on the establishment of the Human Genome Project, see Jerry E. Bishop and Michael Waldholz, *Genome: The Story of the Most Astonishing Scientific Adventure of Our Time* (New York: Simon and Schuster, 1990); Robert Mullan Cook-Deegan, "The Human Genome Project: The Formation of Federal Policies in the United States, 1986–1990," in *Biomedical Politics*, edited by Kathi E. Hanna (Washington, D.C.: National Academy Press, 1991); Joel Davis, *Mapping the Code* (New York: John Wiley and Sons, 1990); and Daniel J. Kelves and Leroy Hood, eds., *The Code of Codes* (Cambridge: Harvard University Press, 1992).

113. The project involves first "mapping" and then "sequencing" the human genome. In "mapping," information from family linkage studies and biochemical measurements is used to determine the location of a gene on a chromosome. "Sequencing" is a more involved and detailed process entailing the breakdown of DNA into its component biochemical parts, nucleotides. Sequencing makes possible the development of drugs or treatments on the molecular level. See John C. Fletcher and Dorothy

C. Wertz, "Ethics, Law, and Medical Genetics: After the Human Genome Is Mapped," *Emory Law Journal* 39 (Summer 1990): 754–55.

114. For discussions of these issues, see Office of Technology Assessment, *Genetic Monitoring and Screening in the Workplace*, OTA-BA-455 (Washington, D.C.: Government Printing Office, 1990), and *The Genome, Ethics, and the Law: Issues in Genetic Testing*, report of Conference on the Ethical and Legal Implications of Genetic Testing, Berkeley Springs, W.V., June 14–16, 1991 (Washington, D.C.: American Association for the Advancement of Science, 1992).

115. U.S. House Committee on Government Operations, *Health Security Act*, 103d Cong., 2d sess., 1994, report 103-601, part 5, p. 86.

116. Ray Moseley et al., "Ethical Implications of a Complete Human Gene Map for Insurance," *Business and Professional Ethics Journal* 10, no. 4 (Winter 1991): 72–73.

117. For discussions of validity and reliability issues generated by genetic testing in the workplace, see Ann Lucas Diamond, "Genetic Testing in Employment Situations," *Journal of Legal Medicine* 4, no. 2 (1983): 231–56, and Laura Rowinski, "Genetic Testing in the Workplace," *Journal of Contemporary Health Law and Policy* 4 (Spring 1988): 375–413.

118. The 1983 survey was sent to the chief executive officers of the 500 largest U.S. industrial companies (the Fortune 500 manufacturing and mining firms), the chief executive officers of the 50 largest private utilities, and the presidents of the 11 major unions that represent the largest numbers of employees in those companies. See Office of Technology Assessment, *The Role of Genetic Testing in the Prevention of Occupational Disease*, OTA-BA-194 (Washington, D.C.: Government Printing Office, 1983).

119. The 1989 survey involved current Fortune 500 companies, the 50 largest utilities, and the 33 largest unions. The comparable population surveyed by the OTA in 1982 was included in this population to provide trend data. See Office of Technology Assessment, *Genetic Monitoring and Screening*, esp. chap. 9.

120. Cited in Larry Gostin, "Genetic Discrimination: The Use of Genetically Based Diagnostic and Prognostic Tests by Employers and Insurers," *American Journal of Law and Medicine* 17, nos. 1 and 2 (1991): 116.

121. Ibid., p. 117.

122. In an interesting and thorough analysis of the discrimination questions posed by the use of genetic information, Larry Gostin concludes that although it is likely that the Americans with Disabilities Act (ADA) of 1990 would apply to discrimination based upon future disability, which could be revealed by genetic testing, an amendment to the ADA may be necessary to prevent any uncertainty. Little congressional attention was given to genetic discrimination during hearings and floor debates, and at this point, it would be left to the courts to decide if discrimination based upon a predicted disability revealed by genetic tests came under the scope of the ADA. See ibid., pp. 109–44. For other discussions regarding the applicability of the ADA to genetic conditions, see David Orentlicher, "Genetic Screening by Employers," *JAMA* 263, no. 7 (Feb. 16, 1990): 1005, 1008. For an earlier discussion of discrimination questions, see Ellen R. Peirce, "The Regulation of Genetic Testing in the Workplace — A Legislative Proposal," *Ohio State Law Journal* 46, no. 4 (1985): 771–843.

1. John W. Kingdon, *Agendas, Alternatives, and Public Policies* (Glenview, Ill.: Scott, Foresman, 1984), p. 115.

2. Martha Derthick and Paul J. Quirk, *The Politics of Deregulation* (Washington, D.C.: Brookings Institution, 1985); Timothy J. Conlan, Margaret T. Wrightson, and David R. Beam, *Taxing Choices* (Washington, D.C.: Congressional Quarterly Press, 1990).

3. Steven Kelman, "Why Public Ideas Matter," in Robert B. Reich, ed., *The Power of Public Ideas* (Cambridge: Harvard University Press, 1990), p. 41.

4. Deborah A. Stone, *Policy Paradox and Political Reason* (Glenview, Ill.: Scott, Foresman, 1988), p. 269.

5. 425 U.S. 435 (1976).

6. If the purpose of a match is to produce evidence that someone has defrauded the government, then a computer match could be regarded as a search under the Fourth Amendment. But if the purpose is to detect and correct errors, then a match would probably not be regarded as a search under the Fourth Amendment.

7. For a discussion of this issue and an argument for restricting direct marketing because of its limited instrumental purpose, see C. Edwin Baker, *Human Liberty and Freedom of Speech* (New York: Oxford University Press, 1984), esp. chap. 9.

8. M. Sean Royall, "Constitutionally Regulating Telephone Harassment: An Exercise in Statutory Precision," *University of Chicago Law Review* 56, no. 4 (1989): 1403–32.

9. Robert B. Reich, introduction to *Power of Public Ideas*, p. 4.

10. Mark Moore, "What Sort of Ideas Become Public Ideas?," in Reich, *Power of Public Ideas*, p. 77.

11. Jane J. Mansbridge, "The Rise and Fall of Self-Interest in the Explanation of Political Life," in *Beyond Self-Interest*, edited by Jane J. Mansbridge (Chicago: University of Chicago Press, 1990).

12. Kelman, "Why Public Ideas Matter," p. 52.

13. Donald N. Michael, "Speculations on the Relation of the Computer to Individual Freedom and the Right to Privacy," *George Washington Law Review* 33 (Oct. 1964): 275.

14. Senator Sam J. Ervin, "The First Amendment: A Living Thought in the Computer Age," *Columbia Human Rights Law Review* 4, no. 1 (1972): 16.

15. U.S. Department of Health, Education, and Welfare, Secretary's Advisory Committee on Automated Personal Data Systems, *Records, Computers, and the Rights of Citizens* (Washington, D.C.: Government Printing Office, 1973), p. xx.

16. Privacy Protection Study Commission, *Technology and Privacy* (Washington, D.C.: Government Printing Office, 1977), appendix 5, p. 1.

17. Office of Technology Assessment, *Federal Government Information Technology: Electronic Record Systems and Individual Privacy*, OTA-CIT-296 (Washington, D.C.: Government Printing Office, 1986).

18. Privacy Act, sec. 3(a)(7).

19. President's Commission on Law Enforcement and the Administration of Jus-

tice, *The Challenge of Crime in a Free Society* (Washington, D.C.: Government Printing Office, 1967), p. 193.

20. U.S. Senate Committee on the Judiciary, Subcommittee on Criminal Law and Procedures, *Controlling Crime through More Effective Law Enforcement: Hearings*, 90th Cong., 2d sess., 1967, pp. 957–58.

21. Herman Schwartz, "Summary of Findings on the Amount, Benefits, and Costs of Official Electronic Surveillance," ACLU report, 1972, cited in Alan LeMond and Ron Fry, *No Place to Hide* (New York: St. Martin's Press, 1975).

22. Samuel Dash, Richard F. Schwartz, and Robert E. Knowlton, *The Eavesdroppers* (New Brunswick: Rutgers University Press, 1959).

23. U.S. Senate Committee on the Judiciary, Subcommittee on Administrative Practice and Procedure, *Invasions of Privacy (Government Agencies): Hearings*, 89th Cong., 1st sess., 1965.

24. Administrative Office of the U.S. Courts, *Report on Applications for Orders Authorizing or Approving the Interception of Wire or Oral Communications, for Calendar Year 1984* (Washington, D.C.: Administrative Office of the U.S. Courts, 1985).

25. Ibid., pp. 6, 7, 21. The figures for arrests and convictions are incomplete because of the time involved in concluding a federal investigation and criminal proceeding.

26. U.S. Senate Committee on the Judiciary, Subcommittee on Patents, Copyrights, and Trademarks, *Electronic Communications Privacy: Hearings*, 99th Cong., 1st sess., Nov. 13, 1985, p. 45.

27. Anne Anastasi, "The Use of Personal Assessment in Industry: Methodological and Interpretive Problems," in *Personality Assessment in Organizations*, edited by H. John Bernardin and David A. Bownas (New York: Praeger, 1985), p. 2.

28. For a discussion of issues regarding access to criminal history records, see Office of Technology Assessment, *An Assessment of Alternatives for a National Computerized Criminal History System*, OTA-CIT-161 (Washington, D.C.: Government Printing Office, 1982).

29. For a discussion of medical screening tests, see Office of Technology Assessment, *Medical Testing and Health Insurance*, OTA-H-384 (Washington, D.C.: Government Printing Office, 1988), chap. 3.

30. One difficulty was the lack of agreement on what constitutes theft. Some analysts define employee theft broadly to include, in addition to stealing money, taking pencils, arriving at work late, and using sick time for personal reasons. Others define it more narrowly as the unauthorized taking of money or property. Some analysts cite only instances of employee theft in which the employee is caught, others cite only employee admissions of theft, and still others cite all unaccounted for inventory shrinkage. Another difficulty in determining an accurate measure of employee theft is that researchers use different definitions of "employee" and examine different sectors of employers. Additionally, the time periods in studies vary. Thus, it is difficult to compare and/or aggregate data on employee theft.

31. See, for example, Christine Gorman, "Honestly, Can We Trust You?," *Time*, Jan. 23, 1989, p. 44. This article begins: "Each year U.S. businesses lose as much as $40 billion to employees who steal."

32. The eleven nonviolent crimes were employee pilferage, kickbacks/bribery, securities theft/fraud, embezzlement, arson, burglary, vandalism, shoplifting, insurance fraud, check fraud, and credit card fraud. American Management Associations, "Summary Overview of the 'State of the Art' Regarding Information Gathering Techniques and Level of Knowledge in Three Areas Concerning Crimes against Business," draft report for the National Institute of Law Enforcement and Criminal Justice, Law Enforcement Assistance Administration, Mar. 1977, and *Crimes against Business: Background, Findings, and Recommendations* (New York: American Management Associations, 1977).

33. Richard C. Hollinger and John P. Clark, *Theft by Employees* (Lexington, Mass.: Lexington Books/D. C. Heath, 1983), originally "Theft by Employees in Work Organizations," report, U.S. Department of Justice, National Institute of Justice, Sept. 1983.

34. R. L. Tatham, "Employee's Views on Theft in Retailing," *Journal of Retailing* 50, no. 3 (Fall 1974): 49–55.

35. National Council on Crime and Delinquency, *Workplace Crime: Systems in Conflict* (Hackensack, N.J.: National Council on Crime and Delinquency, 1976).

36. Hollinger and Clark, *Theft by Employees*, p. 21.

37. Ibid., p. 19.

38. Statement of Jim Krahulec, vice president, Government and Trade Relations, Rite Aid Corporation, representing the National Association of Chain Drug Stores, Inc., in U.S. House Committee on Education and Labor, Subcommittee on Employment Opportunities, *Polygraphs in the Workplace: The Use of "Lie Detectors" in Hiring and Firing: Hearings*, 99th Cong., 1st sess., July 30, Sept. 18, 1985, p. 295.

39. Arthur R. Miller, *The Assault on Privacy: Computers, Data Banks, and Dossiers* (Ann Arbor: University of Michigan Press, 1971), p. x.

40. Statement of Christopher H. Pyle, in U.S. Senate Committee on the Judiciary, Subcommittee on Constitutional Rights, *Federal Data Banks, Computers, and the Bill of Rights: Hearings*, 92d Cong., 1st sess., Feb. 23–25, Mar. 2–4, 9–11, 15, 17, 1971, p. 189.

41. U.S. Senate Committee on Government Operations, Ad Hoc Subcommittee on Privacy and Information Systems, and Committee on the Judiciary, Subcommittee on Constitutional Rights, *Privacy—The Collection, Use, and Computerization of Personal Data: Joint Hearings*, 93d Cong., 2d sess., June 18–20, 1974.

42. Office of Technology Assessment, *Computer-Based National Information Systems*, OTA-CIT-146 (Washington, D.C.: Government Printing Office, 1981).

43. Office of Technology Assessment, *Implications of Electronic Mail and Message Systems for the U.S. Postal Service*, OTA-CIT-183 (Washington, D.C.: Government Printing Office, 1982).

44. Office of Technology Assessment, *Assessment of Alternatives*.

45. Paul A. Sabatier, "An Advocacy Coalition Framework of Policy Change and the Role of Policy-Oriented Learning Therein," *Policy Sciences* 21, nos. 2–3 (1988): 129–68.

46. Kingdon, *Agendas, Alternatives, and Public Policies*.

47. Quoted in Nadine Cohodas, "Congress Races to Stay Ahead of Technology," *Congressional Quarterly Weekly Report*, May 31, 1986, p. 1234.

48. Robert W. Kastenmeier, Deborah Leavy, and David Beier, "Communications Privacy: A Legislative Perspective," *Wisconsin Law Review*, July/Aug. 1989, p. 734.

49. Issues involving computer security and data encryption standards are very complex because of the need to protect national security interests. For good analyses of the issues, see System Security Study Committee et al., *Computers at Risk* (Washington, D.C.: National Academy Press, 1991) and Office of Technology Assessment, *Defending Secrets, Sharing Data: New Locks and Keys for Electronic Information*, OTA-CIT-310 (Washington, D.C.: Government Printing Office, 1987).

50. G. Pascal Zachary, "Personal-Computer Makers Join Forces in Move to Prevent Tampering, Forgery," *Wall Street Journal*, Apr. 29, 1991, p. 5B.

51. David R. Mayhew, *Congress: The Electoral Connection* (New Haven: Yale University Press, 1974).

52. Richard F. Fenno, *Congressmen in Committees* (Boston: Little, Brown, 1973).

53. Morris S. Ogul, *Congress Oversees the Bureaucracy: Studies in Legislative Supervision* (Pittsburgh: University of Pittsburgh Press, 1976), pp. 124–25.

54. Ibid., p. 95.

55. Ibid., p. 118.

56. Alan F. Westin, "The Protection of Privacy in the Public and Private Sectors," in *Effective Social Science: Eight Cases in Economics, Political Science, and Sociology*, edited by Bernard Barber (New York: Russell Sage Foundation, 1987), pp. 143–44.

57. David H. Flaherty, *Protecting Privacy in Surveillance Societies: The Federal Republic of Germany, Sweden, France, Canada, and the United States* (Chapel Hill: University of North Carolina Press, 1989), p. 309.

58. Ogul, *Congress Oversees the Bureaucracy*, p. 98.

59. Ibid., pp. 98–99.

60. R. Douglas Arnold, *The Logic of Congressional Action* (New Haven: Yale University Press, 1990), p. 10.

61. Ogul, *Congress Oversees the Bureaucracy*, p. 103.

62. See, for example, Derthick and Quirk, *Politics of Deregulation*, and Conlan, Wrightson, and Beam, *Taxing Choices*.

63. James Q. Wilson, *The Politics of Regulation* (New York: Basic Books, 1980), p. 370.

64. Burdett Loomis, *The New American Politician: Ambition, Entrepreneurship, and the Changing Face of Political Life* (New York: Basic Books, 1988), p. 6.

65. Ibid., p. 13.

CHAPTER EIGHT

1. Roger Rosenblatt, "Who Killed Privacy?," *New York Times Magazine*, Jan. 31, 1993, pp. 24–28.

2. T. Alexander Aleinikoff, "Constitutional Law in the Age of Balancing," *Yale Law Journal* 96, no. 5 (Apr. 1987): 981.

3. The legal and philosophical literature that emphasizes the importance of privacy to the individual is vast. Among the most important works are Samuel D. Warren and Louis D. Brandeis, "The Right to Privacy," *Harvard Law Review* 4 (Dec. 1890): 193–

220; Charles Fried, "Privacy," *Yale Law Journal* 77, no. 3 (Jan. 1968): 475–93; Alan F. Westin, *Privacy and Freedom* (New York: Atheneum, 1967); Edward J. Bloustein, "Privacy as an Aspect of Human Dignity — An Answer to Dean Prosser," *New York University Law Review* 39 (Dec. 1964): 962–1007; James Rachels, "Why Privacy Is Important," *Philosophy and Public Affairs* 4, no. 4 (Summer 1975): 323–33; and Jeffrey H. Reiman, "Privacy, Intimacy, and Personhood," *Philosophy and Public Affairs* 6, no. 1 (Fall 1976): 26–44. Several edited volumes on privacy also exist, including J. Roland Pennock and John W. Chapman, eds., *Privacy*, Nomos Series 13, Yearbook of the American Society for Political and Legal Philosophy (New York: Atherton Press, 1971), and Ferdinand David Schoeman, ed., *Philosophical Dimensions of Privacy: An Anthology* (Cambridge: Cambridge University Press, 1984).

4. Warren and Brandeis, "The Right to Privacy," p. 193.

5. H. W. Arndt, "The Cult of Privacy," *Australian Quarterly* 21, no. 3 (Sept. 1949): 70–71.

6. See, for example, Fried, "Privacy"; Pennock and Chapman, preface to *Privacy*; and Robert S. Gerstein, "Privacy and Self-Incrimination," *Ethics* 80, no. 2 (1970): 87–101.

7. Richard A. Posner, "An Economic Theory of Privacy," *Regulation* 2, no. 3 (May/June 1978): 20.

8. Ibid., p. 22.

9. Ibid.

10. Ibid., p. 23.

11. Ibid., p. 25.

12. Westin, *Privacy and Freedom*, p. 7.

13. Fried, "Privacy."

14. Spiros Simitis, "Reviewing Privacy in an Information Society," *University of Pennsylvania Law Review* 135 (Mar. 1987): 732.

15. Barrington Moore, Jr., *Privacy: Studies in Social and Cultural History* (Armonk, N.Y.: M. E. Sharpe, 1984), p. 274.

16. John Dewey, *The Public and Its Problems* (Chicago: Swallow Press, 1927), p. 186.

17. Amitai Etzioni, *The Spirit of Community: Rights, Responsibilities, and the Communitarian Agenda* (New York: Crown Publishers, 1993). For philosophical discussions of communitarianism and liberalism, see Michael J. Sandel, *Liberalism and the Limits of Justice* (Cambridge: Cambridge University Press, 1982), and Amy Gutmann, "Communitarian Critics of Liberalism," *Philosophy and Public Affairs* 14, no. 3 (Summer 1985): 308–22.

18. Richard F. Hixson suggests at first that community "turns out to be the best place for personal privacy to thrive, indeed, to survive." But he also states that "were today's society more public and public serving, the individual would be less inclined to put a premium on her or his privacy." Richard F. Hixson, *Privacy in a Public Society: Human Rights in Conflict* (New York: Oxford University Press, 1987), pp. 130, 216.

19. These proposals will be discussed in the next section. As Stephen Macedo points out: "Without some substantial vision of a common political good communitarianism appears to be a rather empty yearning for a golden age of togetherness and harmony, a longing spurred on by dissatisfaction with liberalism rather than the

discovery of a preferable alternative." Stephen Macedo, *Liberal Virtues: Citizenship, Virtue, and Community in Liberal Constitutionalism* (Oxford: Clarendon Press, 1990), p. 17.

20. Fried, "Privacy," p. 212; Rachels, "Why Privacy Is Important," pp. 295–97.

21. Quoted in Dewey, *The Public and Its Problems*, p. 96.

22. Ibid.

23. S. Rodota, "Privacy and Data Surveillance: Growing Public Concern," in *Policy Issues in Data Protection and Privacy*, OECD Information Studies no. 10 (Paris: OECD, 1976), pp. 139–40.

24. Simitis, "Reviewing Privacy," pp. 736–37.

25. Oscar H. Gandy, Jr., *The Panoptic Sort: A Political Economy of Personal Information* (Boulder: Westview Press, 1993), p. 19.

26. Conversations with Helen Nissenbaum at Princeton University's Center for Human Values (spring 1993) were important in the development of this distinction.

27. William A. Galston, *Liberal Purposes: Goods, Virtues, and Diversity in the Liberal State* (Cambridge: Cambridge University Press, 1991), p. 3. Galston's thesis is: "No form of political life can be justified without some view of what is good for individuals. In practice, liberal theorists covertly employ theories of the good. But their insistence that they do not reduces the rigor of their theories and leaves the liberal polity unnecessarily vulnerable to criticism" (ibid., p. 79).

28. Ibid., p. 222.

29. Macedo, *Liberal Virtues*, p. 12. Macedo goes on to argue: "Liberalism is not first and foremost a theory of the relation between the self and its ends; it is most directly a way of organizing political life that stresses the importance of freedom, individual rights, law, limited government, and public reasonableness" (ibid., p. 207).

30. Ibid., p. 201.

31. Ibid., p. 270.

32. John Stuart Mill, "On Liberty" (1859), in *The English Philosophers from Bacon to Mill* (New York: Modern Library, 1939), p. 998.

33. Ruth Gavison, "Privacy and the Limits of the Law," *Yale Law Journal* 89, no. 3 (Jan. 1980): 347.

34. Ibid., p. 369.

35. Dewey, *The Public and Its Problems*, p. 39.

36. Ibid., p. 181.

37. Michael Walzer, "Liberalism and the Art of Separation," *Political Theory* 12, no. 3 (Aug. 1984): 324.

38. Ibid., p. 325.

39. In discussing privacy and libel, Emerson notes that "both deal with interests that are more individual and private in character than social or public. In both the injury is peculiar to the individual, rather than shared with others, and may concern the most intimate aspects of the person's life." Thomas I. Emerson, *The System of Freedom of Expression* (New York: Random House, 1970), p. 517.

40. Ibid., p. 546.

41. *NAACP v. Alabama*, 357 U.S. 449 (1958).

42. *Watkins v. United States*, 354 U.S. 178 (1957); *Sweezy v. New Hampshire*, 354 U.S. 234 (1957).

43. *Talley v. California*, 362 U.S. 60 (1960).

44. Mill, "On Liberty," p. 949.

45. *Wolf v. Colorado*, 338 U.S. 25 (1949).

46. See Anthony G. Amsterdam, "Perspectives on the Fourth Amendment," *Minnesota Law Review* 58 (Jan. 1974): 349–439, and Peter Goldberger, "Consent, Expectation of Privacy, and the Meaning of 'Searches' in the Fourth Amendment," *Journal of Criminal Law and Criminology* 75, no. 2 (1984): 319–62.

47. Hannah Arendt, *The Human Condition* (Chicago: University of Chicago Press, 1958), p. 38. In this dual sense, privacy can be regarded as the opposite of both the public realm and the social realm. At the same time, the social realm threatens to obviate the private and public realm: "Since the rise of society, since the admission of household and housekeeping activities to the public realm, an irresistible tendency to grow, to devour the older realms of the political and private as well as the more recently established sphere of intimacy, has been one of the outstanding characteristics of the new realm" (ibid., p. 45). Within this context, Arendt examines again the relationship between the public and the private and the importance of privacy to that relationship. She points out that the world of the common is not the social realm but the public realm.

48. Ibid., p. 57.

49. Thomas E. McCollough, *The Moral Imagination and Public Life: Raising the Ethical Question* (Chatham, N.J.: Chatham House Publishers, 1991), p. 66.

50. John Rawls, *A Theory of Justice* (Cambridge: Belknap Press of Harvard University Press, 1971), p. 128.

51. Gandy, *The Panoptic Sort*, p. 3.

52. Mary J. Culnan and Priscilla M. Regan, "Privacy Issues and the Creation of Campaign Mailing Lists," *Information Society* 11, no. 2 (Apr.–June 1995): forthcoming.

53. For discussions of this concept, see J. G. Head, "Public Goods and Public Policy," *Public Finance* 17, no. 3 (1962): 197–219; Mancur Olson, *The Logic of Collective Action: Public Goods and the Theory of Groups* (Cambridge: Harvard University Press, 1965); and Vincent Ostrom and Elinor Ostrom, "Public Choice: A Different Approach to the Study of Public Administration," *Public Administration Review* 31 (Mar./Apr. 1971): 203–16.
Ostrom and Ostrom distinguish between "purely private goods" and "purely public goods" as follows: "Purely private goods are defined as those goods and services which are highly divisible and can be (1) packaged, contained, or measured in discrete units, and (2) provided under competitive market conditions where potential consumers can be excluded from enjoying the benefit unless they are willing to pay the price. Purely public goods, by contrast, are highly indivisible goods and services where potential consumers cannot be easily excluded from enjoying the benefits" (ibid., p. 206).

54. In *United States v. Miller*, 425 U.S. 435 (1976), the Supreme Court rejected Miller's claim that he had a Fourth Amendment reasonable expectation of privacy in the handling of records kept by banks "because they are merely copies of personal records that were made available to the banks for a limited purpose" and ruled instead that "checks are not confidential communications but negotiable instruments

to be used in commercial transactions." In response to this decision, Congress passed the Right to Financial Privacy Act of 1978 providing bank customers with some privacy regarding records held by banks and other financial institutions. The records of customers' rental transactions at video stores were similarly regarded as the property of the video store with no protection for the individual until Congress passed the Video Privacy Protection Act of 1988.

55. Mary J. Culnan, "Consumer Attitudes toward Direct Mail, Privacy, and Name Removal: Implications for Direct Marketing" (paper presented at the Symposium on Consumer Privacy, Chicago/Midwest Direct Marketing Days, Chicago, Jan. 20, 1993).

56. Office of Technology Assessment, *Critical Connections: Communicating for the Future*, OTA-CIT-407 (Washington, D.C.: Government Printing Office, 1990).

57. Statement of Carol Knauff, director, Intelligent Network Services, AT&T, before the U.S. Senate Committee on the Judiciary, Subcommittee on Technology and the Law, *Caller-ID Technology: Hearings*, 101st Cong., 2d sess., Aug. 1, 1990, p. 11.

58. James R. Beniger, *The Control Revolution: Technological and Economic Origins of the Information Society* (Cambridge: Harvard University Press, 1986).

59. Alida Brill, *Nobody's Business: Paradoxes of Privacy* (Reading, Mass.: Addison-Wesley Publishing, 1990), pp. xv, xvii.

60. Ibid., p. xix.

61. Simitis, "Reviewing Privacy," p. 709.

62. Colin J. Bennett, *Regulating Privacy: Data Protection and Public Policy in Europe and the United States* (Ithaca: Cornell University Press, 1992), p. 202.

63. Olson, *The Logic of Collective Action.*

64. Jane J. Mansbridge, "The Rise and Fall of Self-Interest in the Explanation of Political Life," in *Beyond Self-Interest*, edited by Jane J. Mansbridge (Chicago: University of Chicago Press, 1990).

65. Meheroo Jussawalla and Chee-Wah Cheah, *The Calculus of International Communications* (Littleton, Colo.: Libraries Unlimited, 1987), p. 89, cited in Gandy, *The Panoptic Sort*, p. 207.

66. "British DMers Are Worried over Europe Data Board," *DM News*, Mar. 5, 1990, pp. 1, 26.

67. Bennett, *Regulating Privacy*; David H. Flaherty, "The Need for an American Privacy Protection Commission," *Government Information Quarterly* 1, no. 3 (1984): 235–58; David H. Flaherty, *Protecting Privacy in Surveillance Societies: The Federal Republic of Germany, Sweden, France, Canada, and the United States* (Chapel Hill: University of North Carolina Press, 1989).

68. Jerry Berman and Janlori Goldman, "A Federal Right of Information Privacy: The Need for Reform," report of the Benton Foundation Project on Communications Information Policy Options (1989); Marc Rotenberg, "In Support of a Data Protection Board in the United States," *Government Information Quarterly* 8, no. 1 (1991): 79–93; "Privacy Law in the United States: Failing to Make the Grade," report of the U.S. Privacy Council and Computer Professionals for Social Responsibility (June 1991).

69. Simitis, "Reviewing Privacy," p. 744.

70. Several studies of the policy implications of these changes have been conducted. See, for example, Office of Technology Assessment, *Critical Connections*, and De-

partment of Commerce, National Telecommunications and Information Administration, *NTIA Telecom 2000: Charting the Course for a New Century* (Washington, D.C.: Government Printing Office, 1988).

71. David B. Hack, "Caller I.D. — Automatic Telephone Number Identification," *CRS Issue Brief* (IB90085), May 18, 1990.

72. Caroline E. Mayer, "For Whom the Bell Tolls?: Companies Also Benefit from Callers' Questions," *Washington Post*, July 15, 1992, pp. E1, E10.

73. John C. Fletcher and Dorothy C. Wertz, "Ethics, Law, and Medical Genetics: After the Human Genome Is Mapped," *Emory Law Journal* 39 (Summer 1990): 748.

74. Some important exceptions exist. In 1989 researchers located the gene associated with most cases of cystic fibrosis; current screening methods yield probabilities, not certainties, about the presence or absence of the gene. The genetic bases for Down's syndrome and sickle-cell anemia have been known for some time, and tests have been available for screening for these genes in fetuses. Some critics caution against a "gene of the week" psychology that may accompany genetic advances. For a discussion of scientific developments and ethical concerns, see Christopher Joyce, "Your Genome in Their Hands," *New Scientist*, Aug. 11, 1990, pp. 52–55.

75. For example, research seems to indicate a connection between certain genetic patterns (not necessarily the presence or absence of a particular gene) and a susceptibility to develop certain kinds of cancers. More detailed knowledge of the genetic basis will increase knowledge of cancer development, cancer risk factors, and approaches to prevention and therapy. See Zbigniew Bankowski, "Genetics, Medicine, and Ethics," *World Health*, Dec. 1988, pp. 3–5.

76. Ellen Goodman, "First the Gene, Then the Cure," *Washington Post*, Sept. 17, 1994, p. A15.

77. Rawls described the question of eugenics and social justice as follows: "In the original position, then, the parties want to insure for their descendants the best genetic endowment (assuming their own to be fixed). The pursuit of reasonable policies in this regard is something that earlier generations owe to later ones, this being a question that arises between generations. Thus over time a society is to take steps to preserve the general level of natural abilities and to prevent the diffusion of serious defects. . . . I mention this speculative and difficult matter to indicate once again the manner in which the difference principle is likely to transform problems of social justice." Rawls, *Theory of Justice*, p. 108.

78. Fletcher and Wertz, "Ethics, Law, and Medical Genetics," p. 757.

79. James Santiago Grisolia, "The Human Genome Project and Our Sense of Self," *Impact of Science on Society* 41, no. 161 (1991): 46.

80. *Business Week*–Louis Harris Poll, "It's OK to 'Play God' — within Limits," summarized in Office of Technology Assessment, *Genetic Monitoring and Screening in the Workplace*, OTA-BA-455 (Washington, D.C.: Government Printing Office, 1990), pp. 171–72.

81. March of Dimes Birth Defects Foundation, "Genetic Testing and Gene Therapy: National Survey Findings and Questionnaire and Responses," conducted by Louis Harris and Associates, Sept. 1992.

82. John Leo, "Genetic Advances, Ethical Risks," *U.S. News and World Report*, Sept. 25, 1989, p. 59.

83. George J. Annas, "Mapping the Human Genome and the Meaning of Monster Mythology," *Emory Law Journal* 39 (Summer 1990): 647.

84. Gerstein refers to the privilege against self-incrimination as a "guilty man's privilege." See Gerstein, "Privacy and Self-Incrimination," pp. 87–101, reprinted in Schoeman, *Philosophical Dimensions of Privacy*, p. 234.

85. Robert Wright, "Achilles' Helix," *New Republic*, July 9, 16, 1990, pp. 21–31. The following scenario regarding health insurance is based on the premise that the "whole idea behind insurance is to pool uncertainty" (p. 26).

86. McCollough, *The Moral Imagination and Public Life*, pp. 69–70.

87. Mansbridge, "Rise and Fall of Self-Interest."

88. James Madison, "Federalist Paper #10," in *The Federalist Papers* (New York: Mentor, 1961), p. 78.

Index

Federal Privacy of Medical Information
 Act of 1980 (H.R. 5935), 104
Federal Register, 87, 97
Federal Trade Commission, 84
Fein, Bruce, 281 (n. 84)
Fenno, Richard, 21, 203
Ferkiss, Victor, 12
Fifth Amendment, 9, 38–39, 153–54,
 178–80
First Amendment, 35, 41, 84, 180–81,
 225, 236–37
Flaherty, David: on European data pro-
 tection, 5, 268 (n. 4); on history of
 privacy, 44, 110, 264 (n. 1); on pri-
 vacy legislation, 99, 206; and policy
 community, 131, 195–96
Fletcher, John, 238–39
Ford, Gerald, 80–82
Foreign Intelligence Surveillance Act of
 1978, 6, 127, 277 (n. 1)
Fourteenth Amendment, 39
Fourth Amendment: and communica-
 tions privacy, 9, 109–12, 121–22,
 128, 137, 142; case law involving,
 35–39, 178–80, 226; historical
 roots of, 44–46; and computer
 matching, 89–90; and personality
 tests, 153–54
Frankfurter, Justice Felix, 226
Franklin, Benjamin, 45–46
Fraud, waste, and abuse, detection of,
 86–100, 185–86. *See also* Computer
 matching
Fried, Charles, xiv, 29, 34, 217–18
Friedrich, Carl, 30, 32, 227
Frye v. United States, 149

Galbraith, John Kenneth, 11
Gallagher, Representative Cornelius,
 21, 72, 123, 144, 151–53, 191,
 202–5
Gallup Organization, 48
Galston, William, 222, 296 (n. 27)
Gandy, Oscar, 2, 12, 48, 51–52, 58,
 220, 227
Gavison, Ruth, 222–23

Gellman, Robert, 197, 205, 275
 (n. 116), 277 (n. 137)
General Accounting Office, 92, 95–96,
 156
Genetic testing, xi, xv, 2; and privacy
 issues, 170, 238–41; validity of,
 171; use in private sector, 171, 290
 (nn. 118, 119); OTA report on, 172
Gerwin, Mary, 197
Glasser, Edward, 12
Glendon, Mary Ann, xiii
Glenn, Senator John, 99
Goldberg, Justice Arthur, 39
Goldman, Janlori, 105–6, 140–41,
 196, 298 (n. 68)
Goldwater, Jr., Representative Barry,
 21, 80, 83–85, 126, 192–93
Gonzales, Representative Henry, 102
Goodman, Ellen, 239
Gore, Al, 139
Gostin, Larry, 172, 290 (n. 122)
Governmental Affairs, Senate Commit-
 tee on, 22, 94; Subcommittee on
 Oversight of Government Manage-
 ment, 91–99, 197
Government Operations, House Com-
 mittee on, 22, 78; Subcommittee on
 Foreign Operations and Government
 Information, 79–81, 150–52, 154;
 Subcommittee on Government Infor-
 mation, Justice, and Agriculture,
 91–92, 97–99, 106, 197, 203; Spe-
 cial Subcommittee on the Invasion of
 Privacy, 123, 152–53, 191, 204–5,
 207–8
Government Operations, Senate Com-
 mittee on: Ad Hoc Subcommittee on
 Privacy and Information Systems,
 77–81; Permanent Subcommittee on
 Investigations, 120
Grace Commission. *See* President's Pri-
 vate Sector Survey on Cost Control
Gramm, Senator Phil, 102
Greenberg, David H., 274 (n. 91)
Grisolia, James Santiago, 239
Griswold v. Connecticut, 39

Gude, Representative Gilbert, 80
Gunderson, Representative Steve,
159–65

Harkins, Anne, 197
Harlan, Justice John Marshall, 36, 122
Harris, Michael, 168
Harris, Richard, 124
Harris-Equifax surveys, 48–68
Harris–March of Dimes survey, 240
Harris–Sentry Insurance survey, 53–54
Hatch, Senator Orrin, 21, 162–65,
202
Hayden, Trudy, 271 (n. 60)
Health, Education, and Welfare
(HEW), Department of: Advisory
Committee on Automated Personal
Data Systems, 75–79, 184, 192–93;
Project Match, 86–87
Health and Human Services (HHS),
Department of, 96, 105–7
Heclo, Hugh, 20
Hendricks, Evan, 193, 197
Hixson, Richard, 295 (n. 18)
Hoffman, Lance, 192–96
Hollings, Senator Ernest, 138
Holmes, Justice Oliver Wendell, 112
Honesty tests, 1, 168–69
Hoover, J. Edgar, 113–15
Horowitz, Donald, 41
House Republican Task Force on Pri-
vacy, 126, 193
Human Genome Privacy Act of 1990:
proposed, 170
Human Genome Project, 169–70
Huxley, Aldous, 13
Hyman, Merton, 52

IBM, 79, 135, 141, 192
Ichord, Representative Richard, 80
Ideas, politics of, 17–19, 68, 72,
175–83, 209–11
Individual rights, 3, 23, 178–81
Information Industry Association, 135
Information superhighway, 139
Inness, Julie, 3, 4, 33

Institute of Medicine (IOM), 105
Integrity tests. *See* Honesty tests
Intelligence, House Select Committee
on, 104
Intelligent Transportation Systems
(ITS), xi, xv, 2, 142–43
Intelligent Vehicular Highway Systems
(IVHS). *See* Intelligent Transporta-
tion Systems
Interests, politics of, 19, 68, 181–90,
209–11
Internal Revenue Service (IRS), 38, 91
International Association of Chiefs of
Police, 116
International Privacy Bulletin, 198

Jaffess v. Secretary HEW, 89
Johnson, Lyndon, 120, 123
Jones, Charles, xii
Judiciary, House Committee on, 22,
94; Subcommittee on Courts, Civil
Liberties, and the Administration of
Justice, 93, 126, 129, 132, 134, 136,
197, 202, 203; Subcommittee on
Civil and Constitutional Rights, 157,
203
Judiciary, Senate Committee on, 22;
Subcommittee on Administrative
Practice and Procedure, 72–73, 119,
123, 191; Subcommittee on Constitutional Rights, 74, 77–81, 152–53,
154, 191, 192, 204; Subcommittee
on Law and Technology, 105; Subcommittee on Criminal Laws and
Procedures, 122; Subcommittee on
Patents, Copyrights, and Trademarks, 136, 197; Subcommittee on
the Constitution, 155
Jussawalla, Meheroo, 233
Justice, Department of: use of wiretapping, 113–16; and electronic communications, 130, 133–36, 180, 188;
and polygraphs, 151, 156, 158,
163–64, 167; and counterterrorism,
200

Kalven, Harry, 34
Kapor, Mitch, 139
Kastenmeier, Representative Robert, 21–22, 93, 127, 129, 132–36, 188, 200, 202–4
Katz, James, 49, 52
Katz v. United States, 9, 36–37, 121–25, 188
Kelman, Steven, 177, 182
Kennedy, Senator Edward, 21, 124, 162, 165–66, 202–3
Kennedy, Robert, 120, 124
Kingdon, John, 17, 19, 175
Kirchner, Jake, 271 (n. 61)
Knapp, James, 133–36
Knowlton, Robert, 13, 119
Koch, Representative Edward, 21, 83–85, 155, 159, 193, 202
Kusserow, Richard, 273 (n. 88)

Labor and Human Resources, Senate Committee on, 22, 165
Larson, John, 145–46
Laudon, Kenneth, 192, 194
Lawton, Mary, 133
Leahy, Senator Patrick, 21, 105, 202
Leavy, Deborah, 197, 200
Legal Action Center, 164
Levin, Senator Carl, 95–99
Liberalism, xiv, 24–25, 43, 214
Lie detectors. *See* Polygraphs
Linowes, David, 5
Long, Senator Edward, 14, 21, 119–20, 187, 191, 202, 208
Loomis, Burdett, 208
Lotus, 139, 141
Louis Harris and Associates. *See* Harris-Equifax surveys; Harris–March of Dimes survey; Harris–Sentry Insurance survey; Public opinion surveys
Lykken, David, 146–47

McBride, Thomas, 273 (n. 88)
McCandless, Representative Al, 101
McClellan, Senator John, 120, 127

McCollough, Thomas, 25
Macedo, Stephen, 222, 295–96 (n. 19), 296 (n. 29)
McKinney, Representative Stewart, 159–60
MacNaughton, Marcia, 91, 191, 194
Macy, John, 153
Madison, James, 23, 243
Mailing lists, 64, 180. *See also* Direct-mail marketing
Mansbridge, Jane, 182, 242
Marcuse, Herbert, 11
Markey, Representative Edward, 138
Markman, Stephen, 288 (n. 80)
Markoff, John, 197
Marston, William, 145
Martinez, Representative Matthew, 159
Marx, Gary, 93, 195
Mathias, Senator Charles McC., 21, 126–27, 129, 133, 202
Meadow, Robert, 264 (n. 18), 265 (n. 27)
Medical privacy, xv, 71, 103–8
Medical records. *See* Records
Meese, Edwin, 134
Merton, Robert, 32
Metalitz, Steve, 197
Mill, John Stuart, 222, 225
Miller, Arthur R., xiv, 14, 35, 70, 78, 191–92, 194, 196
Miller, Michael, 197
Monitoring, public opinion on: workplace, 48, 52–53; telephone, 53
Moore, Jr., Barrington, 217
Moore, Mark, 181
Moorhead, Representative William, 81, 134
Moran, Representative James, 102, 206
Mosley, Ray, 171
Moss, Representative John, 150–53
Mumford, Lewis, 11
Murphy, Walter, 117
Muskie, Senator Edmund, 77, 124

Nardone v. United States, 114–17
National Academy of Sciences, 75, 82

Protection Act of 1977 (S. 1845), 155

Polygraph Control and Privacy Protection Act of 1985 (H.R. 1924), 159

Polygraph Protection Act of 1985 (H.R. 1524), 159, 162

Polygraph Protection Act of 1985 (S. 1815), 162

Polygraph Protection Act of 1987 (S. 1904), 165

Polygraphs, 23, 213; public opinion on, 54–55; theory of, 145–50; reliability and validity of, 149–50, 156–57; use by federal agencies, 150, 154–58, 285 (n. 33); policy debates on, 150–67, 176, 180; use for intelligence purposes, 151, 154, 156–58, 286–87 (n. 52); use in private sector, 153, 158–67

Posner, Richard, 215–16

Postal communications, privacy of, 45–46

Postman, Neil, 12

Post Office and Civil Service, House Committee on, 22, 157; Subcommittee on the Civil Service, 157

President's Commission on Law Enforcement and the Administration of Justice, 120, 186

President's Council on Integrity and Efficiency (PCIE), 86, 91, 96–99, 185–86

President's Council on Management Improvement, 185–86

President's Private Sector Survey on Cost Control, 86, 96, 185–86

Preyer, Representative Richardson, 85, 205

Pritchett, C. Herman, 3

Privacy: history of, 43–47; public opinion on, 48–68; of information, 69–108, 232–35; of communications, 109–43, 235–36; psychological, 144–73, 238–41; latent interest in, 177, 208; as common value, 213, 221–25; as public value, 213, 225–

27; as collective value, 213, 227–31; legal development of, 214; philosophical views of, 214–20; genetic, 238–41

Privacy Act of 1974, 6, 23; politics of, 71–83, 193, 198–99; implementation of, 86–90, 100

Privacy advocates, 101, 105, 108, 196, 212, 234. *See also* Policy communities

Privacy and American Business, 197

Privacy and Technology Project, ACLU, 131, 140, 194, 200

Privacy Council, U.S., 197

Privacy experts, 196. *See also* Policy communities

Privacy Journal, 193

Privacy Protection Act of 1980, 6

Privacy Protection Commission: public opinion on, 61–62; proposals for, 71, 77–83, 185; need for, 233–34

Privacy Protection Study Commission, 8; establishment of, 81–83; recommendations of, 84–86, 104, 155, 184–85; membership of, 193–94

Privacy Times, 193

Prohibition, 109–18

Project Match, 86–87

Property rights, 34–35

Prosser, Dean William, 26, 33–34

Public good, 297 (n. 53)

Public Interest Computer Association (PICA), 93–94, 131, 194

Public Interest Research Group, 198, 201

Public opinion surveys: on privacy, 48–68, 177, 201, 224; on employee monitoring, 53–54, 65; on wiretapping, 54; on use of personal information, 55–60, 64; on computers, 62; and distrust index, 62–63

Pyle, Christopher, 192, 194–95

Quayle, Senator Dan, 165–66

Quirk, Paul, 18

Rachels, James, 32, 218–19
Radio Act of 1927, 114
Rakas v. Illinois, 37
RAND Corporation, 192
Rawls, John, 227, 239, 299 (n. 77)
Reagan, Ronald, 134, 156–57, 166–
    67, 185
Records: third-party, 35, 228–29; pub-
    lic, 38, 64, 102–3; video, 58–59;
    credit, 58–59, 100–102, 229; med-
    ical, 61–62, 103–8; private sector,
    78, 83–85
Regula, Representative Ralph, 81
Rehnquist, Justice William, 37
Reich, Robert, 19, 181
Reichman, Nancy, 93
Rhode Island v. Delaurier, 133, 282
    (n. 92)
Richardson, Elliot, 75, 205
Right to Financial Privacy Act of 1978,
    5, 6, 199
Right to privacy: philosophical, 25–33;
    common law, 33–35; constitutional,
    35–40
Robb, Senator Charles, 1
Roe v. Wade, 39
Rollins, Norma, 160
Roosevelt, Franklin, 115
Roper Center for Public Opinion
    Research, 61, 67
Rosenberg, Jerry, 14
Rosenblatt, Roger, 294 (n. 1)
Rotenberg, Marc, 106, 194, 196
Roth, Senator William, 97
Rothfeder, Jeffrey, 5
Roukema, Representative Marge, 165
"Routine use," 185, 271 (n. 63). *See
    also* Computer matching
RSA Data Security, 200
Rule, James, 92, 193–96
Russell, Cathy, 197
Russell Sage Foundation, 75

Sabatier, Paul, 198
Sackett, Paul, 168
Safire, William, 140

Samar, Vincent, 3, 5, 33
Sandel, Michael, 295 (n. 17)
Scanlon, Thomas, 31–32
Scheingold, Stuart, 258 (n. 14)
Schmerber v. California, 38
Schoeman, Ferdinand, 258 (n. 11)
Schroeder, Representative Patricia, 157
Schuck, Peter, 18
Schwartz, Herman, 124, 127, 187
Schwartz, Richard, 13
Seipp, David, 46
Sensenbrenner, Representative James,
    158
Sessions, William, 140
Shattuck, John, 93, 192, 194, 196, 271
    (n. 65)
Simitis, Spiros, 3, 217, 219, 230, 234
Simmel, Arnold, 30–31
Simpson, Senator Alan, 107
Skolnick, Jerome, 148
Smith, H. Jeff, 5
Smith, Robert Ellis, 193, 197
Social control, 92–95
Social Science Research Council
    (SSRC), 71–73, 191
Social security number, 7, 95
Stark, Representative Pete, 105
Stewart, Justice Potter, 121
Stone, Deborah, 178
Surveillance: database, 23, 90–99, 213;
    electronic, 179, 186–87

Taft, Justice William, 112
Talley v. California, 263 (n. 62), 297
    (n. 43)
Technology and social change, 10–15,
    42, 70, 176–77
Telemarketing, 180
Telemarketing Protections Act of 1991,
    7, 138
Telephone Consumer Privacy Protec-
    tion Act of 1993 (H.R. 3432), 139
Third Amendment, 35
Third-party records. *See* Records
Thomson, Judith Jarvis, 3, 31–32
Thurmond, Senator Strom, 163–66